Mindfulness-Based Strategic Awareness Training

Mindfulness-Based Strategic Awareness Training

A Complete Program for Leaders and Individuals

Juan Humberto Young

WILEY Blackwell

This edition first published 2017

Registered Office
John Wiley & Sons, Ltd, The Atrium, Southern Gate, Chichester, West Sussex, PO19 8SQ, UK

Editorial Offices
350 Main Street, Malden, MA 02148-5020, USA
9600 Garsington Road, Oxford, OX4 2DQ, UK
The Atrium, Southern Gate, Chichester, West Sussex, PO19 8SQ, UK

For details of our global editorial offices, for customer services, and for information about how to apply for permission to reuse the copyright material in this book please see our website at www.wiley.com/wiley-blackwell.

Library of Congress Cataloging-in-Publication Data

Name: Young, Juan Humberto, author.
Title: Mindfulness-based strategic awareness training : a complete program for leaders and individuals / Juan Humberto Young.
Description: Chichester, West Sussex, UK : John Wiley & Sons, Ltd. 2016. | Includes bibliographical references and index.
Identifiers: LCCN 2016016535 (print) | LCCN 2016026146 (ebook) | ISBN 9781118937976 (cloth) | ISBN 9781118937983 (epdf) | ISBN 9781118937990 (epub)
Subjects: LCSH: Leadership–Psychological aspects. | Mindfulness (Psychology) | Meditation.
Classification: LCC HD57.7 .H8494 2016 (print) | LCC HD57.7 (ebook) | DDC 658.4/012–dc23
LC record available at https://lccn.loc.gov/2016016535

A catalogue record for this book is available from the British Library.

Cover image: Yagi Studio/Gettyimages

Set in 10/12pt Minion by SPi Global, Pondicherry, India
Printed and bound in Malaysia by Vivar Printing Sdn Bhd

10 9 8 7 6 5 4 3 2 1

Contents

Boxes, Tables and Figures

Notes and Handouts

Preface

The idea of writing a book originates from people I appreciate and admire. One of the first was my doctoral thesis advisor, Professor John Aram. At the time we were jointly teaching a master level course on leadership at Weatherhead School of Management, Case Western Reserve University, Cleveland, Ohio. John thought I had a gift for simplifying complex theories and integrating diverse disciplines in a coherent, easy to understand, way. Over the years collaborators at work, students, and clients have confirmed John's view and exhorted me to put my reflections down in writing.

At the University of Saint Gallen, Switzerland, my classes on strategies to improve people's and leaders' decision skills leading to happiness stirred keen interest from the students and were always overbooked. Based on this experience I designed a one-year Executive Master program for positive leadership and strategy with positive psychology and mindfulness as the foundations of the curriculum. It is currently running in its fourth year at IE University, Madrid, one of the world's top business schools. The consistent application of positive psychology and mindfulness throughout the program makes it a unique training opportunity for professionals from a wide array of fields and industries. It is taught within a faculty that is composed of the best specialists in their respective fields, all pioneers in implementing positive and mindful approaches.

During studies at Oxford University for a Master's degree in mindfulness-based cognitive therapy it occurred to me that there was a need for shorter training formats like the well-recognized 8-week training protocols common to most mindfulness training courses. Maybe it was time to contemplate writing a book and make the material that I had accumulated over many years into a series of personal journals accessible to people outside academia—not a book about personal exploits, much less an autobiography, but a practical book enriched with human-centered, anecdotal data and with authentic stories that could illustrate abstract concepts and give them a human face. The drive to overcome my doubts and reservations and start writing comes from what I see occurring in the world around me, and I'm not alone in my observations.

In a recent article MIT professors E. Brynjolfsson and A. McAfee, together with M. Spence of NYU, a Nobel laureate in economics, suggest that one of the key challenges in the future will be assuring an acceptable standard of living for the mass of people being squeezed out of the labor market by the forces of technology. Researchers at Oxford University estimate that in the future 45% of US jobs will be computerized, drastically reducing the workforce. Scientists such as Stephen Hawking also warn about the possible negative effects on social life that will result from a trend towards robots in the workplace that will threaten jobs on a massive scale. While writing these lines the Anglo-American mining company announced its intention to shed 85,000 jobs. At the same time huge numbers of immigrants pour into the more industrialized economies in search of better lives, although these countries are already under strain both socially and economically.

There are other troubles emerging, too. We watch in consternation the developments at FIFA, the Football Association, with its new costly head office in Zurich only minutes away from my home, as reports of corrupt behavior and arrests make news. We learn also how companies engage in deceptive policies such as VW with its diesel emissions scandal. Daily we witness, and hear about, the effect of climate change and its devastating consequences for the ecology of the planet.

These and other problems are already weighing on people's well-being and are likely to impact it even more in the future. An inevitable challenge for us all will be how we can confront these issues and work towards solutions. Some people may place their faith in institutions (government and business organizations) hoping that they will come up with appropriate solutions. My personal optimism is not with institutional solutions given the numerous conflicts of interest and the highly polarized context in which they operate. They rarely seem to get things implemented. My preference is for a personal, entrepreneurial approach, one that places responsibility for well-being directly on the individual. No-one can take the need for a person's happiness and well-being more seriously than the person themselves. Individuals and leaders will be required to develop inner abilities to help them to navigate through these demanding times that are increasingly being defined as volatile, uncertain, complex, and ambiguous (VUCA). This is the central thrust of this book.

I see a great need for individuals to cultivate mental, emotional, and behavioral qualities that allow them to make clear decisions during these turbulent times while maintaining a decent level of personal well-being for themselves and their families. For leaders there is the need to cultivate an awareness that allows them to create real value for many: not only shareholder value but also value for clients with good and healthy products and services; value for their employees so that their jobs are protected and new jobs created; value for society by making the appropriate fiscal decisions and contributions. This is a very big call but it is one that is required from post-modern leaders. Individuals able to attain these goals will be sought after and they will be worth the enormous payouts that accompany these positions. Especially in light of the poor record of managers and leaders investigated by Candido and Santos (2015, p. 237) "one of the most challenging and unresolved problems in this area (business strategy) is the apparently high percentage of organizational strategies that fail, with some authors estimating a rate of failure between 50 to 90%. By failure we mean either a new strategy was formulated but not implemented or it was implemented with poor results."

Today there are too many overpaid mediocre leaders with a flawed view of value who are only capable of reducing the workforce to boost profits or making shortcuts compromising the quality of their products and services in order to save costs when what is really needed is job creation and genuine products. In short they manage the profit and loss (P&L) statements of their business mostly from the short-term cost side instead of generating long-term sustainable, organic growth based on a strategy of revenue generation.

The ability to generate genuine value for multiple stakeholders requires a panoramic awareness that I call "strategic awareness". It implies an open awareness infused with clarity of the mind, positive emotionality, friendliness, practical wisdom (in the sense of finding the right way to do the right things), and skillful responses to our socially constructed reality. It is the kind of awareness that allows for decisions that foster personal and social well-being while avoiding two of the most common errors in decision making:

- Errors in forecasting future personal outcomes of decisions taken today (for example, after being overjoyed with the promotion to country manager in Panama feeling unhappy with the suffocating heat and heavy traffic of Panama City).
- Lack of foresight regarding side effects or unintended consequences of their decisions (for example VW's decisions that led to the emission scandal now affecting many other parties including the second-generation VW representative who lives next to me and his employees who are suffering a dramatic collapse in sales).

Mindfulness-based strategic awareness training (MBSAT) is designed to cultivate an open, panoramic awareness using mindfulness and positive psychology as its foundation and behavioral economics, cognitive therapy, finance, risk management, and system dynamics as supporting disciplines. Mindfulness, a millennium old technology of human development, has recently been receiving much attention as one possible way to help individuals cope with the challenges of postmodernity.

J. Sachs, the acclaimed Columbia University professor, speaks of eight dimensions in people's lives that require mindfulness: mindfulness of self, mindfulness of work, mindfulness of knowledge, mindfulness of others, mindfulness of nature, mindfulness of the future, mindfulness of politics, and mindfulness of the world.

Positive psychology, the second pillar of MBSAT, is an already well-established applied science of well-being. It has developed proven interventions for assisting individuals to increase their levels of subjective well-being. In combination with the other disciplines mentioned above MBSAT forms a robust, comprehensive 8-week program that, if followed by the participants, can significantly improve the quality of their lives.

Considerable effort and care has been made to design MBSAT so that it delivers what it intends to do and doesn't become one more program of what critics call "mindfulness McDonaldization" interventions, simplified approaches with promises of fast results, a kind of fast food for the soul.

The author of this book, besides having several years of mindfulness practice, spent two years learning how to design and teach mindfulness interventions at Oxford University and worked for more than a decade with applied positive psychology approaches to human development in various industries. Together with my many years of experience in organizational settings—as employee, leader, business owner, consultant, and teacher at business schools—this gives me a wide background that has helped me to design MBSAT. The course is the result of solid research findings and relevant practical experience. Likewise the book is written for a wide audience: for leaders and individuals alike and can be used as a guide for teachers as well as a manual for individual learning.

The result is a program built on the principles of scholarly design thinking. It provides innovative prescriptive forms of applied science with a vision of a mindful positive individual that can contribute to his or her personal well-being and that of others.

Instead of taking a theoretical approach and seeking to uncover how things are, it proposes an experiential learning approach with practices and exercises. At this point in the history of human sciences including mindfulness and positive psychology there are no reliable answers to the question of how things are anyway. What can be said for sure, however, is that the practices of mindfulness and positive psychology, when done regularly, are highly beneficial to the practitioner. They are not difficult, the challenge is to maintain continuity in doing them and that is hard as there are no shortcuts around this. As a sage once said: "Start by doing what is necessary; then do the possible and suddenly you are doing the impossible."

For those who practice regularly, MBSAT has the potential to generate positive, transformative outcomes for themselves and the world in which they live.

About the Companion Website

This book is accompanied by a companion website:

www.wiley.com/go/humbertoyoung/mbsat

The website includes Handout and Audio files.

Part 1

Foundations for Mindful, Positive Leadership and a Constructive Way of Life

1

The Quest for a Model of Mindful, Positive Leadership and a Constructive Way of Life

1.1 Groundwork for Models of Leading and Living

This book takes the view that human existence should not be compartmentalized. It is hardly possible to be a mindful, positive leader without being a mindful, positive person in private life. Being one without the other is an oxymoron. In fact, everything in life is shaped by the quality of an individual's innermost attitudes and the quality of human existence. From that standpoint the content of this book applies equally to normal individuals' lives as well as the lives of leaders.

Leadership can achieve great things like excellent products, services and dynamic organizations—all of which can make life more enjoyable and enriching. Equally, leadership can be used to damage human experience. Wars, group violence and many different forms of organized, or even disorganized, social destruction can lead to harmful outcomes. However, most of the time leadership is a process that simply sustains the status quo at organizational, group or even individual levels.

In this book I offer a model that, with training, can produce leadership that assists leaders and managers to create value in a positive and sustainable manner. I am particularly grateful for the perspective of the influential management philosopher, Peter Drucker, who defined leadership as "lifting a person's vision to high sights, the raising of a person's performance to a higher standard, the building of a personality beyond its normal limitations." Consequently what I am advocating is that almost everyone involved in any kind of social interaction has the potential to apply this type of leadership.

For example, a mother helping her child to achieve higher grades in school and a colleague helping a team member with problems at work will both benefit from applying these leadership principles. It is a leadership style that produces workable systems within organizations as well as workable solutions for the leaders themselves as for any individual.

Mindfulness-Based Strategic Awareness Training: A Complete Program for Leaders and Individuals, First Edition. Juan Humberto Young.

Companion website: www.wiley.com/go/humbertoyoung/mbsat

Over the years, both in places where I have worked, led and managed groups and at some of the best business schools in the world where I have studied, I have explored a wide range of leadership theories. (Please see Box 1.1 for a brief description of some of the most popular leadership theories.) Careful application of these theories has helped me to improve outcomes for my teams and myself. In terms of standardized measurements, such as return on investment, we performed extremely well. But I wanted to reach beyond standard measures. I was intrigued by the possibility that we could perform more creatively and avoid the emotional problems caused by chronic stress and fatigue. I knew this was possible because of an important personal experience in my youth.

Box 1.1 Leadership Theories

The plethora of existing leadership theories can be subdivided in four core orientations:

1. *Trait Theories*: These are theories that suggest that leaders must have certain personality traits or characteristics that people either have or don't have. These leadership theories have lost their appeal lately and are somewhat outdated in the light of neurological findings concerning the plasticity of the human brain.
2. *Behavioral Theories*: These types of theories focus on how leaders enact leading. An early popular behavioral leadership framework was Kurt Lewin's classification of leaders by their decision-making style. According to Lewin leaders fall into three categories: autocratic leaders (making decisions on their own), democratic leaders (inviting team members to participate in the decision-making process) and laissez-faire leaders (allowing people to make decisions within their own teams).
3. *Contingency Theories*: These theories suggest that there is no ideal leadership style as each situation requires a different type of leading. A well-known framework is Fiedler's contingency leadership model.
4. *Power and Influence Theories*: These theories take the view that the key is how leaders use power and influence to get things done. A well-known framework here is French and Raven's Five Forms of Power. According to Raven three sources of power are positional: "legitimate," "reward," and "coercive," and two sources are personal: "expert power" (knowing your stuff) and "referent power," stemming from a leader's appeal and charm.

In my mind I can still see one of my father's clients, a young businessman, the owner of a large transportation company dedicated to carrying perishable agricultural produce from the rural parts of the country to the capital, coming down the stairs in the office building as I went to see my father one day after school. He had tears in his eyes and was clearly moved, so I asked him what was happening? He answered that he was overjoyed, because his wife was finally pregnant after hoping for a child for years. He told me that he came regularly to see my father, his financial advisor. They had started talking together about everything, not just business, and this had helped to relieve him from the stress and exhaustion produced by long working hours and constant worrying. As a result he had become calmer and more relaxed and he was convinced that this had played an essential, positive role in enabling him and his wife to conceive a baby. He was so grateful to my father. I was only a 15-year-old teenager at the time, but I still remember that I thought "If only my Dad talked to me more often the way he talked with his client, Jorge."

That story has remained with me because, besides illustrating how pernicious stress can be, it taught me something crucial about the importance of caring and loving relationships at work. I learned that there had to be a positive way of leading people so that they could develop and flourish. I simply didn't know the "how" and this is what I set out to discover.

Here are the milestones of my quest. It is my way of highlighting the necessity of a model for mindful, positive leadership, and a constructive way of living with its integral parts. It is also a way to honor my teachers and all the researchers that have contributed directly or indirectly to the conclusions I have reached.

1.2 In Pursuit of Answers to Intriguing Questions

After years managing my own business and having achieved a respectable level of financial success, I felt secure enough to go back to the question: can we have better leadership and management models that benefit all parties?

In this search I studied for my doctorate at Case Western Reserve University's Weatherhead School of Management in Cleveland, Ohio. There I met Professor Suresh Srivastva who thought of organizations as centers of human relatedness where people come together "to learn, to care and to grow, to love and develop, to cooperate and co-create" (as he often used to say during his teachings in class).

At Weatherhead School of Management I also met David Cooperrider, who had the inspiration during a consulting assignment for the Cleveland Clinic, together with Suresh (his PhD supervisor), to invert the question "What problems need to be solved here?" to "What is working well here and how can we replicate it throughout the whole organization?" By inverting the focus they both created the new approach, appreciative inquiry (AI), which is recognized today as one of the most important modern management innovations.

Inspiring ideas also came from other teachers during my doctoral studies. Richard Boyatzis was teaching about the need for leaders' emotional intelligence and John Aram articulated the need to reform the management profession to reflect the needs of not just one stakeholder but society as a whole.

Also working in the field was Richard (Dick) Boland, my other thesis advisor and one of the early advocates of design thinking in management—a way of managing that was oriented toward creating desirable and creative, yet sustainable futures. Dick's inspiration for design thinking came from working with Frank Gehry, the iconoclast architect who designed the avant-garde Weatherhead building, and observing his design methodology and working approach, which involved engaging the actual users of the building in the design process.

The experiences at the Weatherhead School of Management made a deep and lasting impression on me. It became clear that leading and managing well was not about learning and implementing the latest theories and tools on leadership and management but involved something beyond technicalities. Reading about the work of Albert Speer, the Minister of Armaments and War Production in Germany's Third Reich, it became evident that good management tools were not the answer.

Speer explained how he employed advanced management systems such as ad-hoc democratic styles of management control and flat hierarchies. However, as we all know, these innovations were put to use for purposes universally recognized as immoral that led to crimes against humanity. This historic reality highlights how a leader's qualities are a key variable for skillful and sustainable leadership rather than just great leadership tools and models.

1.3 Two Discoveries and their Importance for Good Leadership and Living

Inspired by the ideas and management philosophies I had learned at Case's Weatherhead School of Management I started focusing on ways to improve management. I realized that management was a profession that needed to improve its standing with the public. Many people saw—and still see—managers and leaders as value destroyers rather than value creators.

Searching for answers I made two important theoretical discoveries: first, I became aware of one of the most complete models of human motivation, a rigorously researched theory called self determination theory (SDT), which had been developed by two eminent psychologists, E. Deci and R. Ryan (2000).

Second, I stumbled upon the evolutionary view of leadership (ELT). For me it was the most sensible theory of leadership. While most theories attempt to find a magic bullet that will solve all leadership questions, evolutionary leadership asks why we have leadership and what is its adaptive value, if any, in social behavior.

It is the brainchild of two scientists working independently, the Dutch psychologist Mark van Vugt and the German psychologist Michael Alznauer. It offers a strong theoretical foundation for the kind of alternative model of leadership and human existence that I was looking for.

I knew from experience that a robust scientific foundation was needed and that gut feeling was not enough. Sometimes individuals have intuitions about concepts before having a solid scientific explanation for them; a case in point is Marty Seligman, the founding father of positive psychology (PP). He explains how fortunate he felt when he discovered Barbara Frederickson's theory of positive emotions (2003), which validated his intuition about positive psychology.

During his presidency of the American Psychology Association, Seligman had created the field of PP out of a sense of need for a nonclinical population. When he developed the idea there was no theory supporting the foundation of the discipline.

In the same way David Cooperrider started practicing appreciative inquiry (AI) without a supporting theory. I remember presenting AI in the early years of the discipline to analytically minded managers and when they asked me how the model actually worked, I did not have an explanation. All I could offer was that it was working and producing good results. The breakthrough eventually came with Fredrickson's positive emotions theory. It provided the theoretical underpinnings for both PP and AI.

Based on these experiences I thought that if I wanted to present a leadership model I needed a theoretical anchor. As the late K. Lewin, the pioneer social scientist of MIT, used to say: "Nothing is as practical as a good theory."

My joy at discovering self-determination theory (SDT) and evolutionary leadership (EL) was derived from the realization that they could enable me to answer two key questions about an alternative leadership model:

1. What makes people feel well in life? SDT could show convincingly that well-being results from the satisfaction of three human needs: autonomy, mastery and relatedness.
2. What are impediments to great leadership and why is great leadership so rare? EL suggests three barriers: a biosocial mismatch between modern and ancestral environments, decision-making biases and an ancestral, archaic tendency in human psychological patterns designed to dominate other individuals.

Taken together these two theories provide a solid theoretical framework: If we can find ways to reduce barriers to good leadership and enable managers and leaders to create contexts where people can fulfill their human needs and have good lives at work, then we have a good starting point for a mindful, positive leadership model.

Contemporary surveys in the United States illustrate how high the hurdle for good leadership is: 60–70% of employees indicate that the most stressful aspect of their work is the interaction with their immediate leader (Hogan, 2006). This is almost as high is the failure rate of leaders in organizations—which is around 60% (Hogan & Kaiser, 2005).

Let us look now more closely at both SDT and EL.

1.3.1 Evolutionary Leadership Theory (ELT)

Evolutionary leadership theory argues that good leadership is essential for the effective functioning of societies and organizations. This is why leadership emerged in early human societies (e.g., in tribes, clans and extended families).

Furthermore ELT suggests that leadership is a task, not a trait or a skill, with the purpose of ensuring that the probability of success in a group is higher than they would be without a leader. Leadership in the ELT model involves setting direction, coordination, organization and the allocation of resources to accomplish group goals.

ELT (van Vugt and Ronay, 2014) defines three barriers that potentially inhibit effective leadership:

1. *Biosocial mismatch between modern and ancestral environments*
   In ancestral times leaders were selected by their followers. Today, leaders are chosen by their peers (boards, executive members, etc.)—this inevitably results in modern leaders having a deep sense of loyalty towards their peers instead of their followers (employees, customers, etc.). Furthermore, in ancient times the task of leadership was distributed, as people were chosen to execute leadership tasks according to their skills. In contrast, today's leaders are expected to perform all types of functions (being an expert in multiple areas: markets, products, technology, finance and organization, foreseeing future trends and generating innovative ideas, acting as coach in professional and personal matters, excelling in public relations, etc.), although most modern leaders do not have the broad set of skills required for such a variety of duties (Kaplan & Kaiser, 2006). In today's modern environment this mismatch applies to both formal, explicit leadership functions as well as informal, innocuous relations, for example in family, friendship, or sports teams.
2. *Cognitive biases and errors*
   Evolutionary psychologists (Haselton & Nettle, 2006) argue that cognitive activities are prone to two types of errors: (a) type I errors of false positive (believing in a false belief) like thinking it is a harmless piece of dry wood when in reality it is a venomous snake and (b) type II errors of false negative (not believing in a true belief) like thinking it is a snake when it is in reality a harmless piece of wood. The consequence of making type II errors is mostly anxiety and stress, whereas type I errors can be fatal. Given this asymmetry of consequences, nature has adapted the human brain to err more on the side of type II errors (tending to assume it is a snake, not wood, to be on the safe side) to minimize type I errors. Inevitably this results in a very anxious mind. In today's management environment these types of responses tend to be disproportionate.

Cognitive psychologists have identified specific cognitive biases that can lead to errors. These biases include overconfidence, group thinking, confirmation bias, status quo bias and so on. For a more detailed overview of frequent cognitive biases affecting business leaders and individuals, please see Box 1.2.

Leaders are chosen based on their ability to make good decisions and avoid errors. Aspiring leaders usually seek to project an image of competence and thus tend to succumb to overconfidence about their ability to make the correct decisions. Overconfidence can result in a number of negative traits including lack of self-awareness, inflated self-evaluation, defensiveness in the face of errors and ultimately failure to learn from experience (Hogan & Kaiser, 2005). These weaknesses can have far-reaching consequences. Yet in the hierarchical structure of today's organizations leaders' mistakes are often difficult to trace and frequently have no consequences. The absence of punitive actions for decision errors creates a strong incentive to pretend confidence and seek leadership positions even when this competent image masks incompetence.

In ancient times, however, overconfidence by pretending to have competence was easily observable and the cost of mistakes was often fatal for both the leader and the group. Only people who were certain to accomplish the task had a chance of being selected as leaders.

3. *Human inherent tendency for dominance*

The third barrier identified by ELT is the psychological tendency, inherent in many human beings, to dominate others. In ancient times the dominant figure in the group was better fed, had a higher chance of reproduction and disposed of a larger share of available resources. But any potential excesses were tempered by direct control of the group of followers.

Today the dominance of a leader, which exists in leader–follower relations, is often characterized by a decreasing ability by leaders to empathize with subordinates (Galinsky, Magee, Inesi & Gruenfeld, 2006). The current concentration of power, normally at the top of the hierarchy, can lead to asymmetrical pay-offs between leaders and followers and, if unchecked, to imbalances in the distribution of resources (van Vugt and Ronay, 2014).

As the human species evolved from a life of survival that determined the form of leadership—mostly male, strong and tall as the best guarantors for assuring group survival—to a life beyond the needs of physical existence (at least in many parts of the world), more adaptive forms of leadership are needed. Our brain's natural responses, and consequently the way leadership is executed, seem to be dominated by what neuroscientists call the "reptilian brain," the oldest part of the human brain physiology. The reptilian brain has a predisposition towards attack and defense (fight or flight) and negativism.

Given the accomplishments of modern society, this archaic human proclivity needs to change in the twenty-first century, if people are to live their lives to the fullest.

Box 1.2 Cognitive Biases

Frequent Biases Affecting Decisions

Action-oriented Biases

Excessive Optimism: Tendency for people to be overly optimistic, overestimating the likelihood of positive events and underestimating negative ones.

Overconfidence: Overestimating our skills relative to others' and consequently our ability to affect future outcomes. Taking credit for past outcomes without acknowledging the role of chance.

Perceiving and Judging Biases

Confirmation Bias: Placing extra value on evidence consistent with a favored belief and not enough on evidence that contradicts it. Failing to search impartially for evidence.

Groupthink: Striving for consensus at the cost of a realistic appraisal of alternative courses of action.

Misaligning of Incentives: Seeking outcomes favorable to one's organizational unit or oneself at the expense of collective interests.

Framing Biases

Loss Aversion: Feeling losses more acutely than gains of the same amount, making us more risk-averse than a rational calculation would recommend.

Sunk-Cost Fallacy: Paying attention to historical costs that are not recoverable when considering future courses of action.

Escalation of Commitment: Investing additional resources in an apparently losing proposition because of the effort, money and time already invested.

Controllability Bias: Believing one can control outcomes more than is actually the case, causing one to misjudge the riskiness of a course of action.

Stability Biases

Status Quo Bias: Preferring the status quo in the absence of pressure to change.

Present Bias: Valuing immediate rewards very highly and undervaluing long-term gains.

Anchoring and Insufficient Adjustment: Rooting decisions in an initial value and failing to sufficiently adjust away from that value.

1.3.2 Self-Determination Theory (SDT)

As early as 1943 Hull suggested that when human psychological needs are satisfied they lead to health and well-being. When they are not satisfied they lead to pathology and ill-being.

"Human beings can be proactive and engaged or, alternatively, passive and alienated; it is largely a function of the social condition in which they develop and function" (Ryan and Deci, 2000). SDT shows that the difference between the two motivational states: engaged or disengaged, is closely correlated to an individual's satisfaction of their needs.

Leaders and managers should be familiar with the notion of human needs. Most of us are familiar with Maslow's theory of hierarchical needs (Maslow, 1943), which is still popular in business schools.

Maslow's pyramid of needs takes a progressive approach in which individuals move from satisfying physiological needs to satisfying self-actualization needs. Yet despite its flawless logic (which accounts for its popularity) Maslow's theory was speculative. It was not an empirically tested theory.

On the other hand, SDT has been thoroughly tested in rigorous empirical research carried out over several decades. This makes SDT a very robust model of human behavior.

SDT is a theory that explains the forces that motivate people to do things and analyzes the types of motivation that generate the highest satisfaction. In this sense SDT differentiates between extrinsic (derived from external cues such as fame, money) and intrinsic motivation (derived from internal cues such as fun, interest). Extrinsic motivation is a continuum of external motivations, whereas intrinsic motivation is self-determined and leads to enjoyment and inherent satisfaction in the pursuit of goals.

Thus, for SDT a critical aspect relates to the degree to which individuals can satisfy their basic psychological needs as they act in pursuit of valued goals. SDT suggests three basic psychological needs: autonomy, competence and relatedness.

1. *Need for autonomy*: Harvard Business School Professor Teresa Amabile (1983) found that when people are exposed to external rewards and evaluations, their level of creativity decreases. Creative activities—those things that people do naturally and spontaneously when they feel free—are autonomous. When people are able to self-regulate, their acts represent intrinsically motivated behavior. Self-regulation is reflected in experiences of integrity, volition and vitality.

   Deci and Ryan's (2000) studies show that coercive regulation—such as contingent rewards and evaluations—tend to block and inhibit people's awareness, thus limiting their capacity for autonomy and hence their creative potential.

2. *Need for competence*: The need for competence spurs cognitive, motoric and social development, which gives autonomous people advantages making them more able to adapt to the challenges of today's volatile environment.

   Although Deci and Ryan recognize differences with M. Csikszentmihalyi's (1990) popular flow theory, they also acknowledge similarities such as its focus on intrinsic motivation as a necessity for individuals to attain flow.

   Flow is described as a state in which a person's demands of an activity are in balance with their abilities. This means they become totally absorbed in the activity because they experience non self-conscious enjoyment. It provides a sense and state of mastery and competence often observed in athletes, scientists and artists. SDT suggests that people need a sense of competence for their attainment of well-being.
3. *Need for relatedness*: Intrinsic motivation, the cornerstone of SDT, tends to flourish where people feel a sense of security and relatedness. For example, an infant's sense of curiosity tends to develop if they feel attached to their parents. School students tend to develop a higher level of intrinsic motivation if they feel their teacher is caring.

   My students at the University of Saint Gallen, Switzerland, often tell me that they have never worked so hard for a class that didn't put stringent formal demands, but that they felt individually so valued and cared for in my class that they were motivated to reciprocate by producing outstanding papers, which they did.

It is the balance of people's three psychological needs that leads to a healthy life. A healthy balance emerges when their need for individual autonomy and freedom doesn't collide with their need for relatedness and collective social integration.

Self-determined behavior is therefore self-endorsed, which leads to positive outcomes. This occurs when individuals feel autonomous with enough optimal challenges to support their sense of competence and with enough attachment to close persons in their family, work and social life who provide caring and acceptance.

1.3.3 Modes of human existence and leadership deriving from ELT and SDT

The investigation of the two variables discussed above, barriers to good leadership and human psychological needs for optimal functioning, led me to identify four modes of leadership and human existence (see Figure 1.1):

1. **Unaware Leaders and Individuals:** This type of person shows poor understanding of both life's challenges/barriers and the psychological needs of others. They are totally unaware of their own experience and of the necessities of others (bottom left quadrant).

2. **Self-centered Leaders and Individuals:** They impose themselves with little or no consideration of others' needs. They have not genuinely overcome the barriers, although they may be successful in acquiring power and money. Even though they know that abuse of power and dominance is detrimental to human well-being they don't care much about the fate of others. Therefore they are in the lower right quadrant.
3. **Permissive Leaders and Individuals:** They are not really aware of barriers but are sensitive to other people's needs. They tend to create social contexts of permissiveness where the exercise of required adaptive authority tends to be absent (upper left quadrant).
4. **Mindful, Positive Leaders and Individuals:** Finally, these are the people who are aware of both their own challenges and the needs of their fellow human beings. They are role models for a mindful, positive way of life as they work diligently to manage the complexity of mastering the inherent barriers embedded in their own life and caring for the psychological well-being of others. Leaders operating in this quadrant tend to achieve high performance for their teams because they pay attention to the well-being of the members. This was corroborated by a meta-analysis by Kuoppala, Lamminpää, Liira, & Vainio, (2008) reviewing numerous studies that searched for a correlation between leadership style and job performance but, interestingly, could not find any link. On the other hand, the research found a strong link between leadership style and followers' well-being. The conclusion was that leaders who care about the well-being of their team members tend to positively affect job

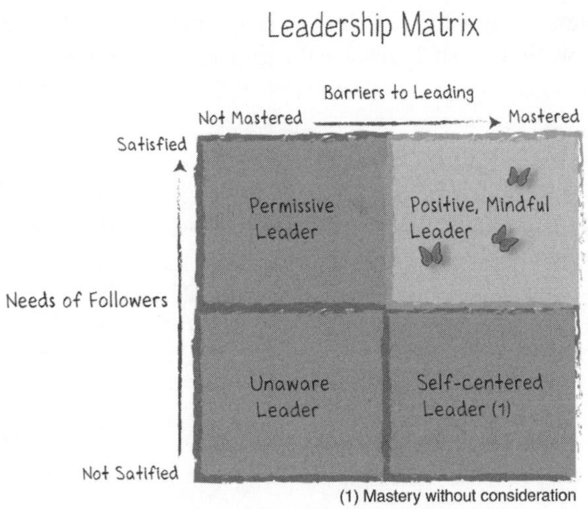

Figure 1.1 Leadership Matrix. *Source*: Juan Humberto Young.

performance in an indirect way. This suggests that only positive, mindful individuals are sustainable value creators, while the others are either destroyers of value or simply do not create any value at all.

1.4 From Groundwork to a Model for Mindful, Positive Leadership and a Constructive Way of Life

Having identified the two main sets of conditions and impediments of an effective postmodern way of life I was still confronted with the task of finding the missing links that could resolve the key challenge—namely how to develop and train for a way of living and leading that masters the challenges: How could the barriers to good life and leadership according to ELT be effectively overcome? And how can the human needs to flourish, according to SDT, be fulfilled in human relations in general and between leaders and followers in particular?

My investigation led me to two areas of human behavior: (i) the contemporary discipline of positive psychology, which prompted me to pursue a Master in applied positive psychology at the University of Pennsylvania in the United States working with the master Positive Psychologist, Marty Seligman, and (ii) a methodology of human development that is over two millennia old and is known as mindfulness. This led me to pursue a Master in mindfulness-based cognitive therapy at Oxford University in England working with Mark Williams, one of the creators of mindfulness-based cognitive therapy. The result was an expansion of the scope of my professional career. From successful corporate finance expert and business strategy practitioner I moved to becoming also a positive psychologist and mindfulness teacher. In the following chapters I explore these two disciplines and suggest how they can help resolve the leadership quandary.

2

What is Positive Psychology?

2.1 Birth of a New Discipline

For half a century, from World War II onwards, large numbers of psychologists have concentrated on healing trauma and curing mental illness. They have established a psychology of victimology and weaknesses.

As the twenty-first century approached, the then-president of the American Psychology Association Martin (Marty) Seligman called upon his colleagues to start focusing on another essential mission of psychology, namely how to make lives of people more fulfilling and how to nurture exceptional talent. He caused controversy among professionals when he declared, in his presidential address at the 1998 annual conference of the American Psychology Association, that it was time to focus on helping build strength, resilience, and health in individuals. These resources were needed to deal with the tribulations of postmodern life by average normal people, not just clinical cases.

This appeal was influential in the creation of positive psychology as a whole new field in psychology, a scientific and practical discipline built around human strengths and individual well-being.

The field of positive psychology generated a large number of research studies and new findings. This process ensured that the new discipline further evolved and refined its focus.

Around 2005, when I was studying for a Master in applied positive psychology (MAPP) at the University of Pennsylvania, positive psychology was primarily concerned with achieving happiness through three basic paths: positive emotions, engagement, and meaning. It was argued that, in combination, these three dimensions led people to achieve higher satisfaction in life.

In a recent book Marty Seligman (2011), the authoritative founder of positive psychology, complemented his views regarding the integral elements of a fulfilling

Mindfulness-Based Strategic Awareness Training: A Complete Program for Leaders and Individuals, First Edition. Juan Humberto Young.

Companion website: www.wiley.com/go/humbertoyoung/mbsat

life when he added two additional dimensions: relationships and accomplishment. The ultimate goal now is well-being in the sense of making people flourish. This is succinctly expressed by the acronym PERMA, which defines the key elements:

Positive emotions: feelings of happiness.
Engagement: psychological connection to one's activities.
Relationships: feeling socially integrated by caring and being supported by others.
Meaning: feeling connected and interested in something greater that one's self.
Accomplishment: feeling capable of moving toward valued goals, having a sense of achievement.

Throughout this book we will revisit the components of PERMA.

One of the most complete recent descriptions of positive psychology can be found at the Positive Psychology Center of the University of Pennsylvania, the place of birth of positive psychology, the wording of which is similar to the definitions of other institutions such as the International Positive Psychology Association and the European Network of Positive Psychology. It reaches beyond the individual and includes institutions and communities and specifies the nature, goals and applications of positive psychology as follows:

> Positive Psychology is founded on the belief that people want … to lead meaningful and fulfilling lives, to cultivate what is best within themselves, to enhance their experiences of love, work, and play… Positive Psychology has three central concerns: positive experiences, positive individual traits, and positive institutions. Understanding positive emotions entails the study of contentment with the past, happiness in the present, and hope for the future. Understanding positive individual traits involves the study of strengths, such as the capacity for love and work, courage, compassion, resilience, creativity, curiosity, integrity, self-knowledge, moderation, self-control, and wisdom.[1] Understanding positive institutions entails the study of the strengths that foster better communities, such as justice, responsibility, civility, parenting, nurturance, work ethic, leadership, teamwork, purpose, and tolerance. (Downloaded from http://www.enpp.eu/research-projects/positive-psychology)

In other words, positive psychology has evolved into a human science that supports and helps individuals, families, schools, workplaces, and society in general to flourish.

In many ways positive psychologists revive the long-standing debate between the renowned Swiss psychologist Carl G. Jung and Sigmund Freud. Jung pointedly remarked that Freud "deserves reproach for over-emphasizing the pathological aspect of life and for interpreting man too exclusively in light of his defects… I (Jung) prefer to look at man in light of what in him is healthy and sound" (1933, p. 117).

[1] In this book I use "wisdom" and "practical wisdom" as interchangeable terms in the sense of finding skillful ways of doing skillful things that increase happiness for oneself and others alike.

Today the field of positive psychology is well developed with a vast body of empirical data about well-being and what makes life worth living. Since 2000 several thousand articles have been written, most of them based on empirical research.

2.2 Positive Emotions: The Cornerstone of Positive Psychology

In my late thirties, shortly after I had taken up the position as Director of Planning at Moevenpick Enterprises (at the time the largest food and beverage conglomerate in Switzerland), Mrs. Prager, CEO and wife of the founder, called me: "Mr. Young, please come to my office, we need to talk! It has been brought to my attention that apparently you are not serious about your work." This took me by surprise, so I asked her what had prompted her remark. She replied that comments were circulating that I was always smiling and greeting everyone cheerfully, even people I didn't know. Now I was even more amazed. After taking a breath I asked her if she knew of any relation between being joyful and performance. She admitted that she didn't. I said that if any correlation existed it would almost certainly be positive. Then I explained to her that in Panama, where I grew up, people greeted each other out of courtesy even without knowing one another personally. I also pointed out to her that I was very content with having the highly qualified job of Director of Planning for the whole organization, a position that corresponded to my qualifications and experience. I was very grateful for that and felt lucky that I had that opportunity when I arrived in Switzerland. She reflected for a moment and then said: "Actually you are right; it is OK, Mr. Young. Just keep being yourself." Next day she circulated an internal memo inviting people to become more welcoming and less stern in their demeanor.

This scene captures a common feeling about expressing positive emotions in public. In Europe and North America people often look oddly at these expressions of happiness in public, especially when there is no clear reason for rejoicing. When I recounted this story to a group of psychologists, a specialist in humor and laughter explained that for many people in the West, as well as in some Asian societies, laughing or smiling faces are related to shallowness and lightness of thinking, especially at workplaces. For him the experience was not so surprising, although he also mentioned that perceptions about public expressions of joy are evolving as people become increasingly aware of the adaptive value of positivity. Popular media has played a major role in this growing awareness.

Let's have a closer look at what emotions are. Since Descartes' famous dictum "Cogito, ergo sum: I think, therefore I am," rational knowledge has been idealized in Western societies and life has been generally based on "rational, logical" thoughts and behaviors.

If a person expresses emotion it is often interpreted as a sign of character instability. This was implicit in the rumors spread by my colleagues at Moevenpick regarding my joyful behavior. They couldn't conceive of the idea that workplaces could be places of both joy and work. It was only after a logical explanation: my gratefulness at having an exciting job, that things began to make sense for them. "Ah! OK. He is happy because he has a top job in our country, so he feels lucky. Now I understand why he is always smiling and friendly. He is not an idiot after all, there is a reason why he is that way."

It is thanks to the work of important psychologists such as Damasio (2005), Ekman (2003), Barrett and Bar (2009), and Kahneman (2003) that emotions are now recognized as basic parameters influencing and shaping cognition. For example, until recently, the field of decision-making theories assumed that individuals evaluate the desirability and probability of alternative outcomes by rational appraisal of the alternatives prior to taking a decision.

However, as Loewenstein, Weber, Hsee, and Welch (2001) have demonstrated, emotional reactions to risky situations often interfere with rational assessments and when this happens it is emotional reactions that tend to drive decisions—a condition the authors call "the risk as feelings hypothesis" (p. 270).

It is research of this kind that is changing the way leaders, managers, and individuals are viewing their actions. They are moving from a purely rational understanding of the human experience to a more holistic concept that incorporates people's entire emotional make-up.

This gives rise to the question as to what sort of emotionality should an individual intentionally cultivate.

Among the models of emotional functioning, Kringelbach and Phillips' (2014) approach stands out because of their robust, yet parsimonious, explanations. They suggest that emotions have the following features:

a. On a timescale they are generally quick and short-lived, but with cognitive input they can be prolonged.
b. They respond to external stimulus as well as to learned internal stimulus.
c. They are subject to appraisal.
d. They are motivated to avoid pain and seek pleasure.
e. They guide behavior and choices.

This implies that emotions are complex phenomena affecting people's thoughts, behaviors, and body sensations and thus are important components of human experience. Taking into account these characteristics it becomes clear that the kind of emotions an individual chooses to cultivate become an important determinant of that person's quality of life. This is where the PERMA model of positive psychology discussed in section 2.1 becomes hugely important: the cultivation of positive emotions becomes a means to help an individual lead a desirable and fulfilling life.

What are the functional beneficial values of positive emotions for humans? This was the question that my friend and colleague at the EXMPLS (Executive Master in Positive Leadership and Strategy) program, Barbara (Barb) Fredrickson, the Kennan Distinguished Professor of Psychology at the University of North Carolina, asked herself. Her scientific research findings led her to develop the so-called broaden-and-build theory of positive emotions. The theory affirms that positive emotions amplify people's awareness and create openness, which facilitates experimenting with new ideas and alternative actions and experiences, thus broadening the processes of thinking, feeling, and behavior generally. As to the "build" part of the broaden-and-build theory, it explains how the frequent experience of positive emotions also helps foster and accumulate resources, in particular:

- **Cognitive resources:** love of learning, capacity to understand and assimilate complex material.
- **Social resources:** good relationships, capacity to connect.
- **Psychological resources:** optimism, resilience, drive.
- **Physical resources:** physical coordination, vitality, health.

Figure 2.1 illustrates the resulting upward spiral. For Barbara Fredrickson positive emotions are the tiny engines of positive psychology that help people thrive and flourish. In Box 2.1 there is an overview of 11 representative positive emotions and their effects.

If, for example, we take the emotions we call hope, optimism, and joyfulness, we can see that they play a key role in challenging or threatening situations. The American TV show *Scorpion* represented a constant belief in hopefulness. Happy Quinn, one of the main protagonists, who plays an ace mechanical engineer always

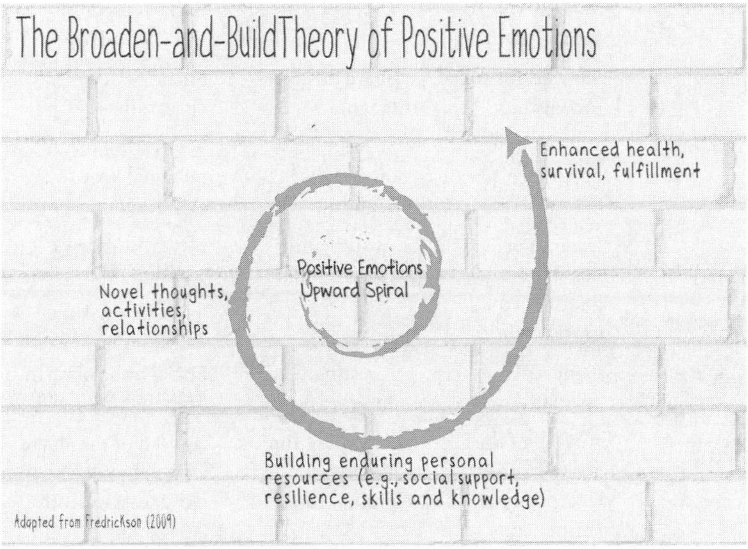

Figure 2.1 The Broaden-and-Build Theory of Positive Emotions. *Source*: Adapted from Cohn and Fredrickson (2009).

Box 2.1 Positive Emotions

Eleven representative positive emotions

Emotion label	*Appraisal theme*	*Thought-action tendency*	*Resources accrued*
Joy	Safe, familiar, unexpectedly good	Play, get involved	Skills gained from experiential learning, happiness
Gratitude	Receive a gift or benefit	Creative urge to be pro-social	Skills for showing care, loyalty, social bonds, gratitude, thankfulness
Serenity, contentment	Safe, familiar, low effort	Savor and integrate	New priorities, new views of self, contentment, peacefulness
Interest	Safe, novel	Explore, learn	Knowledge, curiosity, alertness
Hope	Fearing the worst, yearning for better	Plan for a better future	Resilience, optimism, hopefulness
Pride	Socially valued achievement	Dream big	Achievement motivation, confidence
Amusement	Nonserious social incongruity	Share joviality, laugh	Social bonds, cheerfulness
Inspiration	Witness human excellence	Strive toward own higher ground	Motivation for personal growth
Awe	Encounter beauty or goodness on a grand scale	Absorb and accommodate	New worldviews, wonder
Compassion	Concern, sympathy	Assisting, comforting	Social bonds, warmth, humanity
Love	Any/all of the above in an interpersonal connection	Any/all of the above, with mutual care	Any/all of the above, especially social bonds, closeness, warmth

finds herself in difficult situations but she never loses her optimism and her belief that there would be a good outcome. No matter how dire the situation she always manages to find a solution. She can always find the means to resolve the problem whether it is using an improvised tool or applying intricate scientific knowledge. By facing and embracing difficulty with hope and confidence she taps into her personal emotional reservoir of positivity (optimism, hopefulness, and resilience) that allows her to broaden her awareness while activating all her cognitive, behavioral, and emotional resources. Not surprisingly, she always manages to find a way out of the conundrum.

That is quite a contrast to our normal responses when confronted with difficult situations. In most instances we draw on, and mobilize, our negative emotional base of fear and anger thus narrowing our choices and reducing our viable and rational responses.

President Obama's "Yes, we can" campaign message was loaded with positive emotionality (hope, inspiration, awe, etc.). It represented an excellent example of positive emotions in action, one that helped catapult him to become the first person from an ethnic minority to be elected President of the United States.

On the opposite side of the spectrum there are negative emotions. They reduce people's thoughts, feelings, and actions to two responses: either fight or flee, the common fight-or-flight response.

Nevertheless, negative emotions are not without adaptive value. They are a survival mode. They force us to concentrate narrowly on imminent dangers. But as Baumeister, Bratslavsky, Finkenauer, and Vohs' (2001) research, "Bad is Stronger than Good" reveals, negative emotions tend to stay longer and have a stronger salient effect on humans. Often they become our maladaptive default emotional state. They taint our view of reality in gloomy ways.

Although negative emotions have a useful function, and are necessary for survival, the challenge they pose is that we have to develop the ability to differentiate between appropriate and required responses in the face of real danger. We have to resist the unwarranted negative reactions that often take over in our lives. In *Star Wars* Jedi master Yoda says this about negative emotions: "Fear is the path to the dark side. Fear leads to anger, anger leads to hate and hate leads to suffering." Therefore, in order to avoid unwarranted negative emotions we have to learn how to manage and control the traction and stickiness of negative emotions—that becomes the real challenge.

2.3 Engagement and Flow

Engagement is the second component of PERMA (see section 2.1). Being engaged in an activity or task means being fully committed and focused. It is a more intense form of dedication than merely being motivated. It comprises both cognitive and affective bonding with what we are doing. A prerequisite for engagement is the possibility to use personal strengths: When we can do what we are good at, we thrive and give our best.

For positive psychologists the "engaged" way of life comes about by actively using individual strengths in daily life. Strengths in turn are interconnected with volition. From the point of view of positive psychology strengths are talents and qualities that can be intentionally activated, nurtured, and managed.

Regrettably in today's working environment many people are deprived of the opportunity to use their strengths at work and as a result they become emotionally detached or even languish when they should be shining.

The Gallup organization, which has done extensive research on issues of engagement, discovered that only 13% of the worldwide workforce are engaged in the workplace whereas the vast majority are not engaged or even actively disengaged, that is, so alienated from their work that they actually sabotage the outcome. This is a genuinely sad analysis of the reality of conditions at work and an enormous waste of human productivity.

Most worryingly, Gallup reported in a recent study (2015) that among US leaders and managers only 35% are fully engaged—quite a shocking statistic given the repercussions on the state of the organizations they manage. Estimates of how much this costs the US economy range from $319 billion to $398 billion per annum.

In contrast, organizations with talented and engaged leaders are estimated to achieve a 10% increase in productivity, a 20% increase in revenues, and a 30% rise in profitability. Personnel turnover can be expected to drop by as much as 10% and absenteeism by approximately 25%. Given the huge potential benefits it seems foolish or rather irresponsible not to undertake initiatives to foster engagement, at work as well as in private life.

The second part of this book delves more deeply into the practical aspects of developing people's strengths. Now let us briefly review the basic path to a more engaged life. The first step consists of getting a clearer view of one's own personal strengths. There are several tools and instruments for discovering strengths. My personal preference is for the survey of the VIA Institute on Character (VIA stands for values in action). It is an initiative on a not-for-profit basis designed to disseminate ways of helping people realize their character strengths. Its intentions are open and transparent and the Institute is "proud of offering the only free, online scientifically validated survey of character strengths."

The VIA classification of strengths was developed in a 3-year-long comprehensive research project led by such luminaries as Martin Seligman and the late psychologist Christopher Peterson. The result is a taxonomy of 24 character strengths that are defined by six basic themes that represent the psychological processes that shape people's capacity for thinking, feeling, sensing, and behaving. For example, the theme of humanity comprises love, kindness, and social-intelligence as character strengths, while the theme of wisdom comprises the strengths of creativity, curiosity, open-mindedness, love of learning, and perspective. For a more complete overview, please see Table 2.1.

Table 2.1 VIA–Strengths in six Groups.

VIA-Strengths in 6 Groups

Groups	Positive traits that have to do with:	Character strengths
Wisdom/ Knowledge	acquiring and using information	creativity, curiosity, open-mindedness, judgment, critical thinking, love of learning
Courage	accomplishing goals	persistence, bravery, integrity, authenticity, vitality
Humanity	relating to others	love, kindness, social intelligence
Justice	fostering community life	fairness, leadership, social responsibility, loyalty
Temperance	keeping balance, avoiding excesses	forgiveness, humility, prudence, self-regulation
Transcendence	connecting to the larger universe, provide meaning	sense of beauty, gratitude, hope, humor, spirituality

One of the most powerful examples of engagement I have witnessed occurred while I was working with a Swiss regional hospital, owned and financed by the region's municipalities.

The CEO, a physician-surgeon with an MBA, hired my consulting services to assist him with a program of positive organizational development (POD). In a 2-year whole-organization effort involving all organizational levels and all departments—from surgery to administration and cleaning—we redefined the hospital's mission and strategy. As part of our positive psychology approach all participants took the VIA survey. Among them was Hanspeter (name changed), a fine young man working in the emergency room as a nurse. In addition to his strengths of kindness and spirituality—both important in his function—the VIA test also revealed creativity and appreciation of beauty as two of his top strengths, his so called signature strengths. When we decided to visualize the jointly developed mission and strategy in a movie, Hanspeter took the initiative and committed himself to carry the project forward with total personal engagement: organizing a task force, getting a mini-budget of a few thousand Swiss francs, mobilizing friends as cameramen and sound technicians pro bono, and finally motivating colleagues and the hospital's patients to star in the movie. After several weeks of switching between full-time hospital work and part-time night film studio work, Hanspeter and his crew produced a beautiful, moving film about 24 hours in the hospital that captured the positive spirit of the redefined mission and strategy. Together with the hospital management a festive premiere at a local cinema was launched for all stakeholders and DVDs were sent to all households. A couple of weeks later the CEO called me and mentioned that he was thinking of creating a new position, Director of Marketing and Communication, and promoting Hanspeter to the position. "I think this is where he can really use his special talents for the benefit of the hospital," the CEO explained. For me this represented the essence of managing people according to their strengths, so I encouraged the CEO to make the appointment. Thus an incredible job switch took place from nurse in the emergency room to the hospital's Director of Marketing and Communication where Hanspeter could flourish and realize all of his strengths, including his creative and aesthetic strengths. His example also had a positive effect in the hospital and reinforced the high level of engagement from the POD process. It was noticeable everywhere. It energized all staff and personnel. In fact, the hospital soon turned into one of the most cost-effective institutions in Switzerland and continued to prosper and expand.

Ideally, engagement becomes so powerful that it results in a state called *flow*, which is what the participants in the hospital were actually experiencing during the POD process. They discovered they could all use their personal strengths to achieve good things for the hospital and for themselves.

Flow is the complete involvement and identification with a task so that everything else recedes into the background and becomes unimportant. A person in flow forgets about time and doesn't feel fatigue. They feel elevated, inspired, and energized, which results in them letting go of any insecurity.

2.4 Relationships: The "R" in PERMA

Christopher Peterson, one of the fathers of positive psychology and authors of the VIA survey, had a great impact on me during my studies for the Master's of Applied Positive Psychology at the University of Pennsylvania, Philadelphia. As every positive psychologist knows Christopher Peterson used to say "other people matter" and had the capacity to make everyone feel special and a friend. So I, too, thought of him as a friend and so did many of his other students. One night in one of our conversations over dinner at Susanna Foo in Philadelphia we talked about the need to bring positive psychology to the world of business. We agreed that this could be an interesting joint project. Years later in my role as Academic Director I invited him to participate as a faculty member in a new executive master program of positive leadership and strategy (EXMPLS) at IE University, Madrid, Spain. It was a course set around a curriculum I had designed for professionals searching for novel, positive approaches to leading and managing. Christopher accepted. When we were preparing for the first intake he called me and said: "Juan, you know that I always work with Nansook, my research colleague. I'd like to bring her to Madrid with me."

Sensing that I was concerned about the economics of the situation he added: "And by the way, don't worry about your budget. I will take care of that. I'll share the fees you are paying me." This is how this man was: fair and caring in his relations to the utmost; people were the priority, money never was. Sadly, he never made it to Madrid as he passed away unexpectedly just two months before the start of the program, leaving lots of people mourning including myself.

Chris's attention to people reminded me of my mother. Whenever we children quarreled with personal staff at home she used to tell us that she was not going to take our side, not even if we were actually right.

"We need to be grateful for the kind of privileged life we have," she told us repeatedly. We were growing up in a comparatively well-off world in the 1950s in Panama City. "Therefore we need to treat the people who are here to help us with respect and care and be thoughtful of the tough circumstances they themselves face in their lives."

At the time Panama was a small and tranquil society, strongly influenced by US culture, a consequence of the proximity to the Panama Canal Zone, home to several thousand Americans. The Americans had a more conspicuous lifestyle that affluent Panamanians tried to emulate.

I think that my mother's guidance helps explain why fairness and kindness are an integral part of my signature strengths.

A fulfilling life requires warm, meaningful relationships. Both Chris and Marty have argued that a fulfilling life in line with the PERMA model requires an individual to be socially integrated. They must care for others as well as being cared for by others.

As Humberto Maturana, the Harvard-trained neurobiologist and author of the autopoiesis theory of human behavior, argues positive emotions can only be revealed in relational behavior, thus we learn about our positive emotions only through our relations with others.

2.5 Meaning in Life

The fourth component of the PERMA well-being model is meaning in life. This is represented by using personal strengths to inspire and work toward something bigger than ourselves. I came across the following inspiring case in a small gathering at my home in Zurich.

Several years ago Marty Seligman was scheduled to give a conference in Zurich. Upon hearing about the event I invited him to dinner at my home with a small group of Swiss executives where we could talk in a private circle about his ideas and positive psychology. Among the participants were the CEO of one of the most prestigious Swiss watch companies; the COO of the largest Swiss facility management company, and the Dean of Behavioral Sciences at IE University who had flown in from Madrid. One of my guests was a member of the executive board and Chief Investment Officer of one of the major Swiss private banks. Although I didn't know him well, I had briefly met him at an executive committee meeting where I was invited as an external consultant. A mutual friend told me about his extra-professional activities: he was the founder of a development project in Africa where he and his family regularly spend their vacation. I was really impressed with the work of this man and curious to see and hear what Marty would say about this. In fact, that night at my house it was agreed among all of us that this man truly represents meaningful life: he uses his strengths, his knowledge about finance and quite obviously his highly developed sense of compassion and humanity, for the service of something larger than him—helping African children have a better future. This is in essence what meaningful life means for positive psychology: to use our personal strengths for a cause that is larger than ourselves.

This is a wonderful example of meaningful life—of a man fully integrated into the Western capitalist system at a high level, yet personally engaged with his strengths in a meaningful mission that is beyond his own self. His example demonstrates that it doesn't matter where you are positioned in our society's hierarchy, there is always the possibility of living a meaningful life.

2.6 Positive Accomplishment: Fifth and Last Element of PERMA

Marty defines what he calls "achieving life" as human activity free of coercion, that is, what human beings do when they are dedicated to accomplishment, simply for the sake of accomplishment. The implication is that people do things not only to satisfy biological needs but also to exert mastery and thereby generate subjective well-being.

I like to think of "a person's calling" as a concept that can reflect accomplishment in life. In my view a person's calling includes all four previous elements of PERMA because in following their calling individuals use their strengths (engagement), often with a sense of higher purpose (meaning), and usually within a social context (relationships). This normally leads to experiencing positive emotions, although not always. Sometimes exercising a calling may lead to either physical or emotional suffering.

This connects with the essence of self determination theory (SDT) discussed earlier (see section 1.3.2). SDT argues that mastery is an important human need in people's lives. Positive accomplishment is what gives people this sense of mastery. In turn that generally fosters well-being.

PERMA's five elements: positive emotions, engagement, relationships, meaning, and accomplishment are the vital ways to increase well-being in people's lives. They are, however, not objective parameters, as they are in fact subject to individual interpretations. It is this quality that often renders the pursuit of well-being elusive.

People may believe that they possess what PERMA requires but be out of balance, thus effectively impairing their well-being.

There is, however, a way out of this conundrum. It is the other essential key practice: mindfulness. In my view mindfulness is the bedrock upon which the five elements of PERMA rest. It is the practice that helps people make wiser decisions about the way they lead their lives and consequently increases their chances of flourishing.

Before we discuss mindfulness, let us review some of the most pervasive hindrances of well-being.

2.7 Hindrances to Subjective Well-being

There are factors that hinder people's achievement of higher levels of well-being. I will concentrate here on three that are in my view closely related to choices people make. I believe they can greatly interfere in the quest for well-being.

Paradoxically, the first factor is generally assumed to be beyond our choices: genetic predisposition. How many times have I heard my students and clients say: "Well, Juan, it's just the way I am: I was born pessimistic and negative, always expecting the worse. I have to live with that."

Positive psychologists studying personality traits have discovered that while genetics play a role, their influence on well-being is only around 50%. Another 10% is due to external circumstances—country, health, job, and so forth. An astounding 40% is totally within an individual's control—it relates to how people make use of their autonomous choices. Imagine a person with a complete 50% happiness gene but constantly making the wrong choices. Inevitably that person will end up experiencing a miserable life. Equally, an individual with a 50% predisposition towards a low or negative mood who makes wise choices will still be able to lead a happy and fulfilling life (see Figure 2.2).

The second culprit that makes people go astray in their pursuit of well-being is what positive psychologists call the hedonic treadmill effect. The treadmill is the symbol of constant strenuous running while getting nowhere. When speaking about the hedonic trap with my students and clients I often use the image shown in Figure 2.3 to illustrate the concept. It is very helpful when trying to grasp the idea.

The graphic shows the human tendency to strive constantly for more without ever being fully satisfied. Soon after getting the first egg the emotional pleasure of owning it wears off and an emotional yo-yo effect is set in motion, prompting people to desire ever bigger and better versions of the egg (from lead to silver, gold, and platinum). Marketing experts know very well how to take advantage of this human weakness by adding marginal modifications to products that work perfectly well. The idea is to make the previous version appear outdated in what is known in professional jargon as planned obsolescence.

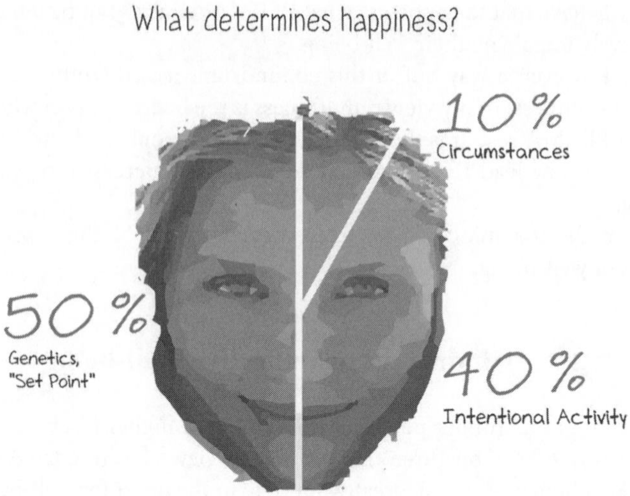

Figure 2.2 What determines happiness? *Source*: Juan Humberto Young, adapted from Lyubomirsky, Sheldon, and Schkade (2005).

Figure 2.3 Clinging and Craving: Hedonic Treadmill. *Source*: Juan Humberto Young.

Brickman and Campbell (1971) first used the term hedonic treadmill in the 1970s to describe how people continually adapt to improvements in their situation to the point where they eventually return to the emotional state where they started. Thus lottery winners, after initially rejoicing, drop back to their customary life. But what about negative events: Do we also adapt to deterioration in our situation? In an oft cited study Brickman, Coates, and Janoff-Bulman (1978) analyzed victims of accidents who became permanently paralyzed. Their findings revealed that after an initial period of sadness these paraplegics adapted to their new situation and their life satisfaction scores returned to their previous levels.

In Switzerland we have all been affected by the example of Silvano Beltrametti, a young ski champion and one of the most talented and promising of the Swiss ski team (bronze medal winner in the world cup at the age of 20), who suffered a terrible accident in a ski race and became paralyzed for life. After the shocking report of the accident there were depressing stories in the media regarding the young man's understandably distraught emotional condition.

In his first public interview, to the surprise of all, we saw a handsome young man full of life, smiling and facing, with good humor, his future in a wheelchair. This confidence and good humor have become his trademark. Today, Silvano is happily married, manages a Swiss mountain hotel, is involved in local politics, coaches young ski talents, and still practices snow ski (mono ski). He is living a wonderful, remarkable life.

In other words joy is not dependent on external conditions or the size of material assets. An ex-collaborator of mine at the Swiss Headquarters of UBS, one of the world's largest banks, who is now in a leading position in a Swiss private bank with the corresponding level of income, recently told me that one of his happiest moments was the time when I paid him a bonus of 3,000 Swiss Francs as member of my young team. He said that never again had he experienced that same exuberant feeling of happiness—even when he later received bonuses many times that amount. This leads to the third barrier to subjective well-being: affective forecasting.

Positive psychologists call affective forecasting people's propensity to misjudge the pleasure or displeasure of future events. These erroneous projections negatively affect their well-being.

Most decisions are based on affective forecasting, even trivial ones such as deciding which restaurant you would like to go; to go out for a IMAX movie or stay home and read. All of these decisions involve some predictions about the "valence" as psychologists call the positive or negative future emotional state resulting from the decision.

Economists also have a term for this type of prediction. They frame decisions in terms of expected utility or prospective satisfaction, based on the assumption of rational decision-makers who will choose the alternative with the highest expected utility.

All of these concepts would be most useful provided we could reliably predict the future. The likelihood of forecasting one's future emotional outcome with some accuracy is, of course, higher in cases where we have some experience concerning possible outcomes or where the outcome is fairly evident. It is relatively easy for example, to predict the feelings if someone were to praise you or criticize you.

It is also relatively easy to forecast the direction of one's emotional reactions, but people in general show poor capacity to predict the intensity and duration of the anticipated emotional state.

In Chapter 1 we looked at cognitive biases (see section 1.3.1, para. 2). In the case of affective forecasting people tend to succumb to the so-called impact bias by overestimating the emotional impact of future events. According to Wilson, Wheatley, Meyers, Gilbert, and Axsom (2000) this happens because people are inclined to preview future events in isolation without taking into consideration peripheral factors. For example, we might predict happy holidays in Panama visualizing the warm weather, sunbathing at beaches, savoring food, and visiting Frank Gehry's Museum of Biodiversity. Once there, however, we might get torrential tropical rain, crowded restaurants, bumper-to-bumper traffic for hours, and so on—all peripheral conditions we had not taken into account when we were planning the trip, thus overestimating our future vacation experience with a detrimental effect on our overall present experience.

As we have seen, the individual genetic components, the hedonic treadmill and affective forecasting, are factors that can severely interfere with an individual's quest for higher levels of well-being. However, there is also good news from positive psychology: these impediments are not immutable; the barriers can be conquered with the help of positive psychology interventions (PPI). The next section explains the nature of PPIs and how to use them to increase subjective well-being.

2.8 Positive Psychology Interventions (PPIs): The Instruments for Increasing Happiness

As an applied positive psychologist, PPIs are my constant working instruments. They are what makes my work meaningful, mindful, zestful, joyful, and real. When I see the results from PPIs—the positive change, personal growth, and increased happiness they bring to clients, friends, and family—I feel truly grateful for my new (well, close to 10 years by now) profession. Now I have two careers as I continue to be active as business consultant and entrepreneur.

When I began practicing and teaching PPIs there was little, if any, empirical and scientific support for them. In what I call the first-generation phase, PPIs were applied without fully understanding how they worked and why they generated good results—a situation quite common for new applied sciences where practice often precedes theory. This was also the case of positive psychology until the broaden-and-build theory provided a robust scientific foundation.

Recently we have gained a better understanding of the factors and processes that work to create the effectiveness of PPIs. Positive psychology researchers such as Layous and Lyubomirsky (2014) have identified that for PPIs to work well there needs to be a fit between:

a. the features of the positive activity that characterize a PPI: duration of the activity, variability of the activity; and

b. the personal features of the subject applying a PPI: type of motivation, capacity to make an effort, affective baseline state, personality.

A good fit of these two dimensions facilitates an effective execution of PPIs by participants and generates the desired results: positive emotions, positive thoughts, positive behaviors, and ultimately greater well-being.

Stanford psychologist James Gross (2002), a leading specialist in the field of affective science, has developed a robust model of emotion regulation that I find particularly attractive because of its rigorous logic. It is also easy to understand. I know this from experience with my clients, mostly business people, as well as students in business schools and nonclinical individuals.

According to Gross "one major aim of emotion regulation, naturally enough, is to modify emotional responding" (p. 283). For example, if I feel sad I might intervene by down-regulating my emotion to feel less sad. If I want to feel more cheerful I might intervene by up-regulating my emotional state to feel more joy. Positive emotion regulation is the target of positive psychology interventions.

Gross's emotion regulation system is composed of several elements. It begins with *situation selection or situation modification,* referring to choosing a situation that hopefully steers towards desirable emotions or—as in the example of reducing sadness—steers towards even undesirable emotions.

The next element is *attention,* more precisely *attention deployment,* referring to orientating attention in a specific direction with the aim of creating a favorable emotional response. A common attention deployment strategy is to use distraction, thus shifting attention away from a situation that is producing an adverse emotional state.

The third element is *cognitive change* and consists of modifying the personal appraisal of a situation in order to change its emotional significance. This is the *modus operandi* of cognitive therapy, which seeks to help individuals change adverse cognitions into more healthy cognitive reappraisals.

Finally, in *response modulation*, the intention is to influence the emotional experience once the emotion is already in place. For example, if you feel angry then go for a brisk walk.

Most of us have a range of personal emotion regulation strategies. These strategies seem to be quite natural given the widely known effects of negative emotions on health and the problems that can ensue if negative emotions are exposed in social contexts. Many people spend a good deal of their time trying to down-regulate negative emotion. However, given what we know now about the benefits of positive emotions, far too little is invested in promoting and up-regulating them in our daily lives.

Bolier et al. (2013) in a meta-analysis of randomized controlled studies on the effectiveness of PPIs concluded that they can be effective for enhancing subjective and psychological well-being as well as helping to reduce depressive symptoms for both the general public and people with specific psycho-social problems.

Therefore, one of the primary concerns is to design optimal interventions for positive emotion regulation taking into account the three time dimensions of human experience: past, present, and future, and the two dimensions of time perspective: short-term versus long-term. Both time and perspective are effective carriers of positive emotions.

2.9 Summarizing Remarks and Outlook

I hope this brief introduction to positive psychology has achieved one essential goal: to enable readers to appreciate the enormous benefits derived from consciously cultivating positive emotions.

Among other benefits there is ample evidence today to ascertain that cultivating positive emotions, positive behaviors, and positive thoughts leads to health benefits. The widely cited "Nun Study" for example (Danner, Snowdon, & Friesen, 2001) showed that nuns with a more positive disposition outlived their sisters by 6 to 9 years. Another study presented evidence that on a scale of five points measuring positivity, moving up one point translated into a 22% reduction of heart disease (Boehm & Kubzanky, 2012).

Many other studies, too numerous to enunciate here, have presented evidence that there are also concrete and measurable positive outcomes in the family, at the workplace, in social networks, and so forth.

My hope is that readers will be able to see that it is worthwhile to invest resources into cultivating personal well-being. Obviously the benefits will not fall right into one's lap. As Nobel Prize winner D. Kahneman and Rabbi Zelig Pliskin tell us: "Happiness is a skill." As such it is learnable but requires practice and hard work.

There is an additional caveat: the practice of positive psychology is not sufficient in itself to ensure sustainable subjective well-being and achieve sensible and successful outcomes. An excess of positive emotions can lead to delusion, the so-called "Pollyanna effect," where one is caught in a rosy world unable to see reality and unable to act accordingly. Furthermore, the overuse of character strengths can backfire and result in adverse situations. For example, too much bravery can lead to dangerous behavior, too much curiosity can lead to gossip. What is required is an additional capacity, an ability to balance and fine-tune our human experience, which tempers our extremes and fosters a calm mind, clarity, and wisdom. Mindfulness has the potential to bring this essential quality to our lives.

The next chapter is therefore dedicated to mindfulness as a necessary complement and companion of positive psychology.

3

What is Mindfulness?

3.1 Rediscovering Personal Practice

Mindfulness, the other pillar of mindful, positive leadership, has become a subject of broad public interest in the past few years and is even marketed as a panacea for many personal and societal afflictions. While it has gained in popularity, mindfulness has also become a subject of controversy. Questions have been asked: What is true mindfulness? What are its real benefits and its ultimate purpose? What is the best (or "right") way to practice it? Who can teach it? How should it be taught? Should ethics be part of the teaching? What is the role of science in mindfulness? With all these challenging questions, the best introduction may be for me to explain how I became acquainted with mindfulness.

In the mid 1970s, when I was studying English and business in California, my roommate Jeff, a Vietnam veteran, suffered from dreadful nightmares every night. Despite this debilitating drain on his energy he studied for his Master in Management Science at the University of California, Berkeley.

One day one of his professors, the late C. West Churchman (co-founder of the field of operations research with Russell Ackoff), invited him to participate in weekly talks on meditation with Eknath Easwaran. Such teachings were novel at the time and Easwaran was probably the first person to teach meditation in a US University.

Jeff became deeply committed to meditation and after a few months his daily nightmares had disappeared. Observing this remarkable recovery I started to go to Easwaran's classes and learned his mindfulness technique called "Passage Meditation," which involves learning by heart inspirational passages from various scriptures and repeating them in meditation. The aim is to use the texts to bend an individual's awareness towards wisdom and well-being.

When I returned to my home country, Panama, my practice of passage meditation, because I was cut off from fresh input, became greatly reduced.

Mindfulness-Based Strategic Awareness Training: A Complete Program for Leaders and Individuals, First Edition. Juan Humberto Young.

Companion website: www.wiley.com/go/humbertoyoung/mbsat

However, the connection was never totally severed and a few years later mindfulness and meditation proved to be of huge value for me.

What happened was that while working on aid programs for poor farmers in Latin America I met my Swiss wife. Later I started a new career with KPMG Consulting. I was promoted rapidly to senior manager. Initially I was stationed in different Latin American countries and then I moved to my own country, Panama, where I was a candidate to become a partner in KPMG.

However, because of my wife's family ties and her commitment to help her aging parents, I found myself living in Switzerland in the mid-1980s. It was a very hard landing for me. I left behind a life of economic and social privilege and a family network of prominent professionals.

Among my family were high achievers including the first non-US president of the International Board of Touche Ross, today Deloitte Touche Tohmatsu Ltd., one of the largest accounting and consulting firms of the world. There was also the founder of the Panama Chamber of Civil Engineers; the Head of the Chest Clinic at the American Panama Canal Zone teaching hospital Gorgas; and the presidents of both the Rotary and Lions Club of Panama City.

In Switzerland I had to start from scratch as an accidental immigrant. I had a short-lived jump-start at the well-known gastronomy chain Moevenpick. Then the reality started to sink in: language difficulties, cultural shock, social isolation.

In this challenging environment, without noticing it myself, I began to change. On one of my mother's visits to Switzerland she took me aside and asked: "Juan, what is going on with you? You have changed, in your body – gaining weight – and also in your temperament. You don't laugh as you used to. This isn't you anymore. You were always athletic, cheerful and in good spirits. If this is what this country does to you, better think about it."

All of a sudden I became fully aware of my pent-up frustration and resentment. I realized that I needed to reorient myself and so I decided to go on a mindfulness retreat at Easwaran's meditation center in California. I decided to resume my long-forgotten practice of mindfulness and meditation where it had started.

I returned to Switzerland with renewed strength and from now on stayed committed to meditation. I also enrolled in Aikido classes. Soon things started to change positively and life became more satisfying for me, personally and professionally. What happened was that I returned to my true nature with the help of mindfulness and Aikido practice and this, in turn, was reflected constructively in my private and professional life.

3.2 Defining Mindfulness

Let us now approach mindfulness from a more scientific angle. The Merriam-Webster dictionary defines mindfulness as "the practice of maintaining a nonjudgmental state of heightened or completed awareness of one's thoughts, emotions, or experiences on a moment-to-moment basis." To grasp the depth of this definition it is necessary to recall the first person in history to use the term: the Buddha.

Over 2,500 years ago, the Buddha in his search for the origin of human suffering identified an affliction he called *Dukkha,*[1] translated from the ancient language of Pali as *dissatisfaction*. The cause of dissatisfaction, the Buddha revealed, is human *desire*, a longing he called *Tanhā*, literally meaning thirst. Three forces fuel this thirst according to his insights: *greed*, *aversion*, and *confusion*.

While these findings were a breakthrough in understanding the human condition, the essence of the Buddha's quest was to find ways to extinguish the three driving forces of desire in order to neutralize *Dukkha*. For that the Buddha developed a practice he called *Sati*, a word most often translated as "mindfulness." For him *Sati* was not just a way of being present (an aspect very strongly emphasized in current mindfulness teachings), but more importantly, a means for "recollecting the fragmented mind," thus helping to create constructive states of mind and protecting those states of mind from adverse emotions, thoughts, and behaviors—for one's own benefit and the benefit of others alike.

In other words, what the Buddha discovered was that human experience is subject to an immanent state of dissatisfaction (*Dukkha*) caused by an unquenchable desire for more (*Tanhā*). At the same time he found that it was possible to end human dissatisfaction (*Dukka-Nirodha*) by developing mindfulness amongst other practices (*Hangika Magga*).

Given his therapeutic orientation some psychologists like to suggest that the Buddha was the first psychologist in human history. I prefer to think that he was the first *positive* psychologist. Through his understanding of the unquenchable desire for things, the idea of the hedonic treadmill is implicit, that is, a never-ending drive for more consumption and more accumulation. The hedonic treadmill as the root of unhappiness (or dissatisfaction—*Dukkha*) is clearly a construct of positive psychology.

In another analogy, the elimination of dissatisfaction in our lives (*Dukka-Nirodha*) through the path of liberation (*Hangika Magga*) corresponds in positive psychology to the paths of PERMA discussed in the previous chapter. Mindfulness is one of the practices that leads to well-being.

Buddhist scholars have advanced classical definitions of mindfulness, for example Añalayo (2004) describes mindfulness as "an alert but receptive equanimous observation" (p. 60). Bhikkhu Bodhi (2011) explains that mindfulness is "watchfulness, the lucid awareness of each event that presents itself on the successive occasions of experience" (p. 21). For Gethin (2015) mindfulness is "a kind of lucid sustaining of attention on the object of awareness, in which the mind is both aware of the object and, in some sense, aware that it is aware" (p. 32).

[1] Pali words used for references purposes only.

Western definitions of mindfulness are numerous. Some of the most cited include:

- Definition by Jon Kabat-Zinn:
  The most popular definition is from Jon Kabat-Zinn (1994, 2013) who described mindfulness as "paying attention in a particular way: on purpose, in the present moment, and non-judgmentally" (p. 4).
- Definition by Bishop et al.:
  For Bishop et. al. (2004, p. 282) mindfulness was composed of two parts:
  - "the self-regulation of the attention so that it is maintained on immediate experience, thereby allowing for increased recognition of mental events in the present moment" and
  - "a particular orientation toward one's experiences in the present moment, an orientation that is characterized by curiosity, openness, and acceptance."
- Definition by Brown and Ryan:
  Brown and Ryan's (2004) definition is "open or receptive attention to and awareness of ongoing events and experience."
- Definition by Ellen Langer:
  For Harvard psychologist Professor Ellen Langer (1989) mindfulness has four characteristics:
  - Continuous creation of new categories for structuring new perceptions
  - More openness to new information
  - Awareness of more than one perspective in problem solving
  - Greater sensitivity to one's environment.

In order to present a consistent view throughout this book I propose the following concise definition, which has been distilled from the authors mentioned above and combines classical and Western aspects of mindfulness:

> Paying attention in the present moment with strategic awareness to ongoing events and experiences both internally and externally with an attitude of curiosity, openness and acceptance.

In mindfulness-based strategic awareness training (MBSAT) the adjective "strategic" represents an evaluative and discriminative quality of awareness, the ability to know what is good or wrong, and hence it is an important quality for the non-clinical readers of this book. This book is intended to help individuals make wise choices in life—for the benefit of themselves and the people they are responsible for. It is precisely this discerning awareness that I call "strategic awareness," which is at the core of the training program proposed in the second part of this book.

It is important to note that the variation proposed as guide for MBSAT in the above definition of mindfulness is not an arbitrary, personal construct but a notion with solid roots in classical mindfulness. According to Dreyfus (2011, p. 48) "Mindfulness is not just present-centred, non-judgmental awareness but involves the mind's ability to attend to and retain whatever experience one is engaged in so as to develop a clear understanding of the experience and the ability to recollect such experience in the future" and as such "it has the capacity to discriminate between positive and negative qualities." He goes further and explains that mindfulness comprises two aspects, (a) mindfulness proper: the ability of the mind to retain an object which provides the basis for clear comprehension, and (b) wise mindfulness, which includes explicitly evaluative and often introspective dimensions, what the Dalai Lama calls analytical mindfulness. As Dreyfus concludes:

> Identification of Mindfulness with present-centred non-judgmental awareness ignores or, at least, underestimates the cognitive implications of Mindfulness, its ability to bring together various aspects of experience as to lead to clear comprehension of the nature of mental and bodily states … so as to free our mind from habits and tendencies that bind us to suffering (p. 52).

It is with this understanding that the construct of strategic awareness is presented as the key ability of MBSAT that needs to be cultivated with both mindfulness proper and wise mindfulness as both facilitate personal transformation and skilful decision-making.

Most secular Western definitions of mindfulness with their sole emphasis on present-centered and nonjudgmental aspects are understandable as most current programs of mindfulness take place in a clinical setting. For example, mindfulness is used to alleviate physical pain, and prevent depression and other mental afflictions. Given that clinical populations are typically locked into a negative emotional and cognitive state, inviting them to intentionally explore a present-centered and nonjudgmental way of being makes obvious sense as the first step in their healing process.

3.3 Some Open Issues of Mindfulness

Mindfulness in its classical form has been part of human knowledge for over 2,500 years. Therefore, we need to ask whether we should adapt it to the needs of the modern Western world and if yes, how. Today mindfulness is often seen as the magic solution for almost any ailment in modern life. Want less stress? Better sleep quality? A life of greater intimacy? Better grades at school? Want kids with less ADHD? Want higher profits and an improved organizational culture? Want to become a better politician? Even a better soldier? In some Western mindfulness circles it is believed that all these wishes can be fulfilled. There is, for example, a monthly journal *Mindful* dedicated to the popular dissemination of mindfulness. There is also an academic journal *Mindfulness* publishing papers that adhere to rigorous APA (American Psychology Association) standards.

Not surprisingly, voices from within the classical Buddhist community are expressing concern about the possible decontextualization of the original intention of mindfulness practices, reducing mindfulness to a simplistic functional technique.

An area of major controversy swirls around the issue of whether ethics should be part of mindfulness teachings. The fear is that in Western societies characterized by individualism, mindfulness could become yet another self-centered pursuit of self-realization. It has been argued that a lack of an ethical component in Western mindfulness programs could impair a wholesome transformation of individuals that would lead to an authentic empathy. An example often cited is the case of snipers trained in mindfulness so they are aware of their breathing and can synchronize that breathing with pulling the trigger so that they can hit their targets with maximum accuracy. While it is true that the snipers may achieve states of mental calmness (a product of mindfulness) the outcome could be obviously questionable.

My understanding of the situation is that most mindfulness programs seek to reconcile individual and societal moral behavior, either explicitly or implicitly. Also, I believe that most people try to act morally, at least from their point of view. In the many years working with leaders and managers I have never met a person who deliberately aimed at behaving immorally. When unethical behavior takes place it is often the result of adverse conditions combined with poor choices that generate negative consequences.

To the extent that living a morally correct life is congruent with having a happy life it makes sense to invite individuals to review their values in mindfulness exercises. In this connection the interrelationship between mindfulness and positive psychology is hugely important. One of the central tenets of positive psychology is the cultivation of character strengths for an engaged life. Character strengths are defined as "values in action" and human virtues are the nutrients of engagement and flow as discussed earlier.

Positive psychology has a solid arsenal of positive interventions that strengthen the link between it and mindfulness. For example, interventions that foster the "strength of courage" can translate simultaneously into helping us stay with our difficulties without despair; interventions promoting the "strength of self-control" help maintain disciplined mindfulness practice; and fostering "strength of curiosity" helps maintain openness to our human experience.

3.4 Operating Mechanisms of Mindfulness

Let us look at how mindfulness actually works: what are its mechanisms, its modus operandi? To analyze the mechanisms of action underlying mindfulness it is appropriate to begin with classical accounts based on Buddhist-oriented views and then move to recent scientific views (neuroscience).

The operating model of Grabovac, Lau, and Willett (2011), which is based on Buddhist tradition, aims at reducing mental proliferation, that is, turning down the constant chatter in our minds that gets us ensnarled with desire (craving, greed) for things we don't have; repulsion (aversion) against things we don't like; and the ensuing confusion (delusion) that results from these driven states. The model defines three mechanisms that can rein-in mental proliferation:

Acceptance: Creating an awareness that helps us to relax and become more flexible, helping perception;
Attention regulation: Pausing, at least temporarily, mental proliferation;
Ethics practice: Creating a life with less guilt, doubt, and worries, thus reducing the baseline of mental proliferation.

As mental proliferation gets reduced in the course of mindfulness practice, the level of well-being increases.

Other accounts of operating mechanisms that allow for and support mindfulness are summarized in Box 3.1.

Based on recent findings in neuroscience newer propositions explicitly relate the components through which mindfulness works with neuronal connections. Hölzel et al. (2014) compiled the overview in Box 3.2.

Tang, Britta, Hölzel, and Posner (2015) suggest that attention control, emotion regulation and self-awareness set in process a motion that enhances the self-regulation necessary for persistent mindfulness practice. Their model presents three stages of mindfulness practice:

Early stage: corresponding to required effortful doing;
Intermediate stage: focusing on the effort to reduce mind wandering; and
Advanced stage: corresponding to effortless being.

Box 3.1 Operating Mechanisms of Mindfulness

Authors	*Suggested mindfulness components*
Shapiro, Carlson, Astin, and Freedman (2006)	Attention, intention, attitude
Brown, Ryan, and Creswell (2007)	Insight, exposure, non-attachment, enhanced mind–body functioning, integrated functioning
Baer (2003)	Exposure, cognitive change, self-management, relaxation, acceptance

Box 3.2 Neuronal Connections of Mindfulness

Mechanism	*Associated brain areas*
Attention regulation	Anterior cingulate cortex
Body awareness	Insula, temporo-parietal junction
Emotion regulation: Reappraisal	(Dorsal) prefrontal cortex
Emotion regulation: Exposure, extinction, and reconsolidation	Ventro-medial prefrontal cortex,hippocampus, amygdala
Change in perspective of the self	Medial prefrontal cortex, posterior cingulate cortex, insula, temporo parietal junction

The model presented by Vago and Silbersweig (2012) includes self-awareness and self-regulation and introduces self-transcendence as a "positive relation between self and others that transcends self-focused needs and increases prosocial characteristics" (p. 1). Clearly it sees self-transcendence as an important quality in social dynamics.

I see the model by Kang, Gruber, and Gray (2013) as particularly valuable. Kang et al.'s model appeals due to its clarity and completeness and its focus on the process of deautomatization, which is so relevant and important since we all are victims of maladaptive automatic reactivity. It suggests that mindfulness supports awareness, attention focus, present moment orientation, and acceptance and that when interacting together these factors lead to the following deautomatization processes: (a) reducing automatic pilot, (b) enhancing cognitive control, (c) decentering and reducing mental storytelling, and (d) preventing thought distortion. This leads to enhanced self-regulation and desirable outcomes.

This brief examination of a number of mindfulness operational models reveals that most of them share the same constructs; therefore the choice of model becomes a matter of personal preference and practical considerations such as, which aspects need to be highlighted, for what purpose, and for what specific audience (clinical, nonclinical, business oriented, spiritual, etc.).

3.5 Benefits from Mindfulness Practice

After, the overview of the operating mechanism of mindfulness it is easy to see the benefits of mindfulness practice.

If you believe the media you would be tempted to conclude that mindfulness is the solution to all the problems of humanity. While this seems to be a gross exaggeration, I admit that I have experienced a number of personal situations where mindfulness has been hugely helpful. At the outset I explained how I believe mindfulness practice helped me to adapt to a foreign cultural setting. On other occasions it helped me deal with life-threatening health issues in my immediate family and to handle, with wisdom, very difficult business situations. However, all this is nothing more than anecdotal evidence. What does scientific research say about the benefits of mindfulness?

3.5.1 Physiological benefits

Sara Lazar et al. (2005) was the first to demonstrate that an important benefit of mindfulness meditation is positive changes in the structure of the brain. With age the cerebral cortex layers grow thinner and it is still unknown what the effect of this process is. However, Lazar et al.'s studies demonstrate that people who meditate have parts of their brain's gray matter that are thicker compared to individuals with no mindfulness meditation experience.

In a recent study Singleton et al. (2014) demonstrated that after a mindfulness program of just 8 weeks participants showed an increase of gray matter in several brain areas. Given that thinning of the cerebral cortex is age-related, gray matter thickness can be interpreted as a sign of healthy physiological brain development.

Brewer et al.'s (2011) research suggested that mindfulness decreased activity in the default-mode network (DMN), a network of the brain in which neural activity correlates self-referential processing (processing information with self in foreground) and mind-wandering, two mental activities that have been associated with lower levels of happiness in individuals. By reducing activity in the DMN, mindfulness leads to higher levels of well-being.

3.5.2 Cognitive, emotional, and health benefits

Stanley and Jha (2009) found that if military personnel who were being prepared for deployment to war zones practiced mindfulness they were better able to maintain their working-memory capacity and positive moods. They were compared with members of the army who had not practiced mindfulness.

Ostafin and Kassman (2012) studied the effects of mindfulness on "insight problem solving," the type of problems Harvard Professor R. Heifetz calls "adaptive challenges" because the solution requires changes in values, relationships, roles, approaches—novel approaches that imply experimentation and discoveries. The results of Ostafin's and Kassman's study showed a positive relation between mindfulness and improvement of insight problem solving, the type related to strategic awareness.

Kiken and Shook (2011) found that mindfulness reduced negativity bias, that is, the tendency to give more weight to negative rather than positive information. In addition, they found that mindfulness increased positive judgments.

Fredrickson et al. (2008) studied the effect of one particular meditation practice: loving-kindness. They reported that this practice led to increases in positive emotions, but more importantly it led to building personal resources that they grouped in two categories: (a) having a loving attitude toward oneself and others including self-acceptance, social support, and positive relations with others and (b) building feelings of competence about one's life, environmental mastery, and purpose in life. All of which leads to increases in life satisfaction.

Let me tell you about one of my clients: yes, a banker (I have several bankers as clients). He came to a course of mine in the midst of a bitter divorce dispute. His wife had demanded the divorce because, as she said, she was fed up with the empty life they were living. For him this was incomprehensible. He had worked hard and in his eyes he had achieved a lot: a beautiful house, extravagant vacations, high disposable income, and so on. "What more does she want?" he asked. "Of course I had to work long hours to achieve all this. And now she does this to me." Several months after finishing the course he contacted me again and told me how instrumental the practices of "meditation on difficulty" (Irimi) and "loving-kindness" (friendliness) that he had learned in the course had been, how they had helped him cope with this difficult time in his life. Best of all, he said, he and his wife were finally able to handle the divorce in a civilized, constructive manner. He was now living in an apartment, while she stayed in their house and together they did all they could to ensure the well-being of their children, without anger or shouting. For me this was an especially powerful example of the benefits of both positive psychology and mindfulness practice because of the intensity of negative emotions and cognitive negativity (worry, anxiety, and rumination) that had to be overcome on both sides, on the one hand the ability to remain calm and on the other to generate positivity in their relationship. Figure 3.1 illustrates the interrelation between positive psychology and mindfulness.

3.5.3 *Benefits in the workplace*

Boyatzis and McKee (2005) argue that mindfulness helps leaders maintain better and more meaningful relationships at work. In another study Hafenbrack, Kinias, and Barsade (2014) established a connection between a series of correlational and experimental studies on debiasing the mind through mindfulness. Their main finding was that increased mindfulness reduces the tendency of irrational,

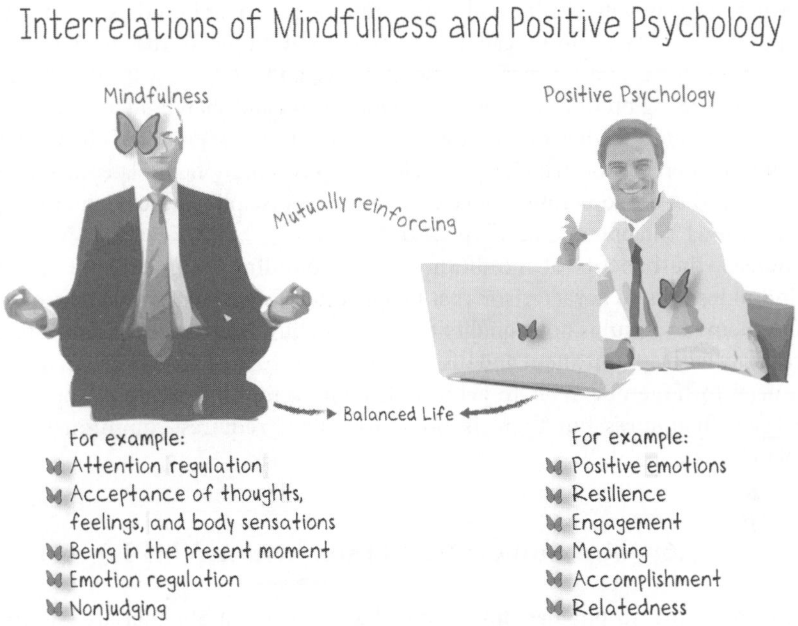

Figure 3.1 Interrelations of Mindfulness and Positive Psychology. *Source*: Juan Humberto Young.

counterproductive financial decisions due to certain cognitive biases. Also Weick and Sutcliffe (2006) suggest that in work environments demanding high reliability (e.g., fire-fighters, pilots) increased level of mindfulness correlate with high performance.

On the topic of mindfulness and decision-making Karelaia and Reb (2014), in a more explorative and speculative article, argue that mindfulness can enhance the consistency of decisions. They demonstrate that a person's fundamental values can help facilitate trade-offs when making decisions.

Sometimes clarification about life decisions can take an unexpected turn. In a case I remember vividly, a participant in a longer training program I conducted at a bank in the city of Geneva, Switzerland, wrote to me after finishing the program that he gained so much courage and clarity about his life that he had decided to abandon his banking career in order to pursue his true passion: an acting career in Paris. He certainly had the looks for it: handsome and tall with a pleasant voice!

Dane and Brummel (2013) in an examination of workplace mindfulness found a positive relationship between mindfulness and job performance. Glomb, Duffy, Bono, and Yang (2011) suggest that mindfulness-based practices improve self-regulation of thoughts, emotions, and behaviors and that these factors are linked to better performance and an employees' sense of well-being in the workplace.

Much of the way in which mindfulness training has so far found its way into the corporate workplace can be called "functional mindfulness," that is, it seeks to improve resilience, performance, personal focus, and attention with the ultimate aim of increasing productivity, organizational profit, and shareholder value.

In a more holistic view on mindfulness Kabat-Zinn (2012) writes: "In a society founded on democratic principles and a love of freedom, sooner or later meditative practices, what are sometimes called consciousness disciplines, are bound to come to the fore as is happening now" (p. 249).

Indeed, the benefits of mindfulness are astounding. But wait, not so fast! Mindfulness has a characteristic that people often forget to mention: it requires work. Being mindful is not a quality that one can buy. It involves persistent practice. Only with commitment and discipline can one reap real benefits. Therefore, we need to hone our skills to achieve it. Being a mindful being is one of the routes to happiness but there is no short cut: it requires commitment and practice.

3.6 Mindfulness-based Interventions (MBIs)

Let us now turn to popular mindfulness-based interventions that are currently being used to ease human distress. While positive psychology interventions (PPIs) cover a broad range of exercises of varying duration, most MBIs follow a generic format following a manual-based approach to teaching that includes: practices in both formal and informal sessions; exercises in sessions; homework reviews, and psycho-educational discussions. The interventions usually last 8 weeks on average with sessions being held once a week.

Formal practices include:

a. Sitting meditations: attention to breath, body sensations, sounds, thoughts, and other phenomena.
b. Moving meditations: walking meditation, mindful yoga.
c. Participant exchanges: guided discussions, experiential learning, and Socratic dialogue.

Informal practices comprise:

a. Mindful activities: eating, driving, cleaning.
b. Mindful reading: mostly poetry.
c. Exercises in class.
d. Mini-meditations: 3-minute breathing spaces.

In the clinical area these 8-week programs usually have core protocols, which include: mindfulness-based stress reduction (MBSR); mindfulness-based cognitive therapy (MBCT); acceptance and commitment therapy (ACT); and dialectical behavior therapy (DBT).

MBSR was developed to help individuals cope with physical distress, especially patients with severe illnesses. Designed in 1979 by Jon Kabat-Zinn as a mindfulness-based intervention (MBI) that combined meditation, yoga, and body awareness, it has been used for over 35 years and has proven successful in helping patients with physical pain. The program is structured yet flexible enough to allow teachers to adapt the course according to what is emerging in classes and what seems most helpful for participants.

Among the other widespread MBI protocols the one I am most familiar with is mindfulness-based cognitive therapy. MBCT began as an offspring of MBSR and was originally developed to help prevent relapses into depression in people with three or more depressive episodes. The authors (Segal, Williams, & Teasdale, 2013) cleverly combined mindfulness with elements of cognitive behavioral therapy and created an 8-week program that almost replicates the structure of MBSR.

In the first four weeks of MBCT participants become familiar with fundamental skills: recognizing automatic pilot behavior; differentiating between "doing" and "being" mode; becoming more aware of their body and beginning to move their focus of attention at will; recognizing when their attention wanders and bringing it gently back to the present; and using their breath to anchor attention. The last four sessions prepare the participants to help them prevent relapses into depression and to cultivate a different, more positive, relation to life in general.

Currently the field of MBIs is evolving as the interventions have called for additional specific applications and program adaptations. Important developments are taking place within the clinical realm and there is also increased involvement from nonclinical fields. I provide here a summary of some of the most important emerging trends beginning with new clinical developments and discussing non-clinical adaptations including the transfer of MBIs to the business community and to the workplace.

Recent clinical developments of MBIs can be subdivided into: field of application, content, and delivery mode and/or format. In the case of the field of application, additional forms of MBIs have been developed for specific, problem-oriented therapies such as, anxiety, intrusions, compulsive behaviors, addictions, issues of relating, and issues of inhibition.

Regarding content and delivery important work has been done concerning psychosis and health anxiety.

Adaptation for psychosis (Chadwick, 2014)

It has been found that mindfulness can be of therapeutic value for psychotic patients, if the duration of practice is shortened and if instructions during meditation follow in shorter intervals and refer explicitly to psychotic sensations. In this adapted form, mindfulness training appears not only to reduce psychotic symptoms but also to increase the general well-being of patients as they learn to respond differently to impulses and thus regain a sense of control.

Mindfulness based for bipolar disorder (Deckersbach, Hölzel, Eisner, Lazar, & Nierenberg, 2014)

Bipolar disorder includes hypomania, elevated and expansive periods of irritable mood, rumination, avoidance, hyper vigilance to body sensations, misinterpretation of such sensations, risk of suicide, and intolerance of uncertainty. Bipolar patients have both manic and depressive symptoms sometime present at the same time. MBIs have been found to be helpful for these conditions through four of its core mechanisms: responding instead of reacting, exploring body sensations, engaging with the present moment, and learning skills that help prevent relapse.

In the second part of this book I present a mindfulness-based intervention: mindfulness-based strategic awareness training (MBSAT) for nonclinical individuals in work settings and in daily life.

There are three nonclinical areas where mindfulness is having a growing impact: in families (parenting), survival training (military), and gradually in business/management.

The use of mindfulness in parenting represents an effort to bring help to stressed families "for the benefit of both the children and their parents" (Bögels & Restifo, 2014, p. v). An eight-session program has been proposed. It is based on MBCT with a clear redirection toward the tasks of parents. The session topics, for sessions 1–4, reflect the fusion of mindfulness training and parenting: automatic pilot parenting, beginner's mind parenting, reconnecting with our body as a parent, and responding versus reacting to parenting stress. Sessions 5–7 move away from MBCT with topics including: parenting patterns and schemas, conflict and parenting, love and limits. Although still in its infancy, it is a compelling illustration of how mindfulness can be of value in all our daily activities and especially in making human relations more enriching and worthwhile.

The US Army has shown an interest in mindfulness. Adaptations of mindfulness training for the military seem surprising or even strange as with the case of snipers. It is fair to ask: What has an approach geared towards generating wholesome mental states, compassion, and self-compassion got to do with violence?

A closer analysis reveals that it is basically a case of promoting stress resilience and coping with trauma (post-traumatic stress disorder, PTSD). Mind fitness seems as important *after* deployment as in the battlefield – particularly as we now know that rampant depression, suicide, violence, and strains in family ties have been sadly commonplace with those members of the US military returning from Iraq and Afghanistan. In fact, because of the military's emphasis on stress management, programs such as mindfulness-based mind fitness training (MMFT) (Stanley, Schaldach, Kiyonage, & Jha, 2011) compare their format and content with mindfulness-based stress reduction (MBSR).

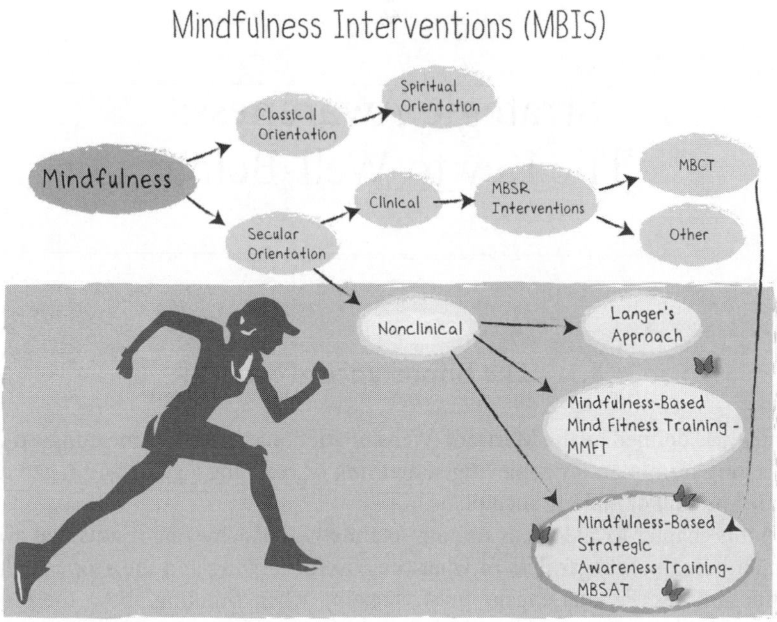

Figure 3.2 Mindfulness Interventions. *Source*: Juan Humberto Young.

The format of MMFT is similar to the standard MBSR protocol, although sessions tend to be shorter and at irregular intervals. The intervention has been adapted to the requirements of the army. The content has also been adjusted. Parallels between physical and mental stress and including concrete military applications and factual knowledge about stress, trauma, and resilience of the body have been highlighted (Stanley et al., p. 571).

For an overview of mindfulness-based interventions (MBIs), see Figure 3.2.

4

Strategic Awareness: The Key to Well-Being[1]

4.1 The Importance of Strategy

Strategy, as defined by the Merriam-Webster Dictionary, has two meanings: It can be "a long term plan for achieving something or reaching a goal" and it can also mean "the skill of making such plans."

In this chapter I will look at strategy as a method of achieving results that every human being uses regardless of what they do for a living and the scope of their responsibilities. Parents engage in strategizing when thinking about the future of their child or when thinking about how to better the family's life, also employs a strategy; even friends making plans for the weekend are essentially engaged in strategizing.

Any manager, shop owner, or leader of an organization, when considering the products and services that would drive demand and make their business prosper, is also strategizing. Likewise any politician, one would hope, is busy strategizing about how to increase his constituents' well-being.

Seen from the larger viewpoint of human history, strategy has always been the primary responsibility of leaders and of every individual thinking about the future. In ancient times it was related to the existential question of movement: when to move, where to move, and how to move to assure survival, either to get food and shelter or avoid dangers such as animal predators or hostile clans. In today's society strategy is still related to movement: the mother worries about the next move forward for her children, the father about his advancement for the happiness of his family, the business leader about his moves in the market to secure the survival of the organization.

[1] Throughout this book "well-being" and "happiness" are used as interchangeable terms. I believe that this is a sensible simplification given that scientific researchers generally use the term "subjective well-being" as synonymous for "happiness."

Mindfulness-Based Strategic Awareness Training: A Complete Program for Leaders and Individuals, First Edition. Juan Humberto Young.

Companion website: www.wiley.com/go/humbertoyoung/mbsat

This relationship between leadership and strategy often implies power play. In his extensive treatise about strategy Professor Freedman of the University of London (2013) argues that the primary features of human strategy—power, partnership, and charade—are common across time and space with only the complexity of specific and unique situations changing.

Historically, strategy was mostly related to war, so much that in its etymology, strategy finds its etymological origins in the Greek word "strategos," meaning "general."

Early writings about the nature of strategy include the Roman Emperor Marco Aurelio's *Meditations*; the treatise by Chinese General Sun Tzu on *The Art of the War* (456 BC); *The Book of Five Rings* (1645) by the Japanese Samurai Miyamoto Musashi; and the book *The Art of War* by Niccolò Machiavelli written in the sixteenth century.

It was in the early-nineteenth century that strategy began to be studied in a systematic manner with the work of the German Major-General C. von Clausewitz, *On War,* and the Swiss Antoine-Henri Jomini with his book also entitled *On War*. These books became texts of learning in military academies and with the migration of military-trained officers to civilian life the ideas and concepts of military strategy were transferred to other societal realms, especially commerce.

Whether it is concerned with existential moves or with leadership and war, strategy always involves a vision of the future. I have always been fascinated by the future. Although history has always interested me since childhood—I used to devour history books as a boy—from an early age I was much more interested in the excitement involved in imaging the future and its possibilities. When I was growing up in Panama, my parents often asked me what I wanted to do or become when I grew up. Like most kids my answers reflected my immediate enthusiasms: I wanted to become a heroic bullfighter as bull fighting was popular in Panama at the time; later I dreamt of becoming a jet pilot; then a flamenco dancer; and even a priest, because I admired a Jesuit math teacher.

Around the age of twelve I gave my parents a definite answer. "I don't want to be a CPA," I said, roundly rejecting the predestined profession of any member of the Young family. My grandpa had been one of the first non-American chief accountants at the payroll department of the Panama Canal company; my uncles were the founders of the highly respected accounting firm Young & Young, the largest in Panama at the time; and my father was a CPA with his own thriving practice.

"I want to work in MCD[2] (management consulting division)," I declared, "because I like to work on things that are going to happen in the future. Accountants only look back to scrutinize the results of the past."

[2] I knew about MCD from reading publications by the auditing and consulting firm Touche Ross (today Deloitte & Touche) which my uncles had brought to my father.

Years later my mother told me that at that moment she became confident that I would make it in life despite my family's image of me as a fidgety, unruly child.

As an adult I took the "strengths finder" survey, a comprehensive test by the Gallup Organization to identify personal strengths and talents. The results revealed that one of my top strengths is strategic thinking. Gallup describes strategic thinking as a perspective that allows some people to see patterns where others simply see complexity. Quite unpretentiously I can say that thinking about the future is indeed a strong and essential part of my personality.

Let me give you an example. As you might recall my first job in Switzerland was Director of Planning at the gastronomy organization Moevenpick which, at the time, was the largest restaurant chain in the country.

At one point the owner, the late Mr Prager, asked me to suggest specific growth strategies for the firm so the company could expand its already sizeable operations. After careful analysis I wrote a brief that included all the corresponding prospective quantitative data and suggested the acquisition of the McDonalds franchise for Switzerland.

My argument was that the level of affluence being experienced in the country couldn't be sustained and eventually people would need lower price alternatives to the high-priced Moevenpick restaurants and the still pricey low-budget restaurant variations, Cindy, and Silberkugel.

A week after submitting my report Mr Prager called me in for a meeting. With all his senior staff present he opened the meeting with this comment: "Dear Mr Young, I can see that you don't understand our culture. We Swiss people will never eat with our hands like the Americans. Even at our fast food places, Cindy and Silberkugel, we serve hamburgers with a knife and fork. It is unthinkable for our people to eat hand to mouth, much less eating a hamburger while walking in the street or taking a train."

In a memorable scene from the movie, *Pretty Woman,* Vivian Ward, played by the actress Julia Roberts, returns to an exclusive store where she was previously denied service because of her modest appearance.

"Big mistake," she calls out to the sales person, swinging in front of her nose the shopping bags full of expensive dresses she just bought from other exclusive stores. It neatly drives home the message of a great opportunity missed.

I have felt many times like swinging my metaphorical shopping bags in the same way and calling out: "Big mistake, Mr Prager! What an opportunity missed."

Today Moevenpick is a minor player in the restaurant business in Switzerland, whereas McDonald's is the most important restaurant operation in Switzerland.

Mr Prager was evaluating my suggestion from an extremely limited awareness as he was blinded by his emotional attachment to his business. He was unable to visualize the opportunity I was presenting to him.

The skill of foresight that helps us navigate into the future is probably one of the most important skills we need to achieve sustainable well-being and continuous growth at both personal and organizational levels.

4.2 The Future—Not the Past, Not even the Present—As Key to Well-Being

It may appear that some ideas presented in this chapter challenge, to some degree, generalize views of the role of mindfulness. That is not the intention. They should be seen as complementary. Fortunately I am not travelling this path alone and therefore feel confident about exploring new areas of awareness. Once again I am in the company of Marty Seligman and others scientists with advanced ideas about the psychology of mindfulness.

I would like to advance two ideas that may appear to diverge from the mainstream views of mindfulness. One involves the "present moment" focus, which is so strongly emphasized in current thinking about mindfulness. Although being in the present moment is necessary to overcome our scattered thoughts it is, in my view, a transitory stage: one that allows gaining the necessary calmness and stability of mind in order to proceed and engage skillfully in further inquiries. Ultimately, it is a question of balance as with all issues. For sustainable well-being you can neither live solely in the present nor solely in the future. The other idea relates to the importance of non-judgment. As with being present, being non-judgmental is required to quiet our busy, highly conditioned minds and getting rid of preconceptions. As such it is also a stage. Having stopped judgmental proliferation and gained stability in our mind, the important next step is to involve the mind's discerning processes to help us perceive reality as it is, free of biases. And this implies wisdom in judgment.

4.2.1 The past: Retrospection

Seligman, Railton, Baumeister, and Sripada (2013) tell us that most of the history of psychology has been dominated by the belief that people are driven by the past. In this view it is a person's past experiences combined with their present circumstances and their inner states that drive their behavior. This reading of human behavior suggests that retrospective analysis provides some of the best clues for the future. However, a clear-eyed assessment of the real world casts doubt on this model. Think about intractable smokers, alcoholics, or workaholics: they all look at their past behavior and would like to change their future actions. Or think about some of the social issues confronting our society: inequality, xenophobia, social services decay, and so on. History is replete with data telling us that the failure to solve these issues could lead to social unrest. However, we all look in amazement at the inability of people to change their course of action and the inability of leaders to solve our social-economic problems. It is as if the forces of the past are not imbued with enough drive and energy to ensure better alternatives for the future.

Thus Seligman et al. (2013) suggest that the past is not what drives action but that it is "a resource from which they (people) selectively extract information about the prospects they face." This suggests that the elements we take from the past are only helpful if: a) we keep an inventory of accurate memories, as they are the raw material that helps us generate accurate prospects and b) if the memory inventory itself stays accurate. Wrong memories (inaccurate and non-factual) are of little help for the future as they may lead to erroneous prospects.

4.2.2 The present: Introspection

Most mindfulness-based interventions (MBIs) are designed to follow Kabat–Zinn's dictum of "paying attention on purpose, in the present moment, and non-judgmentally" (2013, p. xxvii). In Section 3.2 I mentioned that focusing intentionally and non-judgmentally on the present moment seems to provide an adaptive advantage for clinical cases such as for individuals suffering from depression, physical pain, and so on by helping them disconnect from maladaptive emotional and cognitive fabrications. Given the tendency of such patients to get caught in cycles of negativity that confine their perception and ability to sense, the suggestion to ease into a "being mode" by accepting and enhancing their sensory faculties non-judgmentally in the present reality is certainly useful, as the results of multiple studies on the efficacy of these interventions demonstrate.

For non-clinical individuals interested in increasing their well-being and maintaining high levels of flourishing—the kind of readers this book is directed to—the challenge of staying in the present moment non-judgmentally is particularly difficult. Humans are prone to cognitive biases and distortions as explained in Section 1.3.1. What is required to overcome these problems are practices that help individuals reduce biases and distortions and allow them to see reality clearly so that they can make decisions that will lead them to authentic happiness. This implies a considerable degree of discernment.

To achieve a state where you stay in the present moment there are two steps:

1. Move into a neutral state of focused awareness as suggested by most mindfulness-based interventions (MBIs). This allows the individual to reduce distractions and avoid the mental process known as automatic pilot.
2. The second step requires a level of introspection that goes beyond awareness of oneself and staying attentive. It requires that individuals remain unbiased and open their heart so they can refine their perceptions about the experiences of the moment. It is a higher-order cultivation of responsible attention that is the nutrient of cultivating generosity, kindness, and wisdom and generating more skillful prospects about the future. This process has an intentional discerning quality that bends the mind toward wholesome aspects of life.

4.2.3 *The future: Prospection*

Most people are driven by an innate desire to be happy and avoid suffering. This simple fact has been confirmed by psychological research. Yet as Easterlin, Angelescu McVey, Switek, Sawangfa, and Smith Zweig (2010), an economist specializing in well-being issues, suggests it is not the increase in material wealth and improvement in living standards that make people generally happier, although the unceasing desire to increase wealth seems to drive so much of the world. Research findings from the Well-being Institute at Cambridge University reveals that the majority of the population in industrialized countries is actually languishing, in other words feeling utterly dull and drained. Why is that so?

Amongst others factors there is a core problem: people do not fundamentally understand what makes them truly happy; consequently people keep making plans for their future but these plans rarely yield the expected satisfaction. We have already discussed this paradox in Chapter 2 in connection with affective forecasting, that is, the gap between our emotional and cognitive expectations when related to a future event. Economists and psychologists define this gap as the difference between "expected utility or satisfaction" and the real experienced utility.

How often we hear: "I thought that the food here was really great. What a disappointment!" or "I bought a big house in the suburbs because I thought it would make me and my family happy, but now I have to commute to and from my office twice daily for over an hour. I wish I had bought a smaller place in the city and avoided all that traffic."

What we need are robust and realistic expectations about our future that reduce the tendency to make decisions that later impair our well-being and capacity to flourish. Good forecasts for the future require us, among other things, to have high-quality memories about the past so we can accurately simulate potential outcomes for our well-being and create good alternative courses of action.

Gilbert and Wilson (2007) have identified four common errors of simulations when attempting to anticipate future behavior:

a. *Simulations are unrepresentative*: People tend to use their most recent and most memorable experiences to construct their simulations of future events.
b. *Simulations focus only on the essentials*: People leave out incidental, but vital, features in their predictions. For example, if you are going out for dinner to a very popular restaurant you might have forgotten to take the long waiting list into account, or the high noise level, the problem of finding parking, and so on. These are all relatively unimportant components, however, they can have a major impact on the happiness of the experience.
c. *Simulations are abbreviated*: This is due to the natural tendency to simplify. If we were to simulate all details, the simulation would take the same

amount of time as the events themselves. Consequently simulations are brief anticipations of future events, leaving out often vital elements and concentrating on the most recent and significant events.

d. *Finally, simulations are decontextualized*: Often people fail to realize that contextual factors at the moment of exercising a simulation don't have the same effect as when the event actually occurs. For example, having eaten a large meal at a restaurant you may decide not to have the leftovers packaged up because, feeling satiated, you are convinced that eating the same food the next day has no appeal. The next day, however, hungry again, you might regret not having taken home the remains of the meal.

In summary, simulations tend to be deficient because they are based on a small number of memories and features. They do not sustain themselves over time and they lack context.

Marty Seligman et al. (2013) have suggested ways to improve our ability to accurately create simulations:

- One technique is to enhance the alternatives by inviting different people to be involved in empathetic simulation, that is, including other people's perspective.
- Second, we can develop more effective prospection by becoming more skilful in decision tree simulations, the "if–then" approach: if x happens it could lead to y, but if v happens it could lead to w, and so on.
- A third technique is to disconfirm unrealistic prospections, which amounts to helping people get rid of their biases and cognitive distortions.

To achieve these crucial abilities what is needed is a specific kind of consciousness, based on being present non-judgmentally and with a broadening and discerning analytical mindset. It is a distinct type of awareness which I call "strategic awareness"—the focus of this book.

4.3 Strategic Awareness

4.3.1 Differentiating the concept of awareness

Before attempting to define the parameters of strategic awareness let us reflect on the notion of awareness and its multiple facets. The Merriam-Webster dictionary defines awareness as knowing that something (a situation, condition, or problem) exists; also as feeling, experiencing, or noticing something (a sound, sensation, or emotion) and, in a more all-encompassing way, as knowing and understanding what is happening in the world around you.

For the scholar Tse-fu Kuan (2008) awareness comprises four types of functions:

a. *Simple awareness*: Consisting of conscious, non-judgmental registering of whatever is present. This is the way most psychologists understand the practice of mindfulness.
b. *Protective awareness*: Going a step further by consciously registering and observing how the mind reacts, thus relating awareness to restraint and proper judgment. This implies constant practice of mindfulness to protect oneself from unwholesome states of mind such as covetousness and dejection.
c. *Introspective awareness*: Serving as remedial measure when protective awareness fails to act, by activating the faculty of mindfulness to notice and recognize unwholesome states such as anger, envy, and other negative states in one's mind.
d. *Deliberately forming conceptions*: This function is based on constructive memories and constructive imagination. It involves developing friendliness towards all sentient beings including oneself by a process of deliberate constructive conceptualization.

Clearly mindfulness is not a monolithic construct driven exclusively by non-judgmental present awareness. It can involve several other elements. I would suggest that Tse-fu-Kuan's work can best be understood in the following terms:

The practice of mindfulness in the first stage allows practitioners to perceive reality as it is without involving themselves in likes and dislikes about the experiences, while the mind may and, with all probability, will still react.

At the second stage mindfulness protects practitioners by reining in their awareness and keeping them from falling into cycles of negative mental proliferation. If protective awareness is not sufficient to overcome the potential hindrances, mindfulness helps practitioners to access proper retrospection (identifying accurate memories) and introspection to allow the skillful perception of present experiences thus reducing distortions and mental proliferation ingrained in cognitive/emotional patterns.

In the last stage, mindfulness cultivates a lucid and friendly mindset that facilitates positive imagination, builds affirmative images of the private self without cognitive and emotional distortions and fosters healthy social interconnections.

The key functions of awareness are to develop a wholesome cognition, overcome biases and distortions, prevent the mind from going astray and avoid falling into negative conceptual proliferation based on subjective experiences that originate from an unhealthy view of oneself. With this kind of all-encompassing awareness, feelings and mental processes can be freed from the underlying tendencies of craving, hostility, and ignorance; cognitive distortions are dissolved and emotions are more easily regulated—hence the essential barriers to well-being and emotional enrichment are lifted.

4.3.2 *Connections between awareness and well-being*

Awareness and well-being are intertwined because awareness ensures a more wholesome orientation in life, hence more skillful decisions leading towards a greater likelihood of happiness. Without awareness we are blind and hardly capable of strategizing.

Strategizing implies orientation and goals. For strategic awareness to occur we need awareness of our goals in life. When we think of well-being and flourishing as innate human aspirations we need to be aware of two notions of well-being and happiness the mix-up of which often causes mistakes as we travel along life's paths.

One view of well-being is hedonic in nature and assumes that humans are basically concerned with maximizing pleasure and minimizing discomfort. The hedonic tradition goes back to the Greek philosophers Aristippus and Epicurus and carries through to the British thinkers Jeremy Bentham and John Locke in the eighteenth and nineteenth century. Remarkably, recent research has revealed that hedonic well-being is more a function of the frequency of positive affects and not so much their intensity. The wide acceptance of the hedonic view of well-being is largely due to its compatibility with economic theory. Economic models implicitly postulate that man is rational and pursues exclusively personal utility, an assumption named "homo oeconomicus." Quantitative economics models invariably use measurable markers of hedonic happiness: income, wealth, levels of utility, purchasing power, and so on.

A second view of well-being is called "eudemonic" and was first articulated by the Greek philosophers Aristotle and Plato. It argues that a happy life is one that is lived according to an individual's inherent nature. This happy life is produced by a combination of a healthy mind, engagement in activities, and realizing one's highest potential. According to contemporary research by Ryan, Huta, and Deci, (2008) an eudemonic life is characterized by reflection and deliberation concerning one's actions and aims in life.

I hope readers recognize the similarities with the PERMA model explained earlier. Hedonic behavior corresponds to the realm of positive emotions while eudemonic well-being covers meaning and engagement in the PERMA schema. This is not a trivial matter. Knowing which of the two modes of well-being is being employed has significant impact for one's happiness. Normally our limited awareness doesn't allow us to distinguish between the two modes. This leads us to errors of decision and judgment. We might for example invest an enormous amount of time and energy seeking material comfort while neglecting aspects of our life that are important for our humanity, such as true friendship and authentic loving relationships amongst others. This is probably the most common error in decision-making.

A common sense conclusion may be a balanced approach that combines sensible levels of hedonic and eudemonic experiences and produces sustainable well-being. Whatever mixture one chooses (more of one or the other), the main point is that we need to be aware of what we are seeking in life. Without being able to decide which direction we want to go we are likely to end up with disappointment and regrets. This does require a clear, lucid mind which enables us to make skillful decisions to advance our quest for sustainable well-being—and that is what I call strategic awareness.

4.3.3 What is strategic awareness?

The key features of strategic awareness (SA) are wisdom, equanimity, friendliness, and open awareness. It is clean of the cognitive biases and distortions that cloud people's Body sensations, Emotions/feelings, Thoughts and Action/behavioral impulses, what I call people's BETA and it is lucid by being free from unhealthy desires, dislikes, and misconceptions, thus free from the conditioning that leads us to dissatisfaction.

SA is the awareness that travels without limits into the past recollecting accurate memories while staying in the present moment with accurate perceptions. It is capable of projecting into the future, and constructing positive prospects and outcomes.

An entrepreneurial example of SA I have witnessed occurred in the agricultural sector. In the mid-1980s while on a business trip in Kenya I met a Swiss businessman at a dinner party. He was the former General Manager for Africa of the Basel-based chemical company Hoffman before it merged with La Roche to become Hoffman-LaRoche.

After the merger the businessman had launched his own trading business that operated between Africa and Europe. The week we met he was in Nairobi supervising a cargo of mangos from Kenya to Switzerland. At the dinner he explained to the guests that mangos were the fruit of the future. I still remember him saying: "Once the Europeans taste this fruit they will fall in love with it and you will see all kinds of different uses."

He said that mangos reminded him of the first time he ate a fresh orange and how fresh he felt after ingesting it. He genuinely loved all the sensations provided by the taste of the fruit. In this way he was recalling a positive past experience and at the same time seeing the potential of another fruit, the mango, despite the reality in its countries of origin where juicy mangos were eaten in a messy way and often lay rotting on the ground beneath the trees.

He was able to suspend negative judgments and envision the success of the mango in completely different environments. At the time of that conversation in Kenya several decades ago it was almost impossible to find mangos in Switzerland and even in Southern European countries. The businessman's strategic awareness proved to be right: today mangos are one of the most ubiquitous fruits in Europe and even in the United States, available natural and in many processed forms as yoghurt, marmalade, drinks, and so on, all year round. The demand is huge and continually growing, making this man financially well-off—the result of accurate strategic awareness.

4.3.4 *The conditions of strategic awareness*

There are three conditions necessary for strategic awareness to emerge: strategic intent, strategic outlook, and strategic noticing/discerning.

1. Strategic intent

In a Harvard Business Review article published in 1989 the management experts Hamel and the late Prahalad coined the expression "strategic intent." For them it meant an institutional construct referring to a "stretch vision" of what a company could aim for, essentially increasing profits and outperforming their competition. For MBSAT strategic intent is a richer concept and more focused on personal vision. It refers to the intention and desire of individuals and leaders to develop themselves while helping others become mindful, positive individuals, and contributing to well-being in society.

2. Strategic outlook

Strategic awareness involves developing open awareness by being able to suspend judgment and keep an open, probing, and searching disposition toward both our internal phenomena and external happenings. It implies an attitude of friendliness and acceptance, characterized by a beginner's mind and curious spirit even if events differ from personal desires. Mindful, positive individuals, with an intentional strategic outlook, are capable of fine-tuning their own behavior. This means abstaining from striving to fulfill indiscriminately any personal desire or, on the other hand, blindly rejecting personal dislikes. Strategic outlook is infused with equanimity and balance.

3. Strategic noticing and discernment

Finally, out of strategic intent and outlook grows a capacity to notice and discern with lucidity. It is an analytical, practical mindfulness that allows for wise judgment regarding inner and outer phenomena and guides decision-making processes, thus ensuring balanced outcomes.

For example, the head of an organization whose declared intention is to maximize the value of just one part of the stakeholders is more a servant to these stakeholders than a genuine leader. A leader with true strategic intent strives to serve all stakeholders.

Similarly, a leader with a rigid opinion of how a team should be composed, for example, of mostly extrinsically motivated individuals (driven by money and power), gets caught by a conditioned, fixed mindset. This is far from the open awareness required for strategic outlook and is unlikely to develop the ability to lead an organization or even one's own life towards lasting, sustainable well-being. Likewise, if a leader makes decisions based exclusively on so-called hard data and purely quantifiable facts without accessing the wisdom of his or her heart and body they are clearly acting from a restricted awareness.

Strategic awareness feeds holistically in a closed loop of intent, outlook, and noticing/discerning as Figure 4.1 illustrates.

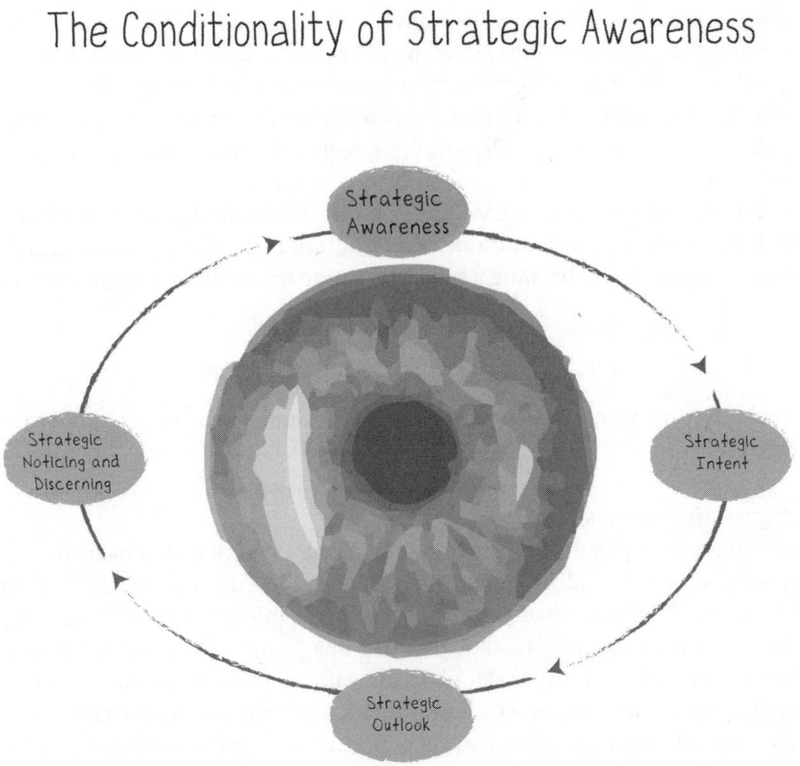

Figure 4.1 The Conditionality of Strategic Awareness. *Source*: Juan Humberto Young.

It is from the fine-tuning of these conditions that strategic awareness emerges as it is not a technique or tool to be learned but a quality that needs to be cultivated over time in order to take effect at the right moment and within the prevailing context. The Swiss entrepreneur growing mangos in Kenya, mentioned in the previous section, was able to see what others couldn't only by understanding the contextual elements of both Europe's and Kenya's fruit markets so that he was able to connect the dots.

Recently I discussed the case of two of my students with my daughter Claudia, a lawyer. The two students had failed the requirements to graduate from the EXMPLS in Madrid, often missing classes, delivering papers late and of mediocre or even poor quality. They wanted to have a second chance to resubmit all the papers that were given a grade of "no pass." For one of them this meant actually redoing half of the program. All of a sudden my grandchild Alejandro, 11-years-old, who was playing with his electronic games but had obviously listened, interrupted us and exclaimed: "But grandpa, that is not fair with the other students who have attended the classes and submitted their papers on time." He had instantly grasped the situation and pointed out an unintended problematic consequence: the likely adverse reaction of the other students if the two were allowed to resubmit. El Bebito, as I call him, knows the context of grading well as most of his time revolves around school and his classmates, essays he has to write, and the grades his parents expect from him. In this context he rapidly, albeit unknowingly, deployed strategic awareness and figured out the implications.

Cultivating the practices of MBSAT, creating the conditions explained above (strategic intent, outlook, and noticing) and understanding the context allow strategic awareness to become a powerful guide for skillful decision-making.

4.3.5 *The elements of strategic awareness*

I would like to propose that strategic awareness can be seen as having four basic elements.

Interpretative awareness

Here I am referring to the process of deploying our cognitive antenna by suspending our preconceived ideas, judgments, dogmas, theories, and beliefs. This suggests that we must learn to suspend and let go of the information and inputs we get from our five senses and our thoughts and imagination. We must intentionally achieve a neutral cognitive state—perhaps with the help of mindfulness of the breath or similar techniques which we will discuss in the following chapters—that directs our attention toward an issue of concern and intentionally begins a hermeneutical/interpretative cognitive exercise by looking at both external and internal phenomena with fresh eyes. It is the awareness that is able to discern between hedonic (pleasurable) and eudaimonic (meaningful) aspects of life and find a skillful balance of these two.

Appreciative awareness

This element involves a positive attitude of the heart, tapping into its innate intelligence.

My friends and teachers, David Cooperrider and the late Suresh Srivastva, refer to appreciative inquiry (AI)—the process methodology they developed (please, see Section 1.2.)—as leading to a personal and organizational life that supports curiosity and openness about relational construction.

It helps us to discover, in relation to others, what could be possible instead of getting stuck by judging what is and should be according to one's limited and fixed opinion.

Thus, instead of asking: "What is wrong with me?" the question becomes "What can I become?" In the same way instead of asking: "What is wrong with this organizational process?" the question becomes "What kind of process can we aspire to achieve?"

I remember my qualms around the year 2000 as I was expanding my consulting practice from corporate finance to positive and appreciative consulting approaches. I was worrying about whether the business world was ready for the change in paradigm and about what model I should use to access the market. And there were many other questions. As I was searching for answers I decided to ask Suresh for advice and visited him at his home in Naples, Florida, where he had moved after his retirement. We spent an entire day engrossed in conversation. At the end of the day Suresh said: "Look, Juan, with this type of work the best advice I can give you is this: just be there with your client with a warm, appreciative heart." I am still learning from this simple and wise suggestion.

Interoceptive awareness

This unusual word, interoceptive, simply means the sensing of signals originating within the body. It explains the third element of strategic awareness. The importance of interoception is one the most recent developments in psychology regarding the connection between body signals and health. Farb et al. (2015) conclude that maladaptive biases about how people perceive, comprehend, and interpret their bodily sensations are at the root of negative health conditions.

On a more serene note falling in love provides a compelling illustration of the interconnection of body sensations, emotions, and cognitive moods: as soon as the adored person appears, the heart races, the skin flushes, butterflies fill the stomach, and nice thoughts pop up in the mind.

It is also true that in everyday life the body sends continuous signals, although we are unaware of them most of the time. One reason why it is important to improve interoceptive awareness has to do with self-regulation: if individuals can accurately read their interoceptive signals they can make decisions that will increase their wellbeing.

Engaged generative awareness

Engaged generative awareness is the awareness of skillful creative action in social contexts. It moves the practitioner beyond the reified (fixed) view of the self that deals primarily with one's own freedom from unhappiness, and uses the newly gained strategic awareness in an all encompassing, friendly way to deal with challenging and difficult situations.

Engaged generative awareness guides the implementation of decisions so that they become skillful and positive actions. Deciding the right thing is not enough; dreadful things can happen while implementing wholesome decisions. It is important that good intentions become real and are not just promises swiftly blown away by the headwinds of life.

Engaged generative awareness keeps people anchored and committed when facing the social realities of family, work, and society. At the same time it helps people to generate skillful positive actions to advance the common good.

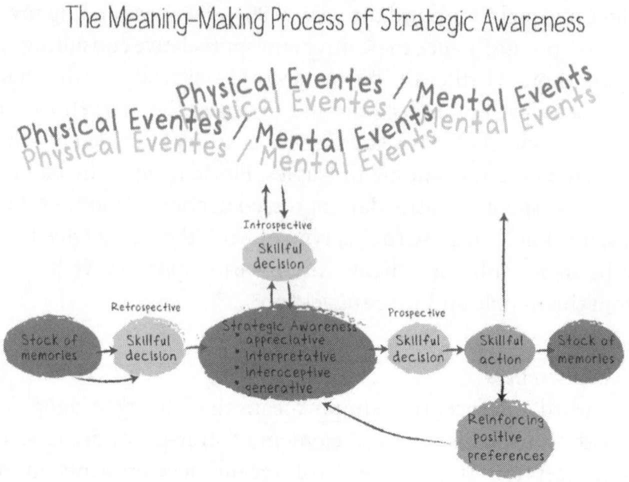

Figure 4.2 The Meaning-Making Process of Strategic Awareness. *Source*: Juan Humberto Young.

Strategic awareness encompasses all four elements: it integrates interpretative, appreciative, interoceptive, and engaged generative awareness to form a meta-awareness. It allows individuals to open their heads, hearts, and bodies to cultivate friendship, wisdom, and equanimity, while reducing aggression, greed, and confusion. In other words it allows us to calm our normally agitated ego and it nudges us towards the development of a flexible, cognitive, and emotional infrastructure that facilitates decision-making and positive behaviors toward others and ourselves.

Figure 4.2 depicts the meaning-making process of SA as a set of skills at the center of people's lives.

SA passes through three stages that represent a process of SA meaning-making:

a. In the retrospective phase it allows a person to trace their past adaptive judgments and decisions retrieving them from the stock of memories to come back to what is before us in the present moment.
b. The introspective phase helps us to see the present without conditioning and with the possibility of seeing the present with new eyes.
c. In the prospective phase individuals are able to build skillful simulations that can guide their actions and enhance their affective forecasting capacity by increasing the probability that their aspirations (plans) will match the reality (facts).

An illustration could be preparations for vacation to one's favorite tropical destination: in the retrospective phase one might recall the wonderful sunny beaches and warm evenings. In the introspective phase one might note one's tendency to remember just the pleasant experiences, and in the prospective phase one might plan to pack a light sweater and a book for rainy days.

In an office setting an illustrative case could be an angry interchange with a colleague: in the retrospective phase one would remember that this same colleague is usually a friendly, likeable person; in the introspective phase one maintains composure despite having the impulse to react in a defensive, blunt way; and in the prospective phase one might decide to invite this colleague to lunch and ask him whether there is something troubling him.

Characteristic of each of these three stages is that the mind is quiet and suffused with strategic awareness. It is in a state of wise composure and it also has a functional quality. The wise frame of mind enables people to maintain a perspicacious, open appreciative, interpretative, interoceptive, and engaged generative awareness, while the functional quality helps people become skillful, strategically aware decision-makers.

The second part of this book is dedicated to developing a practical, detailed program geared towards training SA specifically in Sessions 5, 6, and 7.

Part 2

Mindfulness-Based Strategic Awareness Training (MBSAT)

5

MBSAT: The Program

5.1 Its Origin and Goals

Mindfulness-based strategic awareness training (MBSAT) is a training program designed to help leaders and private individuals improve their decision-making abilities so that they can make choices that enhance their well-being and the well-being of others.

For leaders this means happiness for themselves and for their immediate social circle. It also means happiness for their clients, their employees, suppliers, governments, and society in general. For individuals without organizational leadership functions it means happiness for themselves, their close and extended families, their work colleagues, and friends.

I have spent many years thinking about ways to assist people in the workplace so they become more productive and have authentic, meaningful lives. During my doctoral studies in the United States, I spent several years researching the structures of management practices and concluded that well-being is each individual's responsibility.

Obviously organizations must do their part in mitigating adverse effects on people's lives. However, it is ultimately each individual who needs to take responsibility for his or her own well-being. Organizations can help by creating conditions in which people who take their own well-being seriously can develop and grow. It is observable that happy individuals will contribute to the well-being of their organization, thus establishing sustainable synergetic relationships not only of high economic value but also of social and psychological worth for all parties.

It was in the belief that it would help both individuals and organizations that I designed MBSAT. It is a program designed for individuals who are willing to do the necessary work during 8 weeks at a rate of 5 to 8 hours per week to improve the quality of their lives.

Mindfulness-Based Strategic Awareness Training: A Complete Program for Leaders and Individuals, First Edition. Juan Humberto Young.

Companion website: www.wiley.com/go/humbertoyoung/mbsat

The program is set at the intersection of conditioned life on one hand and reinforced autonomy on the other in line with the already described self-determination theory with its focus on motivation.

Practicing MBSAT reinforces people's sense of autonomy and their will to become happy individuals. At the same time it helps dissolve the elements of undesirable life conditioning. It allows them, as self-directed individuals, to gain an understanding of what is possible for them in a positive and practical way. The program demonstrates that robust self-knowledge allows people to find appropriate answers to how they can live their lives to the best and fullest.

5.2 MBSAT: A Decision-Making Approach

Decision-making involves trade-offs. There are no optimal decisions as they always involve choices: gaining something and losing something. Often people are not aware of these trade-off dynamics in their decision-making processes, which invariably causes dissatisfaction at some point. Making lucid decisions is an ability that is emphasized implicitly in MBSAT, as it is a key skill for leaders and individuals to increase well-being for themselves and the people they are responsible for or close to.

In many instances today's world is the result of choices made in the past. Therefore, placing emphasis on refining people's decision-making skills can prove a sensible and useful strategy. Having skillful decision-making abilities is a key asset for an individual's subjective well-being. Equally, having skillful decision-makers managing societies is crucial for the well-being of all citizens.

Let me give you an example. At the height of the dispute between Panama's former strongman A. Noriega and the United States, the US government offered the General an exit pass, literally assuring him that he could leave the country with his family and the fortune he had amassed during his years in power. He refused and what happened next is history: a military invasion that led according to various news reports to nearly 3,000 fatalities in Panama; Noriega was captured and since then has spent over 20 years in jail, first in the United States, subsequently in France, and lately in a remote prison in Panama City.

I asked one of my brother's college friends, a relative of Noriega, why Noriega refused the US offer to go into exile. He replied: "Imagine you are having a wonderful dream and you find yourself in a country where everything is at your disposal. Just lift a finger and you get what you desire. Would you like to wake up from this dream? Probably not. Well, that was the world of Tony (as Noriega is called by his intimates). It is pretty hard to wake up from such a dream, wouldn't you agree?"

I have been turning this story over in my head for years and for me it demonstrates the pressing need, and enduring importance, of wise decision-making skills. Imagine Noriega had accepted the offer: not only would he still be enjoying his freedom in company of his family, the whole country would have been spared so much horror and suffering. Wrong trade-off!

The world is full of examples like this. An essential feature of MBSAT is to reduce people's reactivity and insensate impulses (Noriega's machismo and decision to challenge the Americans was purely reactive and insensate) and to train and develop spaces in the present moment where people can access their practical wisdom. This will help them reach more skillful responses (Noriega opting for the exit strategy or, in boxing jargon, "throwing in the towel"). In the case of Noriega this would have meant that if he had had the clarity to realize that the dream was turning into a nightmare he would have had time to wake up and develop a beneficial strategy for everyone.

Although it is not the purpose of this book to present a theory on decision-making, it is necessary to comment briefly on the connection between mindfulness and decision-making given MBSAT's orientation towards improving decision-making for well-being.

5.2.1 Decision-making theory

Decision-making theory in its classical form follows the rational economic model. It is based on the assumption that individuals decide rationally and pursue a single goal: to maximize profit (monetary or non-monetary) from their decisions.

Psychologists have long argued that humans do not and cannot make decisions rationally. Even if they were to have all the information required to make a rational decision (which is hardly ever the case, especially in today's complex environment) they simply could not process all that information because of the limited capacity of the human brain. H. Simon, the Nobel Laureate in economics, called this limitation "bounded rationality."

Asian and Buddhist psychology have always recognized the importance of emotional states to decision-making in people's daily lives. They refer to certain emotional states as "feeling tones" that can shape human experience. The West has only recently recognized the influence of emotions on decision-making.

A turning point was the groundbreaking work of Antonio Damasio who studied patients who had suffered damage to those areas of the brain that are responsible for experiencing and expressing emotions. Damasio observed that the decision-making capabilities of these individuals were impaired and that the patients were prone to making poor choices in everything from jobs to marriages. This led him to the conclusion that emotions were important for decision-making. Emotions were possibly a necessity and not, as had been previously thought, an obstacle to rational economic thought.

In 2002 D. Kahneman won the Nobel Prize in economics for his work on the inconsistencies in human decision-making and inspired a whole new field called behavioral economics. Kahneman pointed out that, contrary to the rationality axiom of the utility theory of decision-making, people treat gains and losses of equal amounts differently. This was contrary to what could be expected based on rationality. The example below illustrates this peculiarity of human behavior.

What would you prefer in the examples below: A or B?
Scenario 1:

A. a sure gain of 2,900 or
B. a 70% chance of gaining zero plus
 a 30% chance of gaining 12,000

Scenario 2:

A. a loss of 7,000 or
B. a 70% of losing 10,000 plus
 a 30% chance of losing 0

In the first scenario people tend to spontaneously choose alternative A, because the great majority of people prefer a sure gain over a risky alternative. In the second scenario, however, people tend to choose the risky alternative, because the small probability of having zero loss seems more attractive to them than the prospect of having a sure loss. In other words when dealing with gains people tend to be risk averse, but when confronted with the possibility of avoiding losses they become risk seekers.

Loewenstein, Weber, Hsee, and Welch (2001) developed the risk as feelings hypothesis. The authors argue that most decisions generate heightened emotional arousal as there is always a certain degree of uncertainty involved in decision-making. According to these findings the inevitable emotions of worry, fear and anxiety affect the process of decision-making and, at times, can become the main drivers of behavior.

In addition to the complexities of risk, experts in decision analysis have identified other cognitive biases in decision-making including over-optimism that can result in unrealistic decisions and failure. (For other cognitive biases see Box 1.2 in Chapter 1.)

Alternating between "aversion and fear" and "optimism and hope" people often make decisions they later regret. This can create a misalignment between the satisfaction and enjoyment they originally expected and the real utility they experience as result of their decisions.

This book is written on the premise that improving people's capacity to make mindful decisions in business and their personal life is essential for improving their well-being.

In the ultimatum game, an experiment in economic behavior, one person (the proposer) is given a sum of money to share with a second person (the responder). While the proposer defines the size of what he or she gives away, the responder can reject the offer in which case both parties receive nothing. What to do? The clever aspect of this game is that both parties have power: one may decide how to divide the pie and the other can decide if the portions are acceptable. It has been observed that the responder always rejects the offer if the proposer wants to keep 80% or more for him or herself.

Looked at more closely the responder's behavior is not rational because walking home with 20% in your pocket is better than going home with nothing. Clearly emotions and negative cognitions play a role in distorting the rationally correct course of action: that is, accepting the offer. Can this conundrum be solved? Yes, with mindfulness.

Kirk, Downar, and Montague (2011) designed a study testing the game with a group of meditators and non-meditators and found that meditators were able to accept more unfair offers than the control group of non-meditators. The meditators were able to activate the part of their brain that allows them to uncouple negative emotional reactions from their behavior thus enabling them to accept unfair offers more rationally than non-meditators. In fact the meditators in Kirk's experiments went home with more money in their pockets that the non-meditators.

5.3 MBSAT Principles

Most mindfulness-based interventions emphasize empirical evidence-based approaches and factually oriented scholarship—an understandable focus in view of their target population, mostly clinical, and the need to ensure that the interventions have the healing effect they are designed to achieve.

In contrast a MBSAT program targets non-clinical individuals in their quest for personal growth, hence its design is based on a scholarship of discovery (Boyer, 1997) and it is designed to help the individual explore new possibilities of growing.

Moreover, MBSAT embraces a scholarship of integration, making connections between different disciplines (positive psychology, economics, contemplative sciences, cognitive therapy, and so on) as well as a scholarship of application, making knowledge consequential and of practical use for individuals and organizations.

Finally, MBSAT also pursues a scholarship of teaching with the goal of not only transmitting knowledge but, if possible, extending it. There is a passionate drive in MBSAT to make things better for people in their own working and private environments. That makes participants the ultimate judges of the utility of the program.

MBSAT is based on five core principles, which follow.

5.3.1 Social construction principle

MBSAT takes a social constructionist stand, that is, it aligns with the idea that reality is socially constructed and not a predefined objective reality. Most of what we experience as reality emerges from social interchange, in communication with others, and mostly in relationships. The importance of this principle has became clear after numerous conversations with my friend Dian Marie Hosking, a leading exponent of social construction theories, and reading the work of Kenneth Gergen, also a well-known exponent of the social constructionist paradigm.

People construct the world they live in: whether we think of the everyday life of an individual or larger issues such as human history, culture, economic systems, or social institutions, they are all in some way the outcome of social interaction.

For example, conventional knowledge suggests that the institution of marriage unites two human beings of opposite sex, a woman and a man. Yet, recently I found in my email box a message from Ana Cecilia, my elder daughter, in which she asked me to reserve a date to assist her wedding with Jenny, an American woman with whom she has lived for the past 10 years. The two follow a trend of social reconfiguration as they opt for a same sex union, an act recognized by law in some countries as legitimate—something unthinkable not long ago.

The MBSAT principle of social construction suggests that the program works best as a socially shared activity of experiential learning. In joint inquiries in the sessions, participants achieve an awareness of interdependence that can produce new vistas for both the individual and the social web in which the person is embedded.

Thus MBSAT, anchored in social construction, invites participants to open up to new possibilities of their self; to disrupt their fixed and reified realities; and to embrace alternatives that cater to their full potential and positively influence the larger social realm.

5.3.2 The appreciation and positivity principle

In Chapter 2 we looked into the many benefits of positivity: emotional, cognitive, and physiological. It is evident that MBSAT rests firmly on a positivity principle. In addition MBSAT emphasizes an appreciative stance that is associated with a constructive, generative orientation, that is, appreciation and a positive mindset able to generate novel, more satisfying options. This is the essence of the appreciation and positivity principle.

The late Suresh, my teacher at Case Western Reserve University who developed the methodology of appreciative inquiry, used to equate generativity with reframing. Simply put this involves looking at situations from a different angle, a capacity that helps people renew and expand their awareness and enables them to see physical or mental phenomena with new eyes.

An appreciative mindset can also help individuals discern and observe their own deep-rooted ideas, habits, behaviors, and feelings in new ways so that alternative interpretations can emerge and help them move toward new positive versions of themselves.

Suresh and David Cooperrider from Case always said that social systems move in the direction of questions asked, so people should keep asking positive questions.

In the same way, when individuals have a genuinely positive image of themselves it acts like a magnet and attracts thoughts, feelings, sensations, and actions and turns itself into a positive dynamo of generative energy.

5.3.3 The quantum principle

Why am I introducing this complex subject when, clearly, I am not an expert? Notwithstanding my naïve lay understanding of quantum physics I am convinced that it presents an effective answer to the question: "How can people change and grow so they come closer to realizing their potential?"

While classical physics, with its emphasis on natural determinism, is useful for understanding the material world, the objects of MBSAT: feelings, thoughts, sensations, and possible actions, can better be understood in a less mechanic way and this is why quantum physics seems to be useful.

One of the main differences between classical and quantum physics is that the former views the world as a configuration of particles while the latter looks at the world as representations not only of particles but also of waves which could be closer to the nature of MBSAT (feelings, thoughts, intentions to act, and so on).

Most importantly in the quantum perspective reality is perceived as a world of possibilities and probabilities. As the physicist Amit Goswami explains in his book *The self-aware universe* (1995), in the world of quantum physics waves exist as possibilities that can turn, with a certain probability, into actuality, thus changing from waves to particles.

It would be reasonable to ask: "But how does a wave turn into a particle and a fixed reality?" The answer lies in the influence of the observer over the object observed: the wave. The fact of observation changes the energetic state. So in a quantum world the agents, "we the people," are active participants in the creation of reality.

This view aligns perfectly with the constructionist principle and is also highly relevant to the aims of MBSAT, namely, that of changing and improving the human experience and the condition of individuals.

In many ways quantum physics collapses the dichotomy of an outside objective world and an inside subjective world, typical of deterministic classical physics, and brings about a holistic union between the object–reality and the subject–observer by placing responsibility on the observer/agent.

Given that our lives are mostly reactive patterns to fixed and predetermined or conditioned stimuli from events that we either like or dislike and over which we have little autonomy, an essential aim of MBSAT is to help individuals dissolve their reified chain of automatic reactions that limit their self-determinate and autonomous responses.

It is within the logic of the quantum world of possibilities and probabilities that MBSAT seeks to help increase the possibilities of skillful choices for individuals. For this reason the practices in the program are geared toward increasing the probabilities of people making decisions that will collapse waves of possibilities and turn skillful choices into wholesome realities.

An example illustrating this principle: While working at UBS, I was called into a meeting by one of my superiors, Karl Janjoeri, at the time one of five members of the bank's global executive board. He was a very perceptive man, a sharp old-school Swiss banker, cosmopolitan and familiar with any culture, speaking fluently at least six languages. Before focusing on the business at hand, he asked me: "What is wrong with you? You don't look your usual self." He kept probing for several minutes until I finally told him that I was regularly having lunch at the senior management restaurant and that there was a head waitress who always served me last.

"I don't think she like foreigners," I told my superior. He spontaneously countered: "Nonsense. Have you looked at yourself in the mirror? A tall man like you, athletic and with the kind of tan that the Swiss crave and try to get by skiing in the mountains … I think that women are attracted to you and the waitress is simply bashful and intimidated by your presence and your high rank in the bank."

After this conversation I began to consider this possibility and the fact is that after a short while things started to improve. In quantum language what happened was: as I began to pay attention to the possibility suggested by Mr Janjoeri it gradually became real, because the more I was paying attention the more I was increasing the probability that in the next encounter with the waitress I would act under the possibility that she was nervous and not under the preconception, resulting from my conditioning, that she didn't like me. I was creating a new adaptive and more positive reality.

In essence the quantum world of new possibility (maybe she actually likes me) triumphed over the old deterministic conditioned schemes (she is against me). In this regard the quantum brain is regenerative and important for conscious choice, novelty, and openness.

From a quantum perspective the aim in MBSAT is to reduce the probability of acting on fixed viewpoints to reified conditioned stimuli and instead increase the probabilities of responding skillfully with practical wisdom, equanimity, and friendliness to the challenges of life.

MBSAT strives to achieve this by systematic and sustained training of the practitioner's attention by formal and informal practices detailed in the program.

Figure 5.1 explains graphically how a habitual routine—in this case watching TV—is hardwired into the brain in the form of a thick neural path that results from the frequency of past decisions to watch TV as a pastime, thus becoming a conditioned reaction to the question: "What should I do to relax after coming home from work?" Answer: "Watch TV."

Once the possibility of practicing mindfulness emerges, and provided it is acted upon, a new still fragile neural path begins to form. If attention is paid to regularly practicing mindfulness, the respective neural path will get stronger and, as the practice of mindfulness further increases while the habit of watching TV decreases, the neural path of TV-watching will diminish and become thinner. Ultimately when one asks: "What should I do after work, watch TV or practice mindfulness?" The robust neural path of mindfulness practice enhances the probability of choosing this activity while the conditioned knee-jerk reaction of TV-watching begins to fade.

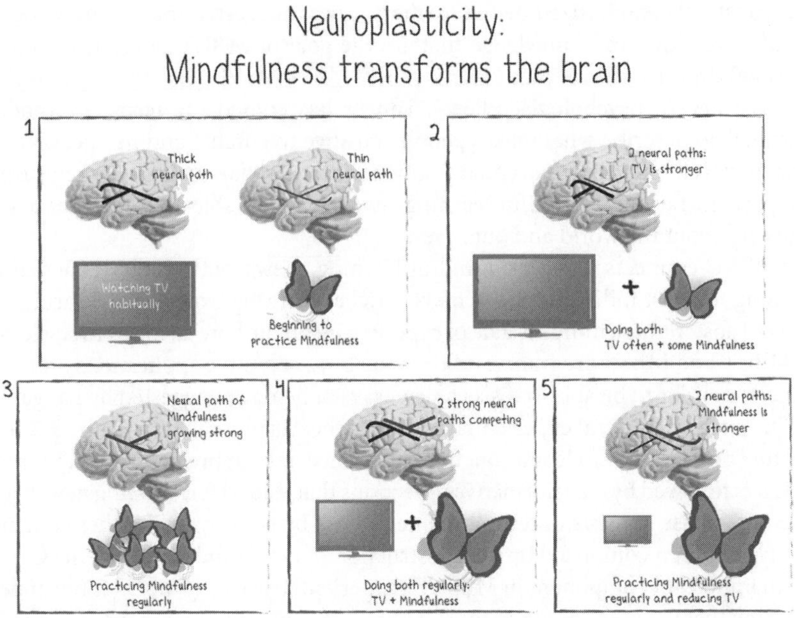

Figure 5.1 Neuroplasticity: Mindfulness transforms the brain. *Source*: Juan Humberto Young.

The MBSAT quantum principle suggests that individuals with sustained attention and appropriate practices can create the conditions for an inner creative revival capable of generating new and more adaptive possibilities for their lives, thus moving them toward a more fulfilling life. It can also help them move away from maladaptive preconditioned patterns and allow them to overcome the drama of an adversely conditioned life.

5.3.4 *The experiential and lifelong learning principle*

The abundance of innovative thinking at Weatherhead School of Management, Case Western Reserve University, Cleveland, Ohio, where I did my doctoral studies, is one of the best kept secrets in the world of academia.

Next to my revered teacher S. Srivastva's office was the office of David Kolb, the originator of the well-known experiential learning theory, hence I was lucky to be exposed to his ideas at the very source. For David Kolb, experiential learning is a process of knowledge creation through transformational experience. It works by embracing an experience, finding new ways of interpreting the knowledge derived from it and acting upon this new, reconfigured knowledge.

In mindfulness-based therapies experiential learning is central to the therapeutic process. During my studies at the University of Oxford in the Masters program of Mindfulness-Based Cognitive Therapy (MBCT) the value of experiential learning was constantly emphasized by the teachers. It was suggested that the only way to acquire the skills and knowledge that are the goal of MBCT programs is direct personal experience.

The Harvard psychologist Ellen J. Langer has coined the term of "mindful learning" to describe what makes people sensitive to context and perspective and what impels them to reach original distinctions rather than to use judgments from the past. In her view mindful learning involves being able to switch modes of thinking about the world and ourselves.

MBSAT connects Langer's mindful-learning views with Kolb's experiential learning to assist individuals to achieve a richer learning experience. Learning in MBSAT fosters: (a) a mindful state of experiencing in the here and now as suggested in MBCT and MBSR programs and (b) a focus on cognitive applications of mindfulness in order to be able to discern new ways of being as suggested by Langer.

The positive mindful experiential learning wheel is presented in Figure 5.2. The starting point of the circle is a concrete experience to be apprehended in a mindful way. It is followed by transformative reflections that lead to formulating new views. The next phase consists of testing the new views by actively trying them out and the cycle is then completed by the construction of new mindful experiences.

An important component in MBSAT's experiential learning model is the understanding that the point of origin must be a mindful experience, because automatic, conditioned behaviors do not provide the richness necessary to become a transformational experience.

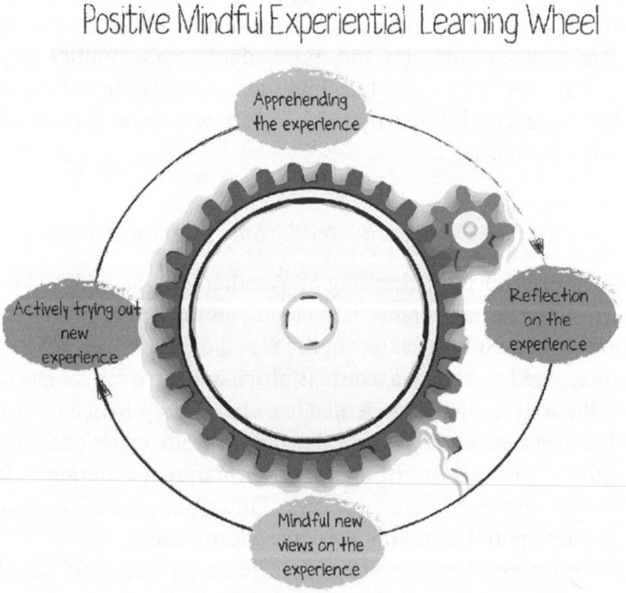

Figure 5.2 Positive Mindful Experiential Learning Wheel. *Source*: Juan Humberto Young.

For example, washing dishes by hand is a simple task mostly done in an automatic pilot mode. While busy washing up, people think about past experiences and how to evaluate them or else they plan ahead and think about what they are going to do later. Thus there are hardly any inputs about the actual experience of washing dishes to create a context for learning. Doing the dishes mindfully on the other hand means staying present and assimilating the experience moment by moment, sensing the water, the changes in temperature, the smell of the detergent, the touch of the porcelain, and so on. No matter how banal the task, if done mindfully it could be the foundation for an experiential learning cycle by becoming an opportunity to practice staying present, thus transforming a rather boring job into something meaningful. Ultimately the focus of MBSAT on mindful experience can help individuals learn ways to integrate personal, economic, and societal values in a coherent form that allows for increases in well-being.

5.3.5 The action orientation principle: The practice

Grounded firmly in experiential learning MBSAT is an action-oriented program where performing an act instead of thinking about it reinforces the program. By engaging in activities participants build a stock of experiences that form the raw material and the basis for transformative learning to occur. It is important to note that in the context of MBSAT I am referring to intentional actions and activities as only conscious acting can provide the raw material for a transformative experience that spurs personal development. We are all acting and thinking constantly so, in a way, we are always practicing something. However, most of the time we are without conscious awareness, acting and thinking in automatic pilot mode.

In MBSAT it is open, intentional conscious practices and actions that are the cornerstones of the learning experience. They help us gain understanding of the patterns of our mind and uncover hidden noxious conditioned habits.

The program is organized around practices that are transformative and generative insofar as they represent a decision to embody BETA (Body sensations, Emotions/feelings, Thoughts and Action impulses) that can help people in whatever situation they find themselves.

In MBSAT a series of mindfulness and meditation practices are practiced with the aim of being able to better deal with the challenges of life whether they are in one's working or private life. As a result of MBSAT one should be able to deal well with a difficult employee at the office or respond wisely to an unruly son or daughter and so on. These are situations that require well balanced responses that integrate emotional, bodily, and cognitive aspects. Systematic and intentional MBSAT practices can help generate benefits for the individual and, in the larger social context, in relation with employees, family, and other persons.

I realize that what is being proposed here is not easy but it is the worthwhile route that will eventually become natural and inevitable. Practice is the way to achieve mastery, autonomy, and healthy social relations in our life—and these are the three essential human needs necessary for well-being in our lives.

Practice has an essential function in any mindfulness-based program and MBSAT is no exception. I have reflected deeply on this issue and how to make it easier for participants. Here are some pieces of practical advice that should be useful.

In making a commitment to practice it is always helpful to establish routines: a place, a time, duration. I will come back to these topics later in the description of the first session of the program.

Another important element is to maintain a flexible approach regarding your aspirations. While one might be sincerely committed to a high-level goal such as becoming a positive mindful person or leader, more modest steps may be needed on the path to the ultimate goal.

I recall the case of one of my students—the CEO of a large Middle Eastern conglomerate who wanted to become more positive and mindful in his relations with his team members. I suggested that he should take a couple of minutes every morning when he comes into his office and just bid his staff good morning and offer other small gestures and pleasantries. For example, if the situation occurs—open the door for members of staff instead of having it held open for him all the time.

He did not object but told me that he found these suggestions trivial and unimportant as he used to rush into his office in the morning in a hurry with no time to greet people. Nevertheless he implemented the small positive interventions and two months later he told me that the favorable changes in his office were beyond his expectations: his colleagues and his staff were opening up, smiling more, and he felt more relaxed and appreciated.

During practice it is common that our shortcomings get in the way of effective practice. Our conditioned self will appear and try to sabotage our good intentions. Instead of achieving the practice our conditioned self will find all sorts of excuses. It will tell us to watch an interesting TV program instead of dedicating whatever time is needed to practice becoming a positive mindful person or leader.

Even if we manage to sit for a mindfulness period of meditation all kinds of distractions will occur: frustration, discomfort, fear, boredom, sleepiness.

However, as we persevere and practice frequently and persistently in the quantum world of MBSAT we will keep expanding the probabilities of choosing to do our practices instead of succumbing to our conditioned self. With time, practice will help create a different kind of self, the one we choose to be. Practice will reframe our mind, feelings, and bodily sensations reaping the transformative effect by embodying a positive and mindful being. As the research by Duke University Fuqua School of Business professor Dan Ariely and Harvard Business School professor Michael Norton (Ariely and Norton 2008) shows: our actions create our preferences.

The principles underlining the structure of MBSAT are geared toward facilitating the integration of the concepts and practices of the program into people's daily activities so they can experience the benefits in their personal and professional lives and help guide other people's lives.

5.4 MBSAT Mindfulness Components

MBSAT comprises three interconnected mindfulness components that are introduced during the 8-week program as follows:

A. Focused mindfulness (FM):
This is the focus of the first four sessions of the MBSAT program with practices geared toward steadying the mind. The purpose of mindfulness practices at this stage is to assist participants to achieve a calmer mind. People's lives, especially nowadays, are saturated with mental conversations about what is happening, what is going to happen or already has happened. To become more mindful and learning to focus attention in the present moment is fundamental, quieting the agitation of the mind and reducing the incidence of distractions and mind wandering. This is the first requirement in any serious project of personal growth or transformation as nothing can change while being in a state of agitation and compulsion. The purpose of FM is to nudge participants from a doing mode of the mind towards a calm being mode that allows participants to sense and observe without judging their experiences to the fullest, including their body sensations, emotions and feelings, thoughts and ideas and action impulses, that I call BETA, as explained below in section 5.5.

B. Analytical mindfulness (AM):
Practices in Sessions 5 and 6 and some elements of previous sessions are directed toward this component of MBSAT. With the practices of AM participants begin to develop a clearer discerning and inquiring capacity that allows observing reality with the eyes of practical wisdom. They also begin to explore new and more skillful ways of regulating their BETA, sensing, feeling, thinking and acting, gradually freeing themselves from what normally conditions people's lives, especially their likes and dislikes. AM allows participants to gain a conscious, analytical understanding of what the causes and effects are that determine their lives. In other words they can start to leverage the clarity gained to disengage from the conditioning that impedes them from living a full and more integral life. With this understanding they can use applied mindful thought and reasoning to create skillful options more likely to achieve high levels of subjective well-being, thus transforming their lives for the better.

C. Relational mindfulness (RM):
Session 7 is specifically designed to help participants open up and become mindful in human relations. Life is enacted and realized in social contexts: in the family, with friends, in teams at work and in society in general. Consequently, to a large extent the quality of people's experience is related to the quality of their relations within their social context. RM helps cultivate a sense of benevolence towards oneself and others. It assists participants to become aware of others and be more gentle to themselves by opening the intelligence of their heart.

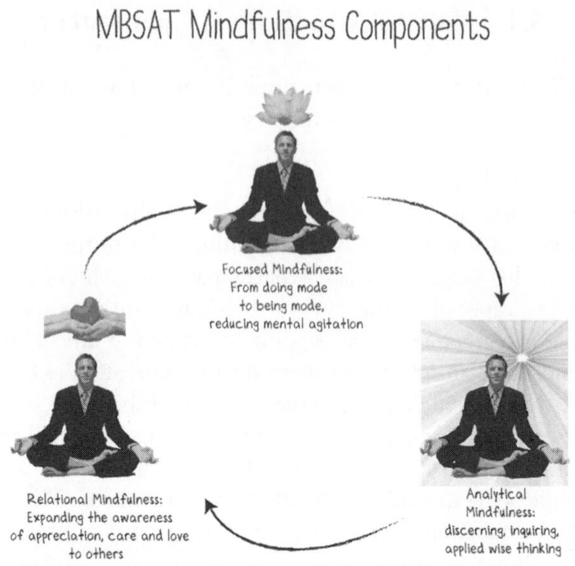

Figure 5.3 MBSAT Mindfulness Components. Source: Juan Humberto Young

The three components—focused mindfulness, analytical mindfulness and relational mindfulness—are the integral parts of MBSAT mindfulness components as a whole. They are closely intertwined and reinforce one another. Figure 5.3 visualizes this dynamic of MBSAT mindfulness components.

5.5 The Locus of MBSAT Practices—Minding BETA

In finance BETA, designated by the sign β, is a measure of risk that gauges the exposure of a company to general market trends. Firms with positive β tend to move in the same direction as the market and those with negative β in opposite direction to the market. Investment advisors establish different combinations of investment instruments with varying βs to satisfy the preferences and risk profiles of individual clients. The variable β is therefore a key measure for investing.

I would like to make an analogy with mindfulness insofar as the locus of mindfulness practices is the human experience as reflected in our Body sensations, our Emotions and feelings, our Thoughts and ideas and our Action impulses and behaviors which yields the same acronym: BETA. In essence the aspiration of a mindful life is to gain the capability to better regulate the human experience by bending it towards a genuinely positive and skillful way of living that can facilitate personal flourishing—including, in addition to the practitioners themselves, any people whose lives are impacted directly or indirectly by the practitioners.

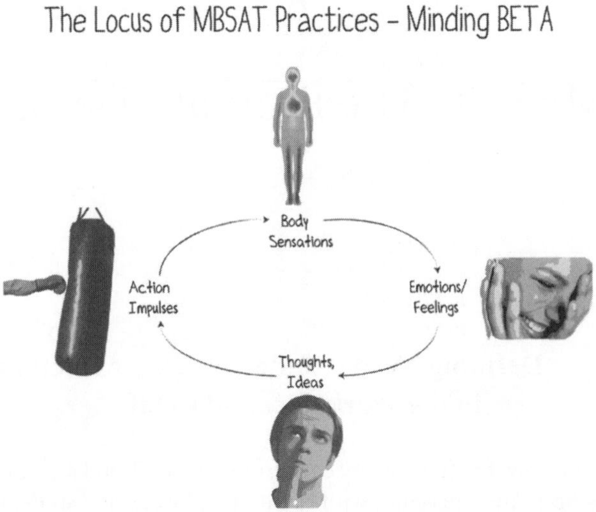

Figure 5.4 The Locus of MBSAT Practices—Minding BETA. *Source*: Juan Humberto Young.

With mindfulness of the body amongst others the intention is to help practitioners focus the scattered attention on a focal bodily point in order to reduce inner agitation and gain inner calm and equanimity. With mindfulness of emotions, practitioners observe their emotional infrastructure, opening their hearts and cultivating positive feelings and emotions toward themselves and others. With mindfulness of thoughts people develop discerning and inquiring capacities to attain practical wisdom and finally with mindfulness of action the ability to observe dispassionately the impulses to act and the corresponding behaviors. The skillful regulation of BETA allows individuals to act skillfully and reduce the risk of making decisional mistakes that could hamper their quest for authentic happiness and well-being.

Figure 5.4, The Locus of MBSAT Practices—Minding BETA, presents the operational closed loop of BETA as the four elements of human experience—body sensations, emotions and feelings, thoughts and ideas and action impulses—feed into one another and in combination construct the quality of people's experiences.

By increasing strategic awareness (practical wisdom, equanimity, friendliness and open awareness) of any or all of these elements the risk of harmful human experiences drops and concurrently the probability of having sustainable positive experiences soars.

It is through MBSAT's mindfulness components that individuals first become familiar with the patterns of their BETA; they become aware of the conditioned reactions of their body sensations, emotions, thoughts and actions and learn based on this knowledge to skillfully regulate their BETA toward what makes them authentically happy.

6

MBSAT: The Program Design

6.1 Defining Needs: Understanding Afflictions in the Workplace and in Life

Workplaces and private life are a key concerns of MBSAT and a major focus of its design. It has been my experience with clients, employees, and students that many of the difficulties and worries in life have a work-related origin. The issues are typically: Can I keep my job? Will I find a job? or Can I have an interesting job?

All of these absolutely fundamental questions have a spillover effect on the private sphere. They inevitably affect the family, relations with friends, in fact almost all in life.

A job, and the importance of employment, is a major determinant of subjective well-being (SWB), as positive psychologists know. The devastating impact of losing a job is one of the most dramatic life experiences. It can have a strong negative effect on an individual's SWB. Recently I watched a British journalist on BBC interviewing a prisoner on death row. When the journalist asked the inmate if he belonged where he was, his answer was yes. "Look," he said, "I'm a kind of a cool guy, but if I try to find a job and I can't find one. Then I go home, get a gun and kill people, because I'm jobless and despairing."

In a case closer to home, a colleague and friend who I worked with at UBS many years ago, a handsome economist and portfolio manager in his early fifties, took his own life, essentially due to issues at work and the hopelessness he felt in his professional life.

One of the central, well-documented problems in the workplace is stress and its effects, in particular burnout. There are also problems with drug addiction and health problems such as nervous breakdowns. Researching the issues MBSAT attempts to address I reached two conclusions.

Mindfulness-Based Strategic Awareness Training: A Complete Program for Leaders and Individuals, First Edition. Juan Humberto Young.

Companion website: www.wiley.com/go/humbertoyoung/mbsat

First, stress is not detrimental in itself. It is chronic stress that is truly and dangerously debilitating because it creates a biological response that stimulates the release of stress hormones such as cortisol which, over time, produces negative physiological and psychological consequences. Healthy stressful responses are adaptive as Stanford's Professor Sapolsky's research reveals in *Why zebras don't get ulcers* (2004). When zebras become stressed at the sight of a hunting lion, stress hormones enable their leg muscles to muster extra strength to sprint and escape the fate of becoming the lion's next lunch. Once the danger is gone (the lion having hunted another zebra) the remaining zebras go back to their normal relaxed state and continue to graze. Unlike this natural alternation in wildlife, most work environments are unstable places prone to chronically stressful situations, not the kind of environments where people can easily level their stress profiles. And stress is only the tip of the iceberg, the visible part of deeper generalized psycho-emotional conditions that will be discussed later in this chapter.

I came to the second conclusion while researching problems in the workplace. It was obvious that if the structural context of organizations could be changed (power dynamics, hiring and firing policies, promotions, compensation policies, and so on) then less toxic work environments would be created and this would have a positive impact on employees and management.

Sadly I am not hopeful about structural change as years of working with positive management approaches (e.g., appreciative inquiry, positive organization scholarship) has demonstrated that while it is true that people in charge are curious about these ideas, most of them are not ready to implement the changes that these advanced systems require.

Recently I was presenting this methodology to the CEO of a large private bank and he accepted that it was convincing and appealing in principle. "But," he then backtracked, "what happens with my job? I am here to create the strategy of the organization and set the direction; this is what I am getting paid for. If my people get involved in strategizing, what am I going to do?" "Very simple", I told him. "You will create the context where your employees can flourish and develop winning strategies—strategies they are eager to implement because they helped define them instead of resisting the execution." In the end the CEO agreed to do some kind of project, however, it was too limited in scope to have an impact, much less to be transformative.

Experiences like this have led me to take another approach that is not dissimilar to quantum physics: the individual agent should take responsibility.

This approach requires every individual to take responsibility by changing, in a positive-adaptive manner, the way they relate to their particular problems. And that is where MBSAT offers support so that everyone can move toward fulfilling their personal aspirations and potential.

Teasdale, Segal, and Williams (2003) suggest that matching mindfulness-based interventions with the related issues or problems must always be based on a clearly formulated understanding of both the underlying problem and the intervention. Before attempting to discuss MBSAT it is therefore important to clearly define the issues that dominate in the workplace in order to ensure an effective match.

A potential mindfulness teacher must have a thorough understanding of the nature of the contemporary workplace within a matrix of economic, social, and psychological conditions and the characteristics of the group he or she is working with. This allows the targeting and emphasizing of specific aspects of MBSAT for the benefit of participants. MBSAT must be geared to the mental and emotional well-being of people in the workplace and in private life.

Independently from each other Leahy, Kets de Vries, and Gino all argue that the predominant, prevailing condition in contemporary workplaces is one of dissatisfaction. They all believe that this can lead to workplaces that are seriously dysfunctional.

For Leahy (2003) dissatisfaction has a number of underlying causes. A primary problem is perfectionism that produces a tendency to be constantly dissatisfied with one's performance as measured against ever higher standards. Another source is early deprivation that haunts people with memories of financial distress and hardship even if they are doing well later in life. Kets de Vries (2006), professor at INSEAD business school, puts it well:

> I have learned that a significant number of [executives] are preoccupied with the idea of obtaining ... money for which they are not beholden to anybody ... Woven in the narratives of many of these executives are childhood experiences centered on a lack of money (p. 7).

Comparisons with other people and perceptions of opportunity also play an important role. Experimental studies conducted by Gino, Harvard Business School professor, and co-researcher Pierce (Gino and Pierce 2009) reveal an abundance effect that describes how in environments of abundant wealth people tend to behave unethically. This appears to Gino to be driven by feelings of envy arising from perceptions of inequality. Admati and Hellwig (2013) follow a similar line of reasoning when explaining the rampant cases of poor ethical conduct amongst bankers.

Amongst senior managers, the ethically compromised have a need to drive for ever more power and money and this leads to behaviors and pathologies that condition much of what is found in the contemporary workplace.

Several years ago I was giving a positive mindful training course at a well-known private bank in Zurich. It was an intense 12-month program with senior managers: several Vice Presidents and Directors, three Managing Directors and one Executive Director: in total 25 participants.

With half of the program completed there was a particular morning, when the mood of the people was downbeat and depressed, quite opposite to the attitude of openness, optimism, sense of possibilities, and the enthusiasm to learn that we had experienced in the previous sessions. This morning the mood of the room was so bad that I started to worry and even doubt myself, thinking that perhaps I was doing something that was unacceptable to the participants. When the lunch break came and I was about to leave the conference room, one of the managing directors approached me and said: "Juan, don't worry. It is not your fault. They are just upset because yesterday was the bonus payout and most of them are disappointed and disgruntled."

What a relief to know! I began to inquire among them and found out that the average payout bonus was around half a million Swiss Francs; nevertheless many were upset because they found that others had received a few thousand francs more. Aware of their pain, when we came back from lunch, I told them to step up to the window, look at the "normal" people in the street and estimate their average annual income. Let me remind you, they were looking at a street in downtown Zurich, one of the wealthiest cities in the world. Their consensus estimate was around 55,000 or 60,000 Swiss Francs.

So I told them: "You guys have bonuses which are ten times the amount you estimate most people make in this city—yet you are unhappy." Complete silence followed. The power of relative wealth dawned on them and they realized how much better off they were when compared to the vast majority of their fellow citizens. When I started the class again their concentration and engagement was back to normal and we could continue as usual.

At one extreme, mostly at the top of the hierarchy, are what INSEAD Professor Kets de Vries (2006) calls "psychopaths lite", a term echoed by Babiak and Hare (2006) who speak of "successful psychopaths."

A study by Board and Fritzon (2005) compared the personality disorders in a population of senior managers with a group of mentally disordered offenders from Broadmoor Special Hospital in England. The study revealed that out of 11 personality disorders three pathological patterns were more common in the group of senior managers than in criminal psychiatric patients. The senior managers were more likely to have histrionic personality disorder (attention seeking, superficial charm, insincerity, and manipulation); narcissistic personality disorder (grandiosity and lack of empathy); and obsessive-compulsive personality disorder (perfectionism, excessive concentration on work, rigidity, and dictatorial tendencies). This is not surprising given the propensity for what Schouten and Silver (2012) call "almost psychopaths" to be attracted to business organizations following their desire for power and money.

Dutton's (2013, chapter 6) study *The Great British Psychopath Survey* found that the most psychopathic profession is a CEO and the least psychopathic one is a care worker. Part of the explanation for this is that the typical traits of psychopaths—ruthlessness, charm, focus, mental toughness, fearlessness, and action—"are also the ones most valued in the world of business and are amongst the most helpful personal assets for advancing a career in this environment," Dutton writes.

Psychopaths lite, lacking empathy and awareness, can do great harm to society. Their decision-making orientation tends to be highly self-centered, dominated by self-serving cognitions and behaviors. In organizations they strive to join the higher echelons in order to gain the power and influence they can use to pursue their own interests. Their lack of empathy and awareness then becomes detrimental to the general well-being of other members of the organization.

Hogan, in a presentation to the American Psychological Association, reported that 75% of people say that the most stressful aspect of their job is their immediate boss, implying an atmosphere where worry and anxiety are pervasive conditions: "Bad managers are a major source of misery for many people" (cited in Jayson, 2012).

It is a fact that a lack of empathy and awareness is a condition prevailing at higher levels in organizational hierarchies. Equally, worry and anxiety often mark the experience of those at lower levels.

Borkovec, Alcaine, and Behar (2004) show how in many organizations people tend to suffer from non-conscious worries that are characterized by a concern for the future and a focus on anticipated threats. This inevitably leads to a conscious motive to anticipate and prepare for potential problems.

In summary, there seem to be two major challenging and difficult issues in the contemporary corporate environment:

1. Addictive behaviors produced by an addiction to power and money: POMO.
2. Anxiety-based conditions, such as worry, produced by conscious and non-conscious insecurity about the future. These anxieties are often linked with the quality of relations with bosses and colleagues, job security, and job performance.

This analysis of conditions prevailing in the workplace demonstrates the need for cognitive and emotional training. These conditions build the case for MBSAT and are the foundation for the design of the program and the importance of its interventions.

The case for MBSAT in the workplace argues that any program that seeks to improve the human experience in workplaces and in private life should include training elements that help participants cultivate qualities including self-knowledge and personal emotional care, mental clarity, kindness and friendliness, personal courage, and strategic decision making. These are the elements that build the bedrock of MBSAT's content.

Before we focus on content, however, here are some preliminary comments on format.

6.2 The Format of MBSAT

MBSAT is modeled on the format of mindfulness-based cognitive therapy (MBCT) in the same way as MBCT is based on mindfulness-based stress reduction (MBSR) programs.

Created in 1979, the MBSR protocol has proven to be highly beneficial for assisting patients suffering from difficult physical conditions. It reduces their stress levels and consequently helps improve their quality of life.

Likewise, MBCT with a successful track record of over 15 years, has helped individuals with three or more periods of depression to reduce the recurrence of depression. It has proven highly beneficial with a treatment that is not invasive and with enough supporting evidence to ensure the potential of changing lives for the better.

Like MBSR and MBCT, MBSAT is a mostly group-oriented intervention with up to 20 participants meeting on a weekly basis for sessions lasting 2–4 hours depending on the curriculum and the needs of the clients. It is structured by a rigorous protocol extending over eight sessions.

MBSAT takes an experiential learning approach like MBCT and MBSR. Methodologically, the starting point is always a concrete experience – for example a meditation practice carried out in the group. Participants then reflect on their experience, guided by the teacher, in a process of joint inquiry out of which they are able to form new conceptualizations about the experience. Subsequently they can actively experiment with the newly gained knowledge.

The didactic in-class format of MBSAT follows the same pattern of most mindfulness-based interventions. Sessions begin with a guided meditation practice followed by an inquiry about it and a review of home practice. Then a new theme or practice is introduced. Each session concludes with homework assignments, a closing meditation, and the distribution of handouts.

6.3 The Content of MBSAT: An Overview

The MBSAT content presented here is clearly influenced by my own life experience. It is marked by my personal pursuit of a good quality of life, from my early years as an idealistic pseudo-hippy in California with the idealism that we could all change the world through "peace and love" (some of the readers might remember the slogan) to the many years in the workplace firstly as an employee and later as a leader in both small businesses and large worldwide organizations. It is also influenced by my years as a consultant helping to improve the functional apparatus of organizations as well as my experience as a coach, business owner, and as teacher in business schools.

The MBSAT protocol draws on multiple disciplines: positive psychology and secular Asian psychology; behavioral economics and finance; coaching psychology; cognitive behavioral therapy; strategic management principles and theories; decision-making analysis; system dynamics; process philosophy, and contemplative sciences (mindfulness and meditation).

An overview of the program and its main parts follows.

6.3.1 Basic know-how and practice

The purpose of Sessions 1–4 is to lay the foundations of mindfulness by introducing participants to key patterns, such as, "mind-wandering" and what is called "automatic pilot" (absent-minded functioning), and familiarizing them with key practices—in particular the body scan (focusing consciously and systematically on body sensations) and sitting meditation. The exercise "three minutes breathing space" provides participants with a mini-meditation they can use whenever they need to decenter from automatic pilot and enter a more mindful mode of being.

Participants also start (a) learning about new ways of "knowing" instead of "living" in their heads, (b) gathering the scattered mind, and (c) relating more skillfully to difficult emotions and situations. In addition, they are introduced to mindful stretching as a way of experiencing the difference between stretching and striving. This is about developing the habit accepting our limits instead of relentlessly pushing ourselves.

With stretching participants learn to approach the edge of their comfort zone and to find some degree of ease of being at that edge. Striving means forcing oneself beyond the natural limits in a way that opens up stubborn, difficult-to-release attitudes. This can, over time, lead to physical harm. Learning to differentiate between these two spreads and triggers different attitudes to a person's work, their private lives and, if applicable, their leadership style. In this way participants become familiar with new ways of taking care of themselves.

Cognitive exercises conducted in these sessions show how the interpretation of facts plays a role in forming one's emotional state.

My view is that first, the likely educational outcomes of these sessions—mindfulness, decentering, care, and self-kindness—are necessary to establish the foundation of mindfulness that the rest of the program depends on. Second, these outcomes are valuable in the workplace as well as in private life.

Typically, in every program there will be a sub-group of participants who are primarily afflicted by worries and anxieties they are trying to escape from. There will be another set of participants who will be driven by their addiction to power and money. Most participants, however, will probably present aspects of both conditions—a sort of co-morbidity effect. Therefore Session 4 is dedicated to the psycho-educational components revealed by mapping the territory of worry.

The corresponding practices consist of 20–40 minutes sitting meditation; shifting the awareness successively from breath to body to sounds and thoughts; open awareness (meditation without any particular focus); three minutes breathing space focused on strengths, Mindful Walking, and Mindful Salsa (being aware of every single movement).

6.3.2 Learning to be mindfully positive

With Session 5, entitled *Strategic Awareness I: Building Mindful Real Options (MROs)*, we begin the strategic awareness series building the decision-making capabilities that can bring us closer to authentic and sustainable well-being and becoming mindful, positive individuals. It initiates a process of personal transformation that results from the groundwork that Sessions 1–4 have created. It takes the learning of the previous sessions further and builds a necessary set of insights and understanding.

This session includes a meditation termed Irimi that is derived from the Japanese martial arts concept describing the Aikido stance of moving forward into a difficult situation to gain flexibility of response and creating a range of MROs instead of fleeing.

The heroic and performative nature of this designation is likely to appeal to the target population of non-clinical people who will see its practical application to their working life.

The core of the session is the counterintuitive insight that allowing difficult states to be as they are, and exploring them as they are reflected in the body and approaching rather than avoiding them, can be a highly effective way of addressing challenging states of mind.

It is a persuasive insight for participants. This allowing mode amplifies their adaptive responsive capabilities as opposed to an avoidance mode that seeks to dissociate and avoid situations when confronted with emotional or situational difficulties.

6.3.3 *Working towards positive transformation*

Sessions 6 and 7 are designed to help participants make shifts in their conditioned ways. This part of MBSAT studies and explains how they relate to certain important facets of their life.

Session 6, entitled *Strategic Awareness II: From POMO (Powerful Money) to MIMO (Mindful Money)*, includes elements of conceptual learning. One of the tenets of MBSAT is that people need to learn to make skillful decisions concerning money in order to become a mindful, positive leader, or individual. It presents evidence of the effects of the pursuit of money on biological and psychological well-being and its repercussions on performance and creativity. Practices in this class include a series of three short sitting meditations on the relation to money. Although it might be argued that a possible downside of this practice could be an increased fixation on money and wealth by focusing on affluence, it is my belief that the practice, provided it is well-guided, will no more bring about such a counterproductive outcome than the sitting with difficulty meditation, a mainstay also in mindfulness-based cognitive therapy (MBCT), would bring about a fixation with difficulty.

It is accepted that skillful teachers will always be alert to the risks they are running in any teaching situation and this is one of the many reasons why MBSAT teachers need to be carefully trained and selected.

The focus of learning in MBSAT Session 6 is to gain clarity and wisdom concerning one of the most potent drivers of human conduct: the pursuit of money. The hope is that the clarity gained and the capacity to discern may translate into other areas of life (family, business, society, and so on) so that leaders and individuals become more likely to make clear decisions beyond self-centered interest. The focus of the session is on money worries and not money troubles or financial problems, i.e., real situations that require direct solutions.

Session 7 of MBSAT, entitled *Strategic Awareness III: Opening the Heart*, deals with the cultivation of friendliness (McCown, 2013). The postulates of mindfulness and positive psychology emphasize the need for kindness and empathy including self-compassion for a well-functioning private, social, and professional life in order to become an authentic, mindful, positive individual. During the session several mindfulness practices are presented for cultivating kindness, starting with being kind to oneself and successively expanding the scope: being kind to the people you lead and manage; to clients; to close friends; to people for whom you have no strong or neutral feelings; and finally to be kind to genuinely difficult persons. These practices then serve as a vehicle for exploring and inquiring into participants' BETA (Body sensations, Emotions/feelings, Thoughts and Action impulses) and the way they express themselves in a variety of situations. In addition Session 7 introduces SOPA Phase I. The acronym SOPA stands for strengths, opportunities, and positive actions, a personal planning exercise.

6.3.4 Integration and conclusion

Session 8, *Minding Your BETA*, is the last session. It is crystallization and distillation of intensive weeks of work with mindfulness, positive psychology, and other disciplines.

Like all sessions it begins with a sitting meditation and the corresponding inquiry. Two final practical instruments will be introduced in this session: (a) Phase II of SOPA—strengths, opportunities, and positive actions, finalizing the personal planning exercise started in the previous session and (b) three-minutes breathing space on strategic awareness (3MSBS), a mini-meditation to use when stuck trying to resolve and develop actions that have implications for the future.

A complete review of the program will also be conducted before ending this final session. Before closing a short body scan and an additional practice, a sitting mediation either on breathing or on friendliness, could be done.

6.4 Expected Benefits from MBSAT

What benefits can a participant in a MBSAT program expect to achieve? There are some distinctive, specific gains from MBSAT in addition to a series of benefits that MBSAT has in common with MBCT and MBSR programs. While all three programs are of great value, the shared benefits are the basis on which the specific gains of MBSAT builds upon.

MBCT and MBSR are designed to combat stress and depression, their benefits are mostly oriented towards a calm and focused mindset, whereas the advantages of MBSAT integrate wise decision-making and action taking.

The starting points and problems of MBSAT are the afflictions prevailing in the workplace. They are seen as pervasive in our society as a whole, spreading from the workplace into families and the entire social fabric. Hence MBSAT is especially beneficial for people in practical struggles, trying to be good bosses or colleagues, good parents, good partners—in short, good and valuable members of society.

Let us start with key advantages that are common to MBSAT and most other mindfulness programs:

1. Reducing the tendency to live on automatic pilot, moving from a frantic and driven doing mode to a being mode.
2. Able to be in the present moment avoiding mind wandering.
3. Improving attention control and working memory capacity.
4. Relating to experience not only cognitively but through our senses.
5. Readiness to relate to negative experiences skillfully.
6. Able to see thoughts as thoughts, not as facts.
7. Accepting of oneself and others more wholeheartedly.
8. Increasing self-regulation of BETA (Body sensations, Emotions/feelings, Thoughts and Action impulses).
9. Gaining acceptance, patience, and wisdom in dealing with difficult challenges in life.
10. Achieving a lifestyle of equanimity conducive to sustainable well-being.

In addition to these advantages MBSAT participants can also expect to gain the following skills that are key to sound decisions and sustainable well-being:

a. Capacity to remain calm and lucid and see possibilities beyond hasty solutions.
b. Capacity to integrate the past (retrospection), the present (introspection), and the future (prospection) into all-encompassing time frameworks to guide skillful decision-making.
c. Capacity to turn risk and adversity into Mindful Real Options (MROs) that can lead to better choices.
d. Capacity to embrace disagreement and conflict and to maintain an open, curious, and friendly approach to life.
e. Capacity to observe conditioning biases and see facts for what they are, thus gaining a debiasing capability.
f. Capacity to strategically discern reality and make sound decisions that benefit oneself and others synergistically.

The combined benefits and skills gained by participating in a MBSAT program lead to a core key skill: strategic awareness composed of practical wisdom (discernment), equanimity (serenity), friendliness (compassion), and open awareness (non-judging) that can improve a participant's ability to make skillful decisions and take constructive action. These are core skills that will nurture in the participant a sense of well-being in their private and working life that will spill over into the well-being of others.

6.5 A Finance View of MBSAT Benefits

When I started to work in the banking industry at UBS my first job was as portfolio manager for a large European fund, in that role I had the opportunity to gain experience buying and selling financial options, usually the option but not the obligation to buy or sell a specific amount of a financial asset, for example the shares of a company. Later, as head of a department in the same bank, I was involved in corporate finance transactions and engaged in applying real options to some of the projects we were involved in. Real options are options to take certain actions such as investing, deferring, downsizing or any other measure in relation to a real project, for example a new factory, a housing project, a software development or any other concrete project.

Real options create flexibility in the future for projects that require actions now in the present. By delaying some action now and combining it with an option the project manager or businessperson gains the ability to make some decision in the future that will be more appropriate for the success of the venture. For example, the person in charge might decide at a later stage to defer a decision about funding the next project phase in order to gather new information about the prospects, thus reducing uncertainty and financial risks. Conversely, the project manager might decide to sequentially scale up a successful project with small operational investments as the demand increases. The qualitative aspects of real options are easy to grasp and the benefits intuitively evident, however, the valuing of real options is a field of expertise by itself as it can require sophisticated quantitative financial and statistical analyses.

Translating the insights of a qualitative understanding of real options highlights the benefits of mindfulness from a different angle as they appear as real options under the lens of finance theory. Thus the systematic practice of mindfulness gives the practitioner the option to stop and pause at will before acting by getting out of automatic pilot. It also provides the option of stepping out of mind wandering and the doing-driven mode of the mind (with its mental factory of likes and dislikes), thus reducing the risk of falling into maladaptive conditioned action patterns that tend to impact negatively the quality of subjective well-being. Furthermore, it allows the practitioner to move into a being mode of the mind, to develop clarity and practical wisdom about the human experiences by stopping the storytelling machine inside the mind that often drives unskillful reactions. Systematic and ongoing practitioners of mindfulness gain autonomy from their reactions and gain the ability to choose how to respond to their experiences, thus de facto creating a range of real options.

The cost of having these mindfulness real options is the premium invested in the present time corresponding to maybe 20 minutes daily of formal practice, an investment that certainly makes sense given the enormity of the payoffs: increasing the probability of making good decisions that foster subjective well-being. Besides, the nature of mindfulness options presents a particular profile—an inverse dynamic—given that with regular practice the costs incurred decrease as it

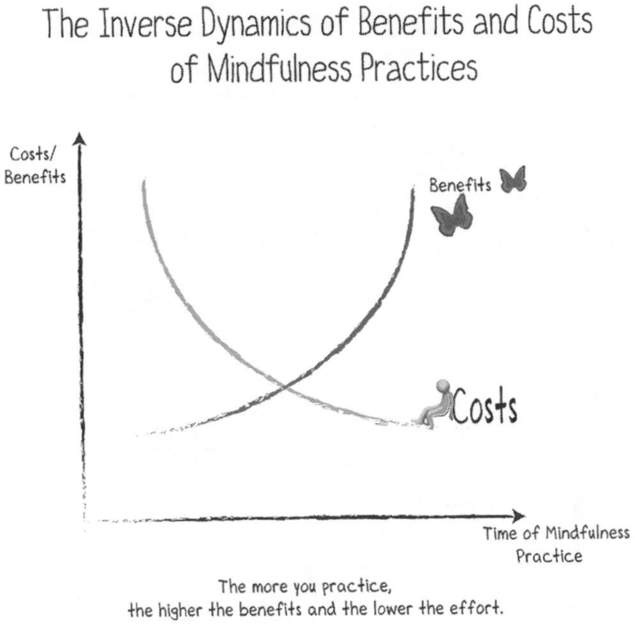

Figure 6.1 The Inverse Dynamics of Benefits and Costs of Mindfulness Practices. *Source*: Juan Humberto Young.

becomes one more customary activity while the returns increase as mindful individuals become more expert in making skillful and wise decisions (see Figure 6.1).

Figure 6.2, mindfulness as real options, depicts the pathways showing how mindfulness translates into real options. In essence it visualizes how mindfulness turns into a skillful regulator of body sensations, emotions (feelings), thoughts and actions impulses, summarized in the acronym BETA. In finance BETA is a measure of risk or volatility of an investment. It is appropriate to use the term for mindfulness as it creates essentially options to better understand and skillfully manage one's body sensations, emotions (feelings), thoughts processes and action impulses, thus reducing the risk of mindless knee-jerk reactions.

As Figure 6.2 illustrates the process begins with inputs from the external or the internal conceptual world when events, situations or thoughts are interpreted either by a mindful or a conditioned mind. If the latter is the case two possible reactions will set in automatically: either one travels the liking path, wanting more of the same with no space in between stimulus and conditioned reaction and further strengthening the components of BETA, that is, reinforcing the prevailing body sensations, emotions, thoughts and action impulses, or one descends the disliking path, thus wanting less of whatever is occupying the attention and subjecting the experience to a conditioned reaction of dislike.

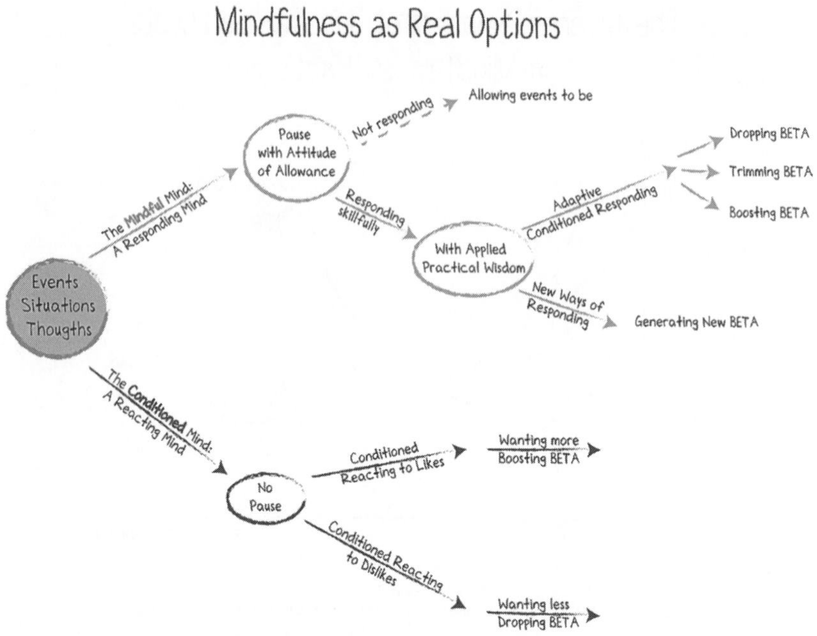

Figure 6.2 Mindfulness as Real Options. *Source*: Juan Humberto Young.

If, on the other hand, the experience is processed by a mindful mind, a range of different options open up to the mindful decision maker. First a pause or space is created after which two options present themselves: a) not responding at all and letting the experience be just as it is with an aptitude of allowance, or b) choosing to respond, creating an additional pause for recollection until another set of options opens up. One of the options consists in responding with a conditioned yet adaptive response, meaning a response that is deliberate and adequate to the particular experience. Depending on the circumstances this may lead to different consequences as existing BETA may be dropped, trimmed or boosted as the case may be. The key is that these choices are deliberate and skillful as a mindful mind exercises agency. Alternatively it could be that a new response is generated, creating a repertoire that transcends the conditioned mind.

In a recent conversation over lunch a participant of one of my MBSAT programs, the vice-president at a well-known, over a century-old Swiss private bank, emphasized how beneficial the program had been for him. One of the main benefits he experienced was the capacity to refrain from reacting impulsively under the stress and time pressure of his hectic business. He now takes a moment and pauses before acting. "Most of the time," he explained, "my first impulse is not optimal. Now, as result of practicing mindfulness regularly, I always pause and then I kind of see more and better possibilities. My relations with my superior, my team and my clients have also become marvelous. And in addition I got a salary increase this year and a prize as the best employee of my division." In other words he not only reaped the inherent benefits of the MBSAT real options approach but was also rewarded with financial gains.

In a nutshell, MBSAT has the potential to help participants gain the skill and capability of strategic awareness by allowing the creation of brief pauses and clarity spaces in their personal BETA (body sensations, emotional awareness, practical wisdom in thoughts and envisioning skillful actions), halting momentarily the vortex of their quotidian VUCA (volatile, uncertain, complex and ambiguous) experiences and avoiding hasty reactions, thus amplifying their decisional responses by facilitating the emergence of a range of options from which to choose.

6.6 The Characteristics of Participants and Related Risks

There is one important caveat regarding the results of MBSAT: the benefits and capacities participants gain are a direct function of the intensity and regularity with which they do the practices advocated by the program.

Although my experience shows that practically every participant reaps certain benefits, there are three typical types of participants.

The dedicated type

Participants with this characteristic are highly engaged and motivated. They do formal exercises such as sitting meditations, body scans, and so on, on a regular basis. Due to the intensity and regularity of practice this type of participant is able to take advantage of the neuroplasticity of the brain. The physiology of their brain starts to change and develop more sound neural pathways that help them gain deeper insights into the essence of reality.

One of my students at the Master's in positive leadership and strategy, a member of a prominent Middle Eastern family, told me how her committed and disciplined mindfulness and positive psychology practices helped her see and understand the loving qualities of her religion rather than only the negative aspects.

The on-and-off type

These participants do not practice regularly but make use of interventions as specific situations arise. Consequently they tend to use more informal interventions. One such popular intervention are the three-minutes breathing spaces (3MBS), brief meditations that help them when they are dealing with a challenging situation to gain control over their frantic thoughts and intense emotions.

Andy, one of my clients, a CEO of a private banking subsidiary, tells me how he has become less angry and choleric with the use of 3MBS. He applies the technique in a situational way. Every time he feels anger mounting in his chest or before difficult discussions with employees or clients, he applies the technique. If necessary he will do it several times a day. The mini-practice helps him to remain calm and react less to his conditioned adverse impulses.

The type that benefits from understanding

This group comprises individuals who employ neither formal nor informal techniques. The benefits they gain are the result of reflecting on, and having a better understanding of, the conceptual variables involved in the process of becoming more balanced and inwardly happy.

For example, they benefit from knowledge gained in the program about the concept of aversion and its negative effects on people's cognitive, emotional, behavioral experiences—experiences that can lead to detrimental reactions. They realize that positivity has the opposite effect and amplifies cognitive, emotional, and behavioral capacities suggesting more adaptive responses to experiences.

This knowledge and raised consciousness serves to mediate detrimental impulses and reaction. Beat, a chef at a restaurant in Zurich and one of my students, told me how even without practicing he feels that he is able to moderate his impulses most of the time, especially during lunch hours when he is under pressure with large numbers of orders pouring into the kitchen. Just by reflecting on the negative effect of his mental state he can moderate his negative, defensive thoughts and bend his mind toward a state that is at least neutral. He says this helps him to remain cool and to better cope with the stress.

To get the best out of the programs it is necessary to train efficiently and smartly. One of my friends, at one time an aspiring concert pianist in Italy and today a management consultant who graduated from Bocconi, the prestigious business school in Milan, told me once: "People who want to learn to play the piano make the mistake of not practicing for days and then doing marathon practices of 5 to 8 hours on weekends. This doesn't work. The trick to learn to play a musical instrument is to practice every day for at least 10 to 20 minutes."

I tell my clients the same, using my friend's principle for the MBSAT practices: "See if you can practice at least a couple of minutes per day instead of doing sporadic longer practices. You will soon note the advantage."

Having discussed the benefits and skills that can be acquired from a MBSAT program, the question remains as to whether there are any risks involved for the participants. As with all human endeavors, especially new ones, there are also some risks in completing a mindfulness training program. The following are possible drawbacks I have observed.

The resignation risk (becoming passive)

Participants can misinterpret two of the most important skills gained in the program: acceptance and positivity. They can interpret these qualities in a way that leads to paralysis, that is, instead of acting and being positive they feel compelled to tolerate inacceptable situations. For example, the managing partner of a small company I know failed to confront under-performing employees thinking that by being accepting and positive the employees would improve their performance. Instead the problem of under-performance only got worse and this had adverse consequences for the company … and the managing partner. In other words, acceptance and positivity do not mean resignation, as we will see later in the program.

The overwhelming risk (hyper-arousal)

Occasionally a participant can get overwhelmed by practices and be unable to complete practices. For example, they find they can't do sitting meditation because they fear that discovering their hidden self could be an experience too difficult to bear. As a result they can become agitated, anxious, and restless. I have experienced only few such cases, but I have had some students who were unable to do the exercises because they triggered emotional distress such as panic. Obviously, MBSAT is not designed for these particular individuals. Other mindfulness interventions are probably more appropriate.

The drowsiness risk

A recurrent problem with some of the practices is the tendency to dullness, drowsiness, and sleep. In the early stages of the learning curve the risk is that people will give up or confuse the exercises with relaxation techniques and use them merely to release tension. The antidote to this risk is simply to persevere and overcome the drowsiness risk with constant practice.

The goal confusion risk

Care should be taking to avoid conflicting goals. Some participants will find that they come to classes with their goals totally out of alignment with the intentions of the program. "I signed up for this class because I thought this could help me with my bipolarity," one of my students told me at the University of Saint Gallen where I was teaching a MBSAT class. The objectives of the course had been clearly articulated in the course description and the main goal of improving the decision-making skills of leaders for both private and organizational life had been clearly stated. Nowhere in the syllabus was there any suggestion that the course would help students with mental problems.

Understanding the potential risks involved in taking or delivering a program like MBSAT is important. The central concern is to realize that MBSAT is not a therapeutic intervention but a mindfulness-based positive psychology intervention. The course is more in line with the principles of coaching, human development and psychological training than with principles of psychotherapy. It is, however, based on robust, evidence-based interventions and employs positive psychology, mindfulness, contemplative sciences, and solidly researched discoveries in social sciences including behavioral economics, management, sociology, and human system dynamics. It is not designed for treatment of clinical psychological conditions for which there are other mindfulness-based interventions.

The main focus of MBSAT is helping individuals improve the quality of their already functioning lives so they can deal better with the many human challenges:

getting a better understanding of themselves; dealing with the sense of personal dissatisfaction that everyone experiences from time to time; coping with impermanence and change; taking appropriate decisions and actions so they achieve and maintain higher levels of subjective well-being—in any final analysis increasing an individual's chances of personal, emotional, and cognitive enrichment. Positive psychologists call this state "flourishing."

6.7 Getting Started: Group Composition and Presession Interviews

Before initiating a MBSAT program it is important to reflect on the composition of the group of participants and clarify some aspects with the participants to ensure an optimal learning process occurs for everyone.

The group composition is especially important, particularly if all participants are from the same employer or organization. My experience has led me to consider the following two criteria: (a) it is preferable to have a group with people from different organizational units, as participants will feel less peer pressure and less threat of competition from colleagues, and (b) it is better to avoid including authority figures in the group such as bosses or HR people involved in evaluations. This allows more open group dynamics and reduces any sense of inhibition.

One issue to consider is preparatory contact with participants. Non-clinical mindfulness initiatives usually omit any type of preinterviews. Despite this tendency in the non-clinical realm I recommend having a presession discussion with each participant. It will help prevent disappointment and potential aggravation during the program.

Here are a series of considerations that should be part of one-to-one conversations with prospective MBSAT participants. In addition, I suggest that you use an interview protocol to guide the discussion. (Please, refer to Section 6.9: Annex to Chapter 6: MBSAT Precourse Interview Template).

Non-clinical cases only

I mentioned the risk of having participants enrolling in a MBSAT program expecting that it will help them with chronic or recurrent mental afflictions including depression, psychosis, and trauma. This point should be addressed explicitly in the precourse interviews and the nature of the program should be emphasized again: the main thrust is to facilitate wise decision-making skills for happiness and sustainable well-being. It is beneficial to explain that the program can be very valuable for individuals going through circumstantial difficulties, for example, job search, relationships issues at work, family concerns, or minor health issues.

Clarifying expectations and risks

It is essential that participants have a clear idea of what they can expect as a result of participating in a MBSAT program. To summarize it once more: it is about helping individuals improve the quality of their normal human experiences by teaching them skills that will assist them with decisions in life so that they have a better chance to achieve their well-being potential. Ultimately, it is a practical and action-oriented intervention with down-to-earth aspirations: to improve a participant's well-being both in everyday life and at important crossroads on life's journey. If the expectation is to reach bliss or a Nirvana-like state (although not excluded—who knows!) there are other more appropriate paths—perhaps going on long retreats, embarking on an ascetic life. Participants must be able to assimilate the program content and exercises even if some difficulties or even emotional issues present themselves during the program.

Finding out about the resolution to practice

In a recent 8-week program I taught to 15 people there was one participant who told me that the program did not have any significant positive effect on him. The others were all very satisfied. Upon talking with this person it became clear that he had never practiced. In fact he had also stayed aloof and passive in the sessions and joint inquiries. "How can you expect to get great benefits from the program and form an opinion about its effectiveness without any practice or engagement?" I asked him. He conceded it was his responsibility to practice and that he could not expect significant positive results as long as he did not do the exercises. It is one of the purposes of the pre session interviews to ascertain the participants' intentions and their determination to engage with the material (practices, exercises, inquiries, and other material).

Perhaps it is useful to reiterate here the vital role of the practices in helping people grow and aligning them with their values. Practices are tools designed to cultivate mental qualities such as attention and strategic awareness as well as affective qualities such as acceptance, friendliness, courage, patience, and equanimity. The practices generate positive cognitive stories, shape people's constructive emotional inclinations, and form positive behaviors.

The importance of a specific intention and resolution is also worthwhile mentioning as the practices work better when inspired by a targeted dedication such as a dedication to become a mindful, positive individual.

Ability to work in group effectively

The program is normally conducted in groups of between 10 to 20 individuals. Group work presents particular challenges and also paradoxes: on the one hand there is the need to belong to the group and on the other the need to assert individuality. Equally, the need to engage with the group is countered by the participants' need for privacy and personal contact. Group work can also involve disclosing private thoughts or ideas and speaking up when faced with unknown or forceful individuals. All of these challenges need to be dealt with skillfully so that individuals feel comfortable working on their personal experiences together with others.

Confidentiality is essential to ensure discretion concerning other people's experiences and to avoid exposing participants' private thoughts. Especially for groups in the same company confidentiality can pose considerable challenges. There is a tendency for participants to become inhibited for fear they could be revealing their vulnerabilities, which in a competitive environment could later turn out to be costly. This not a trivial issue as the risk of losing the instrument of inquiry about the participants' first-person experiences can adversely affect the learning process of the group.

6.8 Teaching MBSAT

Teaching MBSAT is challenging. There are differences to teaching MBCT and MBSR.

Participants in MBCT and MBSR programs come to the sessions already knowing what conditions they seek to resolve: for example, trying to reduce the risk of recurring depression or reducing the impact of physical afflictions and stress. During the program they get to build skills that help them manage their conditions. The information and practices they learn are designed to achieve changes in thoughts, emotions, and behaviors that they have already recognized as inhibiting their well-being.

By contrast, most MBSAT participants, especially individuals in leading positions, come to the program to increase their comparatively high levels of well-being by improving their decision-making skills. Given that they are already successful the question for them is how to maintain their comfort and increase it. They often come with a certain self-confidence. During the course of the program they get exposed to ideas and practices that may challenge their belief system and question their reality and what they thought they knew about what is required for their authentic, sustainable well-being. Thus, in some cases the challenges they face can disconcert them and lead to anxiety, anger, frustration, and other negative states. Skillful teachers with the necessary experience are key to help individuals assimilate their first-person experiences and support them during psycho-education by providing a solid understanding of the material and robust evidence of the conditions that can produce sustainable well-being. If participants are to remain engaged in the program, teachers must also be capable of nurturing curiosity, openness, patience, and embodying the attitudes and the spirit of the program.

Given the high demand for teachers, I do realize that teaching mindfulness has become controversial as criticism is mounting that mindfulness is becoming increasingly distorted and degraded to McMindfulness by the many teaching versions completely disconnected from the historic psychological context and empirical evidence which underpin what is being taught.

At the University of Oxford as part of the Master's in mindfulness-based cognitive therapy, I was not only required to pass the relevant courses but was also obliged to demonstrate competence in teaching mindfulness before being granted the degree. For that purpose a consortium of three British universities (Exeter, Bangor, and Oxford) have developed a rigorous evaluation manual: the "Mindfulness Based Intervention's Teaching Assessment Criteria" (the MBI:TAC). It focuses on testing a teacher's ability to deliver a mindfulness intervention as it was intended. It is a demanding process comprising six evaluative dimensions: (1) coverage, pacing, and organization of session curriculum; (2) relational skills; (3) embodiment of mindfulness; (4) guiding mindfulness practices; (5) conveying course themes through interactive inquiry and didactic teaching; and (6) holding of a group learning environment. Each dimension is evaluated based on at least five key features. For that purpose the full eight sessions of a MBCT program taught by the candidate are video recorded. Between 18 to 20 hours of material is analyzed by two independent assessors who then grade the prospective teacher's level of competence.

For my degree I did two programs, one with a group of high-level Swiss private bankers and the other with professionals from different backgrounds. In both cases I was fortunate to have as my supervisor Dr Esther Riggs, a brilliant psychotherapist, experienced Oxford University mindfulness teacher, and warm-hearted person who guided me competently and gently through this arduous process.

According to the MBI:TAC evaluation process it is possible to pass all the courses but fail the practical part of the teaching. If one is not deemed to have demonstrated sufficient competence in teaching mindfulness one simply doesn't get the degree. One of the critical points in the evaluation of the teacher is Domain 3 of the MBI:TAC, which corresponds to the embodiment of mindfulness. This is a subtle and often elusive criterion that is often difficult to evaluate. It means that the teacher must embody mindfulness in his teachings.

As I am a practitioner of Aikido, the Japanese martial art of defense, and I earned a black belt in this discipline, the MBI:TAC criterion of embodiment often made me think of my Aikido training. In martial arts many techniques are not explained explicitly. The practitioner is supposed to absorb the learning from the sensei (master) who demonstrates the teachings by enacting them. Similarly in mindfulness-based interventions (MBIs) the learning takes place as the teacher subtly articulates and demonstrates the learning process with their inner mindful presence, their whole behavior, and by creating a mindful environment during the sessions. Given the structure of martial arts training, two to three times a week for one-and-a-half to two hours over many years, there are many opportunities to absorb this implicit process of learning. In MBIs, however, contact time between the teacher and the participants is much more limited.

Learning and absorbing these implicit components of mindfulness teaching during the limited duration of the courses poses a challenge. This can be resolved if two important aspects are considered.

A good, sympathetic match between the teacher and the group of participants is crucial. Teaching a group of successful, self-assured business people is not the same as teaching vulnerable, clinical individuals. While an experienced clinical psychologist or even a secular-oriented Buddhist will do an excellent job for a clinical group, they might have a difficult time teaching the group of business people. Thus, a teacher with proper mindfulness experience and training, combined with practical, professional experience with the intricacies and complexities of the corporate and business world, will probably represent a wiser choice as a mindfulness trainer of business people and non-clinical groups.

There is another aspect that I think is important when trying to convey embodied mindfulness effectively to different types of participants. Can the mindfulness-embodied gravitas, which is often apparent in teachers working with clinical groups, be equally effective with non-clinical and business-oriented individuals? My experience is that mindfulness embodiment needs to be contextualized and made explicit. While it is highly desirable to implicitly represent and teach mindfulness, it is sometimes useful and necessary to intervene, albeit briefly, with explicit didactical information in order to avoid losing the trust of the participants, especially when working with business-oriented groups. The appropriate timing and length of these intercessions is a key element that can only be acquired through teaching experience.

Ideally, a combination of qualifications would be desirable for teaching MBSAT: good understanding of MBSAT protocol, be able to follow the TAC mindfulness criteria if possible, several years of mindfulness practice, and good knowledge of business organizations for teaching in those settings. Another desirable requirement is to have proper supervision throughout the delivery of a MBSAT program, especially for teachers without extensive experience.

6.9 The Importance of Inquiry in Sessions

All mindfulness-based programs, whether therapeutic or non-clinical, emphasize the learning that occurs during the practices. The resulting emphasis on inquiry, which occurs after each practice, is driven by two motivations: to help participants discover the full dimension of their living experience and to reinforce their mindful attitudes.

The first aspect—to help participants discover the full dimension of their living experience—implies helping them to live their lives not only with their heads but also with their hearts and bodies. To experience life fully means to connect all the elements that make us human: thoughts, emotions, body sensations, and action/behavioral impulses (BETA).

The second aspect of the inquiry process is to help participants cultivate attitudes that foster the personal development of their mindful lifestyle and encourage regular mindfulness practice.

Leading a mindful life involves the following, indispensable attitudes that should become transparent in the process of inquiry.

6.9.1 Acceptance and non-striving

This is an important skill that helps a person to withstand a situation and remain in a present, being, mode even if they do not like what is happening. It nurtures an attitude of non-striving that helps liberate a person from going into emotional overdrive and wanting to change things. It creates a flexibility of response and a sense of freedom. Any action that follows is likely to be wiser and more effective. It embraces the idea that acceptance does not mean resignation or apathy.

6.9.2 Beginner's mind

This attitude encourages the suspension of preconceptions and fixed ideas and opens up new ways of perceiving and understanding.

6.9.3 Curiosity

Curiosity encourages people to look at their own experiences with a sense of interest and wonder and explore all the learning possibilities those experiences can offer.

6.9.4 Fun

This attitude helps people to experience life with a sense of humor and enjoyment that heightens curiosity and encourages a sense of humility.

6.9.5 Gratitude

It helps people cultivate a sense of thankfulness and gratitude for everything we have.

6.9.6 Kindness

It nurtures a level of kindness that precedes good thoughts, feelings, and caring behavior. Behind all positive experiences is always an act of kindness toward one's self or others.

6.9.7 Love

Love is an emotion that expands intelligence and is an important nutriment for most mindful stances. It actively nurtures goodwill towards others.

6.9.8 Non-judging

A non-judgmental attitude helps reduce a person's internal dialogue, which is commonly overloaded with opinions, judgments, and evaluations.

6.9.9 Patience

Patience encourages people to slow down and enjoy the moment. It reduces the quest for immediate gratification and looks forward to what the future will bring.

These attitudinal stances reinforce each other mutually. Figure 6.1 illustrates the closed loop dynamic in the form of a circle.

How to organize an inquiry effectively? It all begins with the key unit of the analysis: the participant's experience. Whether in self-inquiry or in-group inquiry

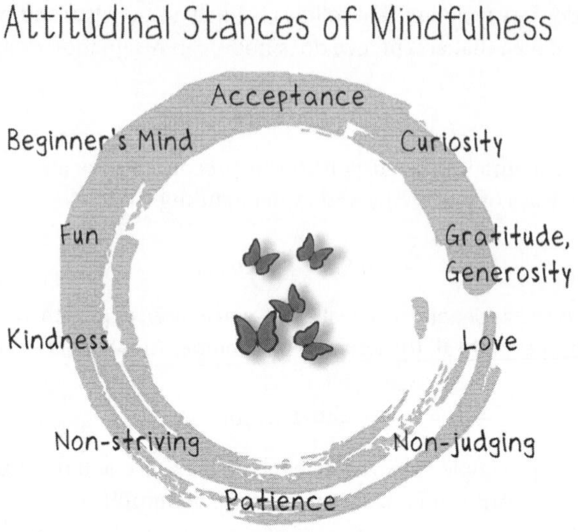

Figure 6.3 Attitudinal Stances of Mindfulness. *Source*: Juan Humberto Young.

(and always supported by a teacher) the starting element is the individual experience. The challenge of this process is to *become aware* of the experience and that is a demanding task. In our head-oriented culture the tendency is to immediately start *thinking about* the experience; instead of being aware we cultivate a kind of attention that immediately turns into an exercise in introspective analysis: "Why do I feel like this?" "Where do these thoughts come from?" Essentially, this creates an additional layer that is concerned with thinking about yourself and this is placed on top of the mental frenzy that is already going on. What this inquiry proposes is something different: becoming aware of yourself without analyzing and judging. This implies noticing and sensing our inner experience: its thoughts, emotions/feelings, body sensations, and behavioral impulses (BETA).

Most mindfulness-based programs follow a 3-stage approach to inquiry which is as follows:

Stage 1 of inquiry

Noticing what is happening or what just happened during the practice or as a direct result of the practice. This should prompt questions such as:

What did you notice? What sensations, emotions, and feelings were aroused? What thoughts? What sounds (in the case of awareness of sounds—see Session 4)?

Did you notice your mind wandering? Where did your mind go: any worries, memories, pain, boredom? Were any emotions attached?

Stage 2 of inquiry

This stage moves from noticing to self-observation, dialoguing mode, and meta-noticing. Typical questions here include:

What did you notice during the practice of awareness? Is it different from a normal state of being? If so, in what way is it different?
When did you notice this? (This question aims at contextualizing the experience.)

What is being trained is the ability to become your own observer, that is, to develop a sense of meta-awareness. It implies the ability to follow the conditioned mind with discernment and investigate the possibilities of liberating it from unhelpful patterns of thinking and reacting.

Stage 3 of inquiry

The third stage of the inquiry relates to new insights from the experiences and how those insights can inform and enrich normal aspects of the participants' lives with questions like: "How can the knowledge gained be of use in the participant's life?"

Normalizing the new learning requires considerable effort. For example, if participants are having issues with excessive worrying and anxiety, relevant questions could include: "How could today's insights be applied to deal skillfully with states of worry and anxiety?" "In what way can the new insights help a person to stay healthy and increase their well-being?" "Can the insights keep a person healthy and increase their sense of well-being?

When guiding the inquiry teachers are encouraged to use verbs such as exploring, investigating, discovering, accepting, letting be, and being with—all forms of language that suggest an invitation without striving, hence a less goal-oriented stance. In short: a being mode. Wordings such as "try to" or "work towards" should be avoided as they convey go-getting messages that could lead to a doing mode and frustration if not attained.

Good practice is to remind participants to focus awareness on their body sensations, to observe without judging, and to stay lucid without wanting to change what is happening. Also, good practice involves identifying any tightness in the body, any inappropriate emotions, and any unwarranted thinking. These are the signs that can help uncover unwanted patterns of the mind.

The essence of inquiry is to help participants increase their awareness of their cognitive and sensorial experiences (their thoughts, emotions, body sensations, and impulses to act—BETA), to help develop their discernment skills, and to improve their insights about what makes them really happy and how they can improve their well-being.

Teachers can help participants achieve this by asking them to move vertically, so to speak, and go deeper into their self-observation in order to extract more information from their experiences. Inquiry also involves a horizontal movement as participants are invited to share among themselves similar, or opposing, insights or experiences that help to broaden the scope of the inquiry. Hence inquiry should be a well-rounded experience involving all participants.

6.10 Homework Assignments

"Happiness is not something readymade. It comes from your own actions," says the Dalai Lama (2010). Improving human experience requires creating conditions that facilitate the emergence of positive qualities in the mind in order to generate creative constructive thoughts that in turn lead to wholesome actions. The emergence of such a cognitive and emotional opening expands our sensory abilities: hearing, smelling, touching, and seeing, and moves us into a sensual realm never experienced before. Our sensitivity and intuition take on new dimensions. For example, you talk to your employee differently and initiate a conversation that leads to constructive and creative solutions; you hear a song with different ears and experience feelings not known before; you touch your significant other differently and both get transported into a realm of new emotional discoveries and bodily sensations; you open your eyes and see a homeless person and buy him a lunch.

Opening head and heart is not easy; it requires genuine courage. Yet for authentic flourishing it is necessary to catalyze our entire being. When Franz Welser-Möst left Zurich's Tonhalle Orchestra to direct the Cleveland Orchestra (CO), one of the top five orchestras in the United States, he was asked what was the secret of CO's great performances. He answered that the musicians of CO had "big ears", allowing them to hear each other well, so they could play great music together. That is what MBSAT's homework and practices aspire to achieve: to open and amplify the individual's cognitive, emotional, and sensory abilities so that they can become better players in the symphony of life. Keeping that in mind, the practices in the program are designed to spur mental creativity, sensuality (the positive and mindful sense of the word), and courage.

MBSAT practices are sometimes adapted from other mindfulness-based interventions, primarily from MBCT and MBSR. In other cases they are designed by drawing from positive psychology, behavioral finance, system dynamics, organizational development, positive design thinking, applied aesthetics, risk management, and process philosophy. They include different meditation and mindfulness practices and can comprise a broad range of other techniques: videos, poems, music, journal writing, short conceptual learning, positive mindful actions, and brief reflection papers.

The focus is always on nudging participants towards first-person experiences. This is the basis for MBSAT's experiential learning model, which is explained in the chapter on MBSAT principles (5.3.4). The goal is to use the participants' own experiences and contributions in inquiry discussions as the central vehicles for knowledge creation and learning.

The homework and practices consist of two basic types: formal and informal practices.

Formal practices are more systematic and done at regular intervals. Typically it is necessary to define a specific time and duration for them. Experience suggests that the best way to maintain adherence and sustain the practice is by creating a routine: always practicing at the same time, in the same place, and for the same duration. For example, every morning before leaving to work in a quiet corner of one's home for several minutes (5, 10, 20, or more). An important consideration is to see the time involved as personal time dedicated to one's well-being with the intention of self-care and renewal.

There are three types of formal practice:

Sitting meditations: Depending on the purpose of the practice, the primary attention in sitting meditation may focus on the breath (inhaling and exhaling consciously and mindfully) or on body sensations, sounds or thoughts as well as other focal points. If no particular focus is chosen the practice is called open awareness meditation.

Movement meditations: These practices consist of doing every single movement very carefully, observing the slightest details in joints and muscles. Typical movement meditations are for example mindful walking, mindful stretching, but also yoga and mindful salsa.

Group learning: The essence of group learning is embedded in frequent inquiries during the sessions about participants' experiences with practices or home assignments. Group learning is an integral part of experiential learning in mindfulness programs, including MBSAT. Moreover, group learning comprises joint exercises, collective reflection, discussions, and so on.

In contrast, informal practices tend to be shorter and are done as a situation arises, that is, in a quiet moment of spare time or when a need for recollection arises, for example, when coping with challenges or intense emotions. Typical informal practices are mini-meditations and mindful concentration on daily activities.

Examples of mini-meditations are the three-minutes breathing space meditations of which several variations are introduced in MBSAT. Other frequently used informal practices are mindful showering, mindful eating, mindful driving, or mindfully doing household chores. There are innumerable possibilities.

However, it is only formal practices that allow for sustainable brain neuroplasticity and the desired quantum changes. As the program unfolds the distinction between these practices becomes apparent, either explicitly or implicitly.

Most importantly, practicing for MBSAT does not mean rehearsing to become a better performer, but engaging with the practice until one eventually embodies it; the practice becomes so natural and intuitive that it feels like an integral part of oneself.

The state can be illustrated by thinking of consummate artists or sport champions who seem to become one with their movements. Aikido, the Japanese defense art, is another example. In Aikido one practices by perceiving what is going on inside and outside of the body, moment by moment, until the practice becomes a part of the practitioner. Thus higher Aikido masters, given their instant and clear perception of a situation no longer rely on predetermined scripts but generate original, spontaneous, and skillful responses. When I asked my sensei: "What would you do if you were attacked by surprise in real life?" she answered: "I cannot tell you in advance; all I know is I would find an effective way to respond in my defense."

Similarly MBSAT practices eventually become second nature to practitioners enabling wise and skillful responses. MBSAT's goal is to assist leaders and individuals to manage their lives positively and mindfully by building skills that help them with choices and decisions that can foster their personal and social well-being. In this respect, becoming the mindful, positive individual is a higher-order achievement that incorporates mindfulness, positive psychology, and decision skills. For the participants it represents the beginning of a process to find a balance between a lifelong, never-ending progression of mastering MBSAT practices and the challenges that the symphony of life presents to them every day.

6.11 Annex to Chapter 6: MBSAT Precourse Interview Template

Mindfulness-based strategic awareness training—MBSAT

Precourse Interview
All information will be treated strictly confidentially.

Name: .... Date:.....................................

Position:................................. Age:......................................

Civil Status:............................ Nationality:...............................

Email:................................... Phone:......................................

Why you registered for this course:

....

....

....

....

....

What you expect to get from this course:

....

....

....

....

....

Major changes have you experienced in the past two years:

....

....

....

....

Five things you would like to change to achieve more happiness/ well-being:

....

....

....

....

....

Most important, helpful persons in your life and what they give you:

....

....

....

....

....

Percentage of your time that you feel is truly YOUR life:

....

....

....

7

Session 1: Robotic Living—Automatic Pilot

7.1 Introduction

"I have been driving from home to work and back for the last ten years without noticing the statue in the middle of the roundabout. Only now, by driving more mindfully, I have become aware of it. Amazing; I was like a robot. How could I be so blind?" Marcus wondered during a homework inquiry in one of my training programs.

I asked him if he could recall what was on his mind while he was driving and lost in his own thoughts. "Not really," he replied. "I must have been mulling over things at work or over issues in my family."

Marcus's experience reveals two distinct facets of the same phenomenon: (a) he was able to drive safely from home to work and back without really paying attention to his surroundings—this suggests that his mind was in automatic-pilot mode, and (b) instead of his mind being present within the driving experience it was wandering and either thinking ahead—the future—or pondering what had happened at home - the past.

Automatic pilot and mind wandering are not conscious mental states. They rob people's immediate thinking and send them into a virtual reality that is driven by a mixture of runaway thoughts, mental plots, and imaginary stories. Thoughts pop up in what some describe as a monkey mind—an allusion to monkeys jumping from tree to tree.

Scientific research by Killingsworth and Gilbert (2010) detected that 47% (i.e., close to half of our time awake) is spent in this automatic/mind-wandering mode. We are more like zombies than living beings.

In the film *Matrix*, Morpheus asks Neo, the hero of the movie: "Do you believe in faith?" to which Neo answers: "No, because I don't like the idea that I am not in control of my life."

Mindfulness-Based Strategic Awareness Training: A Complete Program for Leaders and Individuals, First Edition. Juan Humberto Young.

Companion website: www.wiley.com/go/humbertoyoung/mbsat

Paradoxically, despite this human need for autonomy, it is loss of control that occurs in the automatic-pilot mode when people are reduced to a state of robotic functioning.

The German philosopher, Thomas Metzinger, an expert in the philosophy of the mind, equates these moments to a loss of what he calls M-Autonomy (mental autonomy), that is, the loss of the capacity to control mental abilities such as attention, rational deliberation, planning, and decision-making. He argues that we also lose V-Autonomy (veto autonomy)—the capacity to intentionally inhibit unwarranted mental activities. Two effects are observable: (a) the loss of attention agency or the ability to control our attention, and (b) the loss of cognitive agency or the ability to control the direction of deliberate thinking or stop mindless thinking, such as goal or task orientation.

In view of the ubiquity of automatic pilot this is not a trivial matter. The cognitive psychologists Killingsworth and Gilbert (2010) point out that "a human mind is a wandering mind, and a wandering mind is an unhappy mind. The ability to think about what is not happening is a cognitive achievement that comes at an emotional cost" (2010, p. 932). Jazaieri et al. (2006) in a daily experience sample study on compassion meditation training suggest that a wandering mind is a less caring mind which makes sense since mind wandering implies being unable to pay attention to the surroundings.

In the first chapter (see Section 1.3) I wrote about the well-documented, essential human need for autonomy. When we make the connection between our lack of control over half of our mental activities with our need for autonomy it becomes clear why Neo in the *Matrix* dislikes the idea of not being in control of his life: relinquishing control leads to a state of latent dissatisfaction. It thwarts our autonomy. Paradoxically, this is how we live half of the time unless we become more mindful.

Mind scientists Brewer et al. (2011) discovered that mind wandering while executing activities in automatic pilot correlates to neural activities in the brain that support self-referential processing, known as default-mode network (DMN). The same mental processing also happens to be implicated in attention lapses, anxiety, and even in Alzheimer's disease.

In another study, Epel et al. (2012) discovered that individuals with greater propensity to mind wandering were found to have shorter telomeres, which are DNA caps protecting the end part of chromosomes so that they do not deteriorate. Telomeres shorten with age and with physical and psychological stress. Their length helps in the early prediction of diseases. Shortening is associated with various types of diseases including cardiovascular, cancer, and diabetes. Epel et al. (p. 1) conclude that: "a present attentional state [read mindful] may promote a healthy biochemical milieu and, in turn cell longevity."

This conclusion is promising and hopeful. An essential question is: Why does a mind wander and function in automatic pilot? Nature must have developed this behavior for some adaptive reason. It cannot be all negative.

What are the positive aspects of these otherwise unfavorable mental states? Mooneyham and Schooler (2013) explored this question and came up with several possible benefits:

Mind wandering seems to:

- promote planning and providing for the future,
- enhance creativity, and
- relieve boredom.

Another potential benefit, as Mason et al. (2007) point out, is the creation of subjective coherence when mental links emerge during mind wandering.

In a mindfulness class I noticed how a student brought her journal to mindfulness classes and started writing immediately after meditative practices. I asked her why she did this. She answered: "Whenever my mind starts to wander during meditation many novel and creative ideas surface. I don't want to lose them. So I make notes while they are fresh in my memory." She had fallen for the seductive aspects of mind wandering. "Be careful," I replied, "or you might convert your mindfulness practice into an idea generation exercise and that clearly is not the intention."

Her thought processes had started from stimuli, which had arisen in her mind without any sensorial input such as a smell, sight, sound, or even physical sensations. Those processes are a cognitive function that can create a strategic openness to the future provided that it is the result of ex-post meditative states.

However, a scattered mind has a tendency to kindle dissatisfaction. The focus of mind wandering is on the past and future and this can result in the mind missing the present. The practices in this first session are therefore geared toward reducing the impact of automatic pilot and enabling us to stay in the present moment. This also implies that critical-judgmental attitudes and problem-solving tendencies need to be suspended in order to understand our mental and sensorial experiences from moment to moment.

Out of these practices it is possible to re-engage with life in an unbiased and revitalizing way that can open up new options and possibilities. The point of the practices is to gradually determine a healthy balance between the costs and benefits of mind wandering by finding ways to align our thoughts in a coherent, strategic manner instead of a haphazard, monkey-like jumble. As result of the practices proposed, participants will also increase their memory—a valuable side effect in addition to the other benefits.

This is about finding a balance between *zoning out* (getting away from automatic pilot, mind wandering, and bounded awareness) and *tuning in* (tapping into strategic awareness by being mindfully in the present), thus embarking on a positive mindful life path.

7.2 Session Organization, Coverage, and Sequence

The themes of the first session emanate naturally from the discussion above: they are about recognizing when we operate in automatic pilot mode, discovering the richness of our body sensations, and becoming aware of our mental patterns and strategic resources.

The components and sequence of the two-hour session is as follows:

Session 1: Robotic living/automatic pilot, (Re)discovering body sensations and awareness of strategic sensory resources

	Time suggested in minutes
	Approx. duration 2½ hours
1. Welcome, introductions, and clarifications	25
Introductions of participants (mutually in pairs for 5 minutes, summaries in plenum 10 minutes), need for group work, Rules of privacy and confidentiality, role of teacher, The importance of practice	
2. Raisin exercise Guidance and inquiry about the exercise	35
3. Body scan Guidance and inquiry	50
4. The formal mindfulness practice habit (please, see Handout 1 for definitions and Handout 2)	20
5. Home practice assignments Body scan (6 days a week) and mindfulness of a routine activity (please, see Handout 3, 4, and 5)	5
6. Questions and answers and closing Further explanations and brief final concentration on breath	5

7.3 Exercises and Practices of Session 1

The experiential learning initiated in Session 1 seeks to refine the participants' attention skills by focusing on a single object for a short period of time. While this is a state of narrow focus, participants also get a small foretaste of strategic awareness by observing their body, because observation implies a state of spacious, expansive, and encompassing awareness.

7.3.1 First exercise: The Raisin exercise

The first exercise in the program is the so-called raisin exercise. It was named because of the real, edible raisins that are used in the exercise. It has been part of the long-standing MBSR program for some 40 years. The longevity of the raisin exercise is a testimony to its effectiveness in achieving its key intention: to help participants recognize the difference between their usual unaware automatic pilot and a mindful state of being.

There are several learning outcomes that result from the raisin exercise. Simply put, in the exercise each participant receives one raisin and focuses on it as mindfully and attentively as possible with all senses: observing, touching, smelling, tasting, and even listening to its tiny noises when you squeeze it between your fingers close to the ear. This seemingly trivial experiment brings forth a multitude of discoveries and surprising observations from participants. Below are some examples of the connections that can be expected from the exercise.

Learnings from the raisin exercise

Becoming mindful enriches sensory experiences:

"I normally just eat fast and without thinking. When I slowed down I realized that I normally ignore a lot," Tony, a participant in one of my programs, remarked. Experiencing the vast difference between automatic pilot and mindful attention is an important insight from this exercise. Part of the learning is that being present is a sensory experience that involves all of our senses. It also helps reveal how frequent and ingrained our automatic-pilot habits are.

Mindfulness leads to openness and transformation

"I normally don't eat raisins. I don't like them. But eating one like this, attentively and being present, I discovered that they are not so bad, so I will now start eating them," Meena, one of my students from India, told the class after she had eaten a raisin mindfully. The ability to discern things that we are unable to notice in automatic pilot, but are revealed with a mindful mind state, can have a transformation effect. In Meena's case she moved from disliking raisins to becoming curious about them and then being ready to sample them once more.

Mind wandering is human; the key is to return to being present

Mila, another participant, felt instantly transported home to her country of origin, Georgia by the Black Sea, by the raisin exercise. She remembered happy days with her family eating grapes. She told the class that Georgia is one of the best places in the world for growing grapes. This highlights another learning point: how ubiquitous mind wandering is and how we all make associations, even far-fetched ones, with whatever information we get. Thus, from eating a single raisin in Saint Gallen, Switzerland, Mila transported herself to Georgia in an instant and imagined eating the tastiest grapes with her loved ones.

Being on automatic pilot deprives people of much of their human experience. The mind is constantly exposed to unconscious associative states from all kinds of sensory impulses and memories of the past and consequently people easily succumb to mind wandering. It makes a kind of its own movie before the inner eye and results in people being unable to connect with their real present experience. As people slow down and become curious and mindful about present events and activities they begin to notice and observe the transformational possibilities of mundane, everyday activities and of their potential to promote enrichment in their lives.

Some people may need to overcome deep barriers in order to reap the benefits of the raisin exercise. One of my colleagues in academia, a business school professor with a worldwide reputation, told me that he once invited a famous mindfulness teacher into his organizational behavior class and the first practice the teacher introduced for experiential and perceptual learning was the raisin exercise.

Most of the class found it odd and funny and could not appreciate its potential to reveal experiential insights. This was a class of MBA students at a very competitive, top-ranking US business school. They were a group of highly conceptual learners suddenly confronted with the mindfulness professor's invitation to switch gears from the doing mode to the being mode. It is not surprising that they found the exercise strange. It underlined the difficulty many people have, especially in the world of business, in addressing their sensorial experiences.

Note 1, *The Raisin Exercise*, presents a script to help guide the experience of eating a raisin mindfully.

7.3.2 First mindful practice: The body scan

The Body Scan is the first formal mindfulness practice of the MBSAT program and lays the foundation for the practices in the coming weeks. Essentially it is an attention exercise that consists of shifting the focus of attention consciously from one part of the body to another, normally beginning with the toes and then sequentially moving the attention up through the body towards the head, hence the term scanning.

Awareness of the body seems a sensible way to begin practicing mindfulness. Olendzki (2010) suggests mindfulness of the body is effective because the mind can only be at one place at a time and keeping it in the body is a totally natural experience in the present moment.

In Western society there has been a tradition of focusing on our body only in relation to intimacy, eating, and physical appearance and neglecting other types of information that come from sensory, body experience. This process of disconnecting or ignoring the signals from the body starts early in life: "Mommy, I'm hungry," says the child and the mother replies: "It's not lunch time yet. You have to wait." The mother's answer marks the beginning of our conditioning to override signals from the body, some may be justified, many others unwarranted.

"I am so tired I almost passed out, but I absolutely must keep going until I finish this report," the project leader tells herself, effectively talking herself out of some badly needed rest.

This type of response illustrates how the mind thinks its way out of valuable information coming from the body. Over time this stunts a person's capacity to sense the body's signals.

The body scan is a practice intended to recover the capacity to feel and listen to our body sensations and emotions. At the same time it is a practice to gain autonomy by directing our attention so we stay in the present without judging. Most of our judgments are a result of conditioning and part of our automatic pilot.

Since Kabat-Zinn first designed the practice almost forty years ago its effectiveness has been confirmed by generations of mindfulness teachers. The benefits can be enumerated as follows:

Benefits from the body scan practice

Reconnecting with the body and being fully present: The body scan is an excellent exercise to help participants to become one again with their body and thus, in a certain sense, become whole. "I felt my blood pulsing in my whole body very intensely. I had never realized before that it could be so intense," reported a participant reflecting on the sensations produced by the body scan. It brings participants to the present moment. They experience the body as it is right now, at this point in time. It also teaches participants to observe their sensations with curiosity (I feel a kind of itching in my knee—ok, interesting) and without intellectualizing or thinking about their reactions (I think my knee is itching, because I have been standing for too long; I should avoid that).

Attention training: The body scan trains a person's capacity to engage and disengage their attention. "I cannot sense my toes at all and I have little feeling in my feet," a participant might observe. "But I can clearly feel every part of my legs." Part of the practice involves learning to alter your attention like a spotlight so it can move from a narrow focus like a toe to a wide angle, which encompasses larger parts of the body. It is a dynamic process of sequentially engaging and disengaging attention with regard to different parts of the body. The participants gain more autonomy as they practice.

Learning to relate skillfully to mind wandering: "It feels so reassuring that it is OK to tell myself: if you notice your mind wandering, just acknowledge it and gently bring your attention back to the part of the body that is the focus of attention at the moment. Without these instructions, I would have all kinds of feelings of inadequacy." The participant making this statement voiced a sentiment most practitioners have. It is important to remind participants that mind wandering is normal. In fact, that is what most healthy minds do; it is part of being human. One of the skills being practiced is simply to recognize when our mind wanders and reduce its frequency, if you choose, by gently escorting your attention back to the focus of the practice.

Allowing things to be as they are: "I slept almost all the way through the practice and it made me feel so frustrated because it is not what I wanted. It just felt so relaxing that I could not help it. I'm sorry." Comments like this are often to be heard during the inquiry that follows body-scan meditations. Allowing conditions to be as they are in a non-striving attitude, that is, just accepting conditions the way they are, including the conditions of the body during practice, can be a liberating experience. Relaxation and sleepiness may signal that one is getting out of automatic pilot and the mind is slowing down, ready for new challenges. However, it should be noticed that the purpose of the practice is not relaxation but awareness of the body.

The body scan is a very powerful exercise because of its profound effect on people's health and the added benefits of training attention and developing awareness of the richness of somatic sensations.

Recent studies highlight the beneficial health effects of the body scan. Positive psychologists (Kok et al. 2013) have found a relation between positive emotions, social connections, and the vitality of the vagus nerve, a cranial nerve connecting the brain with the heart and many other inner organs including the lungs, kidneys, liver, spleen, stomach, and colon. The tone of this nerve, called vagal tone, influences the health of all the organs it is connected with. Vagal tone is measured indirectly by recording respiratory sinus arrhythmia (RSA). A pioneering study by Ditto, Eclache, and Goldman (2006) found that 20 minutes of daily body scan meditation over a 4-week period improved the respiratory sinus arrhythmia (RSA), and led to improvements in vagal tone which, in turn, connected to a healthier heart, heightened resilience, and positive coping skills.

In Note 2, you will find instructions and suggestions for in-class body scan meditation.

7.3.3 *The formal mindfulness practice habit: A MBSAT prerequisite*

Mindfulness-based strategic awareness training (MBSAT) is pointless without regular formal mindfulness practice. No amount of knowledge about meditating or smart insights into techniques of breathing and concentration will have any effect if participants don't develop a mindfulness practice habit. It would be like knowing all there is to know about swimming but refusing to practice the actual moves and learn how to keep one's head above water. To reap the benefits of MBSAT and its associated practices, particularly mindfulness practices, it is necessary to do them regularly, preferably every day even if just for a few minutes. My experience in teaching MBSAT and other practices has proven time and again that lack of constant practice derails any aspiration of becoming an authentic mindful positive leader or individual.

Conscious of this challenge I have included a section designed to assist individuals to develop a mindfulness practice habit—the missing link between *learning* the practices and *doing* the practices.

Fortunately the mechanisms that create good habits are now well known. However, given the diversity of people and situations there is no single solution or recipe guaranteed to develop positive habits. What is available and has proved to be very effective is a framework for how habit formation evolves. It can assist people in building a mindfulness practice routine that corresponds to individual motivations and needs and it is designed around incentives and rewards.

In his book *The Power of Habit* Duhigg (2012) presents a habit-development model based on the work of behavioral scientists at MIT and other universities. The model is composed of three observable variables and one invisible element. These, Duhigg argues, are the principal driving forces of habit creation. Figure 7.1 illustrates the model.

The three components are:

The cue: This is the trigger that tells the brain to activate a habit and shifts behavior into automatic pilot, that is, behavior without conscious control. The cue can be either external (sight, sound, smell, amongst others) or internal (a thought, emotions, and sensations).

The routine: This is the customary behavior that leads to a reward. A routine can be physical (drinking a glass of wine at dinner), cognitive (memorizing information for a meeting), or emotional (feeling anxious about speaking in front of an audience). In the case of mindfulness the desired routine consists of mindfulness practices.

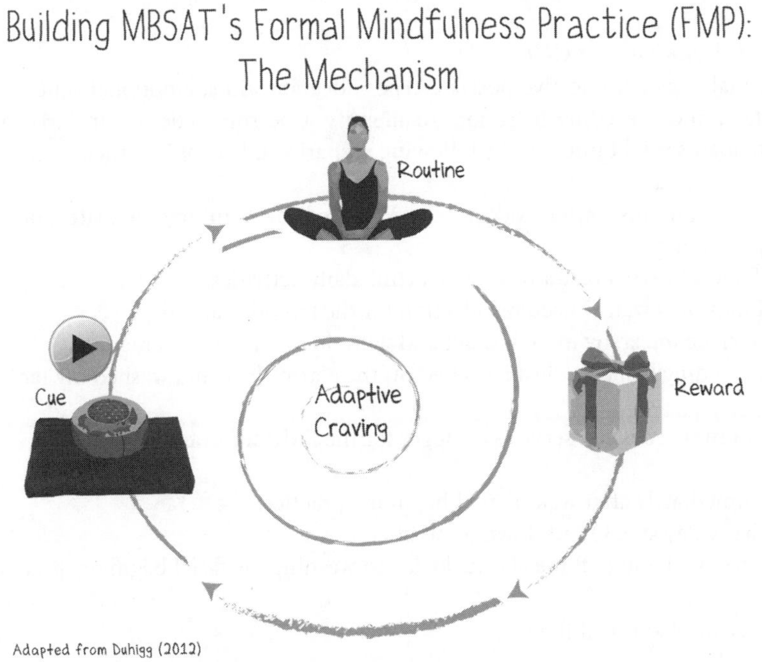

Figure 7.1 Building MBSAT's Formal Mindfulness Practice (FMP): The Mechanism. *Source*: Adapted from Duhigg (2012).

The reward: Like the routine the reward can also be physical (candies or chocolate, going for a walk, etc.), cognitive (doing something interesting or relaxing), or emotional (feeling good about oneself, feeling stimulated, etc.). This reward is crucial because it reinforces the routine loop in the brain, in our case the mindfulness routine loop. From a neurological perspective habits are situated at the basal ganglia at the base of the forebrain. What researchers have discovered is that as behavior becomes a habit the activity in this part of the brain decreases because the routine runs automatically.

Professor Schultz from the University of Cambridge discovered what drives habits: neurological structures in the brain create a craving for rewards and this craving is coupled with routine behavior. For example, it is the craving for the pleasant effects of endorphins released after exercising that fuels enthusiasm for the habit of jogging. Ironically, one of the major aims of mindfulness practice is to develop healthy ways to rein-in craving behavior. Buddhist psychology believes that craving is the origin of human suffering. Here I am talking about adaptive and intentional ways to create a kind of healthy craving in order to sustain mindfulness practice habits.

Handout 2 of Session 1 introduces an exercise on how to build MBSAT's formal mindfulness practice (FMP) habit. It consists of three steps:

Step 1: Defining your CUE

Habitual cues fall into five possible types: location, time, emotional state, social context, and preceding behavior. To identify a personal cue for an FMP habit participants might think of the following scenario and adapt it to their needs:

- Location: just after waking up I settle down in my favorite spot for practicing.
- Time: always at 6.30 am before starting daily activities.
- Emotional state: I need recollection for the busy day ahead.
- Social context: by myself (quiet and with no distracting interactions).
- Preceding behavior: just switched off the alarm clock and washed my face.

Any of these cues can serve as a trigger for the FMP, for example:

- Immediately after waking up I begin my practice.
- Every day at 6.30 I sit down to practice.
- After switching off the alarm clock and washing my face I begin my practice.

Here is another possibility:

- I do my practice when I take my 20 minutes break at work (location).
- It is at 10.30 am or 3.00 pm (time).

- I'm in need of a quiet moment (emotional state).
- I am with a group of colleagues who also practice (social).
- I just finished looking through my emails (preceding activity).

Step 2: Creating the REWARD for your FMP habit

Finding a reward to give yourself for engaging in the routine behavior of FMP is a smart psychological technique. It could include a tasty breakfast, a plan to watch your favorite program in the evening, or a chat with colleagues. Alternatively you might feel rewarded in more intangible ways: by a sense of accomplishment after the practice, a sense of tranquility, the satisfaction of being open in social situations, or being more at ease with yourself and others. It is just a matter of finding the right reward to stimulate the next step that should have a positive momentum so it creates an adaptive craving for the habitual behavior.

Step 3: Define a PLAN to enact the routine

Once Steps 1 and 2 are defined the task is to formulate a statement that is an implementation intention that provides an anchor for the daily routine. For example:

> Every morning after waking up at 6.30 am I will do my mindfulness practice because it provides me with the necessary clarity for the rest of the day.

To further facilitate building the habit one can create additional secondary cues such as placing a meditation cushion next to the bed, getting a meditation clock, or something similar. All of these cues serve as triggers to get firmly accustomed to the routine.

8

Session 2: Living Above the Neck

8.1 Introduction

Session 2 resumes the conversation about our rediscovery of the body. It emphasizes the idea that we are driven by our head as if our body's solitary function is to carry it. When we think carefully about the relationship between our head and our body we realize that our body is a vessel full of experiences. It also holds a mirror up to our mental life. There is a two-way connection between mind and body so that the mind can be used to observe our bodily experience while at the same time mindful observation of the body can help us see what is going on in the mind.

We extend our learning in this session with the first cognitive behavioral training exercise and introduce a practice which helps cultivate positive well-being experiences. In order to be less driven—more in a "being–experiencing" mode than a "doing–inner dialoguing" mode—we also introduce sitting meditation.

When we explore the body scan practice we must first realize that all bodily sensations exist in a precise time and place: the present moment. Usually when we refer to past sensations we are thinking about sensations and modifying them with an evaluative mindset ("an unpleasant sensation," "a wonderful sensation," etc.), which heightens distress or amplifies pleasure.

The sensory-oriented focus of the body scan directs attention to the body in the moment. It is a powerful strategy to help nudge individuals into the present and reduce the possibility of being lost in thought processes that focus on self-referential mental narratives.

The body scan asks participants to move their attention to all the different parts of the body, one after another, in a process that focuses on noticing sensations without trying to change them. As people practice the body scan more regularly they begin to relate to their body sensations in a phenomenological way, sensing and perceiving the sensations instead of thinking about them. Also, as people get

Mindfulness-Based Strategic Awareness Training: A Complete Program for Leaders and Individuals, First Edition. Juan Humberto Young.

Companion website: www.wiley.com/go/humbertoyoung/mbsat

more practice with the body scan, they develop an attitude of allowing and accepting their sensations and integrating the wisdom of the body with the mind.

Participants are invited to observe thoughts and feelings that are attached to their sensations and become familiar with parsing those experiences into different components: Body sensations, Emotions/feelings, Thoughts and Action impulses—BETA.

Another insight from the body scan is the way a participant responds to uneasiness: when in distress, maybe due to uncomfortable sensations or mind-wandering states, participants are invited to move attention to the breath as a neutral focus and useful regulator of the whole experience.

Finally, an important dimension of the practice is the way it focuses on the interoceptive properties of the body. By interoceptive I mean those internal sensations that are different from those generated by the five exteroceptive senses (tasting, touching, hearing, smelling, and seeing), which were the focus of the raisin exercise.

The practical implications of sensing with the body are huge. At UBS I was once trying to close a major deal with an influential businessman. My team and I studied the transaction thoroughly and structured it with tight guarantees and risk management measures that could produce substantial profits. Following the procedures that existed at the time, a board member had to present the deal to the executive board. Given the large amount of money involved, the board member chosen to do the presentation requested a meeting with the client. The client flew in for a one-on-one meeting. After the meeting the board member surprised me with the news that he did not want to go ahead with the deal despite the extensive guarantees and the guaranteed large profit. When I asked why, he told me he just had a hunch and could not offer any specific reason. The due diligence report from a reputable third-party firm gave a favorable assessment of the character and the financial situation of the businessman. Still the board member was reluctant to do the deal. I kept asking him to reconsider. He finally offered a reason for his objection: there was something strange in the man's voice.

"Wow," I thought, "that is incomprehensible. A person's voice cannot be sufficient grounds to reject a deal."

So I continued to insist that we should finalize the deal and the board member kept dragging his feet.

Shortly afterwards we heard from our bank's office abroad that the businessman was being questioned by his country's tax authorities and that he was involved in some dubious financial schemes.

"See, I told you I didn't like the fellow," the board member told me.

He was right. We were lucky not to have done the deal, because we would have lost a large amount of money. The board member had noticed something that could not be identified with a thinking mind but only observed with the senses.

On the other hand, with my MBA and my conceptual, analytically oriented mind, I was blinded by the prospect of the large deal, the profits we could rake in and, maybe, by thoughts about my year-end bonus. I was unable to sense what he sensed.

Some years later I read an interview with S. Porges, the neuropsychologist, who offered a plausible, scientific explanation, interviewed at the NICABM[1] Porges remarked: "You meet someone; the person appears to be bright, attractive, but you don't really like the person because of the way the person is articulating – the lack of prosody and the lack of facial expressivity" (Buczynski & Porges, 2013, p. 13). These subtle signals require an ability to capture information and data through the viscera—an interoceptive way of knowing. This was the case of the board member who connected his impression of the man to his internal sensory perceptions and was therefore able to perceive his intentions and saved the bank millions.

From the perspective of system dynamics, regularly practicing the body scan reinforces a causal loop that generates beneficial outcomes for the practitioner as depicted in Figure 8.1: the body scan has a causal relationship with increases in bodily perceptual abilities (interoception) and volitional attention that leads to a reduction of mind wandering. In turn this engenders increases in alternative ways of relating to mental states and increases an individual's capacity for acceptance. The causal loop is completed because the beneficial outcomes motivate participants to reinforce the practice of the body scan.

The graph shown in Figure 8.2 illustrates the beneficial outcomes of the causal loop with a timeline in an idealized way. It is clear that no matter how intensively one practices mind wandering will never disappear, because that is one of the characteristics of the human mind. However, the idea here is to present a visual aid that reflects intuitively the benefits of practicing: an increase in acceptance, attention, and bodily perception and a different, more positive way of relating. The shape of the curves provides an indication of the changes without representing mathematical functions or data.

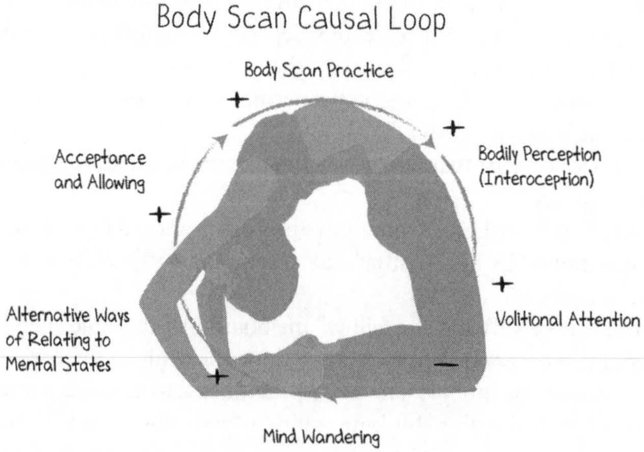

Figure 8.1 Body Scan Causal Loop. *Source*: Juan Humberto Young.

[1] National Institute for the Clinical Application of Behavioral Medicine

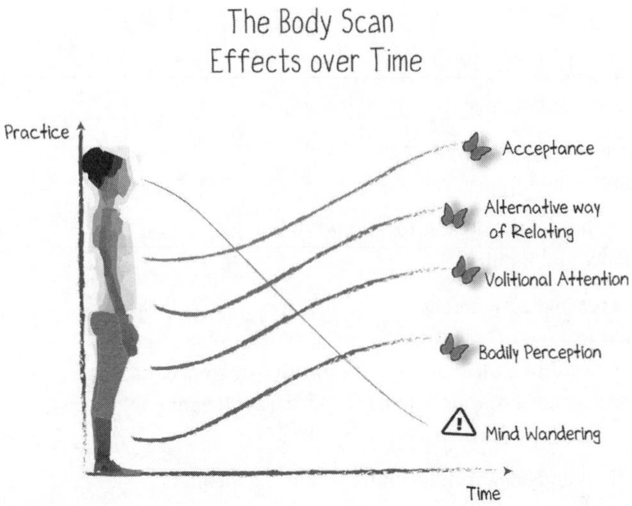

Figure 8.2 Effects of Body Scan Over Time. *Source*: Juan Humberto Young.

8.2 Session Organization, Coverage, and Sequence

In Session 2 we continue to explore the distinction between different modes of the mind: the doing mode; the driven-doing or crazy-busy mode; and the being mode. All of these modes are implicit in the exercises and practices.

It is worth noting that since the first session participants have had a week of practice. They will come to the second session with questions and with issues they are confronting in implementing the practices and integrating them into their daily lives. This provides rich material for exploring skillful ways to manage hurdles that interfere with their progress.

The session plan and sequence:

Session 2: Living Above the Neck: Doing Mode and Being Mode

	Time suggested in minutes
	Duration 2½–3 hours
1. Coming to the session (welcome and settling in)	3
2. Body scan Guidance and inquiry	20
3. Home practice review Inquiry	35

4.	BETA exercise Guidance and inquiry	20
5.	Three good things exercise Guidance and inquiry	20
6.	Mindfulness of the breath: 10 minutes sitting meditation Guidance and inquiry	20
7.	Home practice assignments Body scan 6 out of 7 days 10 minutes sitting meditation of the breath 6 out of 7 days Mindfulness of a routine activity (choosing a different one)	10
8.	Closing Questions and answers and 3 minutes closing meditation	3

8.3 Exercises and Practices of Session 2

The exercises and practices of Session 2 are intended to further refine the participants' attention skills and to open and expand their awareness.

One of the exercises introduced is based on cognitive therapy. Its primary function is to experience the connection between a participant's interpretations and the effect they have on the participant's feelings and behaviors.

Another exercise finds its origins in positive psychology. It seeks to help participants rediscover the pleasant, positive experiences already embedded in their lives but often ignored or taken for granted.

Moreover, the first sitting meditation is introduced.

8.3.1 The BETA exercise

In one of his numerous meetings with scientists, the Dalai Lama met with Dr Aaron Beck, the founder and father of cognitive therapy (CT), specifically to discuss the similarities between Buddhism and cognitive therapy. Dr Beck explained how he helped one of his patients, a Nobel Prize candidate, who became depressed because he was passed over for the prize.

Dr Beck asked the patient how important the Nobel Prize was to him. The candidate put the prize at 100%. "Do you have a family?" Dr Beck asked. As the answer was affirmative, he continued: "How important is it for you?" The patient figured that his wife was around 20% for him. "So now you have 80% for the prize," Dr Beck argued. "And do you have any children?" he continued. "Yes, I have three." He reckoned they were about 40% to him. "Do you get to see your children often?" Dr Beck asked. "No," said the patient, "I'm so dedicated to my physics research, that I really haven't spent much time with them." "And how do you feel about that?" Dr Beck inquired. All of a sudden the patient started to weep. As Dr Beck asked him why he was weeping, he sobbed: "It reminded me that is just the way my father was with me when I was growing up and now I realize what I am missing out on." So Dr Beck asked: "How important are your children to you *now*?" And the patient put the figure at 80%. "Where does that leave your wife?" Dr Beck probed.

As the story went on both Dr Beck and Dr Gyatso (the Dalai Lama) started to laugh. "Anyhow," Dr Beck concluded, "he finally left my office and was not depressed anymore." "Very wise," remarked Dr Gyatso. "I think this is precisely the method we call analytical meditation ... which means analyzing reality and then act accordingly."

What we observe Dr Beck doing in this anecdote is referred to in CT as "Socratic questioning," that is, skillfully asking questions that draw out a person's innermost reality.

It was the method Socrates used over 2,000 years ago with his disciples. It is also called maieutic in Greek, which means, etymologically, midwifery. Maieutic refers to the idea of a teacher being a midwife and helping to give birth to latent knowledge in a person. In the story we saw how Dr Beck, in a masterly therapeutic performance, moved the physicist by a sequence of gentle logical questions from 100% despair to rediscovering his latent reality: his heartwarming, uplifting love for his children.

The significance of the Dalai Lama's succinct reply about analytical meditation is of enormous importance for MBSAT because throughout this book the suggestion is that at the root of most people's difficulties are decision-making errors.

People generally lack the ability to analyze reality as it is, without bias and mental fabrications. Instead they make decisions that are mostly based on delusions. It is only with a good grasp of reality that people can make appropriate decisions that genuinely improve their well-being. It is for this essential reason that MBSAT is implicitly presented as a *decision-making program for well-being based on mindfulness, positive psychology, and other relevant disciplines.*

People's actions are in essence the enactment of decisions with three possible outcomes: mistaken actions with unfortunate consequences; inconsequential, neutral actions that are unfulfilling and boring; and successful actions that lead to well-being and happiness. It is entirely logical and worthwhile to concentrate on honing people's decision-making skills for personal well-being.

The basic assumption of cognitive therapy is that cognition causally influences emotions and behaviors. It is a bidirectional relationship so that emotions in turn also influence cognition but from the CT perspective "it is the way one thinks about a situation or experience that influences the way he or she feels and behaves in the context of the situation or experience" (Hoffman, Asmundson, & Beck, 2013, p. 200). For CT cognitive activity affects the components of BETA: Body sensations, Emotions/feelings, Thoughts and Action impulses. Because cognitive activity can be altered, behavioral and emotional alterations can be achieved. With constructive adjustments of the content of the cognitions (interpretations, judgments, etc.) positive modifications can be achieved at emotional and behavioral levels.

Such changes are not easy, however. R. Baumeister (Baumeister, Bratslavsky, Finkenauer, & Vohs, 2001), while at Case Western Reserve University in Cleveland, Ohio, published a landmark paper entitled *"Bad is Stronger than Good"* in which he shed light on an amazing array of negativity biases typical of the human brain, all of which have far-reaching practical consequences.

Given Baumeister's findings it is not surprising that it is an uphill battle to change our propensity for negative biases or, translated into the language of CT, our negative automatic thoughts (NATs).

Mindfulness-based approaches propose a third wave of cognitive behavioral therapies in the form of meta-cognitive processes focused on an attitude of acceptance instead of efforts to change the content of people's cognitions, which is an almost impossible undertaking anyway.

See Figure 8.3 for the CT generalized ABC model. It works as follows: a situation activates an automatic thought, belief, or interpretation and that leads to an emotional reaction that in turn triggers body sensations and behavioral impulses.

The main learning point here is that situations drive cognitions and cognitions drive emotions. Consequently we must be aware of our interpretations of events because they can shape our lives.

To practice how interpretations influence feelings, body sensations, and impulses to act, the so-called BETA exercise is introduced into the session as experiential learning (please, see Note 3 for guidance on this exercise).

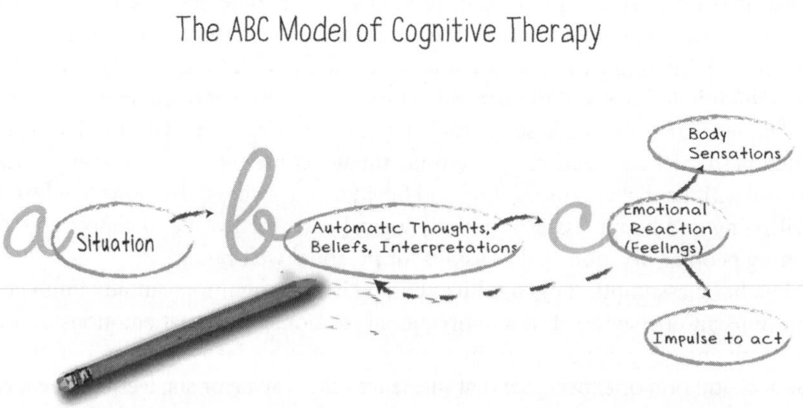

Figure 8.3 The ABC Model of Cognitive Therapy. *Source*: Juan Humberto Young.

8.3.2 Three good things (TGT) exercise

This was originally a positive psychology intervention designed by Marty Seligman and Chris Peterson as a way to cultivate gratitude. Peterson, reporting on their investigation on this practice, found that TGT increased happiness and decreased symptoms of depression for up to six months. Seligman likes to remind his students at the University of Pennsylvania that over 300 years ago William Penn, the English businessman and philosopher who founded the Province of Pennsylvania in the seventeenth century, stated that: "the secret to happiness is to count your blessings while others are adding up their troubles." Seligman also emphasizes that noticing and analyzing what goes well in people's lives builds skills—one more reason to never take it for granted.

TGT is an effective intervention to help combat negativity biases and bend people's minds toward positive states. It is quite simple in design yet extremely effective as empirical tests and my own teaching and coaching experience have demonstrated.

In essence the exercise consists of taking a few minutes every day to think about three good things in one's life and write them down in a journal. It could be something small and recent or something existential, in the past or ongoing—the practitioners are absolutely free to choose. (For further details regarding the practice, see Note 4.)

The underlying quality that is cultivated by TGT is gratitude for the many good events in life that are often obscured by automatic-pilot behavior and mind wandering driven by a biased doing–inner dialoguing mode. It helps to cultivate a mindful awareness of the good things in one's life. Benefits of a grateful attitude and its effect on well-being have been reviewed by Emmons and Mishra (2012). Some of their salient findings include:

a. Gratitude is a virtue, therefore it needs to be regularly cultivated and practiced to become a habit of character.
b. Gratitude not only enhances positive affect but also relieves negative affect. In particular, it reduces toxic emotions such as envy, resentment, and frustration.
c. Gratitude promotes optimal functioning at multiple levels of analysis: experiential, personal, and relational.
d. By building a supply of positive thoughts gratitude supports adaptive coping and personal growth while reducing a maladaptive focus on losses; hence it reduces stress.
e. Gratitude interventions have been shown to increase sleep duration and to reduce complaints about negative body sensations.

Experimental research by McCraty and Childre (2004) suggests gratitude and appreciation can also be beneficial for the health of the heart by lowering systolic blood pressure.

The intentions of the three good things (TGT) exercise are threefold:

a. It helps participants recognize the many good things already present in their lives.
b. It serves as an antidote to prevailing negative automatic thoughts (NATs).
c. The idea is to encourage participants to create space for pleasant and positive activities as they organize and manage their lives.

Note 4 provides suggestions on how to guide this intervention.

8.3.3 Mindfulness of the breath (sitting meditation)

Sitting still, suspending both your biases and your automatic pilot fantasies while connecting the posture of sitting still and focusing on your breath with the aim of maintaining a beginner's mind and patiently remaining in this state: that is what mindfulness of the breath means. In Aikido, the Japanese martial art, becoming aware of the breath (Kokyu in Japanese) is the beginning of a path toward becoming an Aikido master as it is through and with the breath that people merge with the universe. It is with Kokyu or the breath that one can calm the senses, deepen awareness and perception and gain the stability, power and timing required to neutralize negative forces.

As soon as you close your eyes you will make the same discovery as everyone else: there is heavy mental traffic on the mind's superhighway as well as endless mental loops about things one should have done (or done differently) in the past, a to-do list of future projects, and emotions that have become personalized.

After a short trial run of mindfulness of the breath one of my students at the University of St. Gallen in Switzerland complained: "I just can't control what is going on in my mind right now. I try to focus on the breath but I end up thinking about upcoming exams, plans for the weekend, the next visit to my parents, and so on. It is crazy. It makes me frustrated and depressed."

"Welcome to the club," I reassured him. "This is what the mind does when left unattended. It turns into a virtual factory of mental fabrications running at maximum speed and producing mostly rejects. Only occasionally does it produce one or two nice outputs. That is the whole point of the practice: to find out if one can slow down the frenzy of our mental factory and regain some degree of control over our internal processes. That is why this practice is also known as calming the mind."

D. Siegel (2009) explains why most mindfulness-based programs begin with awareness of the breath. He points out that the breath has universal characteristics: it is the interface between the internal and the external world and is the demarcation boundary between involuntary and voluntary actions. The breath is vital and fundamental for life. Its rhythmic quality has an important effect on the human nervous system.

Siegel suggested a possible neurological explanation for the dynamics of mindfulness of the breath. He concluded from his research that there is a set of "mirror neurons." These neurons are activated when they recognize an intentional act and are able to predict the next sequential act. Mirror neurons work through what Siegel calls the sensory implications of motor action (SIMA). In the case of mindfulness practices the intention is to keep the focus on an object of attention and therefore the SIMA network is implicated. In the case of mindfulness of the breath the intention is to attend to the process of the breath. With every in-breath the SIMA is activated to detect the intentional sequence of the out-breath. However, this works only when, and if, the meditator maintains attention on the intention so that the action of the out-breath matches the intention. When that happens there is a match between the activation of the SIMA and the intentionally expected action: out-breath. When this cycle happens repeatedly during a mindfulness of the breath practice the result is an integrative state of the nervous system, a wholesome harmonization.

There are a number of other benefits associated with mindfulness of the breath:

- being in the present,
- calming and settling the mind,
- learning to manage mind wandering,
- understanding the dynamic of the mind,
- learning to deal with distraction,
- cultivating gentleness toward oneself, and
- encouraging attitudes of curiosity and patience.

As mentioned in Session 1 above mind wandering correlates with the neural activities of the default-mode network (DMN), the self-referential narrative center. With mindfulness-of-the-breath as with other mindfulness practices one activates SIMA, the other neural center in the brain that correlates with awareness in the present. Consequently, with mindfulness training one increases the probability of activating more SIMA than DMN, thus increasing the probability of leading a mindful life. See Note 5 for instructions on guiding a mindfulness-of-the-breath practice.

The practices and exercises that have been introduced so far such as the body scan, the raisin exercise, and now mindfulness of the breath are gateways to exploring the difference between the doing mode and the being mode of our mind. The doing mode is a mostly conceptual way of thinking but also tends to proliferate self-created stories, creating mental noise about the future and the past, and keeping us in an agitated state. The being mode is oriented to an experiential moment-to-moment awareness rooted in the present, creating an openness to the world surrounding us. Strategic awareness is a mode of existence that volitionally seeks a balance between these two modes. It is a dynamic and flexible balance insofar as the combination of the two modes can shift: at times the doing mode may be stronger and at other times the being mode may be more pronounced. For example, a state of engagement in a constructive activity—work or hobby—can be a healthy and enriching way of doing mode as the positive psychology suggests with the PERMA model discussed in Chapter 2

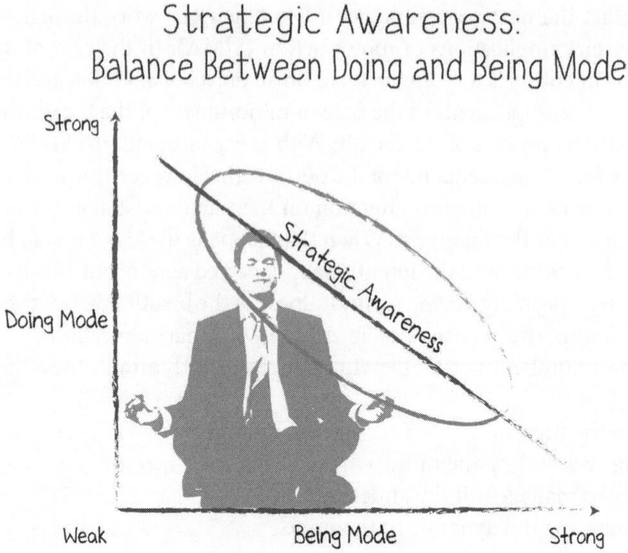

Figure 8.4 Strategic Awareness: The Difference Between Doing and Being Mode. *Source*: Juan Humberto Young.

("E" for engagement and flow). The key is that shifting the balance should be a process directed by volition and awareness. Figure 8.4 visualizes this flexible balance as an area between doing and being mode that is capable of generating strategic awareness.

9

Session 3: Recollecting Our Mind

9.1 Introduction

Session 3 takes a deeper look into the complexity of the mind: dull sometimes but mostly dreaming; straying and busy concocting all sorts of ideas; never quiet but active in its natural proclivity of regretting mistakes made in the past; solving issues with work in progress and making plans for the future—in short, remaining stuck in a doing mode. Mindfulness of our body and breath is suggested as a mechanism of suspending this mental chatter and enabling us to refocus our mind in an effort to regain autonomy over our internal life.

This session also reviews the next component of PERMA. In the previous session participants were introduced to positive emotions (the letter P in PERMA). This session explores engagement, the second element of PERMA. The positive psychology approach to recollection is also presented.

9.1.1 Intention as a driver of practice

After a week of training with mindfulness of the breath participants will bring their questions about this practice to the session and seek guidance. Two areas are frequently addressed. One is about the implementation of the practice itself and concerns issues including mind wandering ("my mind is all over the place") and drowsiness ("I always fall asleep"). The other recurrent line of questioning addresses the challenge of maintaining a disciplined, regular practice. Typical feedback is: "I couldn't do it, because I am really busy at the moment"; "I have a big project at work"; "My kids need me so much right now"; "I was too exhausted to muster the energy to sit."

Jon Kabat-Zinn, known as the father of secular mindfulness, believes that mindfulness follows three core principles: attitude, attention, and intention (2013, Chapter 1 and 2). At this stage of the program it may be important to invite

Mindfulness-Based Strategic Awareness Training: A Complete Program for Leaders and Individuals, First Edition. Juan Humberto Young.

Companion website: www.wiley.com/go/humbertoyoung/mbsat

participants to clarify their personal intentions as this can help them find their own ways of resolving the very real challenges of building a mindfulness practice. Having clearly defined personal intentions is a great asset when trying to conquer the barriers that keep coming up during mindfulness practice.

In a recent conversation with a well-known, reputable European mindfulness teacher I mentioned that my work is predominantly oriented towards people at work, especially leaders and managers. His immediate reaction was: "Well, what is really going on in mindfulness programs in the business community is mostly *attention control* not really mindfulness." In other words, participants should be clear about what their intention is: Is it to improve concentration (attention control) or is it mindfulness in a wider sense?

My father and his older brother, Samuel, used to have long and heated arguments. Uncle Sam was an avid big game hunter, travelling in the late 1960s from the tiny Republic of Panama to places in Africa, Alaska, and India to go hunting. My father, however, abhorred the idea of his brother travelling solely to kill for pleasure.

"Well, Johnny, I don't expect you to understand how I feel," uncle used to say, "the feeling of complete calmness, fully concentrated on waiting for the right moment to shoot. It is obviously beyond your understanding."

And my father would reply: "In my view it is pure cowardice to shoot and kill animals that haven't done anything to you, just for fun, because if what you are looking for is calm and concentration you can do something different that doesn't destroy animal life. Yes, you are right, I can't understand that."

But what was Uncle Sam's real intention: the moments of peace before the shot or the fame that came with the sport? After all he grew up at the time when the African safaris of the US President Teddy Roosevelt were legendary. Maybe this was what inspired him to go hunting in the first place. Roosevelt's trophies ended up in the Smithsonian Museum. Uncle Sam's trophies are still to be seen at the Panamanian National Museum.

Clearly knowing your personal intentions is, I believe, the most useful mechanism to help you progress on the path of establishing a mindfulness practice. Nevertheless my personal view on the value of different intentions is flexible and not dogmatic. We live in a driven world that is highly volatile, uncertain, complex, and ambiguous (often abbreviated as a VUCA world) (Bennett & Lemoine, 2014). In this context it may be too much to ask participants to tackle from the beginning the high ideals of classical mindfulness with its links to wholesome and pure intentions. Simple attention training can be a good starting point. It is certainly beneficial for people if they are able to reduce distractions and increase concentration. It also has a positive impact on their well-being. It can even help people to perform better in their jobs with less effort and stress. These are all constructive outcomes.

Personal intentions are not monolithic or set in stone. They are dynamic constructs that are bound to change. My observation is that as people become more thoughtful and established in their mindfulness practice they tend, quite naturally, to revise and modify their intentions. This is why it is important to present a comprehensive mindfulness program such as MBSAT. Limiting the practices simply to attention training and calling it mindfulness is not only incomplete but it could actually be unethical. It is therefore important to provide participants with an encompassing insight into the vast, transformative possibilities of fully practicing mindfulness, not only training for focusing mindfulness but analytical and relational mindfulness as well. People can then decide how far they want to go. As someone once put it, it is their choice "how far into new territory they want to journey."

In a US symposium for psychotherapists in March 2015, the key speaker Jon Kabat-Zinn noted that: "The only goal of mindfulness is to acquaint people to a whole topology of being that most of us haven't been educated about ... It's entering into a domain of fuller being as opposed to what we do most of the time, which is thinking, thinking, thinking—and then the emoting that goes along with the thinking" (2015, Psychotherapy Networker Symposium, March 26–29, Washington DC).

But how can we be in the being mode when our ingrained habits are towards mental agitation and doing mode and internal dialoguing about problem solving when we are exposed to a bombardment of all kinds of inputs from our environment? One can hardly even watch the news on TV without being distracted by blatant advertisements pressing us to buy this product or that product. They leave us with no time to assimilate, much less to understand, what is going on the world.

Modernity has sold us the belief that we can do several things at the same time. What we call multitasking actually amounts to projecting our scattered mental state into the real world. While we are writing an email to a client we simultaneously think about what stance we are going to take in the upcoming strategy meeting. Scientists tell us that it is an illusion to believe we have the capacity to perform well this way. Research shows that we cannot multitask without compromising the quality of the output. At least one of the activities will diminish in quality.

The same applies to our mind when we fill it with ideas and concepts and try to solve all kinds of problems by churning them around in our head. In the world of matter problem solving has been and will be useful. It is an efficient mechanism when we need to maintain output standards or close the gap between current states and goals. It is a valid approach, called in professional jargon, discrepancy-based processing. It is widely used in financial accounting where actual results are measured against a budget, and where one of the main tasks is looking for discrepancies in execution and taking appropriate correcting measures. However, with mental activities the model of discrepancy processing does not work well. It tends to produce more of the same, that is, just more ideas, without resolution of the issues we find ourselves thinking about and wanting to resolve: our moods, sensations, or behaviors. Hence, the real importance of mindfulness practices as an effective mechanism and strategy to switch our mode of processing from a mental doing mode to a being mode.

9.1.2 The positive psychology approach to recollection

A practical way to recollect a scattered mind can also be found in positive psychology with the concept of engagement, the second element of PERMA. People engage when they get the chance to use their character strengths because what we are good at we usually also like doing. Therefore the use of our character strengths in our daily life is a source of well-being and a path that gets us closer to flourishing.

Character strengths in action are the actual manifestation of engagement, which is a natural mode of behavior for humans. People are surprised when they take the values in action (VIA) test, which helps identify their personal strengths. Some are thrilled by what they discover, others less so. "Oh, I didn't know I have this great quality," someone might say. I have also often heard puzzled comments like: "I am a manager in charge of a major team yet I scored low in the strength of leadership. That's weird."

It is one of the most persistent myths that different tasks or occupations require specific profiles for people to perform well. For example, it is argued that if you want to be a salesman you need to have specific social skills. The fact is that once the desired output is defined it is more a question of allowing people to use their natural strengths to achieve the target. There is an incredible diversity in the ways people find to employ their different strengths to reach their specific goals. This is part of the beauty of letting people do their job their own way.

I tell most of my corporate clients that job descriptions are passé: just set the output to be achieved, set strict rules of conduct (law compliance, ethics, internal policies and so on), and then let people do their job freely. The result is that you will see how, in a natural and happy way, productivity and related results like profit and share value start improving.

For years my friend Michele, a mechanic in a Porsche garage, wanted to work in the sales department so he could make more money and improve his position in the organization. "But," he kept saying, "I don't have the necessary skills. I can't communicate well enough to make sales happen." In one of our conversations I told him: "Look, no one knows these cars better than you. You are curious, always researching and finding out new, interesting stuff about them. The kind of people who buy these cars want to have a salesperson like you with whom they can speak in depth about these cars. Just try. I'm sure it will work." Today Michele, who has been working in sales for the past two years, is one of the high performers in his team. His income has increased and his once shaky marriage is happy again. Every time he sees me, he says: "Hey, Juan. I'm so grateful for the pep talk you gave me. My wife also tells me to thank you." He sells cars using his curiosity, one of his character strengths. His inquisitive spirit led him to accumulate in-depth technical know-how about these technology-oriented cars and the clients feel drawn to him because of his expertise.

When people synchronize their character strengths and professional skills with the appropriate task they can easily reach a state of flow, which is an important

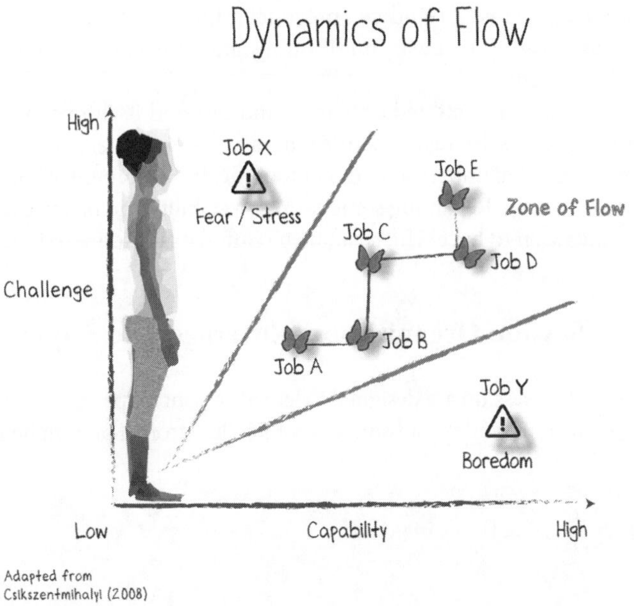

Figure 9.1 Dynamics of Flow. *Source*: Adapted from Csikszentmihalyi (1990, new edition in 2008).

construct of positive psychology. State of flow is characterized by total immersion and absorption in the task at hand. People in flow even tend to forget the time. Flow is sometimes also defined as being in the zone. It is a single-minded mode where the entire range of BETA (Body sensations, Emotions/feelings, Thoughts and Action impulses) converges into a balanced unity. It is one of the few healthy ways of staying in doing mode and at the same time being in the present, totally focused on the task with joyful and enthusiastic emotion. Figure 9.1 depicts the parameters and dynamics of the state of flow.

Flow occurs when a person's capabilities align with the challenges of the task at hand. In this situation he or she feels stimulated and inspired and relishes a feeling of mastery and achievement. This zone is represented in the graph by a triangle that is referred to as the flow funnel. As a person becomes more expert over time the demands of the task should be raised to maintain a level of challenge that is animating and stays in the flow zone. This is visualized in the graph by the path from Job A to Job E.

If the demands of a job exceed a person's skills (Job X above the funnel), that person will become anxious and stressed. On the other hand if the capability exceeds the challenge and a person is overqualified then they will become bored (Job Y below the funnel) and become easily distracted.

Distractions are the quintessential enemy of a mind in training. They are the uninvited, unwelcome, and unruly guests that invade the space of our mind, refusing to go away and preventing us to rid our "mind house" of unwanted and unnecessary cognitions: prejudice, preconceptions, and other impediments that have their origins in past conditioning and prevent us accurately from observing the present.

In this distracted and scattered state the mind can find itself occupied and busy with mostly useless self-created stories in a self-referential unconscious and involuntary process that undermines our autonomy, and autonomy is a key determinant for our well-being. Regaining some degree of stability and balance in our mind is a valuable intention to have which can help reinforce our desire to practice.

9.2 Session Organization, Coverage, and Sequence

The practices of this session are designed to let participants experience the benefits of recollecting their mind and the advantages, which flow from a present being mode.

Session 3: Recollecting our Mind

	Time suggested in minutes Duration 2½–3 hours
1. Arrival meditation	5
2. Sitting mediation of breath and body Dealing with physical sensations Guidance and inquiry	35
3. Home practice review and inquiry	20
4. 3 minutes breathing space (3MBS) Exercise and inquiry	20
5. Two movement exercises Mindful stretching and mindful salsa with short inquiries	40
6. Positive BETA reframing exercise Ratio exercise and inquiry	30
7. Home practice assignments Breath and body sitting meditation: Day 1, 3, and 5 Mindful stretching or mindful salsa exercises: Day 2, 4, and 6 3 minutes breathing space (3MBS): three times daily Reframing one negative event a day Taking VIA character strengths test to bring results to next session	10

9.3 Exercises and Practices of Session 3

The session begins with a five minutes arrival meditation so that participants can settle into the session and open their mind for what is to unfold. The short recollection is followed by a home practice review to share experiences and offer guidance if needed. From now on each session will begin with this duo of arrival meditation and home practice review.

The session continues with a 30-minute breath and body sitting meditation and the corresponding inquiry. Then we introduce four new activities: the 3-minutes breathing space mini-meditation, mindful stretching, mindful salsa, and positive reframing of negative experiences.

9.3.1 Sitting meditation breath and body

When deepening the sitting practice one crucial aspect to be addressed is posture. In longer meditations it is sometimes difficult to maintain the same position without discomfort. Having a balanced posture helps avoid uneasiness and minimizes the effort.

In Aikido, the Japanese defense art, disciples train to develop a posture or stance called *Kamae* that involves centering the body by focusing on its three main centers of gravity: the head, the spinal column, and the abdomen. This stance fosters flexible attention and enables the disciple to respond with speed and precision when necessary. This may be one of the reasons why Aikido is sometimes referred to as meditation in action. The same stance of centered posture can be useful during sitting meditation. Kabat-Zinn recommends an erect and dignified posture for sitting meditation with head, neck, and spine aligned vertically to allow the breath to flow freely and reflect the attitudes of self-reliance, self-acceptance, attention, and alertness.

In sitting meditation breath and body we amplify the practice of mindfulness of the breath (introduced in Session 2) by integrating the body as a whole. In addition to the benefits of meditating on breath already mentioned—being present, calming the mind, and learning to manage mind wandering—focusing the attention on the body provides the following additional, special benefits:

Benefits of breath and body sitting meditation

a. *Learning to sense the body.* The point of the body scan in Sessions 1 and 2 was to learn how to shift attention around the body, training our sense of different parts of the body. With the new practice we train a wider awareness of the body. The whole body normally reflects our emotions. These tend to fall into the three fundamental categories of liking, disliking, or indifference and lead to a wide variety of manifestations in our body. Thus the body is a good place to read our emotions and sense what is going on.

b. *The body as a laboratory for understanding thoughts and feelings.* The ability to understand where thoughts and feelings manifest themselves in the body is a useful tool that allows us to establish a systemic connection between body, thoughts, and feelings. This can be helpful in diffusing negativity in people's lives, especially aversion to strong negative emotions that manifest themselves as physical sensations, typically tightness or tension.
c. *Integrating mind and body.* Marty Seligman has always argued that in Western societies we live predominantly in our head. "We live above our neck," he used to say. The practices of body scan and mindfulness of the body help reintegrate mind and body in a holistic beneficial unity.
d. *Additional benefits.* There are also benefits that come with mindfulness practices in general including learning to be more accepting and more focused.

In the annex to this chapter you will find a pictorial guide to help recognize emotions and sensations in the body (Section 9.4).

For further explanations see Note 6.

9.3.2 The 3-Minutes Breathing Space (3MBS) practice

3MBS is the backbone of the MBCT (Mindfulness-based Cognitive Therapy) protocol because of its effectiveness and the ease with which it can be integrated into one's daily life (Segal, Williams, & Teasdale, 2013, see chapter 18 pages 383–390). It is a way of pausing to recollect the mind and step back from the flux of things when life becomes hectic. When our mindfulness wears down and is on the verge of getting lost, the 3MBS provides a convenient way to recapture our awareness by switching us to a present being mode.

In many ancient faith traditions the value of taking a mental pause has long been recognized. There are many customs of repeating a particular phrase, mostly silently in the mind, to stop the frantic mental activities and recover a sense of psychological stability. Faith-orientated people have a treasure trove of such phrases:

- In Judaism:
  - "Barukh attah Adonai": "Blessed art thou, O Lord."
- In Buddhism:
  - "Om mani padme hum": "Jewel in the lotus of the heart."
- In Christianity:
  - "Lord Jesus Christ, Son of God, have mercy on us."
- In Islam:
  - "Bismillah ir-rahman ir-rahim": "In the name of God, the merciful, the compassionate."
- In Russian Orthodoxy:
  - "Gospodi pomilui": "Lord, have mercy."

All these invocations have the effect of calming and recollecting the scattered mind, especially in moments when things seem to have become out of control. They work as a brake and help gain a moment of respite on the superhighway of the mind.

The 3MBS shares some similarities with these ancient practices in the sense that it is the intention to focus and create a pause in the mind. It is an excellent instrument in today's hectic world, a mini-meditation that can be used at any moment during the day wherever you might happen to be: at work, on a train or plane, in stress situations, and so on.

Here are some recognized benefits of practicing 3MBS regularly:

1. It helps to switch the awareness from a doing mode to a being mode. This allows you to approach the next moment in a mindful way.
2. It offers a way of connecting the mindfulness practice with daily routines and helps increase the awareness of our mind's tendencies in daily life.
3. It enables us to realize that there are always Mindfulness Real Options (MROs) and choices, stepping back from the momentary situation, gaining acceptance, and then skillfully moving into any difficult situation.

See Note 7 for more information and suggestions.

9.3.3 Mindfulness of movement: Mindful stretching and mindful salsa

Mindful movement heightens our awareness of the body in a similar way to the body scan. Some people prefer experiencing the body in motion rather than being in a still posture.

One of the national pastimes in Switzerland, where I have been living for over 30 years, is hiking in the mountains—"Wandern" in German—as the Swiss call it. Even in winter the Swiss enjoy walking for hours. Martha, my mother-in-law, used to go for walks of several hours even when she was well over 70. "It has a soothing effect," she used to say.

On the other side of the Atlantic, in Panama, people just love to dance salsa. Recently my mother told me how she and my sister Gaby went for a Sunday brunch with Rodolfo, my 93-year-old cousin. For many years Rodolfo had been the distinguished Dean of the Faculty of Medicine at the University of Panama. Unfortunately he has been suffering from advanced bone cancer for the past 10 years. At the restaurant where they had Sunday brunch there was live music and a wedding party nearby. Rodolfo, ever the fun-loving gentleman, invited my sister to dance with him and when he spotted the bride of the wedding party a little later he asked her for a dance, too! Apart from being an amazing fellow, I believe that for Rodolfo, although he has a physical ailment, dancing has a soothing and positive, restorative effect.

Music is an active ingredient in the mindful salsa practice proposed in this session. In a review of music interventions Nilsson (2008) found that music reduces and helps control peri-operative anxiety and pain in patients undergoing surgery. This is a scientific confirmation of the restorative power of music.

Moving to music in the mindful salsa practice engages all the aspects of the sensory mind: exteroception (listening), interoception (internal sensing), and proprioception (sensing body movement) are fused into a single activity with multiple benefits:

- Physical benefits—musical rhythm energizes and encourages to be active;
- Social benefits—dance activities usually involve one or more partners;
- Emotional benefits—appropriate music produces emotional states of positive arousal and engagement.

In combination these benefits create a virtuous circle of uplifting energy as people practice mindful salsa with enthusiasm, joy, and focus (concentrating on rhythm and different rhythmic instruments). In the Chinese film *The Emperor's Shadow* Ying Zheng, the king of Qin, kidnaps the musician Gao Jianli and forces him to write the music for a national anthem as he believes that with music he can control the minds and hearts of his people. Centuries later Mao Zedong, embracing the same idea, encouraged the writing of patriotic communist folk songs.

It seems that dancing kindles rejuvenating zest. Just think of the members of the famous Cuban music band Buena Vista Social Club who have spent their whole life playing music, dancing, and singing: members like Señora Omara Portuondo, who is now 84, still perform with élan and so did the remarkable Compay Segundo who kept playing until he died at the age of 95. It is not surprising that President Obama said he wished he could reach their age in as good a shape as them.

Mindful salsa captures this uplifting energy and for some practitioners this form of mindfulness generates an especially positive boost. Sandra, a participant in one of my MBSAT courses, is a case in point. This talented young woman, a Harvard MBA, CEO of a Swiss company and pianist of classical music in her spare time, was troubled by all kinds of anxieties and worries every time she gave a concert. With Mindful salsa, she told me, she learned how to be in the present moment with a sense of calmness, focusing entirely on the music and listening attentively to the other instruments instead of being anxious about her own performance. Liberated from nervousness and apprehension she can enjoy the concerts more fully. Apart from the benefits already known from practicing the body scan, mindfulness of movement can also benefit practitioners because:

1. Mindful movement is an effective and practical way to connect our mind, emotions, and body.
2. Moving the body mindfully can help pick up signals from the body that are in the present and guide us to a healthier way of life.
3. Dancing mindfully can take us to the present and produce a positive and joyful disposition.

4. Mindful movement teaches us to be attentive to our physical limits and to observe how these limits begin to expand with regular practice and how this increases well-being.
5. It is a form of gentle physical conditioning and energy building.
6. Mindful salsa, which I call a self-induced, positive-emotion treat, is a delightful and effortless way of reaping so many positive benefits, especially when defenses are dropped and people are willing to experience the rhythm of the music. It is in fact an ancestral ritual: human beings have been making music and dancing to it since the beginning of time.

See Note 8 for further details.

Pinniger, Brown, Thorsteinsson, and McKinley (2012) conclude in their study that dancing could be an effective complementary adjunct for the treatment of depression and for inclusion in stress-management programs. Also the Harvard Gazette (January 5, 2016) in the article "Strength in Movement" reported how researchers are investigating dance for treating neurodegenerative disorders.

9.3.4 Positive BETA reframing exercise

The positive reframing exercise builds on what we have learnt in the previous session. In Session 2 we explored the BETA exercise (see Section 8.3.1), the main message of which is "that our emotions are consequences of a situation plus an interpretation" (Segal, Williams, & Teasdale, 2013, p. 161). We also discussed the ABC Model of cognitive therapy according to which people find themselves in a situation (A) and end up with a feeling (C) without being aware of the thought (B) that created the link and prompted the feeling.

It is useful to go back to the example of Irene, which was mentioned in Note 3, on guiding the BETA exercise.

Irene said: "I feel irritated by her," referring to the friend who failed to greet her. When I asked her what thoughts went through her mind, she explained: "I think it can't be that she didn't see me. My heart is beating faster and I feel like going over to her and say to her: 'Can't you at least say hello? I know you saw me.'"

The ABC sequence of the incident was:

A = The situation
Irene greets her friend who does not greet her back. (Irene is aware of this part of the sequence.)
B = Interpretation
Irene thought: "It can't be that she didn't see me." This thought was the driver of the subsequent emotional experience. (Irene is probably not aware of this thought.)
C = Feeling
Irene stated: "I feel irritated by her." (Irene clearly expressed her irritation, so she was aware of it.)

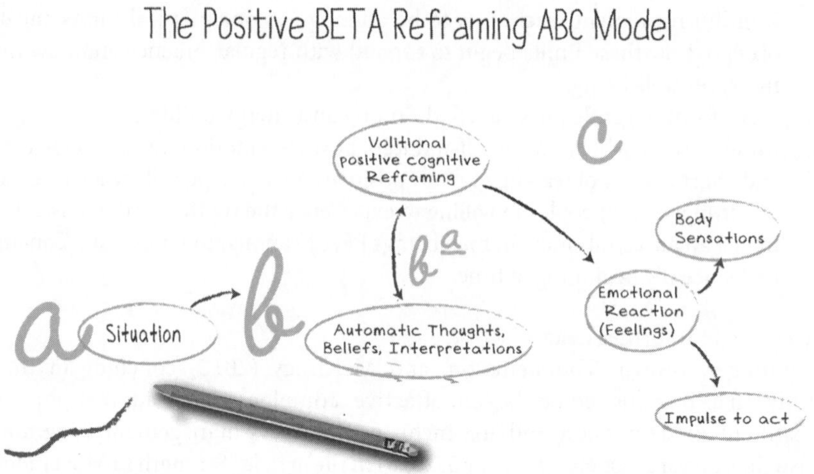

Figure 9.2 The Positive BETA Reframing ABC Model. *Source*: Juan Humberto Young.

This sequence could lead to an action impulse, namely going over to the friend and complaining.

The question is: Could the outcome have been different?

If Irene reframes stage B, the thought that interprets the situation, this could produce an alternative interpretation: "She is so busy, she didn't see me," in which case stage C in the ABC sequence, the emotional reaction, would become more friendly and lead to feelings of kindness and concern: "Poor dear, I feel sorry for her."

Figure 9.2 is a modified version of the original ABC model. It includes the reframing activity as an intermediate stage between B and C. As the figure indicates, situation A stays the same but B splits into two components: the original automatic thoughts, beliefs, and interpretations that are triggered instantaneously by conditioning and cannot be prevented. However, with awareness and volition an additional process B^a can be set in motion that enables the person to reframe the situation and interpret it differently. This leads to changes in C, the emotional reaction, and most importantly in the resulting action impulse. An alternative possible response could be now: "I will call her went I get home and find out how she is doing." This is a very significant modification.

Obviously there will be cases where the negative automatic pilot trumps intentional positive reframing, but the hope is that in those cases the negative interpretations will be tempered by the awareness of automatic triggers and the conscious attempt to look at possible positive interpretations. In the worst case the reframing avoid stacking will lead to a neutral position and prepare the ground for more mindful and positive outcomes in the future.

Positive reframing as proposed here is a simplified, down-to-earth adaptation of more complex models that are used with clinical populations. Once we understand that our emotional responses are determined by our interpretation of events a door opens and as many courses of action as there are possible interpretations become feasible. Here is where we can begin to exert volition: which of several possible interpretations do we choose to give priority? This is not a trivial decision as that choice will produce our emotional state and our action impulses.

Of course there may be occasions where adverse interpretations are the correct ones. We may, for example, have been mistaken to even bother about a person who does not greet us as a friend. This naturally raises a question about how to respond to problems involving objectively negative situations. This is a theme in one of the upcoming more advanced sessions. However, for the target MBSAT population with normal negative conditioning this exercise is an effective way of reframing events, adding constructive meaning, and helps bend their mind towards more healthy states in their lives by reducing the ratio of negative to positive cognitions, welcoming productive thoughts and dismissing corrosive ones. This is one example how a mindful positive leader or individual can create Mindful Real Options (MROs).

For more ideas see the positive reframing exercise in Note 9.

9.4 Annex to Chapter 9: Body Scan: Recognizing Emotions and Sensations in the Body

Figure 9.3 Recognizing Emotions and Sensations in the Body (I). *Source*: Juan Humberto Young.

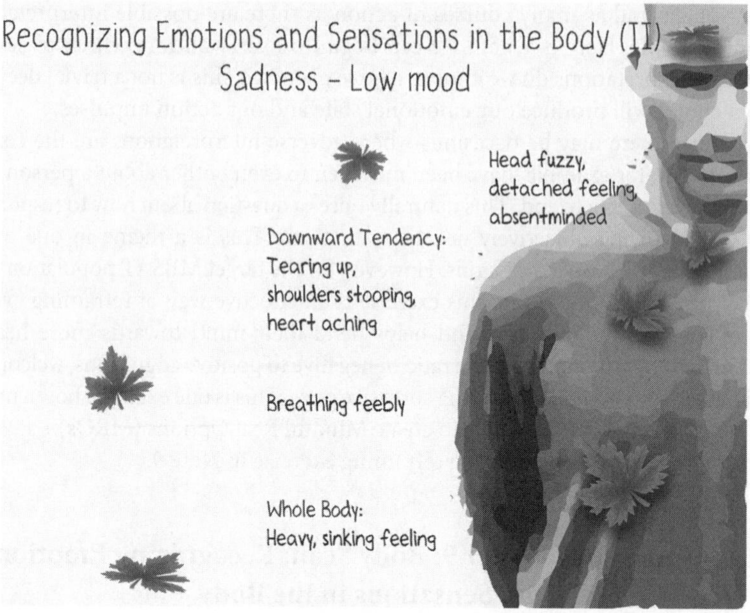

Figure 9.4 Recognizing Emotions and Sensations in the Body (II) Sadness–low mood. *Source*: Juan Humberto Young.

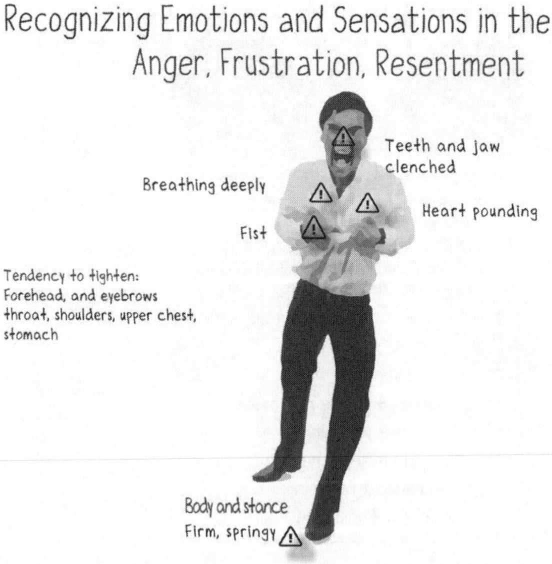

Figure 9.5 Recognizing Emotions and Sensations in the Body (III): Anger, frustration, resentment. *Source*: Juan Humberto Young.

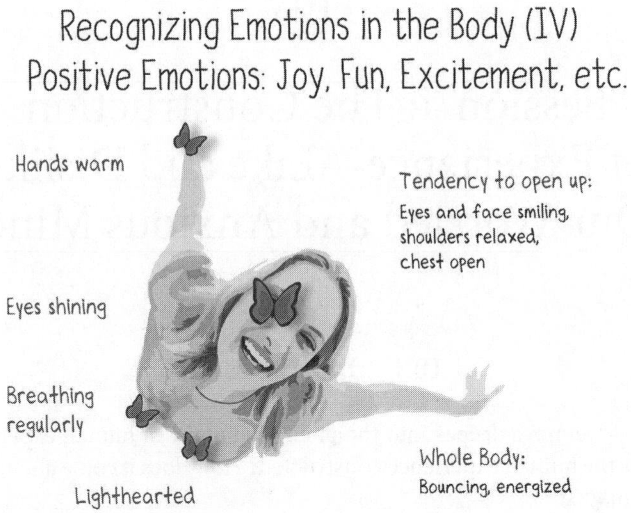

Figure 9.6 Recognizing Emotions and Sensations in the Body (IV) Positive Emotions: Joy, fun, excitement, etc. *Source*: Juan Humberto Young.

10

Session 4: The Construction of Experience—Like and Dislike (Our Worried and Anxious Mind)

10.1 Introduction

In Session 4 we move deeper into the phenomenology of human experience and ask: How is the human experience constructed? How does it come about and what are its hallmarks?

There is a commonly held belief that reality is fixed, existing outside of us and independent from us. MBSAT doesn't adhere to this view. It adopts the view of modern quantum physics that reality is a process that is constantly in the making. It is a succession of cognitive events being constructed moment by moment as our senses interact with external data. The meaning that is given to this external information is what constructs our experience and drives human emotions and actions.

Millennium old conditioning has condensed the interpretation of incoming information into two essential reflexes: like (pleasure) and dislike (pain), complemented by an additional neutral, indifferent state.

Through the course of human evolution these reflexes have served humanity well. In ancient times the notion of liking something and the associated positive emotions would motivate people to make the most of opportunities concerning food, mating, or playing, and so on. They kindled the desire to move towards the object of their liking in anticipation of pleasure.

Dislike on the other hand warned people against threats (rotten food, poisonous animals, and many other potential dangers). It triggered the instinctive, fear-driven mechanisms of flight or fight and activated an urge to move away from the danger to avoid pain.

Over time, the focus on aversive behavior became more accentuated. This has been documented in vivid detail by Baumeister, Bratslavsky, Finkenauer, and Vohs (2001). Clearly it has an adaptive benefit as making mistakes in risky circumstances can have dramatic consequences: what if you are not sure whether the

Mindfulness-Based Strategic Awareness Training: A Complete Program for Leaders and Individuals, First Edition. Juan Humberto Young.

Companion website: www.wiley.com/go/humbertoyoung/mbsat

snake in front of you is harmless or poisonous? Or whether your business partner is trustworthy or treacherous?

Kahneman, the winner of the Nobel prize in economics, demonstrated that losses matter much more for people than gains of an equal amount. In other words, the distress people experience from losing 100 units of value is much greater than the happiness they gain from winning the same amount. The despair over a loss is often so great that people forget about being prudent and make irrational, foolhardy decisions. This explains why gamblers on a losing streak keep betting.

These two forces—attachment to what we like and aversion to what we dislike—have become automatic conditioned reactions and are so ingrained in the human make-up that all human experiences can be classified in three basic categories: I like; I dislike; I don't care.

These conditioned reflexes, which result in humans becoming hooked on likes and dislikes, confine the human experience to a narrow channel that creates frustration and discontent and results in responses like: "I have a nice car but I like this other car better"; "I like this colleague but I can't stand that other one." It is an endless yearning for more and for things to be different from what they are. Sometimes the desire may be justified but most of the time it is simply the result of craving and greedy and/or antagonistic reflexes.

At times the power of dislikes leads to radical aversion: "We mustn't tolerate immigrants, they threaten our culture"; "I can't work with this guy. I can't stand him." The conditioned fixation on likes and dislikes gets people stuck on certain ideas, beliefs, opinions, sensations, and self-images, which are merely mental models of reality yet compel them to reject anything that puts their ego identity into question: "We are cool and they are not, we can't have them with us."

This is the root cause of human suffering, our resistance to change, and our impairment regarding positive thinking. Mindfulness and positive psychology are antidotes that can tackle the human condition at the root—not by changing the object of perception but by inviting people to examine how they perceive things and offering a range of solutions that will help to cultivate wisdom (discernment), equanimity (serenity), friendliness (compassion) and open awareness (non-judging) which are the key features of strategic awareness (see Section 4.3.3).

During the global privatization wave in the 1980s when many public enterprises were up for sale, I met a businessman under unusual circumstances. I was visiting his country on a business trip for my bank. Not knowing the country well I joined a local firm headed by a Stanford-trained management expert with an excellent reputation and good connections. Out of the blue we got a phone call from a person requesting a meeting to explore a big financial transaction. My local partner had never heard of the caller but in the emerging market we were working in this was not unusual. When the man came to see me a day later the immediate impression was total dissonance. While all potential clients I had met during the week represented the country's establishment business people with "de rigueur" Hermes tie, dark suits, and soft spoken ways, this visitor had a very blunt way of expressing himself and wore a polo shirt and jeans. After the meeting everybody in the office shared the same scathing view: "Doing business with this man is out of the question." "Why?" I asked. "It is obvious," they said. "He does not have the profile. He has no manners and this reflects very badly on him as a businessman." "Well," I remarked, "we might just give him credit for his solid ideas, his determination, and down-to-earth way of doing business. He is the cleverest and most serious businessman I have seen this week."

In short this person became a truly outstanding bank client for many years. Like everybody I am prone to fall into the like/dislike trap, but fortunately this time I managed to eschew the pattern and it was a blessing. Otherwise I would have missed a major opportunity of doing business and getting to know one of the most forthright, ethical, and smart businessmen I have encountered on my many business trips all over the world.

The sources of human experience are rich and complex: a sound, a smell, something we see, a thought, or an event can all evoke a "feeling tone." Feeling tones fall into three categories: pleasant, unpleasant, and neutral, which correspond to like, dislike, and indifference. In most cases they are subtle and people remain unaware of both their presence and impact. In the case of the businessman in the polo shirt and jeans my colleagues sensed a definite, unpleasant feeling tone, perhaps there was even some unconscious prejudice, as he did not fit the image of their country's well-mannered business establishment.

Rigid opinions involving likes and dislikes cause people to abandon and lose their awareness and resilience. Life will always present challenging situations and the ability to stay flexible and to see possible solutions beyond rigid norms is one of the attributes of a mindful, positive mind.

Figure 10.1 presents a model showing how feeling tones impact the human experience and how they shape outcomes.

The origin of an experience, a situation, or an event such as a sound, thought, or action must pass through a feeling tone filter where the experience gets classified in like, neutral, or dislike. This happens at an unconscious level, gets interpreted (in accordance with the ABC model discussed in section 8.3.1) and generates a reaction. Each interpretation can lead to a wholesome or unwholesome reaction because not every liking is necessarily helpful and not every aversion must be, by definition, negative.

A positive interpretation can produce a constructive reaction (for example, friendship, collaboration at work) or an excessive, unwholesome liking that can result in addiction, greed, or clinging (compulsive consumer behavior or dependence on substances for example).

Neutral interpretations can lead to a wholesome objective attitude or, on the unwholesome side, to boredom, apathy, procrastination, or lack of sensitivity.

Dislikes, too, can create diverging reactions. On the wholesome side aversion can stimulate defensive and protective behavior (avoiding danger). However, unwholesome aversion can also lead to aggression, actions motivated by hate, and other antagonistic reactions.

In this session we look at reactions to aversion that cause unhealthy feelings but, if left unchecked, can lead to anxiety and worry.

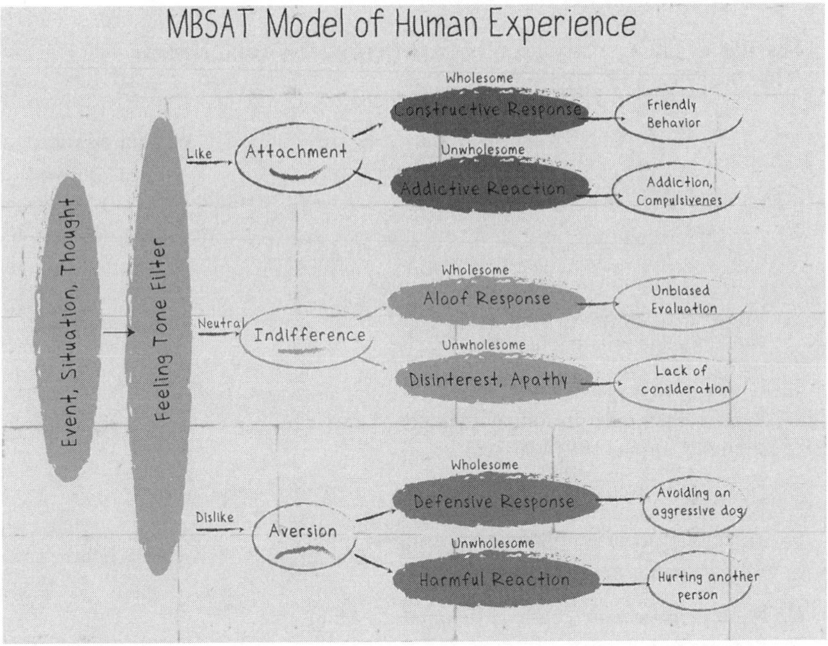

Figure 10.1 MBSAT Model of Human Experience. *Source*: Juan Humberto Young.

10.2 Session Organization, Coverage, and Sequence

The practices presented in this session are oriented towards helping participants recognize experiences of aversion.

10.3 Exercises and Practices of Session 4

After a brief arriving meditation in this session we practice another variation of sitting meditation with multiple focal points: the sitting meditation on breath, body, sounds, thoughts, and open awareness. It is followed by the home practice review that this time includes the inquiry about the results of the VIA strengths survey that the participants were asked to bring with them.

The principal new theme in Session 4 is worry and anxiety. Participants will gain insights about the origin and dynamics of worry and anxiety and about mindfulness-based ways to modify and reduce unnecessary or disproportionate low moods. The focus on strengths can be a helpful antidote.

We will also continue mindful movement by practicing mindful walking and we will learn to apply the 3-minutes breathing space to different situations by focusing on our strengths.

Session 4: The Construction of Experience—Like and Dislike
(Our Worried and Anxious Mind)

		Time allocated in minutes Approx. duration: 2½ to 3 hours
1.	Arrival meditation	5
2.	Sitting meditation on breath, body, sounds, thoughts, and open awareness Guidance and inquiry about the exercise	35
3.	Home practice of Session 3: Review and inquiry including review of character strengths (results of VIA survey)	20
4.	Defining the territory of worry and anxiety (TWA)	30
5.	Three-minutes breathing space focusing on strengths: Exercise and review	15
6.	Mindful movement (continued): mindful walking: Exercise and inquiry	20
7.	Home practice assignment:	5
	Sitting meditation on breath, body, sounds, Thoughts and open awareness (daily, one day of rest)	Days 1–6
	Mindful Walking	preferably daily
	3MBS (regular)	3× daily 9
	3MBS on strengths: whenever you notice unpleasant feelings	Days 1–6

10.3.1 Sitting meditation on breath, body, sounds, thoughts, and open awareness

This session's sitting meditation guides the participants' awareness through different focal points. The intention is to become more skillful in recognizing what strikes us as unpleasant or aversive at a specific moment. Normally, states of aversion are hard to detect because the rapid succession of likes and dislikes has become second nature to humans and is an ongoing, continuous process without conscious awareness.

We begin the sitting meditation by narrowly focusing our attention on the breath so we can recollect ourselves and become fully present. As we continue the practice we can start shifting our awareness progressively to the whole body, then to any sounds in the room, and to any thoughts in our mind. Finally, we stop concentrating on particular things and maintain an open, unfocused awareness.

As we pass through these stages the main idea is to observe, specifically and with heightened interest, whatever seems unpleasant right now. Instead of playing down what bothers us, or trying to amend it in any way (adjusting the posture, dismissing thoughts, or ignoring unpleasant sensations), we try to face the trouble squarely, look at it closely, and admit to ourselves any sensations of dislike and aversion that we have.

Edith (name changed), a participant in one of my mindfulness programs, summed up her displeasure after a practice, when she explained: "It was too long for me. I kept thinking: 'When is the meditation going to be over?' And then I felt discomfort in my buttocks and wanted to move and go home but I knew I had to restrain myself and so I endured it."

She experienced a full spectrum of aversion that resulted in a chain reaction of physical, emotional, and mental responses. She disliked the prolonged sitting (emotion), kept thinking about ending the practice (thoughts), suffered from pain in her buttocks (body sensation), and wanted to leave and go home (impulse to act). Only during the inquiry did she begin to see her own experience from the point of view of an external observer and to recognize that her responses were steeped in a feeling tone of aversion.

This self-observing cognition is referred to as metacognition, a kind of "cognition about cognition" (a cognitive process observing cognition). Likewise the awareness of how one is aware—or is not, as the case may be—is called meta-awareness. With metacognition the chances of picking up unpleasant signals with our senses and becoming aware of aversion is greatly increased. In other words, you look at your own experiences from the vantage point of an impartial observer.

One of the reasons why the earlier sessions emphasized mindfulness of the body is that connecting with physical pain or discomfort is, for most people, the easiest way of recognizing aversion. In this session the primary aim is to learn to recognize when unpleasant situations, thoughts, and emotions arise.

The sitting meditation on breath, body, sounds, thoughts, and open awareness encompasses all the benefits of mindfulness of breath and body and also provides specific additional benefits that are summarized in the following overview.

10.3.2 Benefits of sitting meditation on breath, body, sounds, thoughts, and open awareness

1. This meditation is a powerful way of enhancing the ability to connect emotions and thoughts to sensations in the body and vice versa.
2. Mindfulness of sounds allows us to develop our attention naturally because sounds are always available and they enter our ears without our choosing.

3. Sounds allow us to just be with the sensory experience without having to create any mental stories. This is what makes listening to music so restorative.
4. Central to practicing mindfulness of thoughts is gaining the ability of "decentering" from our own thoughts. This is a very important skill that involves the ability to observe thoughts and see them for what they are: just thoughts, not facts.
5. Simultaneously forming thoughts and being able to observe those thoughts is a metacognitive ability that expands mental possibilities, provides clarity, and eases conditioning. When patterns of conditioning abate it gets easier to recognize the insidious likes and dislikes that rule the mind. The importance of gaining the skill of mental decentering cannot be overestimated. It is one of the most important steps on the path towards becoming a skillful mindful, positive, decision-maker.
6. Mindfulness of thoughts hones the skill of recognizing recurring mental patterns.
7. Mindfulness of open awareness helps us develop an intuitive, natural form of awareness similar to what we experience in daily life where our attention is capable of encompassing multiple aspects of life instead of homing in on a single focal point. Open awareness allows for fluidity in awareness and thus replicates what we do in daily life. It allows for spaciousness in the mind that can generate strategic awareness.

10.3.3 Defining the territory of worry and anxiety (TWA)

There is an ancient parable called *The Two Arrows*. It describes the physical pain of being shot by an arrow—the first arrow—and how this causes obvious, tangible hurt. The question is how a person responds to this painful experience. If the person who is already suffering reacts with indignation, despair, worry, and anxiety then the pain will worsen: it is like being shot and hurt by a second arrow, with the difference that the second wound is largely self-inflicted. It is mental pain. Learning about the pain of the second arrow is the purpose of this segment of the session.

The July–August 2015 cover of the *Atlantic* magazine drew attention to this problem with a startling headline in red that announced "The End of Work." Combining this ominous trend with the unstoppable influx of immigrants, especially in Europe where, in 2015, tens of thousands of refugees were crossing the borders to the EU every day, it is no surprise that the levels of worry, anxiety, and aversion are increasing almost everywhere in the world.

Recognizing aversion can be problematic for individuals working in business and similar organizational settings where the ability to deal with difficulties both mentally and physically is equated with aptitude and resilience. Appearing to lack toughness is often seen as being detrimental to career prospects. Consequently, many people have a long history of sublimating their personal difficulties and keeping them hidden from others. These unspoken situations are often the source of widespread problems of stress, anxiety, and addiction, especially alcohol and drugs. Worries and fears are often nothing more than manifestations of people's untreated problems.

Fritz (not his real name) was a senior engineer in a company where I was one of the three owners. He was a dedicated professional. He was loyal, highly knowledgeable in his field, and delivered work of Swiss precision. In addition he was fluent in English and, among the 90 employees, one of the few team members with international experience. At the time his wife was pregnant with their first child.

His conscientious and meticulous approach to his work gradually put Fritz in a difficult position. The CEO, one of my two partners, began complaining: "He is too slow. He always advances a 'but' at every new project. The other colleagues complain about him."

After a while the CEO escalated his criticism from unappreciative, critical remarks to essentially undermining Fritz's work by withdrawing assistants and withholding resources that he needed for his work. He created a situation that reduced Fritz's productivity. It took me some time to realize what was happening. Fritz was not quite as upbeat as before but he never mentioned anything about his silent struggle. Eventually he had a nervous breakdown, which almost coincided with his wife giving birth to their child.

I went to visit him at the clinic and it was only then that I found out what he had been going through. In the meantime the CEO was making plans to fire him arguing that Fritz lacked the resilience and the competence to do his work well. Naturally I opposed him on this. The consequence was that our differences of opinion became so great we decided to sell the company. We arranged a management employee buyout (MEBO) and sold the company to a group of managers and employees who had been working with the company for over 15 years. Happily they included Fritz.

As awful as this story sounds it is a common drama in many firms. Sadly it is not an unusual situation. On the positive side Fritz became a co-owner, albeit with a small shareholding, and his future was protected.

The late Nolen-Hoeksema and colleagues (Nolen-Hoeksema, Wisco, & Lyubomirsky, 2008) distinguished between the features of worry (the substrate to anxieties) and rumination (the substrate to depression) for the following reasons: worry is future oriented and it is focused on anticipated threats with a conscious motive to prepare for the threat and with a unconscious motive to avoid pain and negative effects. Rumination is more past and present oriented and is focused on themes of loss, meaning, and self-esteem. It has a conscious motive to find meaning in events, insights, and solutions, and an unconscious motive to avoid taking responsible actions and staying away from aversive situations.

The modern world is characterized by VUCA (volatility, uncertainty, complexity, and ambiguity) and consequently most individuals do worry and experience anxiety—this is normal. Only when the situation spins out of control do those elements turn individuals into clinical cases. However, even in their normal milder forms these conditions can have serious drawbacks and impede people from enjoying satisfying lives. Consequently, it becomes important to learn skillful ways to relate to these harmful mental states.

Anxiety and worry are functions of uncertainty and powerlessness—exactly what Fritz experienced in his relationship with his CEO. Thoughts began to trouble Fritz such as "Will I be able to keep my job? What happens if I lose it now that we have a newborn? Should I talk to the partners? Oh no, they are probably all in this together. It would not help much, on the contrary it could aggravate the situation." He told me later that all of these and similar thoughts were occupying more and more of his mind space. Over time he became really anxious and started to have physical discomfort, headaches, and sleepless nights. Eventually, it simply overwhelmed him so that he was required to stay in a clinic for almost a month of rest and recuperation.

It was a typical worry–anxiety vicious circle: Fritz is being badly treated by his boss, a controlling CEO and partner of the firm; thoughts of future threats start entering his mind; the thoughts begin to get traction as he feels a growing uncertainty and a sense of powerlessness. He seeks a possible solution and considers talking to the other partners but then he decides to do nothing because he sees no hope. All this creates more agitation in his already overly excited mind and eventually he becomes so anxious that physical problems appear: headaches, lack of sleep … finally he feels as though he is up a blind alley: a baby on the way and the real prospect of losing his job. So he finally cracks. Fortunately his case ended with a good resolution. If only this was the case more often. Figure 10.2 below shows the vicious circle of worry/anxiety in operation.

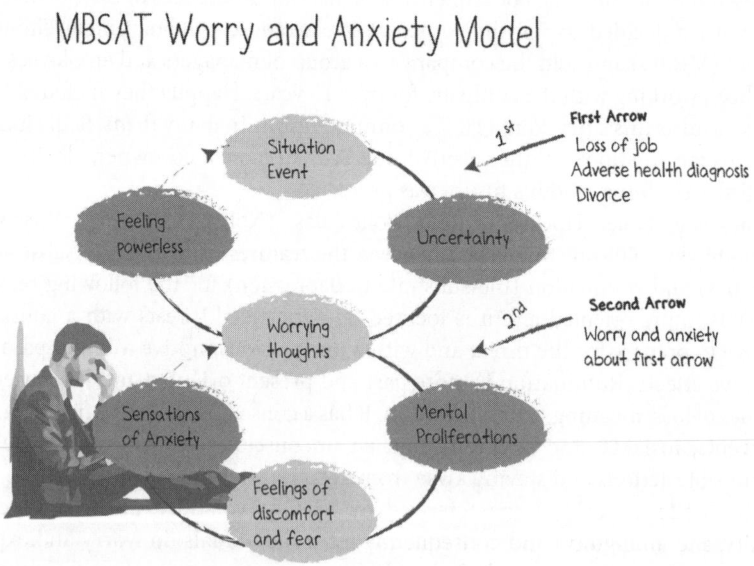

Figure 10.2 MBSAT Worry and Anxiety Model. *Source*: Juan Humberto Young.

The MBSAT model of worry and anxiety consists of two causal loops that correspond to the metaphor of the two arrows. The first arrow represents the initial worry generated by the negative situation that is being confronted. For Fritz it was his realization that he could lose his job. This set the first loop in motion.

The uncertainty of the situation provokes worrying thoughts about seeking solutions ("Could I talk to the partners?"). He was overcome with feelings of powerlessness, because, in his view, this solution was not possible. His worries and anxieties resulted in a second painful arrow. An additional loop opened as his mental condition accelerated and intensified, leading to feelings of discomfort and fear and further increasing his level of anxiety.

Worry and anxiety are insidious aspects of modern society. Everyone seems to have some degree of worry and anxiety. We even worry about good events. The South Korean youth who won the 2015 International Chopin Piano Competition at the age of 21 was interviewed after his performance and the first thing he said was: "I kind of worry now about how I can keep up with the expectations."

Worrying about being perfect is a common problem in modern society: the perfect appearance, the perfect job, the perfect vacation, the perfect school, and so on. In business settings perfection is a generalized condition leading to enormous worries and anxieties. As Charlie Brown, the cartoon character, says: "Worrying won't stop the bad stuff from happening, it just stops you from enjoying the good."

The importance of identifying the second arrow is an essential message in this session. The ability to identify the second arrow is the basic requirement to deal with it and that is the theme of the next session, where we focus on strategies to effectively manage emotional pain—which is the essence of the second arrow.

For an exercise to explore the territory of worry and anxiety (TWA) based on the personal experiences of the participants see Note 11.

10.3.4 3-minutes breathing space for strengths: (3MBS-Strengths)

Participants already know that the 3MBS is considered as the spine of the MBCT protocol. They know that it serves as a pause in daily life and allows a participant to switch from a driven doing mode of the mind to a being present mode.

Throughout the MBSAT program a number of variations of 3MBS's are introduced. These variations look at specific contexts and respond to the reality of the moment. The 3MBS-Strengths is the first of these mini-practices. It is presented in this session after the participants have identified their personal character strengths with the help of the VIA survey.

Here are some recognized benefits of practicing this variation regularly:

a. 3MBS-Strengths helps an individual to step back from a situation for a moment and then return to that situation and move into action using the power of one's strengths.

b. 3MBS-Strengths fosters self-reliance and determination as antidotes against worries and anxieties.
c. 3MBS-Strengths is a reminder for participants to practice their strengths in daily life.

For further information on this practice see Note 12.

10.3.5 Mindful walking

Walking is an activity everyone does with the intention of moving from one place to another: the office or a train station, a store, or a restaurant for lunch, and so on. Consequently, walking meditation is easy to incorporate into your daily life.

Like mindful stretching or mindful salsa the aim of the exercise is to do the same activity but to pay close attention to every single movement. In mindful walking we walk while carefully observing every step and staying present as we lift one foot after another instead of letting our mind wander. It seems to be easy but it is actually a very demanding practice. Masters of this practice display wonderfully harmonious movements that convey a feeling of utter well-being.

Even participants new to the practice derive remarkable insights from it. Regula shared with her colleagues how a deep feeling of gratitude pervaded her during the walking meditation. She told them how she had always taken her feet for granted without realizing how important they were, carrying all her weight and getting her everywhere in her high-speed doing mode. At the end of the inquiry she stood up, bowed to her feet and addressed them directly: "Thank you, thank you, feet, for being so kind to me."

Walking meditation provides an opportunity to experience awareness with an activity that everyone does every day. It serves as experiential learning and demonstrates how other daily activities can be transformed by doing them mindfully.

Note 13 offers additional suggestions for the mindful walking practice.

11

Session 5: Strategic Awareness I—Mindful Real Options (MROs)

11.1 Introduction

With Session 5 we begin the second half of the program.

In the first part of the course we trained and developed the ability to focus our awareness at will. In doing so we learned to recognize our mental patterns and cope with mind wandering. We connected with our breath and body sensations so we could move our attention to the present moment and we switched our way from a frantic doing mode to a being mode. We learned to identify the sources of difficulty and aversion and to decenter our thoughts by looking at them for what they are, just thoughts and not facts. Essentially we learned to calm our busy mind and to reduce the level of automatic impulses and conditioned reactivity, decreasing the incidence of impulsive, misdirected decisions and beginning to gain personal freedom by living our lives more positively and mindfully.

In the second half of the program we consider what this involves when we respond to the unavoidable challenges in life. We will look at how to handle difficulties mindfully and make better decisions, including decisions related to money. Most importantly we will explore how we can make the best of our character strengths and become the best possible versions of ourselves, our mindful positive selves (MPS).

In one of my earliest jobs, when I was a very young man, I worked as the chief financial officer of a construction company in Panama. I was only in my mid-twenties but because the partners of the company were absent on business trips most of the time I became the most senior employee, the de facto boss, who was often in charge of running the whole operation and making difficult personnel decisions.

One afternoon after work, a sales manager came to see me. He was agitated and told me excitedly that he had been with some clients in a night club and had spotted a co-worker, a member of my personal team, dancing with another man in an embarrassingly intimate embrace.

Mindfulness-Based Strategic Awareness Training: A Complete Program for Leaders and Individuals, First Edition. Juan Humberto Young.

Companion website: www.wiley.com/go/humbertoyoung/mbsat

"Clearly we can't have that kind of behavior in the company," he told me. It turned out that my co-worker was gay. I became livid and after a heated discussion I fired him. Yes, I did it, just because of his sexual orientation.

I remember he asked me if I was happy with his work and I told him that I was more than happy—he was one of the best accountants in the company. Then he asked me what his private life had to do with his professional work if he was performing well? Despite his compelling argument nobody was able to make me change my mind. My personal assistant, an elderly lady, begged me to reconsider, but I stuck to my decision.

There is a strange side to this story. When I was growing up—and I remember this perfectly—my cousin Pedro used to spend almost every weekend at our home. He was openly gay. Even as a young boy I was aware of it. He liked to come to our home because, as he explained: "It is only Uncle Johnny (my father) and Auntie Eva (my mother) who really accept me."

For my family it was a delight to spend the weekend with Pedro. He was refined, sophisticated, and an expert hobby cook. So I certainly did not learn this kind of homophobic bigotry from my family.

What happened in my unfortunate clash with the gay staff member was a case of an unwise, unreflecting reaction, which may have been partly incited by the sales manager. I acted out of an intemperate and ill-considered impulse. It was a vulgar act showing that while I was technically competent in finance and accounting, I was utterly incompetent when it came to the challenges of managing complex human relations.

Perhaps I was simply too young to grasp the responsibilities of managing individuals. The fact is that I regret this decision so much and it makes me tremendously sad whenever I think of the suffering that I inflicted on this competent young man, albeit not out of spite but lack of mindfulness. The irony is that years later my older daughter Ana would come out of the closet with my full support.

How do we prevent unskillful decisions? My rash decision in the case of the young accountant haunted me for years. How we can make better decisions is the focus of the next part of the MBSAT program. It builds on the skills learned in the four previous sessions and expands our knowledge and practices to help us cultivate a different way of being that is more conducive to a positive, mindful, and flourishing life. MBSAT's concept of Mindful Real Options (MROs, see Section 6.5) is one of the tools that is helpful in this respect as it opens up a range of flexible responses based on the ability to regulate one's BETA (Body sensations, Emotions/feelings, Thoughts/ideas and Action/behavioral impulses). In this session we look at the conditions that allow MROs to emerge naturally and facilitate a mindful positive life.

In today's society the hero is the doer, the one who makes things happen, the person who can push decisions through and always finds the way ahead when faced with adversity.

This approach tends to work with technical challenges. However, with very complex issues—adaptive challenges as R. Heifetz, the leadership expert from Harvard Kennedy School calls them—it does not work.

For example, in building more equitable and peaceful societies it has yet to demonstrate its usefulness. In the field that concerns us here: issues related to people's emotional and personal growth, it is now well recognized that problem-solving approaches do not work. On the contrary they tend to exacerbate the problems.

Like most mindfulness-based approaches, MBSAT proposes a radically different way of approaching the difficulties and challenges in our lives. Central to the MBSAT approach is a way of relating to human experience that is based on acceptance, allowing, and letting be—it is an attitude that can become a real challenge for most people especially in business organizations where the mantra is "be a doer - nothing will stop you."

Here is what Tanja (name changed), one of the few female Managing Directors (MD) at a prestigious financial institution, said after a meditation practice on difficulties. It occurred during one of my programs (an Irimi meditation practice explained in more detail in Section 11.3.1).

TANJA: This meditation brought to my awareness the situation in my job and I started to feel painful tightness all over my body. It is so distressing what is happening.

TEACHER: Would you like to share more about what it is that you are experiencing?

TANJA: I have been with this company for over 20 years and have been a MD for the last 5 years. Recently new owners have acquired us and it seems that they are not into promoting females. It has been a year now and the CEO hasn't greeted me yet.

TEACHER: And how does that make you feel?

TANJA: I feel betrayed. It is such an unfair situation. I have worked here for 20 years building a portfolio of clients from all over the world and now I am treated as if I don't exist. When you were inviting us to move the attention to where we can feel a difficulty, an indescribable sensation swept all over my whole body. I just trembled from these feelings of unfairness.

TEACHER: Can you say a bit more about that?

TANJA: You work hard for so many years and all of sudden, without any warning, your life is turned upside down by circumstances that are out of your control. All of my clients are males and here I am in this impasse where I just don't know what is going to happen to me—just because I am a woman. I feel so impotent and hopeless. And with the meditation that we just did I haven't found a solution either, so I don't see how this could help me.

TEACHER: You seem to be profoundly disillusioned. Isn't that so?

TANJA: Yes, precisely.

TEACHER: Let me generalize about your experience and see if we can extract some lessons from it. Disillusion or disappointment is nothing more than a disconnection between our expectations and reality. In this case, the expectation that the new owners will honor your many years of highly successful and competent work with the firm. That doesn't look as though it is going to happen. So cognitive and emotional dissonance sets in between reality and expectations and creates a direct path to disappointment and worrying.

What are the choices here? One option is to continue worrying and seeking solutions which adds an 'arrow of pain' to a reality already perceived as painful and which is creating increased anxiety.

The other option is to adopt an accepting stance and trust that practical wisdom will reveal itself and some kind of opening will eventually appear. This is hard for most of us who grow up in a culture of self-reliance and are used to solving problems swiftly. What we are training here is reducing our emotional reactivity and suffering by enabling a calm and lucid mind that opens a range of new possibilities, what I call Mindful Real Options (MROs), creating new spaciousness in the mind from where more constructive responses in the form of skillful decisions can emerge.

Months later Tanja wrote to me. She explained that practicing meditation on acceptance had revealed to her that she needed to stop fighting the situation, accept the reality however difficult and simply move on.

She gained the practical wisdom to realize that after 20 years of hard work her firm was now in a different place. She told me in her mail that she had left the firm and moved to another financial institution taking most of her clients with her and maintaining her rank as Managing Director. She is no doubt an outstanding achiever in the Swiss financial sector.

This story illuminates what acceptance and responding mean: first creating a space by accepting and allowing whatever difficulty you experience and holding it in open awareness (no judging); then, when the time seems appropriate, selecting a skillful response with strategic awareness (practical wisdom). In the case of Tanja, acceptance gave her the emotional stability and spaciousness to gain lucidity and maintain an open awareness (without judging) to her situation. This created MROs for her to strategically plot a skillful response (her strategic awareness in action).

So what is acceptance? It is a multifaceted construct that Hayes, Strosahl, and Wilson (2012, p. 272) define as:

> the voluntary adoption of an intentionally open, receptive, flexible and nonjudgmental posture with respect to moment-to-moment experience. Acceptance is supported by a willingness to make contact with distressing private experiences or situations, events or interactions that will likely trigger them.

A source of confusion is the widespread idea that acceptance equals resignation or failure. However, as Tanja's case demonstrates, it was her ability to allow acceptance that opened the door for her to contemplate other options. Far from being passive or resigned, her accepting attitude restored her calm and gave her the necessary self-assurance to change her employer after two decades in the same workplace.

Acceptance has a kind and gentle quality that allows growth and change to emerge by themselves. However, it is not without challenges as it requires trust in the efficacy of acceptance and gentleness to generate change. From a rational point of view this can be difficult as it is hard to make sense of the idea that by doing less things can move ahead. It is especially difficult for people in organizational and business environments where there is an ingrained disposition to take immediate action to solve issues and where attitudes of acceptance tend to be equated with resignation and failure. Actually, it is almost the opposite: the underlying stance of acceptance is courage and self-assurance as only with these qualities can one resist the urge to react immediately and embrace what acceptance really means.

Another complication with the patterns of the problem-solving doing mode is the tendency to suppress unwanted thoughts and emotions. This actually aggravates the mental and emotional state of individuals confronting difficulties. Wegner's experiments (Wegner, Schneider, Carter III, & White, 1987) on thought suppression led to intriguing findings.

In his experiments Wegner asked participants to *not* think about a white bear. The result was that people had great difficulty avoiding images and thoughts of the bear. This is, Wenger argued, because while one part of the brain bars the forbidden thought, another part of the brain checks every so often to see whether the thought is successfully suppressed. The irony is that in doing so it brings the white bear into the mind again. This phenomenon is called the white bear dilemma. Interestingly, Wenger found that meditation and mindfulness can help people avoid unwanted thoughts. In most mindfulness-based programs reducing unwanted emotions and thoughts is an important part of the curriculum. The therapeutic benefit of an attitude of acceptance is its ability to cope with seemingly unacceptable situations by switching from an automatic reaction to a skillful, responding manner as the case of Tanja beautifully illustrates. Consequently, acceptance should be considered one of the most important skills that can be gained in MBSAT as it is one of the underlying factors of strategic awareness.

According to Williams and Lynn (2010, p. 18) some of the recognized benefits of acceptance include:

1. An expanded range of available experiences;
2. An increased potential for productive action;
3. An increased compassion and reduction in blaming others;
4. An increased serenity and reasonableness;
5. A decrease in distressing negative emotions; and
6. Positive therapeutic outcomes.

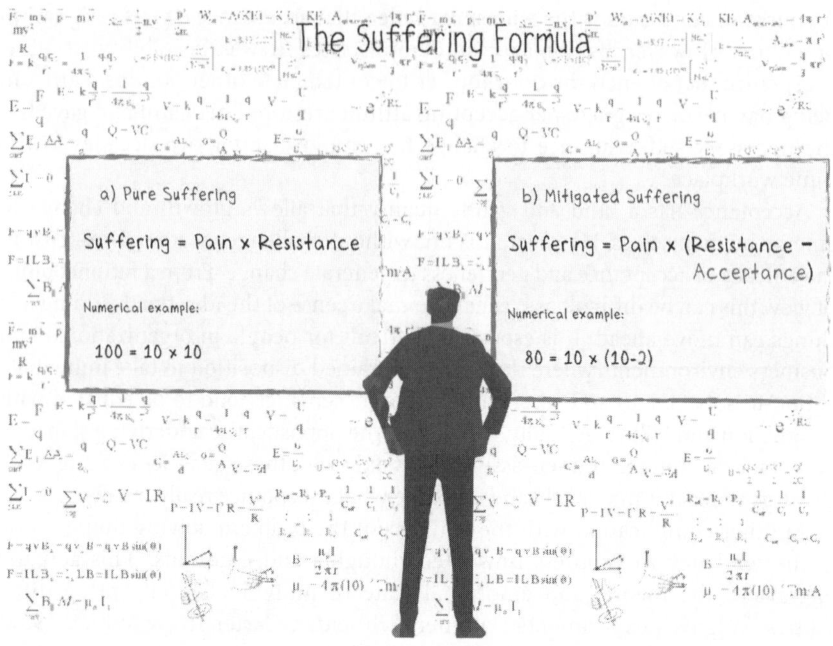

Figure 11.1 The Suffering Formula. *Source*: Juan Humberto Young.

A way of understanding acceptance is by going back to the MBSAT worry and anxiety model explained in Chapter 10, Session 4 (Figure 10.2), the two arrows approach to suffering. The real pain corresponds to the first arrow, in this model an objective factor that could be difficult to change, for example, physical pain or the loss of a job. The second arrow represents resistance and the distress related to the first arrow, that is, more subjective elements but also hard to change and that add to the suffering. Resistance can take different forms: one is frantic problem solving, another is ignoring the first arrow or suppressing the cognitive and emotional effects related to the first arrow.

In Figure 11.1 an easy to understand, straightforward, mathematic formula summarizes the logic and the adaptive value of acceptance, helpful for rationally oriented readers. On the left side of the equation is suffering that equals real pain times resistance. For example, in version (a) of the formula (pure suffering) numerically 10 units of pain times 10 units of resistance result in 100 units of suffering. In version (b) of the formula (mitigated suffering) injecting acceptance transforms the right side of the expression by adding acceptance as a minus term, thus bracketing resistance minus acceptance. Given that resistance stays constant (a fact that reflects the difficulty of changing emotional distress at will) increasing acceptance reduces resistance, hence the left side of the equation results in less suffering. For example, 10 units of pain times 10 units of resistance less 2 units of

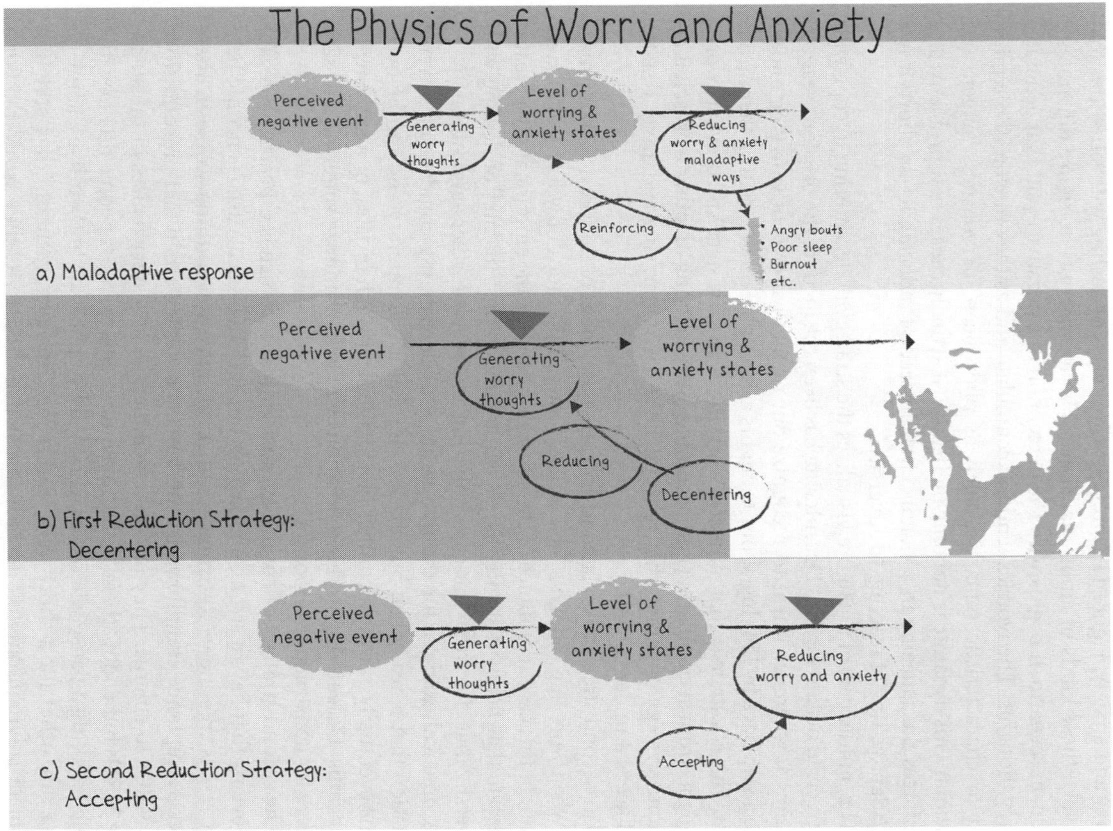

Figure 11.2 The Physics of Worry and Anxiety. *Source*: Juan Humberto Young.

acceptance yields a lower level of suffering of 80 units. This illustrates the beneficial value of acceptance and its impact on strategic awareness as it has a calming effect and reduces the probability of hasty reactive decision-making.

Another useful way of understanding suffering is by looking at the physics of worry and anxiety. Figure 11.2 presents three ways of dealing with situations that provoke these kinds of emotional states. The top part of the figure illustrates a frequent scenario. It begins with the perception of a negative event that generates worry thoughts. The worries tend to accumulate and as they pile up in the mind lead to characteristic outcomes such as poor sleep, nervousness, anger, and burnout. This dynamic is not only ineffective, it actually causes new problems and reinforces the suffering in a vicious circle instead of reducing it—in short, it is a maladaptive way of reacting to adversity.

The middle part of the figure visualizes the strategy of decentering to cope with a perceived negative event. Decentering has been the focus of the previous session, Session 4, where we learnt to recognize our mental patterns of worrying and to take a step back by looking at our thoughts as thoughts differentiating them from facts. This is a strategy that mitigates worrying at an early stage and prevents worry thoughts from accumulating and becoming overwhelming. In other words, it is an ex-ante strategy of coping that reduces the stock of worrying and anxiety states and keeps it under control.

The second strategy is related to accepting, the focus of this Session 5. It is useful when worrying thoughts have already entered the stock of worry and anxiety states. In this case acceptance of the situation as well as the emotional state creates a respite that helps in staying balanced. It is an ex-post manner of dealing with adversity that effectively mitigates suffering and avoids further aggravation.

A practical example for the first strategy of decentering could be an adverse situation that is really bad but chances are that it is temporary and can be overcome eventually: maybe a conflict in a relation, a trough in sales, or a truly awful bronchitis. Decentering in these situations will help minimize suffering and save energy for constructive responses.

The second strategy of coping ex-post with acceptance is especially relevant for events that have a strong and lasting impact. A classical case is chronic pain that resists treatment. Resistance and revolt makes everything worse in these cases. Acceptance and allowance are key factors, they are in fact preconditions for MROs to emerge. They not only facilitate the necessary pauses in the structure MROs but endow them with the required quality. Most people do know the value of taking a pause when overwhelmed by upheavals in their lives; some go for a run, other for a short walk, and so on. However, mentally they stay in a problem-solving/doing mode, they just switch the activity they are doing. For a pause to be truly effective it must create a mental switch from a doing mode to a being mode. Only by generating the condition of acceptance and allowance to whatever difficulty one is confronting can one create an effective, adaptive pause that is conducive to letting MROs emerge.

11.2 Session Organization, Coverage, and Sequence

The practices presented in this session are designed to help participants deal with experiences of aversion in skillful ways, make the best of their character strengths and increase their well-being.

We look at reactions involving feelings of aversion and how they can lead to anxiety and worry when left unchecked and impede skillful decision-making. In a later session we will look at the effect of unhealthy feelings of attachment, the counterpart of aversion.

Session 5: Strategic Awareness I: Mindful Real Options (MROs)

	Time allocated in minutes Duration: 2½ to 3 hours
1. Arrival meditation upon arrival	5
2. Irimi meditation (awareness of breath and body—introducing a difficulty) Guidance and inquiry about the exercise	35
3. Home practice review of Session 4	20
4. 3-minutes breathing space on worry Exercise and review	20
5. Rumi's poem, "The Guest House" Reading and discussion	30
6. Your mindful positive self: first take	30
7. Home practice assignments: Irimi meditation on 6 of 7 days 3MBS—three times daily 3MBS on worry (whenever you start worrying) Practicing one strength a day Practicing transforming dislikes: eating, seeing, hearing, doing Initiating the positive mindful self assignment as a first step towards a meaningful life Watching at least one of the following two movies: *The Great Gatsby* with Robert Redford and Mia Farrow *The Treasure of Sierra Madre* with Humphrey Bogart	5

11.3 Exercises and Practices of Session 5

Upon arrival the session begins with 5 minutes of meditation so participants can settle in. Then we concentrate on meditation on difficulty, a practice I have named Irimi meditation from the Japanese martial art Aikido. After the home practice review we revisit the territory of worry and anxiety and the 3MBS on worry.

The last part of the session focuses on strengths as we introduce an exercise dealing with character strengths for personal development, called mindful positive self. Different phases of this implementation will accompany us to the very end of the MBSAT program.

11.3.1 Irimi meditation: Awareness of breath and body introducing a difficulty

In Aikido, the most recent form of traditional Japanese martial arts, the main focus is to minimize violence by blocking and disabling an aggressive attacker using the attacker's momentum. The intention is not to inflict harm but to hamstring the adversary. Aikido is a defensive system that allows a practitioner to manage an aggressive situation and let things cool down.

The principle is straightforward. In an attack there is energy. It is adversarial, negative energy. The point is to turn this energy around and convert it into a neutral force. By focusing on keeping your balance, being centered and understanding other people's views, Aikido is a study of wisdom based on commonsense and mastery of the body.

In Aikido two essential defensive movements are taught: Irimi and Tenkan. With Irimi one does not move away from an attack but moves towards it on purpose, either straight ahead or at an angle. This is a highly counter-intuitive movement. Practicing Irimi was especially hard for me because when I started to train Aikido I already had over a decade of intense kickboxing training, which employs the opposite tactic: one retreats from an attack and then moves forward with a counterattack, fast and lethal. In my case I had to unlearn my reflex of retreat in order to gain the benefits of Irimi.

Tenkan involves a similar tactic as Irimi. It also involves entering an attack but then you turn around and either approach the attacker from behind or in the same direction.

Ursula Sensei, my teacher, used to say she did not understand why it was so difficult to see the value of Irimi. "After all," she would explain, "most people do it intuitively when walking in the street. When someone comes towards you on the sidewalk, you don't back off. You continue walking in the direction of the other person and just before you bump into each other either one of you, or both of you, move a aside to avoid a collision. Then you both continue with your stride. Well, that is Irimi."

The Irimi meditation practice is built around the Aikido principle of moving into the realm of adversity instead of away from it when you are confronted with difficult situations (first arrow) or emotional and mental difficulties (second

Irimi:
Moving Towards Adversity Instead of Away From It

Figure 11.3 Irimi: Moving Towards Adversity Instead of Away From It. *Source*: Juan Humberto Young.

arrow). In the framework of MBSAT both are considered to be bundles of negative energy. Participants are invited to blend their positive energy with these difficulties to create a generative unity by remaining open, balanced, and maintaining an attitude of acceptance towards the difficulties.

I like this metaphor because it is an analogy with what an Aikidoka defender does in cases of real, physical attacks: he abstains from reacting impulsively and instead responds consciously and deliberately with a positive spirit, seeking to resolve a potentially violent situation harmoniously.

Figure 11.3 illustrates an Irimi movement. The defender first takes a step forward in order to come close to the body of the attacker, thus neutralizing the energy of the attack and serenely opening an array of possible responses for the defender, in this case making the adversary lose balance and fall helplessly backwards to the floor.

When the negative thoughts and emotions we have concerning the difficulties in our lives get out of control it is like inflicting violence on ourselves and our mind. This is why the counterintuitive, soft Aikido approach of moving closer to our own destructive forces (negative thoughts, fearful emotions, painful sensations, or unskillful actions) has a soothing, healing effect and can lead to positive practical outcomes.

In essence Irimi meditation invites a stance of "how to be with" difficulty instead of "what to do about" difficulty. It is, in this respect, completely congruent with the intentions of mindfulness interventions such as MBCT and MBSR.

The soothing, healing effect of Irimi is derived from its many benefits as well as the benefits of meditation which were discussed in detail in Chapter 3.

Benefits of Irimi meditation (awareness of breath and body, introducing a difficulty)

a. Irimi helps participants reduce their tendency to worry and get into an anxious state.
b. It opens up a new, more skillful way of relating to states of anxiety and worry.
c. Although it might not make the difficulty disappear it allows the person to function normally without excessively taxing their cognitive and emotional system.
d. Irimi reinforces the principle of decentering from our adverse experiences and thoughts.
e. It helps promote an attitude of curiosity and kindness towards our adverse experiences.
f. It opens an array of Mindful Real Options (MROs) that can lead to skillful decision-making and helps gain resilience, the ability to bounce back from adversity.

More details are to be found in Note 14.

11.3.2 3-minutes breathing space on worry (3MBS-Worry)

MBSAT presents a series of different 3MBS's that are contextualized within the reality of the moment. The 3MBS on worry is the second contextualized mini-practice designed to assist in moments of worry and anxiety.

Like 3MBS on strengths and the basic 3MBS, the 3MBS on worry has three steps. The difference from the other 3MBS's is that the first step introduces worry as a focal point by suggesting that practitioners identify and label what is worrying them, for example, saying to themselves: "I worry about my job" or "I worry about my relation with X." This creates awareness and allows the practitioner to immediately get out of a worry automatic pilot.

In the second step awareness is shifted to the breath as in the regular 3MBS, but with a slight variation. The idea is to start counting in- and out-breaths or alternatively to silently repeat the words: "exhaling, inhaling, exhaling."

Step 3 is identical to the basic form of 3MBS and consists of awareness of the body (expanding awareness).

Note 15 contains step-by-step instructions and suggestions.

Here are some recognized benefits that can be derived by regularly practicing 3MBS-worry:

1. It helps to switch from a worrying doing mode to a calmer being mode and allows the participant to get out of a worry automatic pilot.
2. It helps to step back from the moment and to look at worry as an external phenomenon created by our thoughts.
3. Perceiving worry thoughts as mental events leads to a sense of allowance and acceptance.

4. 3MBS-Worry changes the time orientation of our thoughts and shifts them from worrying about the future to dealing with them in the present.

11.3.3 The mindful positive self (MPS): First take

In this session participants are introduced to the mindful positive self (MPS). All cultural traditions tell us that the gifts of thinking wisely, feeling extended love, accepting sensations of discomfort with fortitude, and acting with prudent restraint are already within us, but often buried so deep that they find no expression in our daily lives. Too many years of negative self-control and conditioning have numbed these human capabilities.

This is why it is often argued that all that is required is an awakening of the best of our natural human qualities. This is the great value of MPS. It is a kind of mindful, positive self-portrait of what we can be when we are at our best and it serves as beacon for personal growth with the help of an action plan.

We all have moments in life when our BETA (Body sensations, Emotions/feelings, Thoughts and Action impulses) are harmoniously aligned and synchronized. At those times we feel complete and happy and those around us who witness the fulfilling experience are also moved. Sadly for most of us these periods are rare and short-lived. The idea of MPS is to replicate these states of fulfillment. It is a practice that originates from the positive psychology tool box. I have adapted it to the framework of MBSAT.

MPS is defined as a combination of character strengths (an element of positive psychology), equanimity, and clarity of mind (elements of mindfulness practice) all brought together with appropriate and adaptive emotions to facilitate the attainment of strategic awareness.

The main benefit of having a mindful positive self-portrait is its function as a powerful magnet. Having a clearly defined vision of one's possibilities to enact a mindful and positive way of life serves as blueprint for attaining authentic well-being. It then nourishes our BETA with a sense of what we can become. And that represents a motivational force moving us towards the vision.

The exercise consists of two components: a mindful, positive self-portrait of the participant and an action plan for personal development to realize this vision of self. So each participant will take with him, or her, a concrete tool of orientation after the MBSAT program has been completed. It is an invitation for participants to continue cultivating their MPS as a way of enriching their life.

At this point participants have already established their values in action inventory, so by now they have deepened their self-knowledge and are conscious of their character strengths, which are the assets for an engaged and meaningful life and one of the essential inputs in the MPS self-portrait. The process of creating an MPS portrait consists of several building blocks and includes feedback from people who know us well and perceive us from different vantage points (friends and family, colleagues and supervisors at work, contacts from social activities and hobbies, etc.).

This session started with the first steps involved in building the portrait. Note 16 and Handout 2 present guidelines and instructions for this initial phase.

12

Session 6: Strategic Awareness II—From POMO (Powerful Money) to MIMO (Mindful Money)

12.1 Introduction

This is arguably one of the key chapters of this book … and it is probably the most challenging. It deals with one of the most persuasive and potent extrinsic motivational factors: money. So powerful is money that individuals and entire nations are willing to put up with strife and conflict for the sake of it.

It is useful to make the objective of this session clear from the beginning. The intention is to facilitate an inner journey from an obsessive attraction to money—what I call *POMO: Powerful Money*—to a wise relation with money, aware of what money can or cannot provide to its user, that is, *MIMO: Mindful Money*. In order to be able to use money to achieve higher levels of subjective well-being one must know its possibilities and limitations. In the words of INSEAD business school professor De Vries:

> We need to learn how to live with the quest for money without losing ourselves to it. We need to realize that in money matters, it's all a question of balance. If too much money can be demoralizing as too little, how can we juggle our need for it and our fear of it?" (2007, p. 240)

Helping achieve this balance is the purpose of this session.

What I also find of paramount importance and drives me to design this session is the role of money as extrinsic motivator and its implications for outcomes. Money is one of the most powerful forms of extrinsic motivation and yet extrinsic motivation has been proven manifold to hamper creative work. As Teresa Amabile of Harvard Business School writes,

> extrinsic motivation comes from outside the individual … the offer of a bonus… on its own, it can't prompt people to be passionate about their work, in fact it can led

Mindfulness-Based Strategic Awareness Training: A Complete Program for Leaders and Individuals, First Edition. Juan Humberto Young.

Companion website: www.wiley.com/go/humbertoyoung/mbsat

> them to feel bribed and controlled... By contrast intrinsic motivation comes from inside the individual. It's a person's abiding interest in certain activities or deep love of particular challenges. Employees are most creative when they are intrinsically motivated, in other words, when the work itself is motivating. (1998, p. 1)

The extensive research related to Self-Determination Theory (SDT, see section 1.3.2) corroborates these findings.

Undoubtedly today's challenges in business and in private lives require new, innovative ways forward. Almost all industries are facing disruptive forces that put their business models in jeopardy (computerization, big data, new technologies, and global competition amongst other). This reality puts a real premium on finding creative solutions, however fixation on material compensation such as bonuses goes in the opposite direction: ample research suggests that it can restrain creativity.

Money issues are as delicate as they are controversial. In the years that I have been addressing this topic with my business partners, clients, students, and friends it has always aroused a wide range of passionate responses. Commonly these conversations can quickly turn to the accusation that one is simply envious of other people's fortunes. When it becomes clear that a person actually has money people become intrigued and their aggressive tone shifts to curiosity: "Why are you interested in this issue? A person in your position needn't think about this."

I passionately believe that a healthy relationship with money and wealth is essential for people's well-being. If we look at people's problems—tensions at the job, mental problems, marital difficulties, and so on—the underlying root causes are often related to money, either the lack of it or, as ironic as it may sound, not knowing how to sensibly manage an abundance of it.

Without a skillful way of dealing with money (MIMO) every initiative to increase a person's well-being will ultimately be an exercise in futility. In our economy-driven, consumption-loving society where money is omnipresent and permeates all interactions, finding a balance in money issues is an integral part of mindfulness-based strategic awareness and paramount to leading a fulfilling life. This is the reason why an entire session of the MBSAT program is dedicated to developing a mindful relationship to money.

It is worth mentioning that I am in good company regarding my preoccupation with these issues, as renowned social scientists (economists, sociologists, psychologists, etc.), among them Nobel Prize winners, are actively advancing research on the topic (Kahneman, Easterlin, Seligman, Csikszentmihalyi, Kasser, and Frank amongst others). They have made important discoveries connecting happiness, well-being, and money. They have produced scientific evidence demonstrating how we can constructively relate to this all-important societal preoccupation.

In our society a preoccupation with money tends to oscillate between two extremes: there are those of modest means who are constantly preoccupied with how to get more money and those who live in affluence but are still preoccupied with how to get more of it. Both manifest behavior that is clearly

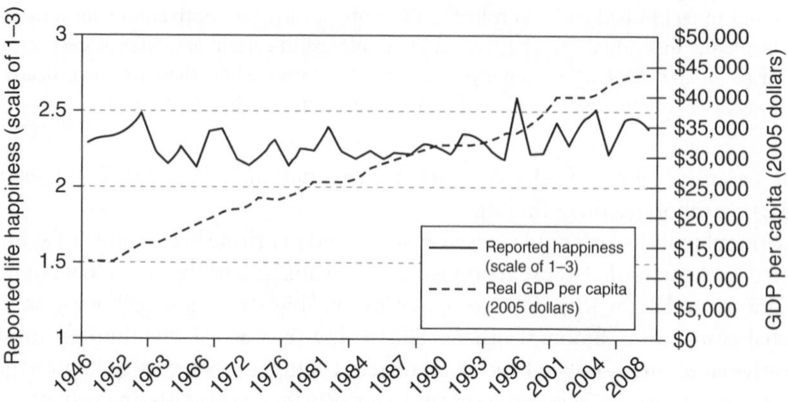

Figure 12.1 Life happiness vs. real GDP per capita, the United States. *Source*: Veenhoven (2008).

addictive. In this chapter I present relevant recent findings about the interrelationship between money and happiness and illustrate those interrelationships with real-life experiences.

Let me make this clear: In no way am I taking a moral stance or suggesting how people should, or should not, relate to income and wealth. Money is such a personal matter that no one can be certain what the "right" way is. I am simply arguing that if people are interested in increasing well-being and achieving a state of personal flourishing—two valued and indisputable desires—then that person needs to look carefully at this very important aspect of life. Achieving clarity of economic aspiration, and understanding its interdependence with other goals, will certainly advance people on the path to what we all want: authentic happiness and satisfaction in life.

MBSAT is based on solid research in the fields of economics of happiness and positive psychology, two fields in which I am an academically trained practitioner. In combination with my life experience as a professional financial specialist dealing with a vast range of money suppliers and users—from the hugely wealthy through economically average individuals to people in dire financial straits—this helps me to enrich academic research with observations and human-centered data (anecdotal evidence), based on years of working in different contexts, functions, and countries.

Let's begin by taking note of a well-documented counterintuitive finding: economic growth does not lead to an increase in happiness. The graph in Figure 12.1, using the United States as an example, demonstrates that the level of subjective well-being has remained relatively constant since the end of World War II despite an unprecedented increase in real GDP per capita. The same holds true for Europe. Sophisticated economic studies have extended the analysis to a greater number of developed countries and added developing countries as well as countries in transition and they have always yielded the same result (Easterlin and Angelescu, 2009): once basic needs are covered, increases in material wealth cannot buy lasting subjective well-being.

If material wealth were to correlate or create more happiness, the curve of well-being should run parallel with the real gross domestic product (GDP) per capita or, at least, show some kind of upward trend over time. The finding that this is not the case challenges the widely accepted assumption that increases in material wealth (money) lead to increases in happiness. Obviously, the perspective here is a longer-term view that presupposes that basic human needs are covered.

We briefly touched upon this phenomenon, named the Easterlin paradox after the economist R.A. Easterlin, in Chapter 4. It is an intriguing question worthy of investigation: Why do people invest so much of their life pursuing material wealth when the emotional rewards fall short of the effort?

Manfred Kets de Vries, the business school professor at INSEAD and one of the world's foremost authorities on the psychology of top executives, has spent decades studying and researching the minds of executives and leaders at the top of the compensation pyramid and summarizes his findings as follows:

> Having met a great many very wealthy individuals, I have come to realize that being wealthy has its own problems. Far too often, money comes to possess the person as opposed to the person possessing the money. Ironically, instead of gaining greater satisfaction through wealth, many people find that the acquisition and position of money creates an even greater state of dissatisfaction. (2007, p. 232)

I couldn't agree more with this statement having seen the same high level of dissatisfaction in partners, clients, and friends—people who have achieved material riches beyond the imagination of average people and are still emotionally dissatisfied. The dissatisfaction stems in part from losing independence: when people are possessed by money they become its servants and in the process lose their autonomy. And autonomy is a very important need according to SDT motivation theory as we have seen in Chapter 1. Focusing on money could mean sacrificing an important route to personal fulfillment.

Let us study the important conditions that lie at the heart of this kind of immanent dissatisfaction: social comparison and envy, privation or want in childhood or youth, and insatiability, amongst others.

12.1.1 Comparing and envy

Panama and Switzerland are the two countries with which I am most closely connected. The contrast of their economic realities could hardly be starker: one nation with the characteristics of a less-developed country and a large number of poor citizens with many material worries, the other with probably the highest standard of living on the planet, and yet both score high on the global happiness scale. Does this make sense? Specialists suggest that Panamanians and Swiss think differently when they answer the question "are you happy?" In Panama people respond based on their emotional state; for them happy may mean sunny weather, friendship and close social ties, a culture of openness, a slight bent for hedonistic enjoyment—all of which they already have. In Switzerland people seem to think more in terms of life satisfaction: no hunger, no wars, reliable public governance assets—these are the assets that come first to their mind.

However, Seligman's PERMA model suggests that a flourishing, fulfilling life is complex and multidimensional, which implies that both the Swiss and the Panamanian concept of happiness are only partially true.

Knowing both cultures and realizing the differences in their psychological, cultural, and economic make-up it had always intrigued me why both countries score so high on worldwide happiness indexes. Then I realized that the two countries give two honest, but different, answers to the same question.

For the Panamanians the answer is an emotional one, coming from what Kahneman would call the "experienced self" (yes, I'm feeling happy) whereas the Swiss give a cognitive, evaluative answer (yes, I reckon I'm better off than people in most other countries) coming from the "remembering self" that people activate when thinking about their life.

When asking Swiss people why they are happy most of them will invariably refer to a referential, evaluative discourse: "The people from our neighboring countries—the Germans, Italians, French, and somewhat less the Austrians—want to come to Switzerland for work," they might say. "Why? Because the situation in Switzerland is better than in their home countries, therefore as Swiss we should be happy; we are better off than all of our neighbors."[1]

Group social reference is the term psychologists use for the social phenomena of comparing ourselves with others and checking how well we are doing in relation to others. If it happens at an individual level it is known in the common vernacular as envy.

Several years ago while working at UBS, a client from overseas called me at my office in Switzerland and said he needed my presence urgently next day to assist with a consortium of businessmen. He had already made the travel arrangements so I could reach the meeting on time. I was to leave on Concorde from London to New York (a three-and-a-half hour flight), transfer to New Jersey's Teterboro airport and board his personal jet.

I flew to the meeting as arranged and was in my client's private office on the next day with two of his partners, like him extremely wealthy individuals, waiting for the senior partner of the transaction, a member of one of the five richest long-established families in the country with interests in vast areas of the economy: oil, banking, beverages, and so on.

When he arrived there was some shoulder patting and small talk before starting the negotiation. During the banter the senior partner asked my client casually: "So what are you flying these days?" My client told him the model of his jet (a

[1] Panamanians fall into social comparison traps as well. They compare themselves with neighboring countries in Central America and with Venezuela and Colombia. They, too, consider themselves as happier when comparing to the situation in those countries. In fact both Switzerland and Panama present the same characteristics of massive immigration from both adjoining and remote states.

name I can't recall) that seated 5–6 passengers. "And you, what are you flying?" asked my client in return. "Oh," he replied, "I have two like yours that I let my employees use. Myself I use a large cabin Grumman (that name I remember); it is faster and has a larger range." Incidentally, it also cost about seven times the amount of my client's jet. I couldn't believe what I just witnessed; it was like a contest to find out who possessed the largest plane. It reminded me of a business school professor who quoted a top executive telling him something along the lines of: "What good is money if it can't inspire envy and terror in your fellow men?"

Later, a colleague, who for many years was the Chief Operating Officer (COO) of one of the top 100 US corporations, told me over dinner he was not surprised by my experience. He saw the same behavior all the time with his fellow US executives. The CEO of his company had decided to buy a bigger and more luxurious corporate jet because in conversations with fellow CEOs they talked endlessly about the size, speed, and comfort of their jets. He concluded that his company needed a more impressive plane for the sake of their reputation, lest his colleagues might think they were in trouble. "They are like kids talking about their toys and each wants to have the best and largest gadget," my friend told me.

On yet another occasion I was having dinner with a limited partner of one of the centuries-old Swiss private banks. He was not a real friend but more than just an acquaintance. He vented his anger about "all these top executives of these large universal banks making many millions in extravagant compensations every year," while he, as he said, made fewer millions although as partner of his bank he had more fiduciary responsibility than the managers of the large banks. This person displayed another variation of disproportionate economic referential behavior.

Where do all these behavioral patterns come from? Nettle (2005) suggests that envy once had an adaptive function. Thousands of years ago observing and following those neighbors with more resources, more food, or better shelter was adaptive, because it could signal better supply sources or better hunting and building methods, hence better chances of survival. However, in today's environment where existential needs are mostly covered, the adaptive value of envious behavior needs to be updated.

Can we learn from experiences of social comparison and envy to ameliorate the human experience without adverse consequences for the individual? If we manage to move away from destructive envy into benign forms of envy learning is under way.

In this session we set out to investigate and train the adverse consequences of envy.

12.1.2 Scarcity and insatiability

For some people their relationship with money is shaped very early in life, in childhood. Children who grow up in an environment of need, experience the pain that a lack of money can produce and the resulting scarcity of essentials can begin to form an attitude imbued with the significance and importance of money that can carry over into adult life. Money becomes consciously or unconsciously the most important factor in their lives.

They become committed to never again experiencing deprivation and as a result they fall into the trap of insatiability, as there will never be enough money to erase their early feelings of deprivation. This is one reason why most of these people, as Schouten and Silver (2012) suggest, are attracted to business organizations because of their desire for power and money. They make the pursuit of POMO their key driving force in life and become, in de Vries' words, possessed by it (see quote in p. 168), in most cases forfeiting their life and true aspirations.

A psychological mechanism that plays a key role in this behavior is the human tendency to use a hierarchical goal system. McIntosh, Harlow, and Martin (1995) write of conditional links between lower-order goals and higher-order goals. In the case of the behavior outlined above, it is the belief that in order to become happy, accepted, or admired a person needs first to have lots of money and power, thus linking the higher goals of life satisfaction to a lower conditional goal of achieving wealth. The problem with this kind of behavior is the danger of dysfunctional consequences when the lower conditional goals are in jeopardy. In the case of individuals the problems begin with negative thoughts and feelings that can lead to worry which, in turn, can end in depression or even suicide if unchecked as some recent high-profile cases in Switzerland demonstrate.

These individuals, known as "linkers" because they link their higher- and lower-order goals, are highly vulnerable because they cannot conceive of any other alternative to reach their higher goals than by achieving their fixed lower conditional goals.

In some cases the difficulty in attaining the conditional goals can produce behavior that breaks the law. We have all heard of cases of ambitious linkers in the financial community whose disastrous actions brought misery to the financial markets and to home owners, pension funds, and the world economy.

Equally, think of the young men who manipulated one of the chief elements of the world financial system: the Libor rate. As one of them, now serving a prison sentence, said: "Point is, you're greedy, you want every little bit of money that you can possibly get." (Downloaded from http://uk.businessinsider.com/libor-rigging-trial-ringmaster-tom-hayes-accused-of-being-dishonest-and-greedy-2015-5)

Another hindrance to subjective well-being is the treadmill effect, discussed previously in Chapter 2. In brief it concerns the tendency of individuals to adapt to previous levels of subjective well-being once the novelty effect of any increase in utility wears off. This leads to a renewed desire to achieve additional utility and creates a never-ending cycle of adaptation leading to experiences of insatiability in a rat race to catch an elusive, short-lived well-being effect.

Reto (a fictitious name) had been a "key child" or "Schluesselchind" in Swiss German, a boy with a key on a string around his neck so he could let himself in when he came home and there was nobody there. Both of his parents worked hard and were away from home until late in the evening as he was growing up. At lunch time he would come home from school to an empty apartment and prepare his own lunch before returning to school. He didn't like studying so he became an apprentice after finishing the compulsory school years.

I met him at a social gathering when he was already in his mid-forties, married with two children and having achieved a relatively high level of success in his life. Because of my background as a businessman and positive psychologist we engaged in a conversation and became regular acquaintances, although there was no professional relationship. Despite his material success—Reto owned his house, had several cars, and money in the bank—he was not happy, always wanting more (insatiate), feeling insecure, and always worrying about what could go wrong and potential catastrophes (thinking of possible catastrophes is typical of linkers).

Having a social intelligence above average he had a network of contacts that were crucial for the business that he owned jointly with several other partners. It was sad to see this likeable and intelligent man, who was haunted by a past of privation and lack of self-esteem, doing all kinds of unnecessary, insensate things like changing his cars three times a year (treadmill effect in action) and changing his lovely house for a larger one that he admitted he would not be able to fully utilize. He was driven by an obsession to be on top and number one (incessant social comparison). He told me seemingly joking yet fundamentally earnest, how he bought two polo shirts, one for his partner and one for him, making sure that his had the number one sewn on the sleeve and the other for his partner the number two. He told me: "I'm showing him who is the number one."

The inability to decouple conditional higher-order goals (be happy) from subordinated linked goals (but I need lots of money for it) and a distorted tendency to nurture the unhealthy feelings of both self-referencing and comparing yourself to others is often at the heart of many personal difficulties. I have often observed this with people who are trying to achieve a more satisfying life. This conditioning is often the source of poor decisions about money.

The impact of such behavior on companies is often magnified because the consequences of unwise decisions by individuals in leadership positions can have repercussions throughout the whole organization.

The recent scandal of the car manufacturer VW is a case in point. It was the consequence of a higher-order goal: an increase in profits is a function of a lower conditional goal: selling the most cars possible to gain market share.

In the VW case at some point in time someone in the value chain of the company must have believed that it was imperative to increase car sales. Confronted with competitive self-referential patterns of thinking (the sales performance of other car brands) an individual or a team of people affected by group-thinking (all thinking alike and not willing to challenge each other's ideas) decided to engage in dubious behavior without having the strategic awareness to consider the damaging potential consequences of their actions on the whole ecology of the firm: customers, suppliers, employees, Germany's reputation as a nation. I think the negative external consequences of poor leaders' decisions, especially if they are driven by self-interest, underscore just how important it is that all leaders and all individuals with responsibility should be trained to develop mental and emotional clarity particularly as it relates to their behavior concerning POMO.

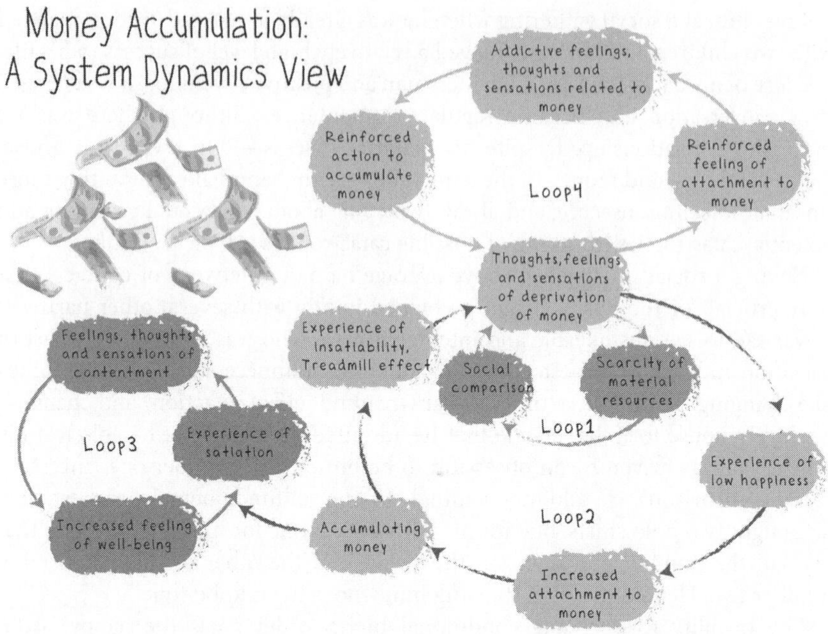

Figure 12.2 Money Accumulation: A Systems Dynamics View. *Source*: Juan Humberto Young.

Figure 12.2 is a system dynamics model of money accumulation.

The first loop at the center of the figure describes an unsatisfied feeling of scarcity which is likely to originate from experiences of material want during childhood. It prompts a person to look upwards for comparisons and check for relative deprivation (am I better or worse off than my neighbor or colleague?). As there will always be people doing "better," this leads to experiences of relative deprivation that compound the original BETA and sensations of real deprivation. This can lead to a feeling of low self-esteem that leads to a second loop which, in turn, is driven by attachment to, and accumulation of, money.

The cycle is only interrupted when complete financial gratification can be achieved. In this case experiences of contentment arise increasing well-being and closing the third loop, which will effectively halt the spiral of money accumulation.

If on the other hand the individual still experiences insatiable desire for money and the associated treadmill effect, the feelings of deprivation are reinforced and this intensifies attachment to money and opens loop number 4. In this case the spiral gains additional momentum by generating addictive feelings, thoughts, and sensations for money that lead to actions driven by the aspiration to accumulate more money. This could eventually lead to questionable behavior if the individual were to believe it was impossible to achieve the money accumulation goals through normal channels.

One important caveat is necessary. The aim of this session is simply to present findings, data and practices about what could represent a more skillful way to relate to money matters by cultivating a MIMO frame of mind. It is not supposed to prescribe solutions. Given the nature of money as a motivating factor it is each individual's responsibility to use the information as he or she finds appropriate. Thus it could well be the case that individuals make a conscious decision to redouble their efforts to increase their material wealth, albeit knowing that their actions might not lead to a sustainable increase in their well-being, as factors of insatiability and treadmill effects could sabotage the long-term result of any increases in wealth. At least they would be mindful and aware of their decisions and choices and that is an experiential gain.

The MBSAT money accumulation model is useful in a number of ways. For individuals it can help gain clarity regarding conditioning and possible strategies to change patterns of perceiving and behaving. For coaches and teachers it reveals ways to structure useful mindfulness-based training and counseling strategies by helping identify the locus of the efforts to promote skillful relations with money: (a) social comparison and (b) insatiability, the two main sources and drivers of dysfunctional patterns.

12.2 Session Organization, Coverage, and Sequence

In this session we look at the relations people have with the most complex external motivator: money. It can increase subjective well-being but it can equally provoke anxiety, worry, and unhappiness. The practices presented are oriented towards helping participants become aware of their BETA patterns and help them relate to experiences with money in more skillful ways.

12.3 Exercises and Practices of Session 6

The customary 5 minutes meditation upon arrival and the home practice review are vital parts of the session. An important practice is the sitting meditation that this time includes thoughts and feelings about how we relate to money. In the next exercise we reflect on the opportunity costs of the pursuit of wealth. It is followed by a variation of the 3MBS, the 3MBS on money worry. Two brief optional mini lectures are suggested on the Easterlin Paradox and the Kahneman–Deaton happiness benchmark. It depends on the teacher's background and inclination whether she or he decides to engage in a discussion of these topics. A section of the home assignments is the second part of the mindful positive self and it may take time to explain how the participants can go about this. Essentially the task is to establish their individual self-portraits from a fulfilling perspective based on their strengths. The session closes with a brief discussion of the other assignments and with a few minutes of closing meditation.

Session 6: Strategic Awareness II—From POMO to MIMO

		Time allocated in minutes Duration: 2½ to 3 hours
1.	Arrival meditation	5
2.	POMO Meditation (awareness of BETA and its relation to money) Guidance and inquiry about the exercise	35
3.	Home practice review Inquiry	20
4.	Exercise on money and opportunity costs: Reflection on scenarios and inquiry	30
5.	3-minutes breathing space on money worry (3MBS-Money Worry): Exercise and inquiry	20
6.	The Easterlin Paradox and the Kahneman–Deaton happiness benchmark: Mini lectures (optional)	20
7.	Your mindful, positive self (MPS): second take Presenting the next steps required for the self-portraits	10
8.	Home practice assignments: Meditation on money 6 of 7 days 3MBS-Money Worry (whenever you notice thoughts about money) Second step of mindful positive self (MPS) assignment: Completing the self-portrait	

12.3.1 POMO Meditation: Awareness of BETA and its relation to money

Money in our contemporary society is basically a source of distress. For those without money it means the constant worry of how to make ends meet and for those with money it involves an enduring preoccupation with not losing it and making it increase. It is almost like a curse: damned if you don't have it and damned if you have it.

The world of money is essentially a world in doing mode, in most cases a *driven* doing mode of the mind. It is a way of experiencing the world with mental narratives revolving around money always in the back of the mind. Money ensures that the brain is steeped in worries and anxiety with a penchant for hyperactivism. Given that most people focus on the outside world of their lives as opposed to the inner aspects of their self, it is hardly surprising that money, as an external driver, takes on such great importance in people's lives.

The intention of this practice is to help individuals switch from a driven doing mode with money as their center of gravity to a mindful being mode. In order to develop more skillful experiences with money people need to (a) give up looking at their thoughts about money as an accepted reality and (b) look at their thoughts about money as mental events, in other words as ideas that emerge and disappear from their awareness.

This way of relating to money will be beneficial for people as they begin to discover new ways of perceiving the significance of money and relating to money issues. I believe that if people want to achieve some relief from their constant thoughts about money they need to shift into a being mode. Being in the present moment helps to move away from addictive to healthy behaviors concerning money. A MIMO relation to money can take many forms; it doesn't necessarily mean aspiring less but can also imply spending more. Recently a participant in one of my MBSAT programs, a young chief marketing officer of a Swiss company, explained to the group how she discovered during the POMO meditation that her relation to money had a dysfunctional aspect: "I kind of realized that I am penny-pinching," she said. "I never spend any money and I really dislike expenditures. During meditation I found out that I need to have a more relaxed attitude towards money. So I decided to give in to a wish and I went and bought myself a bicycle." "Addiction is anything that depletes life while making it appear better," as Clarissa Estés wrote in her book *Women who run with the wolves.*

Benefits of the meditation on money

In an interview at the World Economic Forum in Davos, Switzerland, in January 2015, Mark Bertolini, CEO of Aetna, the world's largest stock quoted insurance company, explained that one of the benefits of mindfulness on economic issues is the possibility of increasing awareness. He told the reporter how he was meditating on economic inequality and as result decided to increase the salaries of his company's lowest-paid employees by 33%. The raise improved the standard of living of 5,700 employees. Clearly, it was not only a compassionate move but also a smart strategy. The decision brought Bertolini and his company enormous gains in reputation. Sharing and generosity often result in benefits that are beyond calculation. It was certainly a win-win situation for all concerned.

Among the specific benefits of meditation on money are the following that go beyond the already known benefits of meditation on breath and body:

a. It helps participants reduce worry and anxiety about money.
b. It opens up new, skillful ways of relating to money and reduces the tendency to become attached to money.

c. The gains in clarity about the significance of money also result in lucidity and increased skillfulness in decision-making, including financial decisions.
d. Meditation on money helps reinforce the idea of decentering from our thoughts about money seeing them for what they are: just thoughts about money.
e. It can lead to creative ways of relating to money that can be more satisfying for the individuals.
f. It helps to differentiate clearly between money problems that are real issues, for example lack of funds to pay the rent, and money worries such as wanting a more luxurious car.

12.3.2 Exercise on money and opportunity costs (MOC)

David was in heaven. He just got the bank's notification that the funds were in his account. This very moment he had become rich. It was the culmination of two years of hard work putting a deal together that made him a millionaire. Now he would be able to realize all his plans: travelling, owning a home, getting a nicer car, and so on. A couple of months after this breakthrough, on the occasion of a routine check up, it turned out that his significant other was diagnosed with a life-threatening illness. It required immediate medical intervention and given the nature of the diagnosis the outcome was uncertain. It could be fatal.

When I met David in one of my positive psychology courses he told me his story and how the shock had changed his life. Suppressing tears he told me about the thoughts that went through his mind at the time—his feelings of guilt, his concern that his partner's disease might be the result of the last two years of intense tension, anxiety, and worry.

Now he had reached his goal of becoming a wealthy, financially independent man, but at what price? I remember him saying that he was ready to swap his hard-earned fortune for a healthy future with his partner. He even told the physician he would give him all the money he had if he could save his partner's life. The physician, a leading authority in the field, told him it was not a question of money but chance; money, he told him, could not buy a way out of the situation, it was a matter of life and death that even he could not control.

Recently, I asked David what he had learned from this experience, looking back after more than 10 years and still with his partner by his side. He answered that the lesson that really struck him was the realization of how relative the value of money is.

"We place so much of our life into the service of it," he said, "and when you most need it, it might not be of help. This discovery has transformed the way I think about money."

It had also impacted his way of living: "I am more relaxed now, living my life as normally as I can, nothing fancy. Most things in life are transient and can change in a moment. In fact," he added, "they are certain to change, and then, my friend, money won't save you. So stop thinking about money worries and enjoy what is now." It sounded very much like Kabat-Zinn, the world-renowned mindfulness teacher.

The point here is not to proselytize but to help participants become aware of their patterns with regard to money and assist them in making informed, mindful, and lucid choices that effectively augment their well-being. Finding a balance between work and the pursuit of money on one side and subjective well-being on the other (family, relationships, sports, leisure) is a challenge.

Figure 12.3 visually depicts the possible trade-offs. It diagrammatically expresses the idea that a certain amount of energy invested in work and getting money is compatible with a certain level of well-being: for example W/M 1 entails SW 1, W/M 2 leads to SW 2, and so on. Obviously, in real life the choices are not as neatly formulated and often they are constrained by circumstances. What the graphic expresses well, however, is that the choices we make come with a cost. In economics the concept is called opportunity costs. Simply put it means that if we choose to increase work and money from W/M 1 to W/M 2, we forego the opportunity to have SW 1. The reduction in the level of well-being from SW 1 to SW 2 is the cost we pay, at the opportunity cost of W/M 2 (Warren et al., 2009).

Hsee (2013) at University of Chicago Booth School of Business has been studying what he calls the over-earning problem or the "extra noise to earn more than

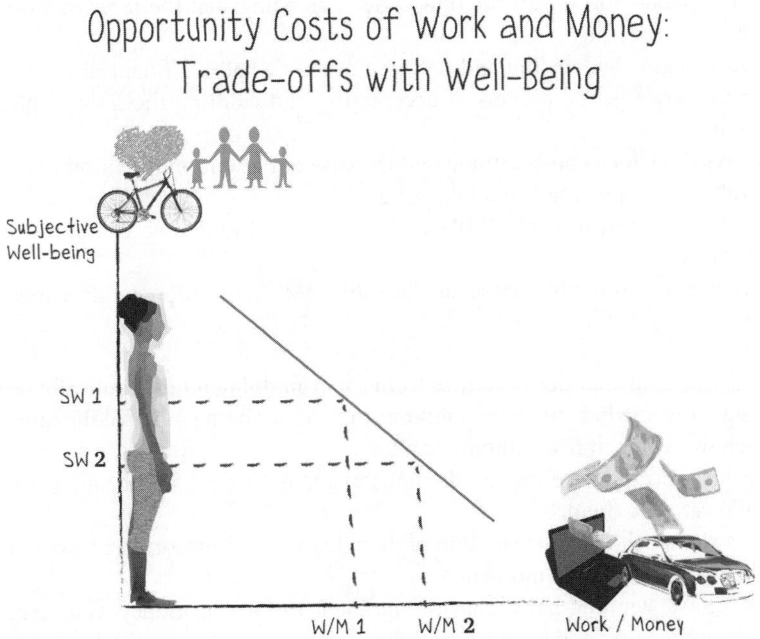

Figure 12.3 Opportunity Costs of Work and Money: Trade-Offs with Well-Being. *Source*: Juan Humberto Young.

what one would consume" (p. 853). He suggests that engaging in overearning causes costs with no apparent benefits and leads to forgoing the pleasure of leisure. He even suggests that over-earners in position of leadership "may lower the well-being of people around them by imposing more pressure on them and by giving less time to their loved ones" (p. 858) and that all of this is happening as result of mindless accumulation, "a tendency to work and earn until feeling tired rather than having enough" (p. 853). Research by Kirk et al. (2015) suggests that mindfulness can moderate excessive reward-seeking behaviors such as classical monetary rewards, which may lead to diminished subjective well-being (p. 752).

In Note 18 the exercise on money and opportunity costs (MOC) is described in more detail. It could be called a reflection exercise as the idea is to present the concept and let the participants discuss possible scenarios or examples from their own experiences in a joint experiential learning process.

12.3.3 3-minutes breathing space on money worry (3MBS-Money Worry)

The 3MBS-Money Worry is the third contextualized mini-practice designed to help with our worries that revolve specifically around our finances. It follows the steps of 3MBS-Worry with the only difference being that the topic of worrying thoughts is predefined.

Step 1 begins by labeling and defining exactly what our financial worry is in order to start a gentle process of decentering and calming the frantic spinning of the mind.

In Step 2 we focus on breathing and increase our attention by counting in- and out-breaths or repeating "inhaling, exhaling."

Step 3 is identical to all 3MBS and consists of expanding awareness to the whole body.

The benefits resemble those of the other 3MBS variations with a focus on money:

1. It helps to switch the awareness from a driven doing mode frantically searching for immediate financial solutions to a calmer being mode of the mind and remove yourself from automatic pilot.
2. It helps to perceive money thoughts as mental events and bring a sense of allowance to them.
3. It switches the time orientation of thoughts from future-oriented worrying to being in the present moment.
4. It allows stepping back from the moment to look at money as an external phenomena shaped by our perception.
5. It promotes an attitude of acceptance to anxious money sensations and reduces unnecessary or disproportionate tension.

12.3.4 The Easterlin paradox and the Kahneman–Deaton happiness benchmark

At this point the participants have gained experiential understanding and exposure to the effect of money on people's lives. The discussion of Easterlin's and Kahneman's research based on the two articles cited brings to the session the findings of a group of heavyweight social scientists. The idea is to provide participants with a wide spectrum of well-grounded, substantiated views as opposed to prescriptions or moralizing.

Richard Easterlin was the first to identify the anomaly that in macro-economics an increase in income doesn't necessarily correlate with an increase in happiness. This is the argument of the first paper.

The second paper presents the findings of extensive research by two Nobel Prize winners. It argues that although increases in income can improve a person's evaluation of their life, it doesn't improve their emotional well-being.

This should allow for an inspiring discussion that the teacher can moderate after briefly explaining the essence of the articles and inviting those who are interested to read the articles for themselves.

a. *The happiness–income paradox revisited.*
   Easterlin, R. A., Angelescu McVey, L., Switek, M., Sawangfa, O., & Smith Zweig, J. (2010). *PNAS, 107*(52), 22463–22468.
b. *High income improves evaluation of life but not emotional well-being.*
   Daniel Kahneman (Nobel Prize, 2000) and Angus Deaton (Nobel Prize 2015). (2010). *PNAS, 107*(38), 16489–16493.

The discussion can also be used to summarize the learning gained in this the session and as a wrap-up of the topic of money.

12.3.5 The mindful positive self (MPS): Second take

When resuming the introduction of MPS (the second take) it may be worthwhile to briefly reiterate that a mindful positive self consists of two components: a self-portrait of how we are in our best moments and an action plan based on how to multiply moments of flourishing and make them more sustainable.

After Session 5 participants will have requested feedback from a number of people in the form of anecdotes and stories that highlight their strengths and special features when they are able to fully deploy their potential.

The task in this second part is to establish the actual self-portrait. A key element is a written description, detailing how a person acts at his or her personal best, based on their strengths and the specific circumstances. The written narrative may be accompanied by whatever the individual thinks will provide further depth to their portrait. It could be anything from mementos to photos or drawings.

To prepare an evocative portrait the participants should be imaginative and use their creative talents.

The main steps in this second part of the process are:

a. Remembering stories of fulfilling moments and adding them to the feedback from contacts.
b. Analyzing all the narratives collected, both your own and feedback from others.
c. Complementing the results with information from other sources (prizes, pictures, quotes from letters or emails, etc.).
d. Establishing a vivid, evocative self-portrait of oneself in moments of fulfillment: The main part will be an essay that can be accompanied or complemented by pictures, mementos, or whatever the participants consider important.

Guidelines that may be useful for teachers can be found in Note 21. Detailed information and tips about individual steps are also provided in Handout 2 for the participants.

Establishing the self-portrait has a healing effect and is a great exercise for experiential learning. We are so used to critical evaluations focusing on shortcomings that most people are full of self-doubts, even reluctant to take a good look at themselves. Defining the mindful positive self opens up new vistas that inspire. The ultimate goal is the integration of the self that one aspires to be with what one really is. When the two coincide there is no more pretending or hiding, no façade or mask, whether conscious or unconscious. The resulting authenticity has an aesthetic quality in my view. I think it corresponds to what the Dutch painter Piet Mondrian called "the aesthetic expression of oneself."

13

Session 7: Strategic Awareness III—Friendliness: Opening the Heart

13.1 Introduction

The friendship that is being offered insistently tends to be opportunistic,
one that sings its deeds is short-lived, a written one is just literary.
Only the friendship that is muted and inconspicuous,
but can be felt by the unselfish reality of its facts, is true friendship.

These verses was dedicated to my mother, Eva Maria, by her literature teacher, Arsenio Blanco. It was written when my mother was growing up in a girl's boarding school and sometimes feeling a bit sad and lonely.

Once upon a time a person who was searching for truth prayed and asked: "Lord, what is the difference between heaven and hell?" And the Lord answered: "It is quite simple. Let me show you." Two doors appeared in front of the seeker. "Let's go through the first door," the Almighty said. They stepped into a room with a large round table and on top of the table was a large dish of delicious food. Sitting around the table were emaciated and feeble looking people. They had very long spoons, so long in fact that it was almost impossible to handle them and put food in their mouths, so they were all on the point of starving. "Now," said the Lord, "let's go to the other room." As they walked through the second door, there was an identical table with the same delicious food. The people seated around the table had the same overly long spoons but they looked happy and healthy and were talking and laughing. "What does this mean?" the seeker asked and God answered: "Wait, you will understand in a moment when they eat their meal." The people picked up the spoons by their long handles, dipped them in the dish and started to feed the person across the table, easily reaching the other's mouth from the distance. Then they took turns and kept feeding each other in this way until the big dish was empty. "In the first room you witnessed hell, here you are experiencing

Mindfulness-Based Strategic Awareness Training: A Complete Program for Leaders and Individuals, First Edition. Juan Humberto Young.

Companion website: www.wiley.com/go/humbertoyoung/mbsat

heaven," said God to the seeker. "In the first room people are greedy, only thinking about themselves and thus creating their own hell. Here they are friends, they love each other, they cooperate and care for one another, creating heaven."

This tale, by an anonymous author, is known as the parable of the long spoons.

Even in nature many species display friendly cooperative behavior. For example an elaborate form of cooperation was discovered among small vampire bats in Panama and Costa Rica. They need to feed on blood every two or three days, otherwise they die. Each evening they go hunting for food and not all are lucky. So in order to survive they have developed a system of mutual support: those who hunted successfully regurgitate food and give it to the unlucky ones so they can survive. However, the little bats keep a record of the less cooperative members. When these selfish bats are unable to find food, the group refuses to share with them in retaliation for their self-serving behavior. This type of reciprocal cooperation is known in game theory as tit for tat. It is a natural way of flushing uncooperative members out of the group and in biology it is considered a most successful natural selection strategy.

13.1.1 Friendliness in organizations (or the lack of it)

In an interview about his book on leadership training—the book was essentially a far-reaching critique of current training practices—the distinguished Stanford Business School Professor J. Pfeffer mentioned an intriguing study. In this study people were asked whether they would forgo a substantial salary increase if instead they could fire their boss. Over a third preferred to dispense with the salary increase in exchange for a chance to fire their bosses, revealing, as Pfeffer observed, a desperate state of affairs in many organizations. Pfeffer also referred to research, by the well-known Center of Creative Leadership, which concluded that one in every two leaders is ineffective in their current role. That's a whopping 50%. It is not hard to imagine the strained working atmosphere and lack of wholehearted cooperation prevailing under such circumstances.

Recently one of my former students at the Master's program of positive leadership and strategy, a chairman of a subsidiary of one of the global universal banks, told me about his constant fights with head office to get resources for the development of his staff. He told me: "The truth is that no one really cares. I have just come from visiting someone who is suffering from burnout having worked for more than 35 years with the bank. He almost cried when I called and told him I wanted to see him, because no-one, not a single team member or colleague, had visited him. Not even his supposed friends. We [meaning his bank] take people, squeeze everything of them and when we don't need them anymore we just discard them like changing a piece of equipment."

If the research of INSEAD Business School Professor de Vries, Oxford University Psychologist Dutton and other eminent researchers is correct about the light psychopathological elements in the personality of many leaders

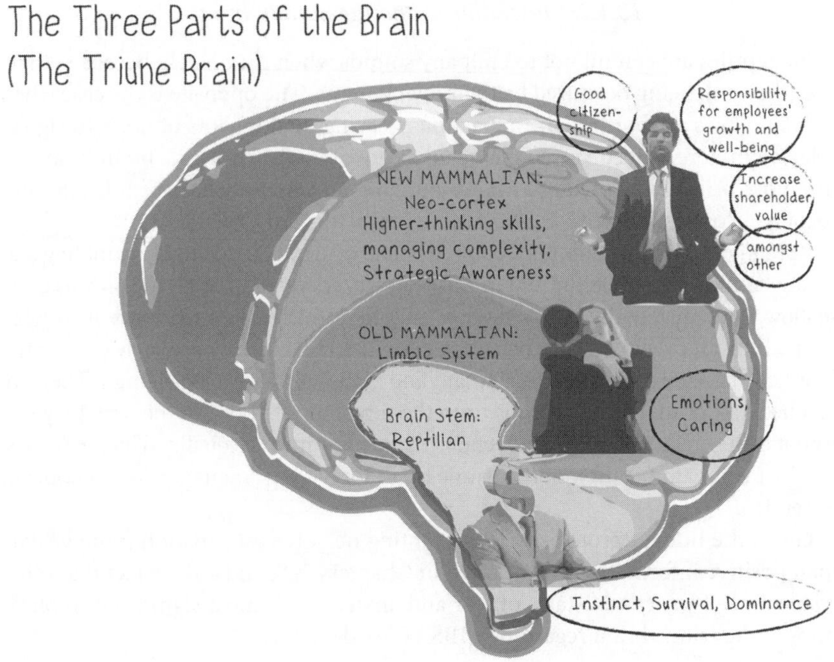

Figure 13.1 The Three Parts of the Brain (The Triune Brain). *Source*: Juan Humberto Young.

(discussed in Chapter 6), then it is a problem that no amount of the normal, management-oriented leadership training at Chicago, Harvard, Stanford, Wharton, IE, and other business schools can solve. The salient features of many successful managers and leaders include narcissistic tendencies, lack of empathy, and a proclivity to manipulation—not the best preconditions to develop genuine cooperation in an organization. These are issues of emotional personality fragmentation that usually date back to the early stages in personal development. Given that there is seldom an opportunity to diagnose the mental conditions of these leaders, what is required are training approaches that are flexible enough to allow participants, if they so choose, to explore their inner life on their own. What is needed are training approaches that help leader personalities expand their self-awareness and enable them to understand and use their underutilized cognitive, emotional, and sensorial capacities. Only this way will it be possible to overcome the hazards and predispositions of those parts of the human brain that have been programmed for survival—often described as the reptilian brain (see "Brain Stem: Reptilian" in Figure 13.1)—and that seem to play an important role in the behavior of these personalities. And that is what the techniques of mindfulness-based training and positive psychology can help achieve on an entirely self-motivated, voluntary basis for both leaders and individuals.

13.1.2 Friendliness and the human brain

Some reptiles are careful not to emit any sounds when they hatch, because otherwise they risk being devoured by their own parents. The opposite is the case when human babies are born: their first action is crying, making lots of noise to signal: "Hey, I am here, I need you to please take care of me." The reptile brain is among the most primitive. Already at birth humans and mammals have a brain with social neurons (see Box 13.1, The Triune Brain, for more details.)

Recently I saw a short film of a baby elephant, evidently a mammal, stumbling and falling halfway in a pit at the zoo in Zurich, Switzerland. Although the pit was quite shallow immediately the baby's mother and an auntie rushed to rescue it in what seemed almost over-protective behavior. The video clip went immediately viral on the Internet with over a million hits. Humans and mammals have a social brain. They live in a network of social connections from the time they are born to the time they die. And it is the quality of these connections that determines the quality of people's lives.

What is the implication of the triune brain for leaders, managers, and people in general?

Given the human propensity for weighting negative information more heavily than positive information (mentioned in Chapters 2, 8, and 10)—a fact that often results in self-generated states of fear and anxiety—the most significant implications of the triune brain regarding MBSAT are described:

Prone to primal reflexes

Commonly we are not fully conscious of our experiences and consequently it is often the most ancient, primal parts of our brain that guide us despite our belief that we are thoughtful and rational. As these parts of our brain, principally the reptilian section, are predisposed to defensive behaviors and territoriality, the question that is raised is whether frequent use of this ancestral part of the brain is adaptive in today's domesticated environment compared to its application in the wilderness in ancient times? Obviously the efficacy of the reptilian brain in today's society is limited. It can still be useful in certain circumstances and might possibly serve in situations of sudden crisis. However, keeping it in overdrive, as is so often the case with many people, especially at work, only creates adverse consequences like stress and anxiety.

Exposed to opposed signals

The other question is: What kind of training is needed to enable people to use the new, more advanced, parts of their brains at their maximum capacity? In tertiary education, for example, in business schools, we supposedly train future leaders and managers to increase their cognitive abilities. In reality what we do is reinforce their less advanced parts of the brain with theories like hyper-competition, first-move advantage, fights for market share, and a war-laden vocabulary. In addition, the evaluation methods prevailing in education, especially the forced-ranking

Box 13.1 The Triune Brain

Paul MacLean, the famous US physician and neuroscientist who taught at the Yale School of Medicine, proposed an evolutionary view of the brain subdividing it into three parts corresponding to the three evolutionary stages of mankind visualized in Figure 13.1 (Newman and Harris, 2009).

The most ancient, primitive part is called the reptilian brain, also known as the R-complex corresponding to the basal ganglia. For MacLean this part of the brain is responsible for instincts and survival behaviors related to dominance, simple reproductive behaviors, arousal (including aggression), territorial behaviors, and similar basic reflexes.

The second part of the brain is what MacLean called the paleo-mammalian brain, also called the limbic system and including the amygdalae, hypothalamus, and cingulate cortex. It corresponds to the evolution of behavior typical of more developed mammals such as motivation, learning, memory, and emotions relating to feeding and other parental behavior.

The third part of the brain, the neomammalian, corresponds to the neocortex found only in higher mammals and human beings. It is the part of the brain responsible for conscious thought, language, planning, abstraction, and self-awareness.

Simply put, the difficulty is that the three parts of the brain do not necessarily work well together. Each has its own purpose and each processes information differently. They also work at different speeds. While the neocortex, where consciousness is located, needs 600 milliseconds to process an experience and take it to conscious awareness, the other more instinctive parts of our brain require only a fraction of that, approximately around 100 milliseconds, which means that when we become conscious of a fact, the amygdala has already processed it and possibly already emitted impulses for action. This implies that people often act on impulses from the more primitive parts of the brain, which explains the habitually agitated and defensive reactions of people instead of serene pacifying responses from their more evolved brain components.

Although MacLean's brain theory has been demonstrated to possess some flaws, it is still popular with the scientific community because it provides a simplified, yet accurate overall, explanation as the reptilian brain is indeed responsible for behavior related to survival and territoriality, the paleo-mammalian for nurturing and reciprocity behaviors, and the neocortex for advanced cognition, planning, and simulations.

systems used at many top universities, stimulate competition instead of cooperation. Therefore it is not surprising that competitive behavior is the norm among students even outside examination rooms. In class discussions during my studies at Chicago Booth and Harvard my classmates' top priority seemed to be scoring points against each other, not exchanging or advancing ideas.

One of MBSAT's implicit intentions is to help participants achieve higher levels of coherence between the three parts of the triune brain, so that each part knows when it is appropriate to act, as it is only by operating within the clarity of a well-integrated triune brain that one can achieve higher levels of well-being for oneself and others.

13.1.3 Friendliness and systemic growth

I believe that complementing the necessary functional knowledge with training for higher levels of consciousness such as mindfulness-based strategic awareness—MBSAT, and self-awareness would be beneficial not only for individuals but also for groups. That is precisely what training in mindfulness and positive psychology can achieve: Mindfulness enhances meta-cognition and positive psychology fosters a constructive, evolutionarily advanced approach to life. Together they can help individuals flourish in today's reality.

"At Apple we believe that work should be more than just improving your own self. It should be about improving the lives of others as well," Tim Cook, Apple's CEO, declared when he referred to a new culture of leadership at the company (*Fortune*, November 1, 2015). Just as Apple is on target with their products, CEO Tim Cook seems to get it right with the new rules of leadership. What he articulates is a model of friendship based on connection and responsibility: the right of individuals to grow and to do so in freedom but in a related, considerate, responsible, and responsive manner by assisting others with their own needs to grow and develop.

How can one grow an organization if the people working in it don't grow or if only one group grows while the others stagnate? Commonsense suggests that if an organizational system wants to grow, all its parts should grow, at least this seems a more efficient and effective way of achieving growth. It is strange how many leaders fail to see this rather simple argument.

The same goes for smaller social structures like teams and families. Improvement in the kids' behavior requires that the parents, too, continue to grow personally. For this reason Bögels and Restifo (2014) have developed a mindfulness-based program for parents and children. As to mindfulness in politics, the US congressman Tim Ryan wrote a book entitled *A mindful nation*. He argues that mindfulness practices are necessary in modern society because it is mindfulness that teaches people how to keep growing personally and how to connect with fellow human beings and be kind to them. Ryan also says we must learn to see the problems other people have and how they deal with them. It is a way of learning to respond more compassionately.

13.1.4 Suppressing friendliness

How people cope with the distressing situations around them has always been something I have sought to understand. "How can you live with so much distress around you?" is a question I have asked people from all over the world: people living in developing and emerging economies with endemic poverty; people in Europe confronted with depressing issues of unemployment in their neighborhood; people living in cities with countless homeless and beggars on the streets. Here are some of the answers: "You just need to close your eyes." "Stop thinking about it and close your heart." "It's their own fault, if they are in this dire situation."

An elderly lady in Tel Aviv told me: "You get used to it. I was in a Nazi concentration camp," and with these words she showed me the indelible identification number on her arm. "You just suppress your emotions and close your heart. The world is cynical. Look," she went on jovially being amused to talk German with a Latin American, "when I came here in the fifties, women from Europe like me could not marry local Jews. Orientals we called them and we considered ourselves as better educated. In the meantime they have become rich because they are better at business and now it is OK to marry them with their money."

On another occasion I was talking to one of my clients in Geneva—he was the head of a company that was merging with one of its competitors. "So many people are going to lose their jobs, many middle-aged employees for whom it will be really tough to find work again," I commented as he told me about his plans to fire redundant personnel. "Look," he replied, "we are in Switzerland. They will get generous unemployment benefits and after a while they will find other opportunities. In any case I need to do this and I can't put my heart and emotions into it. I need to act rationally, from my head and for the benefit of the company."

The father of my godchild, a retired managing director of a Swiss universal bank, told me about a conference he attended where the CEO of his institution responded to requests from employees that the senior management should pay more attention to the personnel's well-being. The CEO told the team leaders: "Neither I nor any of you are responsible for the well-being of the bank's employees. They come here to work. If they need love or attention, they can buy themselves a dog and get from it all the attention and love they want, but not here."

All of these responses to the suffering of others boil down to a single strategy: suppressing one's emotions by closing one's heart. If everybody does it, it must be efficient, right? But wait, isn't the heart the origin of humans' most powerful positive emotion, love? This means that all of these acts of suppression are, in reality, unloving acts. And isn't it also true that positive emotions are the source of constructive, creative acts? As positive psychologists have discovered, it is with positive emotions that we open our cognitive and emotional capacities to a range of skillful possibilities. Consequently, acting from a closed heart must result in poor, uncreative acting—isn't that so? Syllogistically, as the logical opposite to constructive behaviors that build, grow, and expand, uncreative behavior must imply a destructive dimension.

The Dalai Lama often says that the seeds of compassion and friendliness—wanting people not to suffer, being kind to them, and being pleased when others are happy—are already inside us. If this is true (and I believe it is) then when people speak of suppressing the emotions of caring, compassion, and friendliness, they are actually saying that they have a positive core that they need to suppress in order to get on with their lives in this harsh world, which now, more than ever, is characterized by VUCA (volatility, uncertainty, complexity, and ambiguity).

Even nice people sometimes simply forget about friendliness. A friend of mine, also a high-level manager in an organization with a staff of several hundred, told me recently: "It is strange, in my company almost everyone is unhappy, but some of us, a very small group, are doing extremely well." I asked him: "And what are you doing to better the situation of the others, the unhappy ones?" He looked at me and, somewhat ashamed, replied: "Nothing really. I should be doing something for them, you are right."

13.1.5 Human nature and the cultivation of compassion

So what are we humans after all: hard and uncaring beings or loving souls? Different thinkers at different times have found opposing answers. Adam Smith, the great eighteenth-century economist and philosopher wrote: "People of the same trade seldom meet together, even for merriment and diversion, but the conversation ends in a conspiracy against the public, or in some contrivance to raise prices" (1776).

Humberto Maturana, the Harvard-educated evolutionary biologist, in his book *Liebe und Spiele* (1997) came to different conclusions. He described human nature as "loving animals," because, as he noted, they have the physiology of loving beings, no matter at what age. What people want in life is love. Everything people do is about being loved. People enjoy caring for others and want to be cared for; they enjoy being caressed and long to be caressed; they like to cooperate and do things together with others. Under competition people suffer, even if the winners get some joy out it. People don't enjoy relations that present them with demands and exigencies but what they enjoy is being invited.

Maturana's description aligns itself perfectly with the human needs identified by the self determination theory (SDT) discussed in Chapter 1: we want to be in relationships, and we want to be autonomous and competent at what we do. Love does not require learning, either we allow it to grow or deny it; aggression on the other hand needs to be cultivated. Maturana maintained that love is the emotion that expands human intelligence while aggression restrains it, a fact that positive psychology later demonstrated based on painstaking empiric research.

The neuroscientist R. Davison (Weng et al., 2013) at the University of Wisconsin, one of the most experienced and knowledgeable researchers regarding the effects of compassion on the brain, has observed that meditation on friendliness activates the insula, which is involved in social emotions, the amygdala as part of the network of empathy, and the right temporal-parietal junction crucial for perspective taking.

Perspective taking is particularly significant in connection with MBSAT. Davison's findings not only confirm the results of positive psychology that positive emotions expand awareness, but they also establish a connection between meditation on friendliness and strategic awareness.

Although still too early to provide definitive answers, research into compassion suggests that the practice of friendliness has the potential to generate positive effects on others as well as on the practitioners themselves.

Kuyken et al. (2010) suggest that in MBCT (mindfulness-based cognitive therapy) one of the mechanisms for the prevention of depression is cultivating self-compassion for the whole duration of the therapy and the capacity to embrace whatever difficulty is present. According to their research this creates a powerful healing effect for people who have suffered episodes of depression in the past.

At Stanford Medical School the Center for Compassion and Altruism Research and Education (CCARE) is producing careful and rigorous research on ways of cultivating compassion for individuals and society, honoring the Dalai Lama's (n.d.) statement that "the cultivation of compassion is no longer a luxury, but a necessity, if our species is to survive."

One of CCARE's recent findings relates to the detrimental effects of mind wandering. Their study revealed that a wandering mind is not only an unhappy mind but also a less-caring mind. Training in compassion was found to reduce mind wandering on unpleasant thoughts and increase mind wandering on pleasant thoughts. CCARE also worked with Dr T. Jinpa, an eminent Buddhist, translator, and editor for the Dalai Lama and holder of a PhD in theology from Cambridge University. Together they developed an 8-weeks protocol, compassion cultivation training, to spread the benefits of practicing and cultivating compassion. CCARE is precisely at the epicenter of today's most technologically advanced business organizations in Silicon Valley. Perhaps it can have a countervailing effect in a culture driven by personal success and individualism.

13.1.6 Obstacles in training and cultivating friendliness

If friendliness and compassion have such an enormous healing and well-being potential the question is why are they not more prevalent. Based on what we have seen and discussed it seems that culturally driven factors are at work. In a world of VUCA it seems there are a series of obstacles that may prevent people from developing and cultivating friendliness. Some of the barriers have their origin in doctrines and theories that are taught at business schools and in economics. Other barriers are the result of long-held cultural views concerning what is appropriate behavior for living in an increasingly complicated, competitive, and volatile world where a dog-eat-dog mentality is on the ascendancy. The following factors all contribute to impeding compassion and friendliness.

Factors detrimental to compassion and friendliness

1. *Zero-sum-games*: Despite the trend to talk about win-win approaches, most behavior is characterized by zero-sum games where one person's gain is another person's loss. In part this is due to our primal reflexes as discussed above. In addition it is ingrained in many processes and structures. The principal of competition is largely based on the premise of "either you or me." This personal utility maximization is often shortsighted. And that is the reason why lawyers, according to Seligman, are prone to depression and other mental afflictions as they work in a system geared towards zero-sum games, either losing or winning for their clients.
2. *Moral hazard*: People in positions of power are most exposed to situations of moral hazard. They can take all types of risky decisions knowing that even if they are wrong the consequences will be borne by someone else. It is the privatization of benefits for the decision-makers if things go well; if things go wrong, however, it is the public or public institutions that are burdened with the cost or damage. It was moral hazard in combination with other systemic flaws that was at the heart of the financial crisis in the early 2000s. Bankers took all kinds of risks knowing that big bonuses were there for them if things kept running and someone else would pay the bill if the system was to collapse. Under these circumstances there is little or no incentive to behave with compassion and friendliness.
3. *Valuing being tough*: The capacities to endure and persist are highly regarded qualities. The strength to endure whatever hardship comes our way is seen as a winning quality in today's working environment and even in the private sphere. "She is tough, she can take it," is a great compliment. It is the idea that with sheer determination one can overcome without complaint whatever adversities are thrown at you.
4. *Rationality*: Previously in this book we have discussed the limitations of what we consider to be rational (Chapter 1, biases) and the potential deformation stemming from being driven by our head (Chapter 8). Rationality, as a prime guiding force in people's lives, is well received in our society as it comes from the head. That which comes from the heart is considered emotional, not well planned, and perceived as a weakness. "He takes decisions too personally. He is emotional and impulsive" are comments that can damage a career. Given that compassion is an innate quality in humans it often conveys an impression of being impulsive, which makes it an unwelcome quality in a postmodern world emphasizing rationality. A case in point was the mixed public reaction in October 2015, when John Boehner, the long-standing Speaker of the US House of Representatives, a warm and sensitive man, was being deeply moved by the words of Pope Francis to the US Congress. Boehner's tears were the topic of conversation everywhere for days and they marked Boehner's decision to resign from the position of speaker. However, as Damasio (2006) with his studies has amply demonstrated, rationality cannot exist without emotions.

5. *Perfectionism*: The widespread praise of perfectionism puts demands on people to be perfect in every aspect of their lives. This implies an ability to adapt and comply with the prevailing ideals of society: having the right look, the right job, and so on. As it is almost impossible to live up to the ever-expanding standards of success and to achieve all that seems necessary to attain happiness in this society, many people slip into self-criticism and states of low self-esteem, even self-hatred, that prevent the seeds of compassion from germinating. It impedes kindness and friendliness to others as well as to oneself.
6. *Glorifying ambition and greed*: Success and money are seen as the real motivators. In the movie *Wall Street*, actor Michael Douglas as the financial tycoon, Gordon Gekko, says to an assembly of investors: "Greed, for lack of a better word, is good. Greed is right. Greed works. Greed clarifies, cuts through, and captures the essence of the evolutionary spirit." It is in fact a fictional replication of a real speech given by Ivan Boesky a year earlier to the graduation class of 1986 at the University of California Berkeley School of Business. At the time Boesky was at the peak of his career in finance that was in fact built on illegal insider trading. Literally Boesky said: "I think greed is healthy. You can be greedy and still feel good about yourself." That year he was on the cover of *Time* magazine; a few years later he went to prison for securities fraud. Anomalous forms of greed seem to me the antithesis of compassion. By worshipping greed popular culture adds to the deformation and stigmatizes compassionate people as losers and weaklings. However, nothing needs more courage and bravery than responding with caring to uncaring acts.

These factors are socially constructed. They are part of the conditioning that directs people's BETA (Body sensations, Emotions/feelings, Thoughts and Action Impulses) towards suppressing their natural, biological disposition of friendliness that human beings possess from birth. However, as we start to build layers of behavioral, emotional, and cognitive restraint we immunize our hearts, firstly to our own suffering and then to the suffering of others. We simple lose the capacity to fully experience being the loving creatures that we are.

13.1.7 Friendliness as a choice to make

In the ancient Greek epic *Iliad* Homer tells how Hephaestus, the God of blacksmiths and craftsmen, creates a shield for Achilles, the hero. Engraved on the shield is the picture of two cities, one prosperous, in peace, ruled with care and justice; the other in chaos, ruled by warriors pillaging their own people, driven by avarice and brutality. The second dismal city was the world of the Iliad in which even the supposedly invincible Achilles ends up dead. As powerful a warrior as he was, he had one weak spot where he could be wounded: his heel.

In his other epic, the *Odyssey*, Homer presents the reader with polar opposites: on one side are the terrifying challenges the hero Odysseus has to overcome: the one-eyed Cyclops, terrifying beings of huge proportions, and the witch-goddess

Circe who turns half of Odysseus' crew into swine, because of their greed, desire, and lack of awareness. On the other side is Odysseus, the hero: aware, emotionally balanced, and skillful, mastering all ordeals with bravery, and with a strong sense of purpose. After years of tribulations he returns home and takes his homeland back from the traitors pillaging his palace. With the support, generosity, and compassion of his loyal friends the years of pilgrimage end in peace and Odysseus comes home to his true nature of an open heart.

These mythical stories seek to confront us with the fundamental questions: What role do we want to play in the often compulsive chain of life events and what is the role of caring and friendliness in our lives? With the advances in mindfulness and positive psychology technologies and their scientifically proven benefits, it should be a relatively easy choice to aspire to the life of Odysseus.

In this session we look at friendliness as an expression of our social brain. We learn that when we are attuned to other people's social neural circuitry it helps us expand our awareness beyond self-centered needs, encompassing fellow human beings in our closer collective groups (organizations, family and friends, etc.) as well as in broader society. In the process we will become more loving beings.

Mark Bertolini, the CEO of Aetna, is for me the prototype of the leaders of the future. He represents a wonderful living example of what I have tried to explain here. As result of his expanded strategic awareness from practicing mindfulness he decided to ameliorate the economic conditions of his employees (friendliness in action), a decision that had side effects in other areas (the strategic awareness dimension), and translated into benefits (more motivated, creative, engaged employees) for his organization as a whole.

With Bertolini's example we can see strategic awareness in action. With the technology of mindfulness and an attitude of caring Bertolini was able to expand his awareness beyond an immediate concern for short-term financial results and transcend any institutionalized barriers such as the capital market opinions and pressure. He was able to take a strategically aware decision that could position his firm on a solid and sustainable footing for the future. He gained the respect and commitment of 5,700 employees and that is not a trivial achievement in today's environment where more than a third of employees would swap a salary raise for an opportunity to fire their boss (see Section 13.1.1).

13.2 Session Organization, Coverage, and Sequence

The practices in this session introduce a different form of mindfulness practice geared towards opening people's hearts. It also introduces friendliness in communication based on a positive psychology approach to communicating. As the 8-week program draws to a close we begin to work toward the last session by preparing a planning exercise to enhance individual flourishing and personal growth after the program is finished.

Session 7: Strategic Awareness III—Friendliness: Opening the Heart

		Time allocated in minutes Duration: 2½ to 3 hours
1.	Arrival meditation	5
2.	Meditation on friendliness Guidance and inquiry about the exercise	35
3.	Active constructive responding: Connecting a friendly heart with a friendly tongue	15
4.	Home practice review and inquiry including discussion on the mindful positive self assignment (participants' final version)	20
5.	Is the universe friendly? A reflection by A. Einstein	15
6.	SOPA Part I (strengths, opportunities, and positive actions): Inventories of activities, assets, and opportunities exercise	20
7.	3-minutes breathing space on friendliness (3MBS-Friendliness)	20
8.	The Oishi poem for getting talented people: Reading on site session	10
9.	Home practice assignment:	5
	Friendliness meditation	4 of 7 days
	3MBS-Friendliness	(whenever needed)
	Practicing positive communication with the active/constructive approach	continuously
	Practicing a strength	daily
	Completing SOPA Part I	

13.3 Exercises and Practices of Session 7

In this session the sitting meditation focuses on friendliness following the usual brief arriving meditation. Then we focus on a mindful, positive communication practice to sensitize participants to what genuinely friendly communication entails, namely actively constructive responses. After the home practice review and inquiry we read together Albert Einstein's reflection on friendliness and the universe. We start to work with a tool called SOPA: strengths, opportunities, and positive actions, essentially a planning exercise for the mindful positive self (MPS) to be continued in Session 8. Here in Session 7 we start with the basis for SOPA, an individual inventory of activities, assets, and opportunities. SOPA is followed by another variation of 3MBS, the 3-minutes breathing space on friendliness. The session concludes with an ancient poem on how to recruit talented people followed by the homework assignments.

13.3.1 Meditation on friendliness

Until now the practices have been geared towards developing and cultivating attention in the tradition described by William James (n.d.), the father of modern psychology: "The faculty of voluntarily bringing back a wandering attention, over and over again, is the very root of judgment, character, and will ... An education which should improve this faculty would be education par excellence" (James, 1961). The past six weeks have been exactly this: an education of attention and awareness escorting the mind back again and again to the intended focus of the practice and observing without judging whatever arises in our awareness with acceptance and curiosity. This helps us to realize that difficulties often arise in the mind (not as external phenomena as we often assume) and that our BETA (Body sensations, Emotions/feelings, Thoughts and Action impulses) are temporary and impermanent, causing our own self to change constantly. The practical outcomes of intentional attention regulation and awareness should result in new views of personal experiences with heightened clarity and the ability to respond to those experiences with equanimity and a sense of balance instead of being pulled back and forth between the two diametrically opposed forces dominating our life: likes and dislikes.

In addition to the transformative influence on the practitioner's self, the practices presented here will have a direct impact on relationships with others. What is being cultivated is an opening of the heart and the capacity for friendliness with others.

Considering what social scientists predict regarding the changing nature of our society, particularly involving the ongoing "second machine revolution," our future challenges are mind-boggling. The foundations of our economy, work, and the availability of jobs are starting to erode. Recently, the physicist Stephen Hawking observed:

> If machines produce everything we need, the outcome will depend on how things are distributed. Everyone can enjoy a life of luxurious leisure if the machine-produced wealth is shared, or most people can end up miserably poor if the machine-owners successfully lobby against wealth distribution. So far, the trend seems to be toward the second option, with technology driving ever-increasing inequality. (Kaufman, 2015)

If this is the future of humanity I believe we will need to open not only our minds but also our hearts to find compelling solutions that accommodate people in the turbulent times ahead.

What is being cultivated here is a friendly heart capable of empathizing with its own distress and with that of others as well as enjoying its own good fortune and the happiness of others. The two orientations of friendliness—kindness to oneself and kindness to the world around us—are necessary complements.

Without self-awareness of our own feelings and needs it would be impossible to be sensitive to the people we interact with. Conversely it would be hard or even impossible to develop a healthy and balanced consideration for our own needs. Figure 13.2 visualizes these two dimensions and establishes four types of heart in four quadrants.

The upper-left quadrant symbolizes the friendly heart that is high in both friendliness to self and others. To the right is the narcissistic heart, high in self-love and low in friendliness to others. In this quadrant are the people that Professor de Vries from INSEAD called psychopaths lite (see Chapter 6). Cold hearts in the adjoining quadrant are low in friendliness to themselves and to others. Professor Dutton of the University of Oxford would call them definite psychopaths. Finally, the servile heart is high in friendliness to others and low in friendliness to self. Individuals with these characteristics often operate as lackeys to people in higher positions.

Except for people with pathological conditions most individuals in real life will have a default quadrant but will also manifest behavior from other quadrants. For example, a narcissistic person might execute acts of magnanimity that the beneficiaries will interpret as generous but those acts will be more about reinforcing their ego than being genuinely magnanimous. Nudging and bending our hearts to

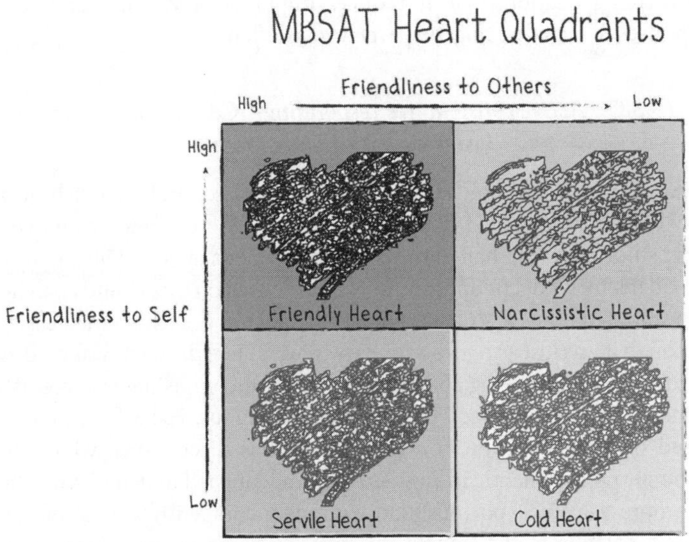

Figure 13.2 MBSAT Heart Quadrants. *Source*: Juan Humberto Young.

the higher-left quadrant (the friendly-heart quadrant) is the intention of the practices presented in this session.

Benefits of meditation on friendliness

In addition to the great personal gains all mindfulness practices provide, this practice generates invaluable benefits that are urgently needed in today's complex world:

a. Meditation on friendliness helps to counterbalance the tendency for people to close their hearts. It helps cultivate an attitude of openness.
b. It promotes a constructive stance of self-friendliness that mitigates aspirations of perfectionism. It reduces the negative effects of low self-friendliness including a lack of self-confidence and self-hatred. Consequently it nurtures self-esteem.
c. It cultivates openness towards others that can result in positive actions. Marc Benioff, CEO of salesforce.com decided to make adjustments to the salary scale in his company to ensure that women and men receive equal pay. He had been involved in mindfulness activities for years and had monks living in some of his houses. This is not to say that for people to be open-hearted they must necessarily be dedicated to mindfulness. However, observing people with advanced mindfulness attitudes one notices that all of them are to some degree involved in technologies of higher consciousness (of the mind, body, and heart).
d. Meditation on friendliness connects heart, mind, and body and thus helps people live more coherent lives. This improves the chances of achieving higher levels of flourishing.
e. Meditation on friendliness promotes a quality of forgiveness, which is crucial for thriving relationships. It reduces impulses of violence and revenge as responses to acts that may be perceived as offensive.

13.3.2 Active constructive responding—Connecting a friendly heart with a friendly tongue

At Harvard Kennedy School (HKS) my tutor Professor Robert Reich, former US Secretary of Labor, suggested that I take classes at the business school (HBS). He signed my study plan with half of the classes to be taken at HBS. During my time the schools had distinct didactic approaches. HKS focused on theory and analytics, while HBS concentrated on case studies. The case studies approach seemed easier at first sight although it was just as rigorous in its own way. Here the focus was on discussion, class participation, and being able to bring forward compelling arguments to solve the business cases, an approach that made HBS famous. Half of each course grade was based on how well you contributed to class discussions, which created a point–counterpoint dynamic in class as each student tried to demonstrate his or her point as more valuable—obviously an extremely competitive mode of communicating. As a reaction to the competitive pressure some students formed groups to discuss the cases in advance and prepare class-participation strategies. Often we decided on what points we should make. During class discussions we supported each other's points. This is how an informal cooperative communication strategy developed to counter the competitive, adversarial style of the school. Once I asked Professor Cash, at the time the star of the HBS information technology group, why the school cultivated this strong emphasis on class participation that was driving those who were not native English speakers crazy. He responded: "What is the value of great ideas, if they are confined in a person's head? We train people to communicate their ideas forcefully and with good arguments effect change." I had to agree with him. However, the way you communicate makes all the difference, it effects change. As Lieberman (2013) says: "A kind word is worth as much to the brain in terms of rewards as a certain amount of money" (p. 78).

Positive psychologist Shelley Gable's research identifies communication along two dimensions. One dimension is the intensity of action, going from active to passive forms of communication. The other dimension refers to communication content that can be either destructive or constructive. This results in four permutations, which are illustrated in Figure 13.3.

a. The active/constructive quadrant means communication that is unmistakably supportive and accompanied by gestures and body language that clearly expresses empathy.

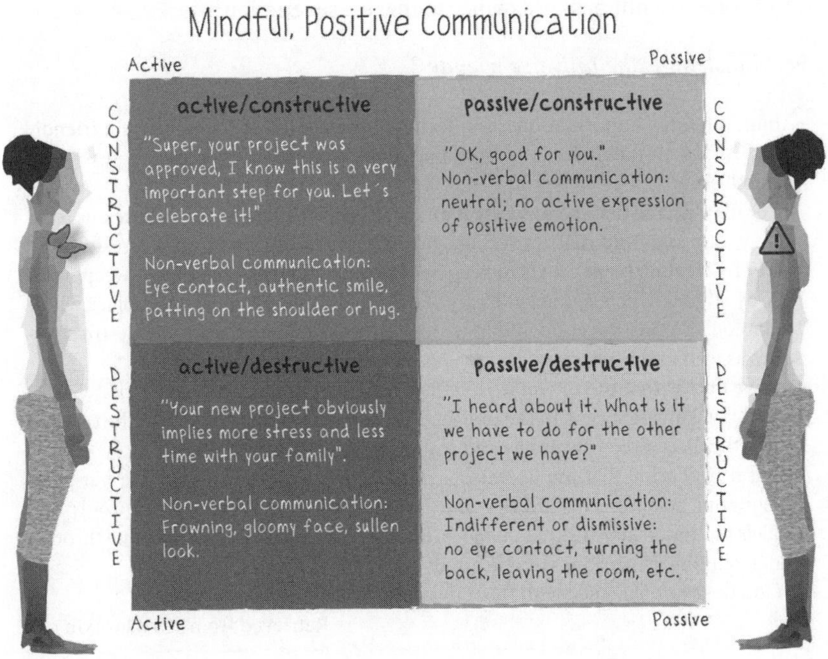

Figure 13.3 Mindful, Positive Communication. *Source*: Juan Humberto Young.

b. Active/destructive implies negative utterances that are further reinforced by disparaging body signals like sneering facial expressions.
c. Passive/constructive refers to utterances that are positive on the surface but put forward in such a lethargic way that the overall impression is close to neutral. It is an indifferent way of communicating that shows little or no emotional involvement.
d. Passive/destructive communication expresses indifference but with a negative tone. In this quadrant a person advancing joy or sorrow would probably feel let down by the passive/destructive response without being able to pinpoint exactly why.

With an exercise based on this classification we can train the ability to connect friendly tongues to their friendly hearts. We can create positive communities of inquiry that can communicate mindfully and effectively on countless issues: work, family, society, economy, business, and so forth.

13.3.3 Albert Einstein: Is the universe friendly?

In this powerful reflection Albert Einstein invites us all to reflect on what kind of world we want to have—a friendly one or an unfriendly one and the consequences of each. Indirectly, yet forcefully, the reflection also makes the point that we do have a choice: friendliness is a choice to make—see Section 13.1.7.

Albert Einstein: Is the universe friendly?

> I think the most important question facing humanity is: "Is the universe a friendly place?" This is the first and most basic question all people must answer for themselves.
>
> For if we decide that the universe is an unfriendly place, then we will use our technology, our scientific discoveries and our natural resources to achieve safety and power by creating bigger walls to keep out the unfriendliness and bigger weapons to destroy all that which is unfriendly and I believe that we are getting to a place where technology is powerful enough that we may either completely isolate or destroy ourselves as well in this process.
>
> If we decide that the universe is neither friendly nor unfriendly and that God is essentially "playing dice with the universe," then we are simply victims to the random toss of the dice and our lives have no real purpose or meaning.
>
> But if we decide that the universe is a friendly place, then we will use our technology, our scientific discoveries and our natural resources to create tools and models for understanding that universe. Because power and safety will come through understanding its workings and its motives.
>
> God does not play dice with the universe.
>
> Retrieved from www.awakin.org

The intention is to read Einstein's reflection together in the session and discuss it in a brief inquiry.

13.3.4 Strengths, opportunities and positive actions—SOPA Part I—Inventory of activities, assets, and opportunities exercise

In this session participants are introduced to a strategic tool, SOPA, for their own personal development and growth, using as base and vision their self-portraits they have been working on for the past two weeks and that serve as visions of their personal mindful positive selves. The idea is to create a practical, personalized plan that can help them realize their visions. In addition, the plan can help them develop their mindfulness-based strategic awareness and deepen their practice after the completion of the MBSAT course.

For the past 5–6 years I have been developing, implementing, and continuously refining this working model. It is called strengths, opportunities, and positive actions, in short SOPA (see Figure 13.4). (Incidentally, in my mother tongue Spanish "sopa" means "soup" and the hope is that this tool functions like a kind of "chicken soup for the soul," i.e., a strengthening and nourishing potion.) It helps individuals combine the three elements necessary to develop a strategic plan as a blueprint to guide them on their path towards leveraging their character strengths and other assets (first element), taking advantage of opportunities in their environment (second element), and defining the positive actions (third element) that they need to implement in order to realize their vision of a mindful, positive self (MPS).

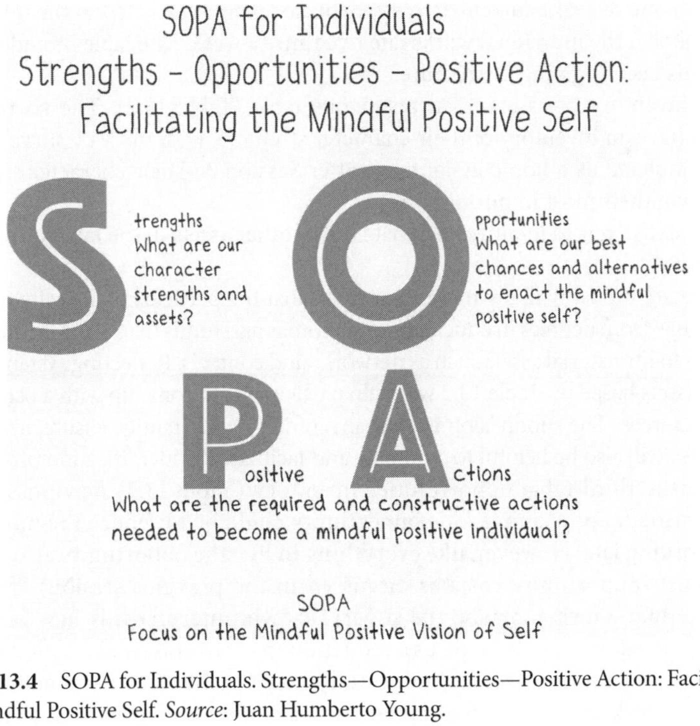

SOPA for Individuals
Strengths - Opportunities - Positive Action:
Facilitating the Mindful Positive Self
S
trengths
What are our character strengths and assets?
O
pportunities
What are our best chances and alternatives to enact the mindful positive self?
P
ositive
A
ctions
What are the required and constructive actions needed to become a mindful positive individual?
SOPA
Focus on the Mindful Positive Vision of Self

Figure 13.4 SOPA for Individuals. Strengths—Opportunities—Positive Action: Facilitating the Mindful Positive Self. *Source*: Juan Humberto Young.

The process comprises two phases.

1. The first phase consists of taking stock of what is present: (a) current activities (what the individual is currently doing daily, weekly, or in even longer intervals), (b) assets available including character strengths, and (c) existing opportunities in the environment. This phase includes elements of analysis and prospection, for example, to identify assets and opportunities.
2. The second phase is the actual planning stage. Based on an overview of the inventories and on explicit criteria for flourishing (derived from self-determination theory; SDT) and evolutionary leadership theory (ELT discussed in Chapter 1), the task is to decide what positive actions should be undertaken to enhance the chances of personal flourishing. What new activities should be generated? What existing activities can be expanded or contracted or even dropped? This phase is reserved for Session 8: the completion of the MBSAT program.

Here in Session 7 we start by establishing the inventories.

The easiest is the inventory of activities (Table 13.1). In the table provided in Handout 5 each participant establishes an inventory of the different activities in his or her life. This inventory should be created around the main domains of life: work, family, leisure, and social activities and subdivided by frequency (daily, weekly, monthly, yearly). The inventory is essentially a list of current activities. For example, one relevant current activity identified, and to be listed in the inventory, might be that the individual works late five times a week. The table provided facilitates this task by giving it structure.

The inventory of assets is an analogous table (Table 13.2). The participants already have an inventory of their character strengths with the VIA survey which they completed as a home assignment after Session 3. Their character strengths are among their most important assets.

The next step is to identify and write down other assets in the table provided in Handout 6.

There are probably many more than those that the participants initially think of. They range from degrees in education or diplomas and funds that could be mobilized through to immaterial assets such as networks and contacts. Reflecting systematically on the assets based on Table 13.2 will help participants to come up with a list of multiple resources. The subdivision in domains of life (work, family, leisure, and social activities) will also be helpful to stimulate and facilitate the identification process.

With the third table opportunities inventory (Table 13.3) new possibilities are identified. For example, one opportunity could be to reduce the number of days working late. However, like everything in life, the opportunity also implies some cost (opportunity costs as discussed in the previous session). The cost can take many forms: maybe the supervisor will interpret this new course of action, if it is followed through, as a reduction in motivation and might decide to postpone a promotion or salary raise, and so on. On the other hand maintaining the same work schedule including late hours could also have a cost as it could

Table 13.1 SOPA (Strengths, Opportunities, and Positive Actions) Phase I: Inventory of Activities. *Source*: Juan Humberto Young.

SOPA (Strengths, Opportunities, and Positive Actions) Phase I: Inventory of Activities				
	Activities			
	Work	Family	Leisure	Social
Daily Activities	Driving to work	Dinner with family	Watching the news	Texting or calling friends
Weekly Activities	Planning the following week	Grocery shopping for a week	Playing tennis	Going out with friends
Monthly Activities	Review of monthly performance	Checking and paying bills	Concert	Volunteering in foundation
Yearly Activities	Yearly personnel evaluation	Family vacation	Spa treatment	Annual meeting of alumni association

Table 13.2 SOPA (Strengths, Opportunities, and Positive Actions) Phase I: Inventory of Assets. *Source*: Juan Humberto Young.

SOPA (Strengths, Opportunities, and Positive Actions) Phase I: Inventory of Assets											
Assets											
Work	Mobilization of Asset		Family	Mobilization of Asset		Leisure (Personal Hobbies)	Mobilization of Asset		Social (Group and Civic Activities Social Projects)	Mobilization of Asset	
	Easy	Difficult		Easy	Difficult		Easy	Difficult		Easy	Difficult
Professional training	✔		Cooking abilities	✔		Kindle reader / ibook	✔		Facebook account	✔	

Table 13.3 SOPA (Strengths, Opportunities, and Positive Actions) Phase I: Inventory of Opportunities. *Source*: Juan Humberto Young.

SOPA (Strengths, Opportunities, and Positive Actions) Phase I: Inventory of Opportunities											
Opportunities											
Work	Cost of Realization		Family	Cost of Realization		Leisure (Personal Hobbies)	Cost of Realization		Social (Group and Civic Activities, Social Projects)	Cost of Realization	
	High	Low		High	Low		High	Low		High	Low
Promotion to vacant higher position	✔		Gourmet cooking once a week		✔	Learning Aikido	✔		Foundation for helping immigrants	✔	

affect family relations, social networks, or fitness and health. Therefore there are columns in the table to report whether the cost is considered to be high or low.

Filling in the three tables is an important home assignment. The results are the basis for the actual strategic awareness planning phase in Session 8. In Handout 8 the participants find some practical tips and examples.

13.3.5 *3-minutes breathing space on friendliness (3MBS-Friendliness)*

This variation of the 3-minutes breathing space has an expanding and uplifting quality that can provide much needed relief, for example, when we feel emotionally depleted or harassed or when we see others struggling and are not sure how to help. It is also useful to simply connect with oneself or others. It is a very versatile 3MBS. It can even be used in situations when we feel a low level of anxiety and simply have the feeling that we need to look after ourselves.

The approach is similar to previous 3MBS with the three steps from wide to narrow and to wide again but it does not have labeling or counting as in 3MBS-Worry and 3MBS-Money Worry.

Friendliness is introduced in Step 3 by invoking wishes of well-being either for oneself or for others. It is similar to the meditation on friendliness. If the practice is directed towards others it can focus on a specific person, a group, or even a larger community. It could be individuals we know personally or people who are only acquaintances.

Pope Francis is a great believer in the power of friendliness practice. It is moving to observe how he regularly and emphatically asks the audiences at the end of his talks and sermons to either pray for him or, in the Pope's words, for those "who do not or cannot pray," send friendly thoughts and wishes his way.

The fact is that this small practice can generate big changes in us and around us. There are several specific benefits:

a. It changes the emotional state from criticism, including self-criticism, to gentleness and kindness.
b. It creates warm connections with others that can improve relations and facilitate communication.
c. It fosters more acceptance for the way we are and the way others are.
d. When there are feelings of fragmentation it provides balance and re-establishes the feeling of being whole.
e. It helps to find balance in the goals for both ourselves and expectations from others by being more gentle and comprehensive.

Practical advice for the practice is provided in Note 26.

13.3.6 How to acquire talented people

Friendliness transforms our relations with fellow human beings. The tale of a Japanese Samurai illustrates that this wisdom is centuries old. It is the tale of a dying Samurai clan leader who explains to his son the secret of recruiting and retaining talented people. His profound wisdom could be used as practical advice for anyone working in a modern organization.

How to acquire talented people: A sixteenth-century Samurai tale

> Before Lord Katsushige passed on his position as lord to his son, he gave him a note consisting of twenty items. All of the items were recommendations from Lord Katsushige's own father, Naoshige, the revered founder of the clan. Now his advice was being handed down to the third generation.
>
> Among the items was the recounting of a father-to-son talk between Naoshige, the then Lord and clan leader, and Katsushige when he was a young man.
>
> Lord Naoshige: "In order to rule the nation, you should have able men."
>
> Son Katsushige: "Do you mean I have to pray to Buddha and the gods for the appearance of these men?"
>
> Lord Naoshige: "You pray to God for things beyond human power and endeavor. Yet it is within your power to get talented people to appear."
>
> Son Katsushige: "How is this possible?"
>
> Lord Naoshige: "Irrespective of any matter, things gather around him who loves them. If he loves flowers, every variety of flower will begin to gather around him,

even though he has not had a single seed until that time. And, in due course, there will grow a flower of the rarest kind. Likewise, if you love people, the result will be the same. Make a point of loving and respecting."

Source: Yamamoto, edited by Stone (2002, pp. 40–41)

As with Einstein's reflection, the aim is to read the tale together and briefly discuss its implications.

14

Session 8: Minding Your BETA

14.1 Introduction

Eight weeks, the duration of the MBSAT course, is a very small part of a person's life and a very short time to establish a lasting mindfulness practice. Nevertheless it is assumed that positive habits have taken root and that the participants have been able to build the foundation for a sustainable practice using the science of habit formation that was presented in Session 1. The hope is therefore that this last session is a beginning and not an end: the beginning of a new way of leading your life and continuing to grow personally.

When I got my black belt in Aikido after almost 8 years of practicing twice weekly, my Sensei told me: "Now the real learning begins." Every time I get on the mat I realize it is true and I learn something new. Developing strategic awareness is similar. All the practices learnt over the past 7 weeks are just the beginning. The decisive phase for participants begins now with the challenge of incorporating the practices into their daily lives and sustaining their personal growth as they develop their mindful positive selves.

The psychologist C. Dweck (2006) subdivides people into two categories according to their mental patterns: those with a fixed mindset and those with a growth mindset. People with a fixed mindset tend to avoid challenges out of fear of failure. They prefer looking for opportunities that will make them look smart. They give-up easily as effort means they may not be smart enough. They assume that learning is easy and effortless for smart people. Individuals with this kind of mindset also ignore useful feedback and feel threatened by the success of others.

On the other hand individuals with a growth mindset are driven by a desire to learn. They look at obstacles as challenges to embrace and barriers to overcome. Effort for them is the natural path to mastery by practicing. They learn from criticism and find inspiration in the success of others.

Mindfulness-Based Strategic Awareness Training: A Complete Program for Leaders and Individuals, First Edition. Juan Humberto Young.

Companion website: www.wiley.com/go/humbertoyoung/mbsat

Probably everyone with work experience has encountered bosses, colleagues, or even members of the human resources department who firmly believe that people cannot change: they are the way they are and nothing can be done about it.

In the course of my professional life I have heard endless stories about people's inability to change. It is exceedingly demotivating for people to work in an environment where the mindset of leaders is that their people have permanent limitations and that the role of the manager is to manage around these unalterable flaws.

Dweck's research findings put this attitude in perspective by demonstrating that the type of mindset affects people's lives profoundly. Fixed-mindset individuals believe that work is all about proving how smart they are and they have a disproportionate need to be right so they can validate their value. Moreover, most of the time fixed-mindset people live in fear of being wrong about something or of not being able to cope with the challenges of life. In relationships they go to great lengths to find the ideal partner or collaborator, the one with just the right characteristics for the job or for private life. When things break down they see no hope of fixing the problem and are not willing to invest the time and effort required to make things different in a constructive way.

By contrast, growth-mindset individuals take it for granted that things change continuously and that one needs to invest energy to make them work. They make partnerships grow by working together with their business or life partners.

The final session of this program is an invitation to participants to continue on the path of personal growth. It encourages participants to work diligently towards accomplishing their vision of mindful positive self by using their strengths and skills to attain a level of mastery in their lives. Hopefully participants will be able to achieve or maintain a healthy level of autonomy by finding a good balance in life between their financial needs and their aspirations and emotional needs. With mindful positive approaches they can hopefully relate to colleagues, bosses, friends, and family in a skillful way. They should notice that in fixed-mindset relations it is easy to slip into the pitfall of activating the worst in our self. In growth-mindset types of relationships it is obviously easier to unfold strategic awareness and skillfully orient your life. Ultimately the aim is to have positive behaviors and relations, with others as well as ourselves, and to experience life to the fullest, without being confined to doing mode and living above the neck (see Session 2), in other words creating the conditions for minding our BETA (Body sensations, Emotions/feelings, Thoughts and Action impulses) in our daily lives.

14.2 Session Organization, Coverage, and Sequence

Part of this session takes a more didactic approach by assisting participants to complete their plans for personal growth corresponding to Part II of SOPA (strengths, opportunities, and positive action). Implicit in this focus is the last element of PERMA: accomplishment. It suggests that diligence, courage, and grit

Session 8: Minding Your BETA

		Time allocated in minutes
		Duration: 3 to 3½ hours
1.	Arrival meditation	5
2.	Meditation on breath, body, sounds, thoughts, and open awareness Guidance and inquiry	20
3.	Home practice review and inquiry	10
4.	Strengths, opportunities, and positive actions—SOPA Part II: Building a plan for personal growth	60
5.	Review of the 8-week program and discussion of "The living zone of the mindful positive individual"	45
6.	3-minutes breathing space on strategic awareness – 3MBS-Strategic Awareness	15
7.	*Good thing, bad thing* – A tale of equanimity and growth mindset	10
8.	Discussion in pairs: How to keep the practices alive and active	20
9.	Course evaluation by the participants	10
10.	Closing meditation of the program and presenting participants with a memento	10

are to be cultivated consciously as participants return to the complexity of their daily lives. The aim is to carry on with the practices they have learned.

14.3 Exercises and Practices of Session 8

Following the meditation of breath, body, sounds, thoughts, and open awareness we dedicate a significant part of the session to Part II of SOPA, building the templates for the participants' future personal growth. We reflect on the living zone of the mindful positive individual that puts strategic awareness in the context of life's challenges and we introduce a 3-minutes space on strategic awareness. Following a tale of positivity we discuss in pairs strategies to maintain a thriving practice after the course. Finally we complete the program with a memento.

14.3.1 Meditation on breath, body, sounds, thoughts, and open awareness

In this eighth and last session of MBSAT we conclude with the comprehensive meditation on breath, body, sounds, thoughts, and open awareness that we first practiced in Session 4. As it comprises open awareness it is an ideal transition to the mindful positive self that is the focus the next exercise, SOPA Part II—building a plan for personal growth.

For specific details on the meditation refer to Session 4.

14.3.2 SOPA Part II: Building a plan for personal growth

SOPA Part II is the completion of the mindful positive self plan. By now participants have three basic documents: (a) a well-defined inventory of their activities (daily, weekly, monthly, yearly), (b) an inventory of the assets they possess (intrinsic, extrinsic), and (c) a list of the opportunities they have identified to achieve more mindfulness and positivity in their lives. With this preparation in place, we can now turn to SOPA II.

An interesting approach to planning for personal growth is to think of your actions as psychological moments occurring during the day. The Nobel laureate Kahneman suggests that people's lives can be described as a string of psychological moments. It has been estimated that each of these moments lasts around 3 seconds thus in a waking day an individual has around 20,000 such moments. They can be thought of as spotlights of immediate experience or sensation. I have recalculated this number. There are 1,200 moments per hour, 600 moments per half hour, and 300 every 15 minutes. With these calculations participants can assign psychological values to each of their activities. For example, if you were to assign 15 minutes to cultivating relations with work colleagues you would be investing 300 moments worth of your experience. This means that from the initial balance of 20,000 moments you now have 300 less—19,700.

This quantifying of daily moments can be useful because it can encourage us to be careful about what we do with these moments. An important caveat: the values assigned to activities only have true meaning if the person is engaged. Mind wandering will decrease the utility of the activity and mind wandering is, as we know, inevitable. But at least by cultivating awareness we can contain these effects.

Essentially the question is: "What are you going to do with the daily 20,000 available moments you can allocate?" This question will help when we are planning activities to realize our mindful positive self. It can become a way of keeping a record of the psychological moments invested in each activity selected.

SOPA Part II is comprised of two phases:

Phase 1

The first task of participants is to assign a tag to each activity on their personal inventory lists, specifying what we plan to do with it. For this purpose we use a tool to determine the appropriate action as presented in Figure 14.1. The mindful

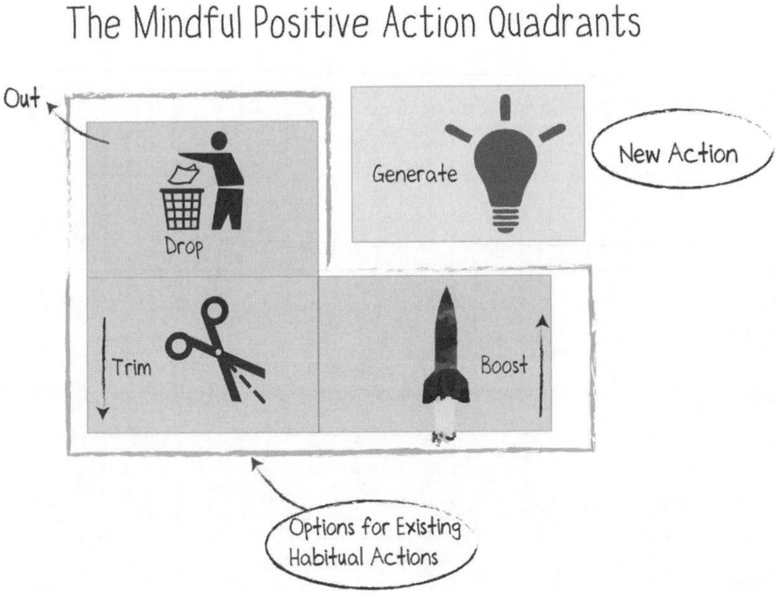

Figure 14.1 The Mindful Positive Action Quadrants. *Source*: Juan Humberto Young.

positive action quadrants define four essential types of actions of which three relate to existing activities and one to new activities yet to be created:

- **Drop:** This means cutting and eliminating entirely an existing activity when the action of cutting would considerably increase the person's well-being, for example, smoking.
- **Trim:** This means reducing existing activities. It means that by reducing their frequency, intensity, or duration it would significantly improve well-being, for example, eating sugary snacks daily.
- **Boost:** This means increasing activities and results in a boost to the quality of life, for example, spending more time with the family.
- **Generate:** These are activities that are not part of a participant's present activity inventory but they have been recognized as a way to improve the quality of life, for example, developing the habit of visiting concerts, museums, and other cultural activities, intellectual activities such as taking courses on subjects of interest.

The participants now have the task of going through their inventories of activities and deciding where each activity belongs in the four quadrants. They should do this in the context of the opportunities they have identified in a separate inventory. For this purpose they can use the MBSAT SOPA Worksheet in Table 14.1. On the left they can report individual activities according to their inventory and on the right they can record their choices of drop, trim, boost, or generate in the columns provided under positive actions.

Table 14.1 MBSAT SOPA Worksheet (SOPA Phase II). *Source*: Juan Humberto Young.

MBSAT SOPA Worksheet (SOPA Phase II)												
Activities	Opportunities	Character Strengths and other Assets	Flourishing Function						Positive Actions			
			Reducing Evolutionary Barriers			Fulfilling SDT Needs						
			Bio-social Mismatch	Cognitive Biases	Human Tendency for Dominance	Need for Autonomy	Need for Competence	Need for Relatedness	Generate	Boost	Trim	Drop
Spending more time with family	Longer dinner at home	Love, Kindness, Cooking abilities			✓			✓		✓		
Diet: eating less meat	Meat substitutes readily available in supermarkets	Persistence		✓			✓				✓	
Communication: Interrupting others while they speak	Meeting at the office, conversation with family	Self-regulation, Social Intelligence, MBSAT Training		✓	✓			✓				✓
Working mindfully and positively to compete for a new opening in the organization	Opening of a higher position in the organization	Social Intelligence, Leadership, etc. Additional professional training.			✓	✓	✓	✓	✓	✓		

Note: Please go to the book's website and kindly download a larger size copy of this table.

As they reflect on the four options they may think of the limited budget of psychological moments available as discussed above.

Phase 2

In Phase 2 of SOPA Part II we continue to complete the MBSAT SOPA worksheet.

a. We start by conne ting the activities already filled in with the opportunities identified in the inventory of opportunities. For each activity we ask: What opportunity does it support? The respective opportunity is entered in the column next to the activity.
b. Then we identify and register the assets and character strengths that support each activity and give it a positive, fulfilling quality.
c. Next we define the flourishing function of the activities by indicating which of the three evolutionary barriers they help reduce: the evolutionary bio-social mismatch, cognitive biases, or the human tendency to dominate.
d. We finish by determining which of the fundamental human needs they fulfill according to the self determination theory (SDT): the need for autonomy, the need for competence, or the need for relatedness.

Let's take an example.

a. *Activity*: A possible activity could be "working mindfully and positively to take on more responsibility within the organization or company." This means honest work; no back-stabbing or engaging in destructive internal politics; and maintaining a constructive work–life balance.
b. *Opportunity*: This activity could be connected with an opening in the organization, which would allow the participant to be promoted to team leader or assigned as the head of a strategic project.
c. *Assets and character strengths*: Assets might be the appropriate professional training as well as additional education such as the executive master in positive leadership and strategy (EXMPLS) or mindfulness-based strategic awareness training (MBSAT). Relevant character strengths could be social intelligence and leadership or other outcomes of the VIA survey such as social responsibility, fairness, and judgment among others, depending on how a person utilizes these qualities. Strengths tend to be much more flexible than is usually assumed.
d. *Reducing evolutionary barriers*: The evolutionary barrier that is likely to be reduced is the human tendency to dominate for the sake of power.
e. *Fulfilling SDT needs*: If the opportunity is realized all three needs are fulfilled: the need for autonomy, competence, and relatedness. It is also the case that just being mindful and positive, even if the participant does not get the position, allows the participant to fulfill the SDT needs.
f. *Positive actions*: This activity will require you to boost certain subordinated tasks to achieve the realization of the opportunity, for example, it may require working some overtime and it may also require you to acquire new knowledge about the position you are seeking.

The teacher may work through some examples from the participants' inventories of activities to allow them to experiment with the worksheet and gain some practice. The aim is to enable participants to complete their personal worksheets later at home or at work.

It is a process that fosters strategic awareness for professional and private life by guiding a participant through a structured and conscious analysis. This exercise will have a powerful impact on the future of the participants because its effect will not stop when the worksheet is filled in. The exercise also trains participants to think differently about their choices in life and this is one of the most important benefits of the MBSAT course.

14.3.3 Review of the 8-week MBSAT program

As the program draws to a close, we take stock of what we have learned in the past 8 weeks and reflect on the essence of the MBSAT program. We start by looking at an overview of all the practices and exercises of the program and their multiple benefits.

We analyze benefits from different perspectives and, most importantly, we connect all the different dimensions of the program including the scientific foundations and theoretical frameworks discussed at the beginning of this book:

- We check what **goals** of mindfulness and positive psychology are served by the practices and exercises.
- We analyze what evolutionary **barriers** to leading a mindful and positive life are reduced by the program.
- We determine what fundamental human **needs** are fulfilled by the practices and exercises.

All these aspects are presented in a synopsis of the MBSAT program in Table 14.2. Here is a brief description of the structure of the table and its main sections. There are four major subdivisions:

a. Session themes, practices, and exercises.
b. MBSAT's scientific foundations: mindfulness and positive psychology.
c. Mindful positive function:
   Reducing evolutionary barriers to mindful life and fulfilling fundamental human needs (needs according to self determination theory (SDT)).
d. Benefits: Skills and insights.

These major subdivisions are further differentiated to reflect essential learning outcomes:

Mindfulness is classified in the four classic mindfulness areas of BETA: Body sensations, Emotions/feelings, Thoughts and Action impulses. These are the areas that meditation makes us aware of. Here we register what aspects of mindfulness are covered by individual practices and exercises.

Table 14.2 MBSAT Program Overview. *Source*: Juan Humberto Young.

MBSAT´s Program Overview																				
8-Week Program				MBSAT´s Scientific Foundation									Mindful Positive Function							
				Mindfulness - BETA				Positive Psychology					Reducing Evolutionary Barriers			Fulfilling SDT Needs				
Session No	Theme	Practices	Exercises	Body	Emotions	Thoughts	Action Impulses	P	E	R	M	A	Bio-Social Interaction Mismatch	Cognitive Biases and Errors	Human Tendency for Dominance	Need for Autonomy	Need for Competence	Need for Relatedness	Skills	Insights
1	Robotic Living - Automatic Pilot	Body Scan		✓	✓									✓		✓			Directing attention volitionally	Awareness of Body sensations
			Raisin Exercise	✓	✓	✓	✓							✓		✓			Shifting from doing to being mode	Experiencing the richness of life in the present moment
			Building MBSAT´s Formal Mindfulness Practice Habit	✓	✓	✓	✓	✓	✓	✓	✓	✓	✓	✓	✓	✓	✓	✓	Building a mindful positive habit	Adaptive craving for a positive purpose
2	Living Above the Neck		Three Good Things (TGT)					✓						✓		✓	✓		Cultivating gratitude	So many good things in life we normally don´t see
		Mindfulness of the Breath		✓	✓									✓		✓	✓		Dealing with mind wandering	Awareness of the patterns of the mind
			BETA Exercise		✓	✓								✓		✓	✓		Connecting thoughts, emotions, body senstions and behavioral impulses	Our interpretations of events influence our experience
3	Recollecting Our Mind	Breath-and-Body Sitting Meditation		✓	✓									✓		✓	✓		Using breath and body sensations to focus awareness	Becoming aware of patterns of the mind and how they connect with body sensations
		Three-Minutes Breathing Space (3MBS)		✓	✓	✓	✓							✓			✓		Using Mindfulness in daily life	Moving into the present moment and away form doing into being mode
		Mindful Stretching and Mindful Salsa		✓	✓			✓		✓				✓				✓	Awareness of body in movement	The richness of body sensations and the accompanying healing effects
			Positive BETA Reframing					✓	✓					✓		✓	✓		Switching mood from negative to positive	Ability to increase the positivity ratio (ratio of positive to negative events or emotions)
			Character Strengths						✓				✓	✓	✓	✓	✓	✓	Identifying and learning to better use character strengths	Living an engaged life and living in "flow"
4	Contraction of Experience- Like and Dislike (Our worried and Anxious Mind)	Sitting Meditation on Breath, Body, Sounds, Thoughts and Open Awareness		✓	✓	✓	✓							✓		✓	✓		Using the breath, sounds, thoughts, and open awareness to be present to our moment-to moment experience	Recognition of our full experiences in awareness including worries and difficulties; decentering fro thougts by bringing attention to our body
		Mindful Walking		✓									✓			✓			Awareness of body in movement	Managing mind wandering and staying present with daily activities
			Defining the territory of anxiety and worry									✓		✓		✓	✓		Identiying the cyles of worry and anxiety	Ability to exit the worry cycle
		Three Minutes Breathing Space Focusing on Strengths		✓	✓	✓	✓		✓				✓			✓	✓	✓	Moving from doing to being mode and responding skilfully with strengths	Ability to respond to fifficulty skilfully and from character strengths
5	Strategic Awareness I: Mindful Real Options (MROs)	Triml Meditation		✓	✓	✓	✓					✓		✓		✓	✓		Ability to rerecognize aversion patterns and moving directly into difficulty	Allowing difficulties and opening up Mindful Real Options (MROs)
		Three-Minutes-Breathing Space on Worry		✓	✓	✓	✓					✓	✓	✓		✓	✓		Switching form a driven worrying-doing mode to an accepting being mode	Responding skilfully with acceptance
			Mindful Positive Self (First Take)									✓	✓	✓	✓	✓	✓	✓	A mindful positive vision of oneself	The mindful positive self is achievable
6	Strategic Awareness II: From POMO (Powerful Money) to MIMO (Mindful Money)	POMO Meditation I, II and III		✓	✓	✓	✓	✓	✓	✓	✓	✓	✓	✓	✓	✓	✓	✓	Recognizing cognitive, emotional and behavioral patterns related to money	Using awarness of the relation to money to change patterns of behavior (MIMO)
		Three-Minutes-Breathing-Space on Money		✓	✓	✓	✓	✓	✓	✓	✓	✓	✓	✓	✓	✓	✓	✓	Switching mindset away from money worries	Eneterig a zone of being with expanded awareness about more skilful ways with money
			Money and Opportunity Costs			✓	✓				✓			✓	✓	✓	✓	✓	Trade-offs of money	Recognizing the relative value of money
			Mindful Positive Self (Second Take)									✓	✓	✓	✓	✓	✓	✓	Desingning the mindful positive vision blueprint	The magnet effect of mindful positive vision (motivating towards achieving the vision)
7	Strategic Awareness III: Opening the Heart	Meditation on Friendliness			✓	✓	✓			✓					✓			✓	Opening the heart: developing friendliness to others and to self	Befriending ourselves and the world is possible
		Three Minutes Breathing Space on Friendliness			✓	✓	✓			✓					✓			✓	Befriending ourselves and others in a moment	Befriending ourselves and others in a brief moment in daily life is possible
			Active/Constructive Responding							✓					✓			✓	Connecting a friendly heart with a friendly tongue	Changing pattern of communication is possible and desirable
			Strengths, Opportunities and Positive Actions-SOPA Part I	✓	✓	✓	✓	✓	✓	✓	✓	✓	✓	✓	✓	✓	✓	✓	Designing the Mindful Positive Plan for personal growth	Discovering the growth mindset of perceiving multiple possibilities
8	Minding Your BETA	Three Minutes Breathing Space on Strategic Awareness		✓	✓	✓	✓							✓		✓	✓	✓	Switching from doing mode to being mode with strategic awareness	Strategic awareness as prospection in being mode and in the present moment
			Strengths, Opportunities and Positive Actions-SOPA Part II	✓	✓	✓	✓	✓	✓	✓	✓	✓	✓	✓	✓	✓	✓	✓	Accomplishing the Mindful Positive Plan for personal growth	Discovery of one´s potential to become a mindful positive self

Note: Please go to the book's website and kindly download a larger size copy of this table.

Positive psychology is schematized according to PERMA: positive emotions, engagement and flow, relationships, meaning in life, and positive accomplishment. Again we report on what areas the practices and exercises contribute to. For example, the three good things exercise of Session 2 connects with the P of PERMA, namely the positive emotion.

Reducing evolutionary barriers—part of the heading mindful positive function—is subdivided into three categories as discussed in Chapter 1 based on evolutionary leadership theory (ELT): bio-social mismatch, cognitive biases and errors, and human tendency for dominance. Each practice and exercise is analyzed from the vantage point of which barrier it helps to reduce.

The second part of mindful positive function is fulfilling SDT needs, that is, the fundamental human needs of autonomy, competence, and relatedness according to SDT. We check what fundamental needs are fulfilled by these practices and exercises.

Clearly the practices and exercises can have multiple effects: they can reduce evolutionary barriers and at the same time help fulfill one or more needs for positive functioning. For example, Irimi meditation can reduce cognitive biases and errors that are often the source of our difficulties. At the same time it fulfills our needs of autonomy and competence as it helps us acquire the ability to handle difficulties skillfully.

Finally, the benefits of the MBSAT program are subdivided into the skills and insights gained. For example, with the meditation on the participant's relation with money one of the skills gained is the ability to recognize what one's cognitive, emotional, and behavioral patterns related to money are. The insight is that you can use this awareness to change those patterns, if you want to.

This synopsis can be used as a template to initiate a review conversation of the whole MBSAT program.

14.3.4 The living zone of the mindful, positive individual

The MBSAT program culminates with the participants' personal visions based on their mindful, positive self-portraits and their plans for personal growth based on SOPA. These blueprints highlight the true meaning of MBSAT.

The purpose of the MBSAT program is to provide training for practices and skills that allow individuals to make decisions that lead to a life characterized by mindful and positive states.

With MBSAT there are three essential zones into which a person's life unfolds, depicted in Figure 14.2:

- *The Zone of Aversion*: Whenever dislike arises in us we are in the zone of aversion. We try to stay away from what we dislike or ban it altogether from our lives.
- *The Zone of Attachment*: We enter the zone of attachment when we like something and wish to keep it and preserve the pleasurable feeling that comes with it.

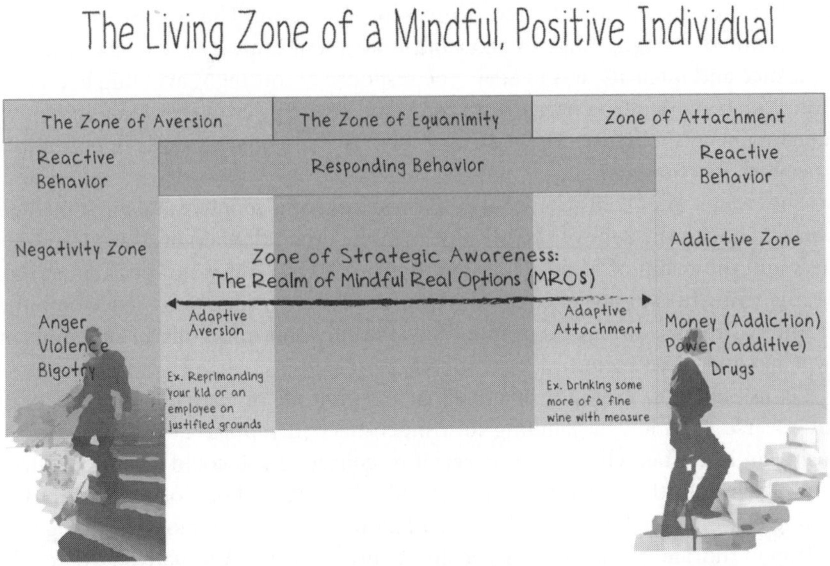

Figure 14.2 The Living Zone of a Mindful, Positve Individual. *Source*: Juan Humberto Young.

- *The Zone of Equanimity*: This is the zone of balance and serenity where ideally the lives of mindful, positive individuals can develop. I agree with G. Desbordes et al. (in press) that equanimity is probably the most important psychological element in the improvement of well-being. MBSAT further expands this view by defining a zone of strategic awareness that encompasses equanimity and zones of adaptive transition toward aversion and attachment. For MBSAT living in this extended zone of strategic awareness may help most people to maintain enduring well-being.

Life in the first two zones, aversion and attachment, is characterized by reactive behavior: doing mode in automatic pilot, impulsiveness with little awareness, and compulsive patterns. It is a life of reactivity.

In the zone of equanimity individuals live their lives more consciously and calmly. It is a zone of balance, tolerance, and serenity even when facing provoking events. Equanimity is the ability to regulate our cognitive and emotional state and to adapt the intensity and quality of our responses, based on strategic awareness that allows for lucidity, a wider perspective, and greater objectivity. Thus individuals in the zone of equanimity are aware of their actions and capable of responding mindfully to life's events instead of being driven by impulses. When they respond to events around them, their equanimous BETA are congruent and measured.

The art of living most of the time in the zone of equanimity implies that you are able to respond adaptively when the inevitable happens and life's events carry us into the zones of aversion or attachment. The normal tendency is to get caught in negativity or mired in different degrees of addiction. The artistic element of equanimity is to realize that aversion and attachment can vary considerably in significance and intensity and to adapt the response accordingly, avoiding overreactions. Such moderate responses are indicated as adaptive aversion and adaptive attachment in the figure. These areas imply responsive behavior as opposed to a knee-jerk reaction.

The two areas of transition of adaptive aversion and adaptive attachment when combined with the zone of equanimity form the broad domain of strategic awareness and the realm of Mindful Real Options (MROs). If it is not possible to stay permanently in the zone of equanimity, we can however maintain ourselves in the realm of strategic awareness, responding skillfully and mindfully to situations of aversion and attachment.

Let us look at an example. Imagine that an employee or team member provokes an adverse situation by handing in a much-needed report late or, even worse, losing an important client. As supervisor or colleague you could let yourself drift completely into the negativity zone, go red with anger, shout, or even insult the failing person, which could make the situation worse (the employee walking out, a drop in morale, or many other negative consequences). Alternatively you could reprimand him or her with fairness albeit firmly, pointing out the damage and taking measures to prevent similar situations happening in the future (e.g., regular checks before the deadline or additional personnel training). With these responses you remain clearly in the zone of strategic awareness and correct the situation with wisdom and friendliness.

The same applies to situations in the zone of attachment, for example, going out for dinner with friends and having more than usual of a very fine wine in the animated ambience of the group without losing your composure or doing something foolish.

Obviously, the aim is to stay in the zone of strategic awareness that coincides with the zone of responding behavior.

By continuing the practices of MBSAT the ability to avoid reactive behavior and avert negativity or addiction will rise. Over time we can build a special space within the world around us, a personal world that acts as an antidote to the world's turmoil.

If the world we live in is characterized by VUCA (volatility, uncertainty, complexity, and ambiguity) our personal world of mindful, positive practitioner has the qualities of WECO (wisdom, equanimity, compassion, and open awareness). An illustration of these two contrasting worlds is presented in Figure 14.3 as well as the last handout (Handout 6).

Figure 14.2, the living zone of a mindful, positive individual, is contained in Handout 3 of this session. The teacher may either distribute the handout or beam the graphic on a screen or wall and discuss it with the participants. Then participants may be invited to share their own examples that occurred in the different zones of equanimity, attachment, or aversion.

Figure 14.3 The Institutionalized World of VUCA/The Goal. *Source*: Juan Humberto Young.

14.3.5 3-minutes breathing space on strategic awareness (3MBS-Strategic Awareness)

Strategic awareness, as trained in MBSAT, has a practical and discerning quality to it. It makes us lucid and alert to the implications of our decisions for both others and ourselves and conveys a subtle distinction between what is constructive and beneficial in the longer run and what is detrimental, even if it is only latently so.

This makes the 3-minutes-breathing space on strategic awareness an invaluable mini practice for all kinds of situations. It is easy to integrate at work and in your private life.

As in all 3MBS practices we start in Step 1 by gathering our scattered mind and shifting from a doing mode to a being mode. Then in Step 2 we focus on breathing, becoming aware of the in-flow and out-flow of air and the contraction and expansion of the abdomen.

In Step 3 we expand the awareness to whatever issue of strategic significance we may be confronting with an attitude of acceptance, openness, and patience. We are not looking for solutions but holding the situation in mind with gentle curiosity, staying with it in this moment, without judging, simply keeping it in awareness for a few moments and breathing with it. When we feel ready we slowly open our eyes, calm and refreshed and ready to take up where we left off before the practice.

14.3.6 "Good thing, bad thing"—A tale of equanimity and growth mindset

All good qualities need to be cultivated to keep them vibrant. Reading aloud the following Sufi tale can foster equanimity and the openness for diverse possibilities that is typical of a growth mindset, especially because the refrain "Good thing, bad thing – who knows?" is likely to lodge in the memory and turn into a kind of comforting mantra when we experience a mishap or a setback.

Good thing, bad thing, who knows (A Sufi Tale)

> There was once a farmer who owned a horse and had a son.
>
> One day his horse ran away. The neighbors came to express their concern: "Oh, that's too bad. How are you going to work the fields now?" The farmer replied: "Good thing, bad thing – who knows?"
>
> In a few days, his horse came back and brought another horse with her. Now, the neighbors were glad: "Oh, how lucky! Now you can do twice as much work as before!" The farmer replied: "Good thing, bad thing – who knows?"
>
> The next day, the farmer's son fell off the new horse and broke his leg. The neighbors were concerned again: "Now that he is incapacitated, he can't help you around the farm, that's too bad." The farmer replied: "Good thing, bad thing – who knows?"
>
> Soon, the news came that a war broke out, and all the young men were required to join the army. The villagers were sad because they knew that many of the young men would not come back. The farmer's son could not be drafted because of his broken leg. His neighbors were envious: "How lucky! You get to keep your only son." The farmer replied: "Good thing, bad thing – who knows?"
>
> *Source*: YogiMir (2013)

The tale is included in Handout 4. The text can be distributed and read together or projected on a screen or wall. After the reading, participants could be invited to share experiences of their own lives that echo the theme of the tale.

14.3.7 How to keep the practices alive and active: Discussion in pairs

For sustainable benefits from the MBSAT program it is important to find ways to maintain the practices despite the many demands of daily tasks and the scarcity of free moments. Hopefully, 8 weeks after starting to practice, and implementing the formal mindfulness practice habit, some of the participants will have an established practice and others might be heading towards regular practice.

To maintain the practice, pairs of participants can be invited to discuss strategies to ensure continuity and discipline. Often it can strengthen our good intentions if we can co-create plans and resolutions with colleagues instead of thinking about them on our own. To stimulate the exchange the teacher could provide a targeted proposition to consider, for example:

"Please, discuss in pairs your experience in establishing a formal practice habit. The suggestion is to focus the conversation on the model presented in Session 1 of MBSAT, so the discussion will be around establishing cues, rewards, and a positive craving element."

In the inquiry following the discussion the goal is to share as many effective strategies as possible so that the participants get a wide range of practical advice.

14.3.8 Course evaluation by the participants

At the end of the course it can be useful to gather feedback and evaluations from course participants. Below is a suggested template that participants can fill in. Depending on the intentions of the teacher and the learning goals and intentions of participants, the template can be extended or modified.

Value of the Program

How beneficial have the following themes been for you?

Please give a score from 1 through 10 where 1 means "not at all beneficial" and 10 means "extremely beneficial."

Theme **Score (1–10)**

Living with awareness and conscious choice
(*versus* being on automatic pilot)..

Knowing experience directly through your senses
(*versus* through thinking) ....

Being here, now, in this moment
(*versus* dwelling in the past or future) ....

Approaching all experience with interest
(*versus* avoiding the unpleasant) ....

Allowing things to be as they are
(*versus* needing them to be different) ....

Seeing thoughts as mental events
(*versus* as necessarily true and real)..

Taking care of yourself with kindness and compassion
(*versus* focusing on achieving goals regardless of the cost to you and others) ....

Relating skillfully to money
(*versus* being driven by compulsion or reaction in relation to money) ....
....

Overall, has MBSAT improved your decision-making skills for well-being?
(*versus* no improvement at all) ....

Has your strategic awareness increased in your opinion?
(*versus* no increase at all) ....

14.3.9 *Closing meditation of the program and presenting participants with a memento*

Before the group departs a closing meditation can provide a worthwhile conclusion to the shared 8-week journey. It may be just a few minutes of awareness on breathing, staying once more for a moment together in awareness.

It is also a suitably gracious gesture to distribute a memento to remember the course and as a gentle reminder to keep doing the practices. It could be a poem or an inspiring quote or also a small gift, a welcome keepsake that will later wake positive associations.

The overall goal of MBSAT that participants hopefully keep in mind could be summarized as follows: Moving from VUCA to WECO with the eye of strategic awareness (see Figure 14.4).

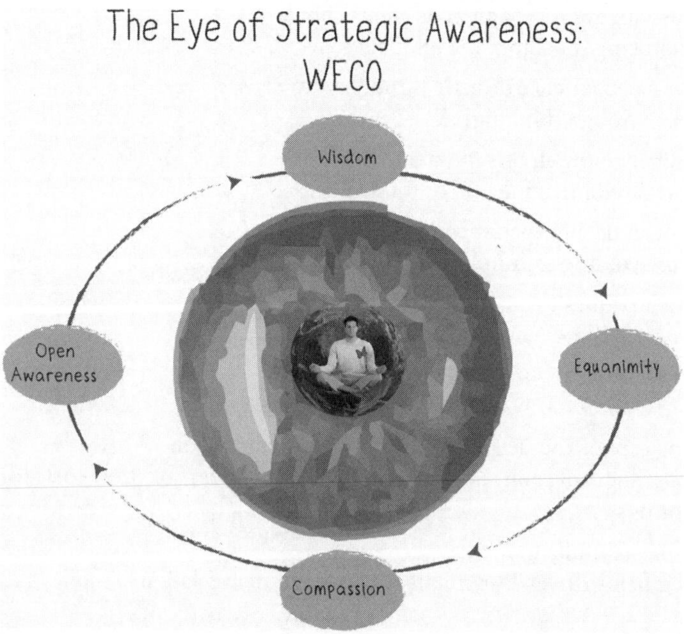

Figure 14.4 The Eye of Strategic Awareness: WECO. *Source*: Juan Humberto Young.

From VUCA to WECO:

From the VUCA world around us
(a world of Volatility, Uncertainty, Complexity, Ambiguity)
To a personal world of WECO
(Wisdom, Equanimity, Compassion and Open Awareness)

Session 1

Note 1: The Raisin Exercise

1. *The script*

Each person in the exercise receives one raisin and starts exploring it full of wonder and curiosity, as if it was the first time they had encountered this little object, like a Martian on Earth trying to find out as much as possible with all their senses.

Holding it quietly in your palm or between your fingers, take your time to feel, notice, and discover.

Then, by moving it slightly between your fingers, what else can you discover?

And what impressions arise when, taking time with every step, you hold the raisin close to your nose, then to the ears, then to the lips?

If any thoughts arise such as "this is an odd exercise" or "this is too slow for me" just acknowledge this idea and return to the process of exploring.

After inspecting the raisin thoroughly, and resisting the impulse to gulp it down, place it in your mouth and carefully and patiently explore all the sensations produced by having it on your tongue, between your teeth, or on the palate.

Then start chewing it very slowly and notice all the sensations that emerge now including the impulse to eat it.

Finally, swallow it and, for as long as possible, follow the remainders of the raisin on their way to the stomach.

Once you have completed every step, carefully reflect on the experience:

Have you discovered something new or surprising?

How do you feel after the exercise?

Mindfulness-Based Strategic Awareness Training: A Complete Program for Leaders and Individuals, First Edition. Juan Humberto Young.

Companion website: www.wiley.com/go/humbertoyoung/mbsat

2. *Guidelines for conducting the exercise*

Here are some suggestions for guiding the exercise that might be useful for everyone from mindfulness teachers to readers curious about the experiment:

a. The key is a "beginner's mind," inviting participants to see the raisin as a new object and forgetting their preconceptions of likes and dislikes.
b. The emphasis is on curiosity and the exploration of all possible sensations, even less obvious ones such as the weight of the raisin, the temperature, the texture, the sound as you gently squeeze it.
c. If it is appropriate an additional raisin can be distributed.
d. The raisin has proved to be very conducive to the process of exploration, but other options are not excluded, for example, dates or other dried fruits, or even small wrapped chocolates.
e. On the practical side mindfulness teachers must remember to bring enough raisins to the session and a spoon to distribute them. A non-sticky variety makes it easier to distribute the raisins.

3. *Inquiry*

In the inquiry that follows the exercise there are two points of special importance:

a. The inquiry should focus on the sensorial aspects of the experience (sweetness, translucent color, etc.) as opposed to *thinking* about the experience (I liked or disliked the feeling, comparing to other fruit, etc.).
b. The exercise should help participants to explore how our minds normally work, how easily automatic pilot sets in, and how this influences subjective well-being, for example, comparing eating in automatic pilot and eating mindfully.

4. *Psycho-educational points*

The main learning outcomes from the raisin exercise relate to automatic-pilot.

a. When we do things mindfully instead of functioning in automatic-pilot mode a whole spectrum of perceptions opens up to us so that we can recognize the total symphony of life.
b. In automatic pilot our perception is narrow, poor, and stereotypical. Our autonomy is reduced to a mechanical state.
c. The exercise may also help illustrate how the automatic-pilot mode induces us to bring up stories of the past (memories related to raisins) and plans about the future (intentions regarding food), thus inhibiting the experiences of the present.

Note 2: The Body Scan

1. The script

For the body scan the most convenient position may be lying flat on your back with your legs and feet slightly apart and your arms alongside your body. Make yourself comfortable.

If you have a quiet moment at work and would like to do the practice in the office, a conference room, or some other location where you won't be disturbed you can also do it in a sitting position, with your back and neck upright, your feet firmly on the floor, and your hands on your knees. Whatever position works best for you.

Take a few moments to settle into the posture, become aware of where your body touches the floor or chair, and feel how you are supported. If possible, close your eyes.

Now starting to pay attention to your breathing and the gentle movements of your body as you inhale and exhale. Feel the slight expansion and contraction of the abdomen with each breath.

Then directing your attention to the big toe of your left foot. Can you feel it? What sensation can you detect? Maybe you feel the blood pulsing or can detect some warmth or some coolness. Whatever it is, just take note of it with interest and acceptance, even if you cannot feel anything in particular right now. Do the same for your other toes.

Next you may experiment with "breathing into your foot," inhaling and imagining the oxygen from the fresh air flowing down from the lungs through the leg and into the foot and the toes. As you exhale imagine the warmth returning from the toes and the foot upwards through the leg and out of the nose. This idea is in fact not fantasy. The blood actually transports oxygen from your lungs down to the tiniest blood vessels at the tip of your toes. It is likely that you will notice slight changes after further inhaling and exhaling while focusing attention on your toes.

When you feel ready to move further up your body, you may disengage with an out-breath from the toes, engaging your attention on the next in-breath with the other parts of the foot, one by one: the sole, the instep, the heel, the top of the foot, and the ankle, exploring with curiosity what you can feel in these regions and keep "breathing with them," sending them some extra oxygen in your imagination.

With the next in-breath the body scan continues, expanding your attention and beginning to scan your lower leg, your knee, and your upper leg, always in the same fashion, exploring and breathing. Continue with your right foot and right leg.

By now you might feel drowsy as you start letting go of tension. If this is the case you might open your eyes to help you stay awake. The main purpose of the body scan is not relaxation, although this may be a pleasant side effect.

You may also feel like changing your position. If you need to, you may do it consciously and mindfully with minimal adjustments. Here, too, making sure you notice what you feel and acknowledge it. If your mind wanders, become aware of where it took you and bring it gently back to the focus of the practice.

Continue by scanning the pelvic area, breathing in and out, then the buttocks, hips, abdomen, and lower back. As you continue to breathe moving up through your torso, directing your attention to your chest, your ribs, the upper back, and the shoulders. Carefully observe the sensations in these parts of the body.

When you reach the shoulders experiment with moving your attention downwards once again and focus on your fingers, hands, and arms in the same way as you scanned your feet and legs, only this time focus on the left and right sides together. Keeping your breath while gradually shifting your attention from one part of your body to another.

Next moving your focus to the neck and head and give them the same detailed attention with which you started the body scan. With gentle curiosity explore all the sensations in your jaw, your face, your eyeballs, your forehead, and your scalp as you shift your attention sequentially. Always breathe with the part of your body you're focusing on.

The last focus is on the top of your head. Perhaps you can identify the spot by exploring any sensation you can detect. Then breathing through your whole body by imagining that air is seeping in through the crown of your head and ventilating your whole body. You are exhaling through the soles of your feet and then inverting the flow—inhaling through the feet and exhaling through the crown. Give yourself some time to do some breathing in this way.

To complete the practice the suggestion is to slowly return to normal breathing, lying, or sitting for a few more moments with your awareness covering your entire body, sensing its wholeness. Then, when you feel ready, starting to move gently and resume your normal activities as calmly and mindfully as possible.

2. Guidelines for conducting the practice

Here are some essential suggestions to help facilitate the body scan:

- It is important to view any lack of sensation in a particular body part as a valuable insight, just like any other discovery. In the beginning of the practice it is quite common that participants have difficulties in sensing certain parts of the body. If this happens then just the attempt to focus attention on that spot, however numb it may seem, is already an achievement. General body awareness will gradually increase and return to long-neglected parts if the participants regularly maintain the practice. The key to the practice is to explore your body with kindness and generous acceptance, the way one would treat a loved one. Therefore, it is forgivable if someone falls asleep although the intention of the practice is to stay awake and attentive. It is inevitable that some participants will get drowsy, especially those who have come from work. The main thing is to maintain gentle curiosity in observing our bodies.

- There are two ways of focusing: the attention can be very narrow on a small area of the body, for example, a toe or the knee cap, or it can be expanded to wide angle attention and encompass larger parts, for example a whole leg or the torso. The widest possible angle is feeling the whole body in its entirety.
- Mindfulness teachers can help participants by mentioning every single tiny body part and giving examples of feelings such as tingling, twitching, numbness, cold, warmth.
- Other important practical aspects for mindfulness teachers are logistics and organization: there must be enough room for participants to lie down. Mats and blankets may be necessary unless the participants bring their own. Establish a consensus about dealing with noise or snoring if someone falls into deep sleep.

3. *Inquiry*

- The key points of the inquiry are the experiences of noticing, acknowledging, and bringing the attention back from mind wandering.
- An interesting point of discussion is the difference between narrow and wide-angle attention and how the participants experience these aspects during the practice.
- In order to be able to shift the attention to the next body part and engage in exploring this new area, the attention has to disengage from the previous point of focus. It can be worthwhile to discuss with the participants how they experienced this process of disengaging and engaging.

4. *Psycho-educational points*

- Most importantly, the practice helps us develop and cultivate direct sensorial knowledge as opposed to thinking.
- With the body scan we learn that our body is an ally. It sends us information that can be useful for our well-being.
- With this practice we learn to recognize mind wandering and to acknowledge it as something fundamentally human.

Session 1—Handouts and Homework

Handout 1 of Session 1: Foundations

1. *A definition of mindfulness*

Paying attention in the present moment with strategic awareness to ongoing events and experiences both internally and externally with an attitude of curiosity, openness and acceptance.

2. *What is positive psychology?*

According to the International Positive Psychology Association (http://www.enpp.eu/research-projects/positive-psychology):

> Positive psychology is founded on the belief that people want to lead meaningful and fulfilling lives, to cultivate what is best within themselves and to enhance their experiences of love, work, and play. Positive psychology has three concerns: positive emotions, individual traits, and positive institutions. Understanding positive emotions includes the study of contentment with the past, happiness in the present, and hope for the future. Understanding positive traits consists of the study of strengths and virtues, such as the capacity for love and work, courage, compassion, resilience, creativity, curiosity, integrity, self-knowledge, moderation, self-control, and wisdom. Understanding positive institutions entails the study of elements like justice, responsibility, civility, parenting, nurturance, work ethic, leadership, teamwork, purpose, and tolerance, which lead to better communities.

3. *The PERMA-model of well-being*

- **P**ositive emotions: feelings of happiness
- **E**ngagement: psychological connection to one's activities
- **R**elationships: feeling socially integrated by caring and being supported by others
- **M**eaning: feeling connected and interested in something greater that one self
- **A**ccomplishment: feeling capable of moving toward valued goals, having a sense of achievement.

Handout 2 of Session 1: Building the Formal Mindfulness Practice Habit

Strategic awareness is like a muscle: even if you feel very fit today, if you don't keep up your training your fitness declines, your muscles become weak and atrophic.

Therefore, if you want to really benefit from MBSAT, it is key to establish a habit of practicing and integrating it in your daily routines. You can use recent insights of neurology and psychology to facilitate this process. It is known that routines are driven and kept in motion by the dynamic of cues triggering the habitual behavior and enticing rewards that awaken our craving again and again.

Here we define and formulate the three elements of habit dynamics: the routine, the cue, and the reward for integrating formal mindfulness practice in your activities. While the routine is a given, the cues and rewards are personal. It is up to you to define your cues and rewards.

Please, use the space below to draft a first version of what you think are your best cues and rewards. Throughout the MBSAT course, as you keep practicing, you can keep modifying and adjusting them. This is a natural process.

My routine: Integrating mindfulness-based strategic awareness practices and exercises in my daily activities

My Cues (First Take)

Location:..

....

Time:..

....

Emotional state:...

....

Social context:..

....

Preceding action:..

....

My Rewards (First Take)

Extrinsic rewards:..

....

....

Intrinsicrewards:...

....

....

Handout 3 of Session 1: Home Practice for the Week Following Session 1

1. Do the body scan with the audio files provided six times per week (one day of rest) without evaluating yourself or trying to get it right. Just notice, with curiosity, what you experience and how it makes you feel. Then we can talk about it in Session 2. The main thing is that you keep doing it.
2. Every day choose a routine activity that you normally do in automatic pilot and instead do it mindfully, staying present and aware while you execute the task. It can be any activity: brushing your teeth or taking a shower, driving to or from work, eating lunch or dinner, doing household chores like cleaning the kitchen. You may choose the same activity for the whole week or a different one every day.

On the home practice record form each day note what you have done (the body scan and which routine activity?) and make brief comments on the experience so that we can build on it in Session 2.

Handout 4 of Session 1: Optional Reading

Article: *A wandering mind is an unhappy mind* (one-page article)
by Killingsworth, M. A., & Gilbert, D. T. (2010). *Science, 330*, 932. http://www.danielgilbert.com/KILLINGSWORTH%20&%20GILBERT%20(2010).pdf

Handout 5 of Session 1: Home Practice Record Form

Name:..

Please, record each time you practice or do an exercise on the home practice record form. Also, make a note of anything that comes up in the home practice so that we can talk about it at the next session.

Day/Date	Assignments: Type of practice and exercise	Yes/No	Comments
Monday	–		
Date:	–		
	–		
Tuesday	–		
Date:	–		
	–		
Wednesday	–		
Date:	–		
	–		
Thursday	–		
Date:	–		
	–		
Friday	–		
Date:	–		
	–		
Saturday	–		
Date:	–		
	–		
Sunday	–		
Date:	–		
	–		
Monday	–		
Date:	–		
	–		

Session 2

Note 3: The BETA Exercise

1. The script

The BETA exercise is designed to sample and explore the effect of rapid interpretations and how those rapid interpretations shape emotional reactions and become part of a person's experience by manifesting in the body and creating the urge to act.

The exercise starts by presenting a brief scenario and then asking the participants to share their reactions: What thoughts came up? What feelings, body sensations, and impulses to act?

The classic scenario used in mindfulness-based cognitive therapy (MBCT) is the following: "You are walking down the street and notice someone you know on the other side. You wave and smile, but the other person just passes by without acknowledging you."

You can also choose a different scenario, for example: "You are walking down a hallway and notice a colleague going in the opposite direction. You greet him or her but the other person does not respond and just keeps going."

The main point is to make sure that the description of the story is as neutral as possible and does not tilt the participants' interpretation in one direction or another.

To gather the participants' observations it is necessary to have a board to write on such as a white- or black-board and to take notes using a simple grid with separate columns for thoughts, feelings, sensations, and impulses to act.

The inquiry is a core element in this exercise and the participants should be invited to vent a wide array of reactions. The diversity of the comments provides rich material for the subsequent discussion of psycho-educational conclusions.

2. Guidelines for the exercise and inquiry

When teaching this exercise I have found it useful to help participants unpack their experience in all its dimensions and complexities. It is common for some individuals to have difficulty registering and articulating the effects of the event at a sensorial level. By gently asking people to go deeper and explore the effect of the thoughts and feelings evoked by the event you can help them realize the impact that even trivial incidents can have and how an interpretation can color their BETA (Body sensations, Emotions/feelings, Thoughts and Action impulses).

It is useful to begin with bland, inoffensive, open questions such as: What do you think happened here? and then follow up with additional questions like: How does it make you feel? Any sensations noticeable in your body? Then finish the questions by asking: What did you feel like doing? This way you cover the full spectrum of the experience. It may be useful to invite participants to join into a conversation while being careful to leave space for quiet individuals who find it difficult to voice their feelings.

Usually a wide diversity of reactions will emerge. Some people with a small emotional response to the incident may see it as harmless or understandable and they might conclude: "She didn't see me. Maybe she is absentminded for some reason." Others may have very intense responses: "She ignores me! What an arrogant person…." Naturally the variety of reactions is part of the learning of the exercise. A brief verbatim interchange between two participants and myself as the teacher in one of my training programs demonstrates this:

IRENE: I feel irritation.

TEACHER: Is it you who is irritated or is the situation irritating?

IRENE: I feel irritated *by her*.

TEACHER: Something seems to be on your mind. Would you like you tell us about it?

IRENE: Yes, sure. I think it can't be that she hasn't seen me. My heart is beating faster and I feel like going over to her and saying: "Can't you at least say hello? I know you saw me."

STEPHAN: I guess the person didn't recognize me because she was absorbed by something. She is a friend and I feel surprised that she didn't see me, but on the other hand I feel happy because I didn't have time to chat anyway.

The wide variety of possible reactions provides fertile soil for exploring the themes of the exercise.

3. *Psycho-educational points*

a. It is the interpretation and meaning attached to events that determines our reactions.
b. There is no right meaning or interpretation for the events, only consequences.
c. People's reactions are often part of a matrix of established patterns.
d. The reactions can be determined by the mood of the day. In Stephan's case it was convenient not to get a response from the person he greeted, so his reaction was relaxed.

Note 4: Three Good Things (TGT) Exercise

1. The script

In practical terms this exercise consists of two steps: (1) a brief daily reflection and (2) making notes in a journal to record the highlights.

Step 1 involves taking a few minutes every day to think about three good things in one's life. The choice has no limits. It can be something small, it can be recent, it can be ongoing, or perhaps something from the past. You can choose an event or a relationship; a fortunate circumstance you are grateful for; or something beautiful you enjoyed. Experience shows that the best time of the day for this short practice is either in the morning as you prepare for the day or in the evening when you are reflecting on the day's events.

In step 2 you write the three good things you identified in a journal and reflect on why they are special to you. It is known that journal writing amplifies the positive impact of the practice and helps to produce a calm and more mindful disposition. There is abundant scientific literature on the benefits of journal writing. Reflecting on why something feels good to you also has an enhancing effect and can strengthen links to other people in your life.

2. Guidelines and inquiry

It can be helpful to invite participants to bring their journals along to the next session. The idea is not to read these personal notes but to encourage a commitment from participants and encourage the practice of writing.

A tip to make the practice more pleasant is for participants to buy a journal they like to look at and touch, so that it is always enjoyable to handle.

In the inquiry the focus might be on the changes that were triggered through the practice, perhaps a more positive mood or improved personal relations. A recurrent challenge is the issue of how to maintain the practice regularly. The best advice is to make the notes very short, particularly when there is a lot of pressure on time.

3. Psycho-educational points

a. The attitude cultivated by the TGT practice is gratitude. We learn not to compare ourselves to others and to appreciate what we have.
b. The practice makes us aware of good things we usually ignore or take for granted.
c. The practice opens our eyes and helps us consciously register the small nice things that happen to us during the day. Repeated positive emotions are scientifically proven to increase overall well-being.

Note 5: Mindfulness of the Breath Practice

In mindfulness of the breath the attention is focused on our habitual breathing. There is no need for a special breathing technique. The goal is simply to follow, intentionally and attentively, the rhythm of our normal breathing. The breath is a great companion in mindfulness training because it is easily accessible and with us all the time.

1. *The script*

Participants are invited to assume an upright sitting position either on cushions on the floor or in their chairs. The position should be comfortable enough so the participant can maintain it without straining. If participants are seated in their chairs, the normal posture is with feet firmly on the floor, hands on the knees and shoulders relaxed, preferably with closed eyes. Then the practice can begin. It consists of concentrating on the breath without altering it, just breathing normally, following in- and out-breaths as the abdomen expands and recedes and observing whatever happens with an attitude of acceptance and curiosity.

As simple as this may seem, the practice has its challenges as our busy lifestyle makes it hard for us to sit still in a being mode and with a single point of attention for any length of time. In Session 2 the duration of the practice is set at 10 minutes.

2. *Guidelines for the practice*

Gentle guidance can greatly facilitate this practice for participants. In guiding participants through the 10 minutes there are four points of importance:

a. Begin by assisting with settling into the posture.
b. Remind them from time to time where to focus their attention.
c. Offer suggestions about handling mind wandering.
d. Highlight the attitudes to be cultivated in this practice: Non-judging, patience, non-striving, acceptance, letting go.

Here are some additional details regarding each of these points:

a. *Posture*

Begin the practice with mindfulness of the participant's posture by highlighting awareness of the sensations involved in sitting. Suggest an erect posture with head, neck, and back aligned vertically. Invite participants to reach the mode of being that is about to be cultivated in this practice.

Demonstrate the different possibilities of sitting: chair, cushion, or stool. Encourage experimentation with different alternatives until participants find what is most suitable for them. In the course of the practice remind participants to stay aware of the posture.

b. *Focus of attention*
Emphasize the importance of finding a balance between a state of comfort and wakefulness. Invite participants to focus on the breath in different parts of the body where they can feel the flow of air: the belly, the nose, the chest, or throat. This can facilitate attention. Encourage awareness of the breath by following the movement of the belly, expanding with in-breaths and contracting with out-breaths. If necessary participants may place a hand directly on the abdomen.

c. *Mind wandering*
Remember to offer guidance when dealing with mind wandering: acknowledge, without passing judgment, that the mind is wandering off. Bring it gently back, as many times as needed, with patience and perseverance.

d. *Practical concerns*
Make sure that the practice room is neither noisy, too bright (facilitating calmness), nor too dark (avoiding drowsiness) and that it is comfortably warm in winter and fresh in summer. In other words the place should be conducive to the type of practice.

3. *Inquiry*

Here are some brief suggestions regarding key themes to explore during inquiry:

a. It is important to start with open questions: What did the participants notice?
b. The general focus of the inquiry is on noticing, acknowledging, and helping participants bring back attention from mind wandering: What did they experience? What can be learnt by accepting whatever the experience has been?
c. Participants are encouraged to explore where their minds went in their moments of wandering: memories, worries, pain?
d. In addition participants might share any particular sensations that emerged.

4. Psycho-educational points

a. The breath serves to anchor practitioners in the present.
b. The breath helps to deal with mind wandering.
c. The breath has a calming effect on the mind.
d. Being mindful of breathing helps promote patience and curiosity, thus changing the nature of whatever one is experiencing by giving more space and appreciative perspective.

Session 2—Handouts and Homework

Handout 1 of Session 2: Content of Home Practice and Practical Considerations

1. From doing–inner dialoguing mode to being-experiential mode

With Session 2 we delve more deeply into a state of being in the present, mindful and accepting of where we are and how we feel. This is the opposite of being driven by our head into a frantic doing and inner dialoguing mode where we are planning ahead or ruminating about the past.

To strengthen this ability we continue the body scan practice and initiate a sitting meditation with concentration on breathing, the mindfulness of the breath practice. These two practices complement each other by bringing awareness to our whole being from head to toe.

2. Pleasurable present

Session 2 also introduces the three good things (TGT) practice that helps us regain awareness of what is good in our lives. Our habitual mode of striving to change and improve things inevitably carries a level of unsatisfactoriness, the idea that we must set things right, which does not help us to realize what is already good.

At the same time we continue to do a daily activity mindfully as in the home assignments of Session 1.

In combination these two practices help us reconnect with the agreeable side of the present and help us appreciate and accept what is right now.

3. Time management

Time management may become more demanding as you do several practices daily. You may need to experiment with how to best organize your time. One obvious option is to do one of the assignments in the morning and another in the evening. If a particular working day is especially stressful you might also practice on a Sunday (normally a day of rest) instead of during the week. As the practice will increase your well-being you will still have a relaxing weekend.

Handout 2 of Session 2: Home Practice for the Week Following Session 2

Whenever you practice use the home practice record form handed out in Session 1 to keep track of your activities. The form is an adjustable standard template that can be used for all sessions until the end of the program. If you need more space you can easily add lines and reprint or photocopy the form.

1. Continue to do the **body scan** daily. Remember to let go of any expectations about how you should feel. There is no right way and no goal to achieve other than just being there, right now, in your body, without having to do anything or to change things.
2. Get into the habit of doing the **mindfulness of the breath** sitting meditation every day for 10 minutes—always choosing a quiet spot where you can feel safe and uninterrupted. The audio file provided will guide you to find the appropriate upright posture, whether you choose to do the practice seated in a chair or on a cushion on the floor. It will also assist you to keep the focus on your breathing and gently remind you to lead your mind back to the practice if it has wandered off.
3. Always start with the **three good things** exercise. It is a very pleasant, short, and easy practice consisting of two steps: (i) reflecting on three things that are good in your life and (ii) making notes in a journal.

   The reflection will take you only a few moments. The choice is limitless. It could be something small and recent or something existential, in the past or ongoing. You could choose an event or a relationship, a fortunate circumstance that you are grateful for, or something beautiful you enjoyed.

   When you have identified three good things and thought about them make short notes in your journal, paying special attention to why each particular good thing is so valuable to you: In what way does it make your life richer or more enjoyable? How did the blessing come about? Is it a gift? The fruit of someone's effort? A happy circumstance or something else?

This exercise helps us to become aware of all the good things in our life that we usually take for granted or ignore in our quest for more. It cultivates an attitude of gratefulness that greatly contributes to well-being. By becoming more appreciative we also improve our relationships.

The best time of the day for this short practice is either in the morning while preparing for the day or in the evening as you are reflecting on the day's events.

4. Choose **another routine activity** to do mindfully every day, perhaps one you don't particularly like. If you give it a special twist by being mindful then maybe something will change.

Handout 3 of Session 2: Optional Material

Article

(Neuroscience, with illustrations)

Ricard, M., Lutz, A., & Davidson, R. J. (2014) Mind of the meditator – Contemplative practices that extend back thousands of years and show a multitude of benefits for both the body and the mind. *Scientific American*, November.

http://www.nature.com/scientificamerican/journal/v311/n5/full/scientificamerican1114-38.html

Session 3

Note 6: Breath and Body Sitting Mediation

1. The script

As always in sitting meditations, the first step is to get into an upright posture with the spine, neck, and head in a vertical line. Tucking the chin in towards the chest makes it easier. It also helps to imagine the vertebrae resting one on top of the other like little building blocks so they are not strained during prolonged sitting. The eyes may be gently closed.

We begin the practice by breathing mindfully for a few minutes in the same way as we do with mindfulness of the breath. We are simply following the natural flow of breath as we inhale and exhale, sensing the air streaming in, expanding our abdomen and then leaving our body again as the abdomen flattens.

When we feel that our awareness has deepened we expand it from the breath to the entire body, sensing the body as a whole. We register, if possible, with heightened interest the different sensations throughout the body. Perhaps you can feel the body moving with the breath and gently follow the rhythm of ebb and flow, contraction and expansion. Maybe your attention is drawn to some part of the body where there are more intense sensations or even discomfort. In this case it may be worthwhile to stay with the sensation with acceptance and curiosity. If the discomfort increases and the meditation begins to strain then an option is to carefully and mindfully adjust the posture.

We maintain, if possible, this wider awareness by pulling back from mind wandering whenever our attention gets distracted, again and again, as often as necessary and without blaming ourselves.

When the practice draws to a close we gently return to mindfulness of the breath, letting our awareness come back to the plain movements of in-breaths and out-breaths and focusing once more on the abdomen and the sensations related to inhaling and exhaling, savoring the feeling of staying calmly present in a being mode.

As we return to our normal busy lives we may hold onto this experience and remind ourselves from time to time that we can always tap into this feeling again.

2. *Guidelines for conducting the practice*

The following practical suggestions can help facilitate the practice for teachers guiding a session as well as readers practicing personally.

a. To make it easier to expand awareness a simple and practical way is to widen the attention in several steps from attention *on* the breath to sensations *around* the breath and then expanding to the body as a whole.
b. To widen their awareness participants may be invited to feel their bodies in the space: the contact with the floor, cushion, or chair; clothes touching the skin; the touch of their hands resting on their knees or thighs, and so on. They can also be guided to experience their bodies from the inside: any tingling, pulsing, tightness, or other sensations.
c. As the period of sitting gets longer participants may begin to feel discomfort or pain. The teacher needs to provide guidance on how to deal with these sensations, both physically or emotionally. Even if there seems to be no particular sign of discomfort, it is advisable to offer guidance. The first step is to acknowledge whatever distracting sensations there might be and stay with that acknowledgement for a moment. Additional options include:
    - Adjusting the posture mindfully by being aware of the intention to move and of the movement itself and then returning to stillness and observing the effect of having moved.
    - Staying without moving and calmly bringing awareness to the place where the discomfort is concentrated. This involves exploring the sensation and using the breath as a resource by imagining how to "breathe into the area" and observing the effect this has. Usually participants notice an opening and softening around the experience.
    - Inviting participants to anchor their awareness in the breath, thus moving attention away from the area of discomfort.

3. *Inquiry*

In the inquiry after the exercise several points are of special importance:

- Looking at the body as a container of varying experiences can heighten bodily awareness.
- Both the body and the breath can be used as anchors for our attention.

- The practice enables us to read the patterns of breath and body sensations.
- Learning how to deal mindfully with discomfort is a valuable insight.
- Curiosity can help change how one relates to the experiences.
- Attentive observation shows that internal experiences are continuously changing. By learning to be a keen observer of their internal experiences participants become their own internal detectives.
- The mind is difficult to keep steady or to control. It simply has a tendency to wander.
- The enduring point is to persist in learning to focus and learning to recollect the mind.

4. Psycho-educational points

The breath and body meditation deepens and expands the lessons of the preceding sessions. The main themes are:

a. Recollecting and calming the mind.
b. Dealing with mind wandering.
c. Increasing physical awareness focusing on breath and body.
d. Recognizing the quality of an experience: liking, disliking, or indifference—the three typical categories of human experience.
e. Learning to deal with discomfort by enhancing curiosity.

Note 7: 3-Minutes Breathing Space—3MBS

The 3-Minutes Breathing Space practice is a mini-meditation that is particularly practical for busy people because it is short and versatile: it can be performed seated or standing and with eyes closed or open depending on where you are at that moment. So people next to you, for example, in a commuter train, might not even notice that you are meditating. It lends itself to be implemented several times a day, whenever the need to be mindful, calm, and focused urges you to recollect the mind.

1. The script

The 3MBS practice consists of three steps or stages:

Step 1

Awareness of BETA: From doing mode to being mode: In this phase the idea is to simply become aware of the present moment, taking the whole spectrum of our feelings and sensations in and acknowledging them with gentleness and acceptance.

Step 2

Focus: Concentrating on breathing, abdomen rising and falling: In this phase we narrow our attention and focus on breathing in the same way as we did in awareness of the breath (Session1) and mindfulness of the breath (Session2). The breath is the anchor to help us concentrate and stay in the present moment, aware of each in-breath and out-breath.

Step 3

Expanding: Widening the awareness to the whole body: Just as in the practice of mindfulness of breath and body, the next step consists of widening the attention and becoming aware of the whole body, feeling from the inside what our body is telling us right now. If we feel tightness, bracing, or other uncomfortable sensations in some parts, we experiment with breathing into these areas and out from them, so that the sensation can soften as we let go of unnecessary tightness with our out-breath. Then the idea is to hold onto this regained mindful awareness as we surface from the mini-meditation and get back to the challenges awaiting us.

The sequence of these three steps can be summarized as a movement "from wide to narrow and back to wide," which is why the 3MBS is often visualized as a sandglass where sand trickles from the wide top half through a narrow passage into the spacious bottom half.

The illustration below Figure 9.7 is a memory aid for participants. It reinforces the insight that the 3MBS is a handy tool that is within reach throughout the day.

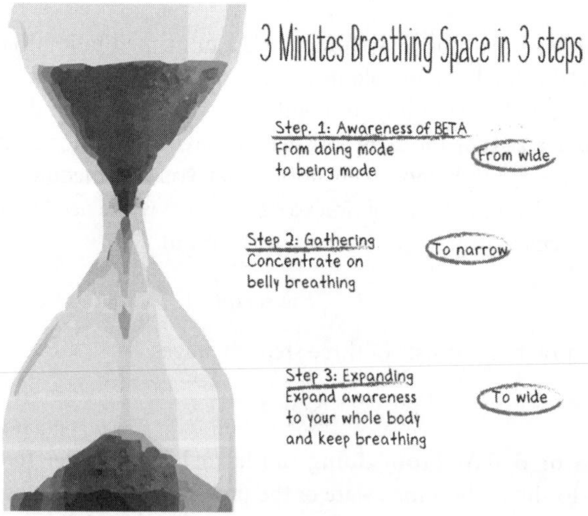

Figure 9.7 3 Minutes Breathing Space in 3 Steps. *Source*: Juan Humberto Young.

2. *Guidelines for conducting the practice*

Here are some suggestions as to how you can apply and guide this practical and compact meditation form:

1. Although the 3MBS can be practiced almost anywhere and at anytime it is still essential to have an erect posture. The upright, dignified posture enhances present moment awareness and also opens the chest and with it our mind. The first move therefore is to become aware of what posture we are in.
2. The practice is most effective when the three steps are clearly marked. Consequently, it is useful if teachers clearly announce each step and label it: Step 1, Awareness of BETA; Step 2, Gathering; Step 3, Expanding. This helps participants know where they are in the meditation. Likewise participants practicing on their own should consciously mark in their mind the passage from one step to the next.
3. It is important to realize that the three minutes are more a figure of speech than a precise measure. It could just as well be longer or shorter according to the unique situation. The number three is only indicative.

3. *Inquiry*

In the inquiry after the exercise several points should be highlighted:

a. The biggest gain from this brief practice occurs when it is integrated in daily life and becomes a frequent habit.
b. Participants may think of 3MBS as a moment to pause.
c. 3MBS is not a problem-solving tool but a method to switch from doing to being mode. Only as a secondary effect, and because of the resulting mindful attitude, solving an issue may become easier. This, however, is not a primary goal.
d. The 3MBS can be performed during sessions if the need arises.

4. *Psycho-educational points*

Here is an overview of the main insights gained by practicing 3MBS.

a. 3MBS is a practice that can be done during the day, even multiple times.
b. Its essence is moving from doing to being mode in just a few moments.
c. 3MBS helps participants to move towards impending upcoming situations with a different, more mindful and constructive attitude.

d. With 3MBS we learn to use wide-angle awareness to find out what is going on in mind and body in the present moment (step one).
e. We practice narrow angle attention by anchoring our mind on breathing (step two).
f. Subsequently we return to wide-angle awareness by widening our attention to the whole body thus creating a more comprehensive perspective of the present moment (step 3).

Note 8: Mindful Stretching and Mindful Salsa

Being mindful of our body in movement has a different quality of awareness and sensitivity when compared to motionless practices like the body scan.

Mindfulness programs usually begin with motionless practices because it is easier to concentrate on different body parts and explore the sensations in them. Moving practices provide alternative experiences involving coordination and the emergence of other emotions and mental patterns. For example, pleasurable feelings may intensify for those of us who like physical activities but aches and pains may become more noticeable, too, as we activate joints, tendons, and muscles.

In this session two mindful movement practices are introduced: mindful stretching and mindful salsa. Later in the program we will look at mindful walking. An age-old and very effective form of mindful movement is yoga, which is sometimes called meditation in motion. If it is feasible it would be ideal for participants to take some yoga lessons, which would perfectly complement the present program. Yoga is highly compatible with MBSAT and with mindfulness in general as yoga teaches participants to listen to their body without comparing it to others.

1. *The script*

a. *Mindful stretching*

Given that many of us have sedentary occupations, mindful stretching is a healthy and practical exercise. In this session we focus on the body parts that do not get a lot of stretching and can suffer from too much sitting: the neck and shoulders and the whole upper part of the body.

Start by standing upright with your feet firmly grounded and slightly apart. You can be either barefoot or in socks. On an in-breath slowly and mindfully lift your arms sideways until they are stretched out at the height of your shoulders and parallel to the floor. On the next in-breath keep lifting further until your arms are vertical and your hands touch each other. Keep this position for a few moments and explore the sensations of the stretch in your whole body while breathing normally. Observe how the sensations change over time as you maintain the stretch. The essence of the exercise is awareness.

When you feel the time is right, slowly and mindfully start lowering the arms until they are again parallel to the floor, but this time with the palms pushing outward and your fingers upward as indicated in Figure 9.8, while pushing firmly for an extra stretch.

Then lower your arms until you are back in the starting position. Take a moment to close your eyes and become aware of any changes in your sensations.

When you feel ready, you may begin the next stretching exercises.

Raising first one arm and then the other as if you were reaching a piece of fruit hanging in a tree. Imagine that the fruit is quite high so that you must lift a heel to reach it. While you are attempting these movements, it is important to stay attentive to your breath and the sensations in your body that have been created by these movements.

For the next stretch lift both arms and bend first to one side, creating an arch that goes from your legs through your torso and arms and up to the fingertips. On an out-breath returning to the center and with the next in-breath bending your body to the other side. Figure 9.8 explains the movements.

After returning to the starting position with your arms beside your body we then move on to shoulder rolls (see Figure 9.9). Imagine that you are

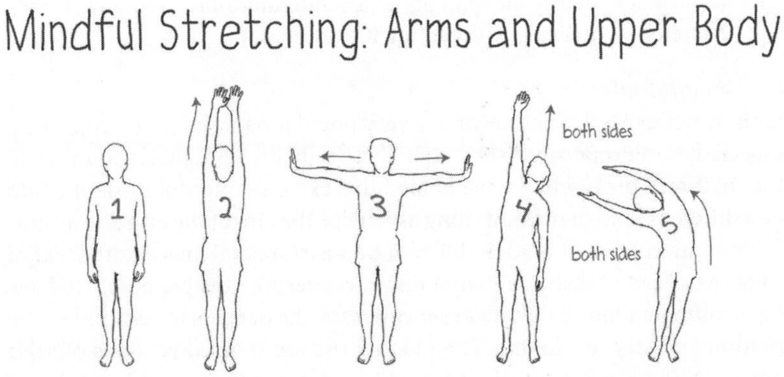

Figure 9.8 Mindful Stretching: Arms and Upper Body. *Source*: Juan Humberto Young.

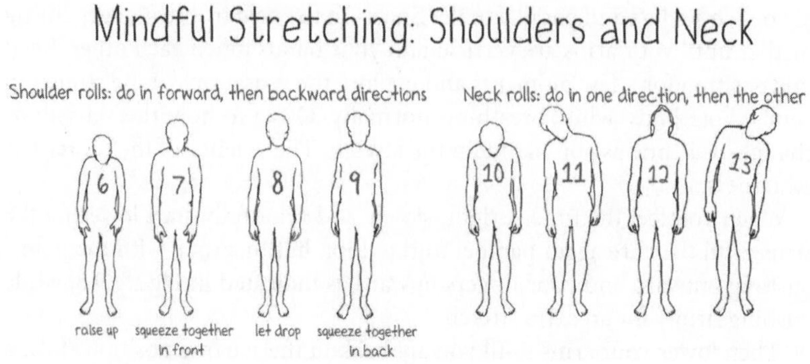

Figure 9.9 Mindful Stretching: Shoulders and Neck. *Source*: Juan Humberto Young.

drawing a circle with your shoulders by first pulling them up as much as you can towards your ears, then rotating them forward and pressing them together in front of your chest. From this position rolling them backwards in a circular movement until your shoulder blades are squeezed together behind your back. This completes the first part of the exercise. Now you may add some more rounds, always with your arms hanging and relaxed. After a few rounds change the direction of the rolls.

After a few rounds in each direction relax for a few moments and carefully observe your sensations.

The last stretching exercise involves head rolls, starting in a neutral and relaxed position and gently drawing circles in the air with your chin, first in one direction and then in the other. In this part of the exercise it is particularly important to do the movements gently and mindfully, giving your neck a good stretch yet delicately protecting it from injury.

b. *Mindful salsa*

Latin American Salsa has become a very popular dance in many countries, especially in Europe, and it is a style that really invites dancers to move to the rhythm. This is why I have named this exercise mindful salsa. It could be a different kind of music as long as it helps the aim of the exercise: mindful body awareness. It is advisable to have instrumental music as the text of songs may lead to distraction and mind wandering. It is preferable to have light, animated music that makes it easier for the dancers to respond to the rhythm and stay in motion. The pieces I use are stylized versions of salsa music. With true salsa music it would turn into a fitness exercise. A list of pieces that work well based on my experience, are given later.

There are two ways to do mindful salsa. At the beginning of the exercise it is useful to invite participants to move freely just following their emotions and keeping their attention centered on their body sensations. This helps produce a present being mode and overcomes any shyness or other inhibitions.

The second variation involves participants being invited to focus their attention on specific instruments, for example, the bass, saxophone, or percussion and moving to the rhythm of different instruments. This approach requires careful listening and full attention because ideally participants should incorporate the beat and feel their whole bodies resonating as opposed to just performing the movements mechanically.

2. *Guidelines for conducting the practice*

Some practical comments and suggestions may help participants to enjoy these active exercises.

a. *The challenge of giving instructions*
People who guide mindful stretching will find that it is useful to have taken yoga lessons. They are an ideal way to become familiar with how to give precise instructions for movements. Although I have been practicing yoga regularly for several years and practicing kick boxing and martial arts for a long time, even earning a black belt in Aikido, I am still careful when guiding mindful stretching. This is one of the reasons I developed mindful salsa. It allows a teacher to work with the same intentions but in a softer way and having fun. Participants are usually in a good mood after 10 minutes of moving to music. (I recently worked with a group of 14 top bankers who did mindful salsa and after the exercise they all were in good spirits and more communicative during the inquiry—conditions that are compatible with MBSAT's purpose of increasing people's well-being.)

b. *Non-competitive attitude*
It is important to remind participants that the mindful movement exercises are not sports events or competitions. Participants should be focused on their own experience without comparing themselves to others and most of all without judging themselves. Whatever a person is capable of doing is acceptable. What is important is the exploration of body sensations without thinking in terms of achievement. Mindful movement exercises are also a way of cultivating kindness to oneself. During stretching the teacher should remind participants from time to

time that it is up to them to set their own limits. They are in charge of their own body. They can decide when they wish to stop a stretch.

c. *Mindful movement and breathing*
It is useful to advise participants to inhale when they stretch and to exhale when they return to a normal posture or, when the stretch is prolonged, during the actual movement. This is the general rule that many people implement intuitively. Personally I tell participants to use their natural tendencies but with awareness. When doing mindful salsa the breath may flow naturally with the continuous movement without paying much attention to in- and out-breaths.

d. *Awareness of liking and disliking*
With the different stretches, and particularly with mindful salsa, the teacher should remind participants to pay attention to their likes and dislikes. It is easy to be diverted by thoughts such as "I like this sound, it is smooth" or "I don't like the trumpet, it sounds shrill in my ears." Our tendency to evaluate and judge takes us away from the being mode. Similarly you should invite participants to watch out for "I can" and "I can't." Remind them that this is an exercise of being mindful in movement and to observe our internal experiences. It is not about prowess.

e. *Suggestions for music*
Prepare a selection of music for the session. The following is a list of pieces I have used personally and that have worked well in my programs (my favorite titles are underlined):

Music Band	Title of piece
A Million Flavours	The Last Wave
Dziha Kamien	Homebase (live), Live in Vienna
Fattburger	Spice
Gabin	La Maison
Green Empathy	Airport
High End	After Traffic (soft)
Jazeboo Havana Moon	Acapulco
Jens Buchert	Mélange Eclectique (soft)
Joe McBride	Oi Gata (soft)
Johann Asmundsson	So low (fast)
Joyce Cooling	Global Cooling (short)

Music Band	Title of piece
Peter White	Déjà vu (soft)
Pune Desire	Hourglass
Renato Falaschi	Summer Rain, Travelling Lite
Steve Oliver	Positive Energy
Tom Grant	Generous Heart
2-Man Legends	Made 4 U

3. *Inquiry*

In the inquiry after the exercises several points are of special significance:

a. Working with the awareness of the body in motion:
What differences were evident between these two practices and the body scan? Where did the participants discover more sensations—in movement or in resting as in the body scan?
b. What did the participants observe regarding balance in mindful salsa and in mindful stretching?
c. Was there more or less mind wandering?
d. What thoughts, feelings, and sensations were identified relating to discomfort during stretches or triggered by perceived clumsiness during salsa?
e. Was there any tendency to become judgmental with regard to fitness or skills?
f. Participants should share their observations about how attention can be moved from one part of the body to another following the breath and the rhythm and cadence of the music.

4. *Psycho-educational points*

Essential insights from mindful stretching and salsa include:

a. Further cultivating and deepening awareness of the body.
b. Learning to notice the mental patterns of striving.
c. Learning to accept limits.
d. Learning to be kind to ourselves.

Note 9: Positive BETA Reframing Exercise

1. *Script*

Positive psychologists have discovered that an effective strategy to increase well-being is brief, but frequent, experiences of positive emotions, sensations, and thoughts in daily life. The positive BETA reframing exercise seeks to assist individuals by multiplying such moments of positivity. It aims to provide a mechanism to reframe negative automatic thoughts that are often unconscious. Negative automatic thoughts reflect the patterns of our conditioning and dominate and shape our BETA, often producing unskillful reactions.

The exercise consists of two steps:

Step 1: As objectively as you can, describe a situation that has generated a negative reaction from you.

Now describe the feelings and sensations generated by the experience and possibly your impulse to act resulting from those feelings and sensations.

Try to remember what negative automatic thoughts sprang up in your mind.

Step 2: Reimagine the situation as it originally occurred.

Constructively and positively try to re-engineer your thoughts, finding possible alternative explanations and interpretations.

Describe what your emotions are now and what impulses to act you feel. If you find it difficult to fathom your feelings based on the re-engineered thoughts you might describe the *expected* BETA: Body sensations, Emotions/feelings, Thoughts and Action impulses that would be likely to result from reframing the same situation.

2. *Guidelines for conducting the exercise*

Ask participants to start the exercise by thinking about a real situation that was a negative experience for them. Guide them through remembering and describing their feelings and sensations, thoughts and impulses to act as vividly as possible. Let them write their experience down by filling in Part 1 of Handout 1 (without handing out Part 2, reserved for the second part of the exercise).

Then introduce the participants to Step 2.

While the situation described in Step 1 remains the same, let the participants imagine that they just won the lottery and are in a joyful mood as they will be able to do something they always dreamt of doing.

Let them reflect on how they would feel if the same situation happened again now that they have a new context (just having been informed of winning the lottery): what would their feelings and sensations be now? What would be their thoughts and impulses to act? Let the participants write down their reflection in Part 2 of Handout 1. (The form does not mention the lottery winnings, but the participants will already be in a different mood as a result of its introduction by the teacher.)

To facilitate a lively discussion you might present during the exercise the visualization of Figure 9.2, the positive reframing ABC model.

3. *Inquiry*

Several issues should emerge in the discussion:

a. The power of automatic thinking and how it shapes the experience, most often in a negative, defensive way.
b. The hidden, unconscious nature of cognition and how it shapes our experience.
c. How mood and feelings can influence our cognition, effectively creating a reverse loop: automatic thoughts shape our feelings and vice versa: feelings can also shape our cognition.
d. How contextual phenomena such as winning the lottery can greatly influence our experience by altering our emotional state.

4. *Psycho-educational points*

a. The quality of thoughts shapes our experience.
b. Thoughts have a malleable characteristic.
c. There is a bidirectional connection between thoughts and feelings, which provides two gates to reframing the experience from negative to positive/constructive.
d. A third gate is context: given the contextual influences on mood and feelings one can auto-engineer the mood and bend it towards appreciation by intentionally creating more positive contexts and thus amplifying the well-being zone.
e. Learning new forms of taking care of themselves.

Session 3—Handouts and Homework

Handout 1 of Session 3: Positive BETA Reframing Part 1

a. As objectively as you can, briefly describe a situation that has generated a negative reaction from you. What happened?

....

....

b. Try to remember, as vividly as you can, the feelings and sensations that were triggered by the situation and possibly your impulses to act resulting from those feelings and sensations.

....

....

c. What was the first thought that crossed your mind as you experienced the situation unfolding?

....

....

Part 2: Positive BETA Reframing Part 2

a. Think again about the situation you described in Part 1 and the thoughts that crossed your mind at the time.
Can you think of other explanations or other possible viewpoints than the ones that occurred to you—more positive ones? What would they be?

....

....

b. Imagine that your alternative interpretations are actually your true beliefs. How does this alter your feelings and sensations? And what is your impulse to act now?
Tip: If you find it hard to imagine your feelings under these new circumstances, describe what feelings and sensations you would *normally expect* from a person looking at the situation from this new angle.

....

....

Handout 2 of Session 3: Home Practice for the Week Following Session 3

Until next session the plan is to alternate sitting and moving practices by doing a sitting meditation on odd days and mindful movement practices on even days. This way you can experiment with both forms.

Please remember to keep track of your practice by recording your activities in the home practice record form handed out in Session 1. As new exercises are introduced it becomes even more important to maintain an overview.

You will also do two informal, shorter practices and do a survey to deepen your self-knowledge.

1. Please, do the **breath and body** sitting meditation we initiated today on days 1, 3, and 5 with the help of the audio file provided.
2. Days 2, 4, and 6 are dedicated to mindful movement and you can choose between **mindful stretching and mindful salsa**. It is recommended, however, that you do each at least once. When you do it, remember to be kind to yourself by neither overdoing it nor judging yourself. After all it should be a pleasurable practice.
3. Whenever you feel the need arise, please, do the **3-minutes breathing space**, for example, when you need a restorative break or would like to calm down, gain more clarity, and so on. As a rule of thumb you should do the 3MBS at least three times a day.
4. Every day select one event and reflect on it from the vantage point of **positively reframing** your BETA using the 2-step method you experimented with in today's Session 3. As guidance you may use the forms you filled in today. In your home practice you can use your journal (the one you started with the three good things (TGT) practice in Session 2) to write down brief summaries of your reframing episodes. This will make your insights more durable, as they enter into your long-term memory.
5. Please, do the **VIA character strengths survey** that is available in 34 languages. You find it under the following link:

   https://www.viacharacter.org/survey/account/register

   On the homepage you will also find a lot of interesting information about the definition of strengths and the structure and validity of the survey. The survey is free of charge and fun to do, because it has no connection whatsoever with job evaluation. It is more about fundamental human virtues and that is why it is called VIA for values in action. You can go through the questions quickly and will probably need no more than 30 minutes. Please, bring a copy of the outcome to the next session.

Looking forward to see you again in Session 4!

Session 4

Note 10: Sitting Meditation on Breath, Body, Sounds, Thoughts, and Open Awareness

1. The script

After assuming an upright position, the meditation starts by becoming aware of our breathing and then expanding that awareness to the entire body in the same way as in the mindfulness of breath and body practice in Session 3.

When you feel fully present in your body you may shift your awareness to your ears and to your hearing, without making a particular effort to listen, being open to any sounds and registering their quality: loud or barely audible, harsh or soft, close by or farther away, long or short. There is rarely complete silence, but if it is really quiet, you may also listen to the stillness in the room or be attentive to intervals between sounds. Staying focused on your sensation of hearing rather than thinking about the sounds and analyzing them.

Thoughts are the focal point of the next stage in this meditation. When you feel ready you can let go of hearing sensations and become aware of your thoughts with the same effortless openness you registered with sounds, that is, don't try to control them. Against the backdrop of your recollected and quiet mind, thoughts will appear by themselves. When this happens you may simply watch them with curiosity as if through the lens of a researcher who studies exotic butterflies or a rare species of hummingbird, being aware of the thoughts and letting them go without becoming emotionally involved in the stories they convey. When this proves difficult, and if you get drawn deeper into the thoughts, you might return to awareness by sensing the changes in your body that reflect your thoughts: can you recognize the sensations resulting from the thoughts?

For the last stage of this practice you may bring the same kind of friendly awareness to your whole being and your surroundings as you sit in stillness, alert and taking note of any external or internal perceptions that might emerge. There is no need to do anything specific, just be present in the here and now.

You might like to close the practice by breathing mindfully for a few rounds of in- and out-breaths before slowly opening your eyes.

2. *Guidelines for conducting the practice*

The first part of this meditation focuses on **breath and body**. You will need to apply the guidelines for the breath and body sitting meditation that were described in Session 3 (Note 6). The following suggestions refer to the second part of the meditation and involve sounds, thoughts, and open awareness.

1. For **mindfulness of sound** participants are invited to simply receive sounds as they become audible, without interfering or judging. In order to train this attitude participants can first start by recognizing their personal reactions to sounds: what they like or dislike and what leaves them indifferent. Then the teacher can ask the participants to let go of this labeling and cultivate an open and accepting attitude that helps them to listen with genuine curiosity.
2. **Mindfulness of thoughts** requires special guidance:
    a. Invite participants to see thoughts as elements of a transitory mental process. They are thoughts that arise, pass, and disappear. They should avoid getting involved in the content of the thoughts.
    b. Invite participants to see their thoughts as clouds that arrive, drift, and disappear in front of a backdrop of a steady bright blue sky, which represents the mind. Sometimes the clouds are light, at other times dark and somber, and the participants simply observe the spectacle. Another useful metaphor that appeals to business people relates to the cinema. Invite participants to imagine that they are in a movie theater and on the screen they watch their thoughts taking shape and disappearing like fleeting images.
    c. People will invariably get involved in their thoughts, mentally and emotionally, as they observe them. When this happens it is necessary to acknowledge the involvement and return to seeing the thoughts just as thoughts, repeating the same steps as many times as necessary.
    d. Instead of getting involved in the content of thoughts it can be revealing to look at the relationship between emotions and thoughts and how they shape each other. Thinking and judging can invade emotions (I like this emotion, I don't like this one, etc.) and emotions can color and influence thought. It is important to learn to recognize the judging mind.
    e. Finally remind the participants that the breath is always there as an anchor if they get distracted, so they can come back to breathing mindfully if necessary.
3. For **mindfulness of open awareness** inviting participants to simply be with whatever arises in the moment, developing a wide and spacious sense of the mind, observing whatever experience is emerging in the moment and how it changes and affects the mind and the body.

3. Inquiry

The inquiry focuses on the following essential aspects:

a. What have the participants experienced as they shifted their attention from breath to body, sounds, thoughts, emotions, and open awareness?
b. What did they experience when decentering from thoughts as discussed above (noticing thoughts as thoughts, not facts)?
c. Have they been able to notice how emotions are attached to thoughts and vice versa?
d. This meditation is an effective practice which allows participants to observe recurrent patterns of the mind.
e. With this practice, especially with the introduction of meditation on sounds and open awareness, the participants will notice the feeling of spaciousness that comes with a calm, yet open and alert, mind.

4. Psycho-educational points

In addition to the insights related to breath and body discussed in Session 3 from this practice you will also learn:

a. Open awareness: which is mindfulness with a friendly awareness of your whole being and your surroundings.
b. To register experiences with an open and receptive mind without labeling or creating stories.
c. To notice the patterns of your mind.
d. To understand the key concept of decentering, which means that you learn to relate to thoughts as thoughts, not facts.
e. To relate thoughts and emotions to body sensations.
f. To develop a spaciousness of the mind by looking at experiences as they arise and pass.
g. To develop the ability to be more aware of the human experience.

Note 11: Exercise to Define the Territory of Worry and Anxiety (TWA)

1. The script

The TWA exercise is designed to explore personal experiences with worry and anxiety and to assist participants to recognize and identify aversion when it manifests itself in the form of worry and anxiety.

The exercise begins by asking participants to close their eyes and bring to their mind an experience they are currently confronting. (In the unlikely case that someone cannot think of a current difficulty, it is acceptable to choose a trying situation from the past.) The mental picture of the issue or situation should be as vivid and real as possible. When the participants are fully immersed in the challenges they are facing, the teacher asks them to explore individually and silently all the sensations, thoughts, feelings, and behavioral reactions they can identify. After a few moments the teacher invites the participants to slowly and gently open their eyes.

In the joint inquiry the participants share, as openly and honestly as possible, their discoveries. They can leave out specific details to protect their privacy. This exchange may appear difficult but it has a comforting effect because, most commonly, the participants discover that their colleagues have similar mental and emotional difficulties.

After the inquiry the teacher can explain the dynamics of worry and anxiety using the MBSAT worry and anxiety model presented in Figure 10.2 and included in Handout 2.

On a board (whiteboard or blackboard) the teacher then draws a table and in conversation with the participants enters the participants' experiences: their thoughts, feelings, body sensations, and behavioral impulses. Figure 10.3 is an easy-to-follow example. There is a separate column for each type of experience headed "Type of Arrow," and participants determine whether they consider the respective elements as an arrow 1 or an arrow 2 item: an arrow 1 type of suffering or arrow 2 type of suffering. These inputs should be reached as a joint experiential learning process with the teacher as facilitator.

After the data gathering and discussion the teacher distributes Handout 1, "Some of the ways that worry can affect you," and reads it with the participants. This allows the teacher and participants to establish recognition of commonalities by generalizing the learning.

2. *Guidelines for conducting the practice*

Here are some suggestions that might be helpful for mindfulness teachers:

a. Invite participants to bring to their awareness to a situation they find difficult to manage. Make them aware that the MBSAT program provides them with a safe context for exploration. It will help them learn to cope with worry and anxiety with confidence.
b. Once they have explored their difficult experience invite them to investigate the messages ensuing from their awareness.

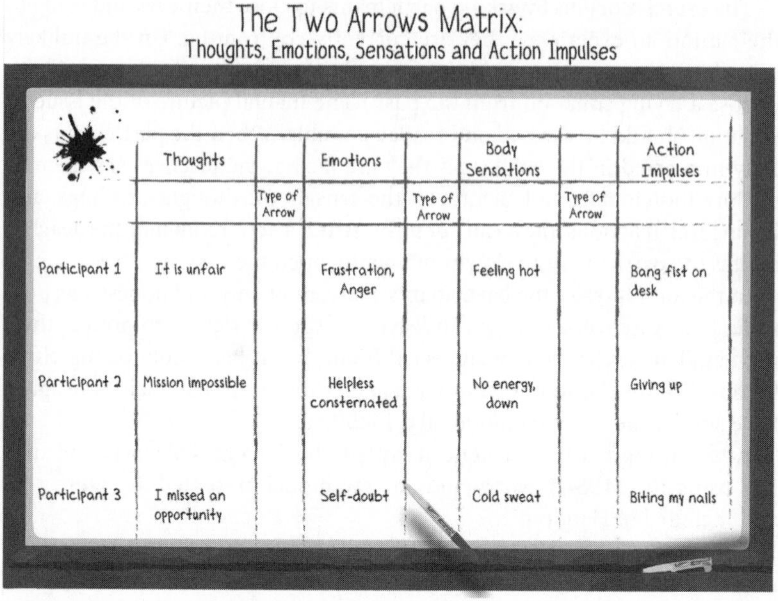
The Two Arrows Matrix:
Thoughts, Emotions, Sensations and Action Impulses

	Thoughts	Type of Arrow	Emotions	Type of Arrow	Body Sensations	Type of Arrow	Action Impulses
Participant 1	It is unfair		Frustration, Anger		Feeling hot		Bang fist on desk
Participant 2	Mission impossible		Helpless consternated		No energy, down		Giving up
Participant 3	I missed an opportunity		Self-doubt		Cold sweat		Biting my nails

Figure 10.3 The Two Arrows Matrix: Thoughts, Emotions, Body Sensations, and Action Impulses. *Source*: Juan Humberto Young.

c. The exercise should help participants observe the feelings that emerge around the experience.
d. Invite participants to sense the effects of the experience on their body sensations.
e. Ask participants to determine the elements of their experience that represent a first arrow suffering and those that represent a second arrow suffering.
f. Remind participants of an attitude of openness and curiosity towards the experience.

3. *Inquiry*

In the inquiry after the completion of the exercise there are several points of special importance:

a. Notice what drives the experience (thoughts, emotions, sensations).
b. Notice emotions are attached to thoughts and vice versa (this is the same as the sitting meditation).
c. Notice aversion in the body.

d. Help participants make connections between the experience of the exercise and their daily lives.
e. Connect the experience to the metaphor of the two arrows (visualized in the MBSAT Model of Worry and Anxiety in Figure 10.2).

4. Psycho-educational points

a. Worry and anxiety are complex emotional states that consist of multiple elements.
b. Aversion can manifest itself in the body.
c. Recognizing aversion and dislike requires awareness and practice.

Note 12: 3-Minutes Breathing Space on Strengths—3MBSS

1. The script

3MBSS is a practice designed for challenging situations where a person needs to remain calm while mobilizing personal resources to cope skillfully.

Like the regular 3MBS, which was introduced in Session 3, the strengths version, known as 3MBSS, consists of three steps. The first two steps are identical to 3MBS. For easy reference we have briefly summarized Step 1 and 2. Readers who want more details may refer to Note 7 of Session 3 and the introduction to 3MBS in Section 9.3.2.

Step 1: Awareness of BETA This step acknowledges the present situation and recognizes the relevant feelings and sensations without judging (this is a wide-angle perspective).

Step 2: Concentrating on breathing This step focuses attention on breathing by letting the abdomen rise and fall again and again until the mind becomes calm.

Step 3: Expanding the awareness and incorporating a strength Having expanded the participant's attention to the whole body (breathing in and breathing out as in the regular 3MBS) bring the specific challenging difficulty into your mind and begin to investigate which of your top five signature strengths could be useful to help cope with the present situation. When you feel that you are aware of a strength slowly open your eyes and return to your normal activities. As you do so keep the strength you have identified in your mind and during the day keep thinking about the connections between this strength and the difficulty you are trying to cope with.

You can repeat the practice as often as you like and you can implement it flexibly either by exploring additional strengths or by focusing on a specific connection between a strength and a challenge.

2. *Guidelines for conducting the practice*

There are two main guidelines for this practice:

a. Given that this is a brief practice to be integrated in people's daily lives there is not much time or opportunity to concentrate on details about posture. Nevertheless, it is important to remind participants of the importance of consciously assuming an attentive posture. The first move is to become aware of your posture—only then can the practice begin.
b. A clear distinction between the three steps is a key element of the practice. A useful rule is to announce and label each step: Step 1: noticing BETA, Step 2: breathing, Step 3: expanding awareness. This can help guide one's awareness in the meditation. It is also essential to remind participants that 3 minutes is just an approximate time. The practice can be longer if they desire: 5 minutes or more depending on the practitioner's needs.

3. *Inquiry*

Points to consider in the inquiry after the exercise include:

a. How to integrate the practice into daily life.
b. How to use the practice as a moment for pausing and recollection.
c. How to use the awareness of character strengths to discover new possibilities and avenues to help deal with your daily difficulties.

4. *Psycho-educational points*

The main points to be learnt from 3MBSS:

a. It is a practice that can be done during the day.
b. It is possible to move from doing to being in a very short time.
c. It is an opportunity to pause and move with constructive engagement by using character strengths consciously and volitionally.

Note 13: Mindful Walking

1. *The script*

Although the practice appears to be simple, mindful walking is actually a complex meditation comprising four principal movements that involve multiple minute moves of muscles, joints, and tendons, which need to be executed with clear awareness and intention.

First movement: Lifting the foot and sensing the lightness in the upward movement.

Second movement: Moving the foot forward and sensing it floating in the air.

Third movement: Putting the foot down and sensing the heaviness as the foot moves down to the ground.

Fourth movement: Sensing the foot touching the ground, either hard (wood, concrete, etc.) or soft (lawn, sand, carpet), then bending the sole of the foot in preparation for the next step.

2. *Guidelines for conducting the practice*

Here are some suggestions for guiding the practice:

a. Guide the practice by mentioning the four movements aloud: lifting, moving, posing, and grounding the feet.
b. After a while invite people to adjust their walking speed as they feel comfortable.
c. Make participants aware of the rhythm and suppleness of their movements as they take one step after another.

3. *Inquiry*

In the inquiry after the exercise several points should be raised:

a. Invite the participants to notice the difference between normal walking and mindful walking.
b. Invite them to experiment with the speed of walking and to adjust it if necessary to maintain focused attention.

4. Psycho-educational points

a. Every activity is a chance to be mindful.
b. The importance of maintaining awareness of breath and body during mindful walking.
c. The connection between breath and walking speed.
d. Additional insights similar to the other movement practices in Session 3.

Session 4—Handouts and Homework

Handout 1 of Session 4: Some of the Ways that Worry Can Affect You

How worry affects your thinking: What is on your mind?

- Worry keeps you on the lookout for problems, difficulties, or disasters (hyper-vigilance).
- Worry interferes with concentration and with your ability to give something your full attention.
- Worry focuses your attention onto yourself and your specific concerns.
- Worry makes it hard to make decisions.
- Worry increases your ability to notice things and to worry about these more than other things (selective attention).
- Worry makes you more pessimistic, so you tend to predict the worst.
- Worry makes you problem-focused, so your mind leaps from one worry to the next.

How worry affects your behavior: The things you do

- Worry makes you less efficient (either over-careful, or unwittingly careless).
- Worry interferes with your performance.
- Worry makes you rely more on others and less on yourself.
- Worry leads you to do things less confidently.

How worry affects your feelings: Your emotions

- Worry makes you feel muddled or confused.
- Worry makes you feel apprehensive and fearful.
- Worry makes you feel out of control.
- Worry makes you feel overwhelmed, or that you can't cope.

How worry affects your body

- Worry reduces your ability to relax and to sleep well.
- Worry makes you weary and tired.
- Worry makes you tense.
- Worry gives you headaches.

Adapted from Butler and Hope (2005)

Handout 2 of Session 4: The Self-Reinforcing Dynamics of Worry and Anxiety

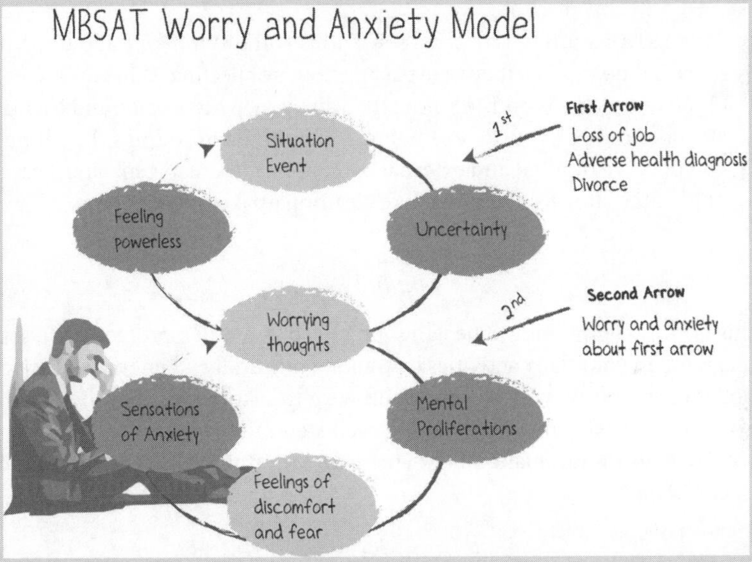

Figure 10.2 MBSAT Worry and Anxiety Model. *Source*: Juan Humberto Young.

Handout 3 of Session 4: Home Practice for the Week Following Session 4

In this week's session the comprehensive sitting meditation of breath, body, sounds, thoughts, and open awareness is a key element and is assigned as daily practice from day 1–6.

It is complemented by Mindful Walking and two 3-minutes breathing spaces: the regular 3-minutes breathing space and the special 3MBS on Strengths—two forms of mini-meditations that are easy to integrate in daily life and designed for frequent use. Mindful Walking can also be easily integrated into daily activities. For further suggestions see below.

1. *Sitting meditation on breath, body, sounds, thoughts, and open awareness*

Practicing this multi-faceted meditation regularly, days 1–6, will take your awareness to the next level. The audio files provided will guide you through it (duration 20–30 minutes).

Essential points to remember from Session 4:

- Try to savor sounds as hearing sensations without *thinking* about them.
- Look at thoughts as if they were passing clouds or fleeting scenes on a screen.
- Open awareness is nothing more than an open, wide-awake, and friendly attitude towards your whole being and your surroundings. It will help you observe internal and external perceptions. It creates spaciousness in one's mind. It feels liberating, like cleaning up a cluttered room.

2. *Mindful Walking*

This home assignment can be either practiced in a quiet, protected place or integrated in your daily activities by walking mindfully whenever you are on foot, for example on your way to the office or to a store, by simply being fully aware of each movement and taking each step mindfully instead of getting from A to B in automatic pilot. This way Mindful Walking can easily be practiced daily.

3. *3-Minutes Breathing Space (3MBS regular)*

Continue your practice. Give yourself a mental break with a 3MBS at least three times a day.

4. *3-Minutes Breathing Space on Strengths (3MBSS)*

3MBSS is designed as a strategy to deal with challenging situations where you need to remain calm and mobilize personal resources to cope with those challenges.

Like the regular 3MBS, the 3MBSS consists of three steps:

Step 1: Awareness of BETA
This step acknowledges the present situation and recognizes the relevant feelings and sensations without judging (this is a wide-angle perspective).

Step 2: Concentrating on breathing
This step focuses attention on breathing by letting the abdomen rise and fall again and again until the mind becomes calm (narrow-angle perspective).

Step 3: Expanding the awareness and incorporating a strength
Having expanded the participant's attention to the whole body (breathing in and breathing out as in the regular 3MBS) bring the specific challenging difficulty into your mind and begin to investigate which of your top 5 signature strengths could be useful to help cope with the situation. When you feel that you are aware of a strength slowly open your eyes and return to your normal activities. As you do so keep the strength you have identified in your mind and during the day keep thinking about the connections between this strength and the difficulty you are trying to cope with.

You can repeat the practice as often as you like and you can implement it flexibly either by exploring additional strengths or by focusing on a specific connection between a strength and a challenge.

Session 5

Note 14: Irimi Meditation: Awareness of Breath and Body Introducing a Difficulty

1. The script

Irimi meditation starts like the meditation on breath and body by bringing the awareness to your breathing in alignment with the rhythm of your abdomen and then expanding your attention to the whole of your body.

When you are ready you may turn your mind to some difficult situation that you are trying to deal with—something that makes you feel puzzled, angry, sad, or feeling guilty, and so on. Normally a person would let go of such thoughts and move their attention back to the focus of the meditation. This time we do the opposite: we move towards the thoughts and feelings of adversity that trigger dislike in us and approach them as if we were Aikido masters, getting closer to the adversary with the intention of gently disempowering him.

Then staying with the unpleasant thoughts and emotions discovering where they manifest themselves in the body. Can we detect tightness, bracing, or physical discomfort? What happens with our breathing? Do we feel colder now or, alternatively, hotter and sweatier? Whatever it is, we stay with our awareness on our emotions and bodily sensations and simply acknowledge them without judging.

Any sensations we might discover have probably been part of us for quite a while, but they are stored away and ignored in the same way we try to avoid unpleasant experiences. This time we stay with them. Whatever it is, it is already there. We are just cultivating body awareness from a different perspective.

In the body scan we learnt to use our imagination to breathe into different parts of the body and out from them. Now we apply this breathing method to the sensations we notice in connection with difficulty. We breathe in and out from where the most intense sensations come—maybe the shoulders and neck, or the stomach, or the heart region. We gently acknowledge any pain or discomfort.

We give this process time and just keep breathing. As we remain seated our feelings and sensations will gradually change and soften as we accept them. What we are accepting in this moment is our feelings and sensations and not the situation or event that triggered them. We observe and acknowledge any changes in our emotional state and body sensation, no matter how subtle they may be.

What is being cultivated here is not an intention to change the nature of the sensations but a gentle way of relating to those sensations and keeping them in our awareness with an attitude of acceptance and allowance.

When we feel that our emotional, mental, or physical upheaval has abated and our mind has become calmer, we can slowly return to our normal breathing and after a few moments of awareness on breathing we can let the meditation come to a close. Give yourself time to slowly open your eyes and adjust before you get up.

2. *Guidelines for conducting the practice*

Irimi can be a demanding meditation for some participants depending on the severity of the difficulties they decide to focus on. It is helpful that by this time (the second part of the program) all of the participants have some practice with calming their mind. It is also important that the participants have become familiar with each other and with the teacher by Session 5. The resulting increase in trust may help soften the intensity of the meditation.

In addition to the guidelines for awareness of breath and body in Session 3 here are some specific suggestions to help make Irimi meditation insightful and effective for the participants.

a. Before initiating the meditation distribute the drawing of a typical Irimi movement above (Handout 1), where the defendant moves towards the body of the opponent. Tell the participants to keep this picture in mind when they start to direct their awareness to the specific difficulty that is in their thoughts, feelings, or body sensations.
b. Always remind participants that they have the choice to get back to mindful breathing if the experience gets too intense.
c. Ask participants to observe where the difficulties manifest themselves in their bodies.
d. Explain to the participants that the intention is not to change body sensations or their intensity, but to soften the way they are held in awareness and the way we relate to them.
e. Suggest that they imagine difficulties as bundles of energy that can be transformed with an attitude of acceptance and allowing.
f. Remind participants to breathe into sensations of difficulties in their body and breathe out from them with an attitude of curiosity and acceptance.

g. Guide the timing of the meditation by allowing time for meditating on breath and body (approximately a third of the projected duration) and then inviting the participants to bring their awareness to a difficulty they are experiencing. If they cannot bring to their awareness a current difficulty, they can recall a difficult situation of the past.
h. Reserve enough time for an inquiry after the meditation to help the participants absorb their experiences.

3. *Inquiry*

In this meditation it is especially useful to wait for the participants to share their observations, even if this leads to longer silences than usual. The following points may be important to discuss:

a. Every experience is important. Maybe there are commonalities among the participants or maybe not. There is no judging.
b. By observing themselves during the meditation, have they discovered patterns that are typical and will help them relate to difficulties in life?
c. What experiences have they had with breathing in and breathing out from intense feelings and sensations?
d. How do they feel now, after ending the practice?

4. *Psycho-educational points*

Essential learnings from the Irimi practice include:

a. The practice is not designed to eliminate difficulty, but to learn how to relate with acceptance to whatever difficulty we may experience and how to reduce vulnerability to worries and anxiety.
b. Focusing on the body allows us to disengage from complex worrying thoughts.
c. Irimi allows us to respond with acceptance and curiosity instead of aversion and judgment.
d. Worries are patterns of the mind.
e. Looking at worry as another mental pattern helps develop a spacious quality of the mind.
f. Decentering means that a participant can relate to worry thoughts as thoughts rather than suppress or negate them.
g. Irimi reinforces the way we relate emotions and thoughts to body sensations.
h. Irimi helps develop a more aware mind about negative human experiences.

Note 15: 3-Minutes Breathing Space on Worry (3MBS-Worry)

1. *The script*

This variation of 3MBS is designed to be used every time you feel that worries are beginning to overwhelm you. In other words the starting point are worry thoughts or feelings of anxiety. This is why the focal point of the first step is to deal with worry from the beginning.

Step 1: Start directing your attention to your present inner experiences: becoming aware of your BETA. Just notice and acknowledge them. Whatever you observe is already there. Try to identify what you detect. You might ask yourself: What thoughts, what bleak scenarios, or negative predictions are worrying me right now? Then put your worry into words, for example: "I worry about my job" or "I worry about my relation with X," "I worry about being late," and so on. Try to be as specific as you can. If it is something about your job that worries you, try to define it precisely: Maybe an upcoming review? Or the latest changes in the organization? This process is called labeling. Giving your worry a name facilitates decentering and helps to calm your mind.

Step 2: Shift your awareness to your breath and follow the flow of air and the rhythm of your abdomen as it expands and contracts. It is recommended that you start counting silently: in 1, out 1—in 2, out 2—and so on. When you reach 5 start again with: in 1, out 1, etc. If you find the counting annoying or distracting, you may silently repeat the words: inhaling, exhaling, inhaling, etc.

Step 3: When you are ready, expand your awareness to your whole body, noticing your sensations, your posture, and facial expression with gentle acceptance. Then carrying this idea of acceptance and allowance into your activities, as you resume what you have been doing.

2. *Guidelines*

a. As with the other forms of 3MBS you should clearly announce each step.
b. Give some examples regarding how to identify and label worries but allow for enough time so that participants can find their own examples.
c. Invite participants to be as specific as possible in labeling. Saying "it is about my job" is not specific enough.

3. *Inquiry*

a. Find out what the participants' experience has been with their identification and labeling process.
b. If necessary help them put their worries into words.
c. Remind them that accepting their inner experience does not mean accepting the situation. It is only about avoiding the second arrow of mental torment.
d. Ask the participants about their experience with counting their breaths or with the repetition of "inhaling, exhaling, inhaling." It may be a question of getting used to this.
e. Suggest participants abstain from judgments about liking or disliking this practice. With further practice their relation to 3MBS-Worry may change.

4. *Psycho-educational points*

a. Switching from a worrying doing mode to a calmer being mode of the mind and escaping the worry automatic pilot.
b. Stepping back from the situation and looking at worry as a phenomenon created by our thoughts.
c. Looking at worry thoughts as mental events and bringing a sense of allowance and acceptance to them.
d. 3MBS-Worry changes the time orientation from worrying about the future to being in the present moment.

Note 16: Mindful Positive Self (MPS) Portrait: The Launch

The MPS is designed as a practical tool that participants can take with them after the MBSAT program has ended. Together with an action plan for flourishing built on the basis of the MPS (the focus of Sessions 7 and 8) it will provide the participants with lasting benefits and support them on their personal growth path. Positive psychology has demonstrated that the MPS is an effective tool to foster sustainable well-being.

As the participants have to establish their self-portrait they need precise instructions on how to proceed. Handout 2 is therefore more extensive than usual.

The comments and guidelines that would normally be part of this Note 15 are, in this case, identical with Handout 2. Hence readers may directly turn to Handout 2 for further explanations and suggestions.

Session 5—Handouts and Homework

Handout 1 of Session 5: Irimi Meditation on Difficulty

The Irimi meditation practice is built around the Aikido principle of moving into the realm of adversity when we are confronted with difficult situations (first arrow) or mental difficulties (second arrow).

Irimi:
Moving Towards Adversity Instead of Away From It

Figure 11.3 Irimi: Moving Towards Adversity Instead of Away From It. *Source*: Juan Humberto Young.

When the negative thoughts and emotions we have concerning the difficulties in our lives get out of control it is like inflicting violence on ourselves and our mind. This is why the counterintuitive, soft Aikido approach of moving closer to our own destructive forces (negative thoughts, fearful emotions, painful sensations, or unskillful actions) has a soothing, healing effect that can lead to positive practical outcomes.

Handout 2 of Session 5: The First Steps of Mindful Positive Self (MPS) Portrait

Introduction

All of us can recall extraordinary moments when we felt we could mobilize our best qualities and felt inspired and good about ourselves while doing something worthwhile. These memories stay in our minds as times when we have felt alive, true to our deepest selves, and committed to pursuing our full potential as human beings. We can collect these experiences into a portrait of ourselves when we were at our personal best. In addition to our own memories it is important to draw on the perceptions of others who know us well and may have valuable insights regarding our strengths and talents. Their feedback will complement our image.

Collecting the feedback is the first task in establishing a MPS portrait. The process of creating a MPS consists of the following steps:

- Collecting feedback about our strengths from people who know us.
- Writing down our narratives of those times when we felt at our best.
- Analyzing the data we gathered and combining it with other sources of information such as our character strengths resulting from the VIA survey.
- Creating the portrait: a description of who we are when we are in a state of flourishing.
- Creating an action plan to multiply the experiences of flourishing and make them durable.

Guidelines to start the MPS portrait

In this session we start with the first step: collecting data from others. From this range of feedback you will learn important things about yourself:

- The responses from your contacts will generate awareness of how others see you when you are at your best.
- The responses will enhance your understanding of what kind of work and life situations bring out the best in you.
- The responses can help you create personal and career development plans and implement actions based upon the reflections that your MPS portrait generates.
- The responses provide a resource for future times when you may be discouraged and need to get back on track.
- The responses can strengthen your ties with the people you ask for honest feedback.

Here is what you need to do in concrete terms:

1. *Identify respondents*: Identify 10–15 people who know you well. These may be colleagues (former or current), friends (old or recent), family members, customers, or anyone who has had extended contact with you. Think about who will give you an honest opinion: the more diverse the group, the better. Ideally, you need at least ten responses to get a sufficiently rich picture of yourself in different situations, so ask enough people to ensure at least ten responses, taking into account that not everyone might get back to you in time.
2. *Compose a short text to ask for feedback*: Formulate a brief feedback request that you can adjust for each person you write to. It should explain what the feedback is for and why the person's input is important. An example of such a text, for more formal relationships, is below. It can easily be adjusted for closer, more informal relations.

   Mail or email your request to the 10–15 people you have identified and ask each person to provide *two* stories to get sufficient data. Although this request may at first seem a bit awkward, experience has shown that most people carefully chosen are happy to assist with the exercise.

   Sample email request for feedback:

   With the goal of continued learning and personal development I am currently participating in a training program called mindfulness-based strategic awareness training—MBSAT. It is based on mindfulness practices and positive psychology. As part of the program I have to establish a self-portrait of myself in my best moments, when my talents and human qualities shine through. It will serve later as basis for an action plan to make the best of my strengths and increase my life satisfaction.

   To generate an accurate portrait I need the input of people like you who have known me for some time. I would very much appreciate it if you could recall three anecdotes where you think I demonstrated what is good in me. Please provide stories and examples rather than just characteristics so I can understand the situation and what it is that you have observed. You could say for instance something like this: "I think one of your strengths is X, because I remember the time when …."

   I would very much appreciate you taking time to do this for me as I have always valued your opinion. Could you possibly provide a feedback within a week or 10 days? The training program has a deadline that I have to meet.

   Thank you very much for your support and warmest regards.

3. *Get in contact with your feedback addressees*: With this preparation you are ready to send your emails. Depending on the people you choose you might also call them and ask them for answers in writing. Respondents who are very close or who you have difficulty emailing might be receptive to an interview. Then you can write down the stories you are given. This should be an exception, however.

   Once you have instigated your requests keep track of the answers so that you can gently nudge respondents who are behind schedule. **Timely answers are important, because your mindful positive self-portrait will be the focus of Sessions 7 and 8 and there are only three weeks left in the MBSAT program.**

Handout 3 of Session 5: Home Practice for the Week following Session 5

Because of the short deadline it is important that you start right away with step 1 of the mindful positive self portrait as it is detailed in Handout 2.

The main formal practice assignment until the next session is the Irimi sitting meditation on difficulty. Several other shorter practices are of the kind that can easily be integrated in daily life. There is also an entertaining assignment: watching a movie or, if you like, even two movies. The second one is optional.

Please, remember to use the home practice record form to keep track of your progress.

1. Starting the mindful positive self portrait

Please, read Handout 2 carefully and start to make a list of respondents and contact them.

2. Irimi sitting meditation on difficulty

Irimi meditation starts like awareness of breath and body. This is a practice you are already familiar with. Give yourself some time to settle into awareness of breath and body before you start focusing on a difficulty in your life. This will facilitate the practice. In addition you have the audio files provided that guide you through the different stages.

Maybe you already know what difficulty you would like to focus on or maybe you can leave it open and let a theme emerge after sitting for a while in awareness of breath and body. It depends on you and the challenges that life confronts you with.

When you start focusing on the difficulty you have chosen remember to observe where it manifests itself in your body. Explore the sensations and acknowledge them. The intention of the practice is not to change the body sensations or their intensity, but to soften the way they are held in awareness and the way we relate to them. You may imagine the difficulty as a bundle of energy that can be transformed with an attitude of acceptance and allowance.

It is helpful if you breathe into your body sensations and breathe out from them with an attitude of curiosity and acceptance in the same way as you practiced in the body scan. You always have the choice to get back to mindful breathing, should the experience get too intense.

Most importantly remember that the practice is not designed to eliminate difficulty, but to teach you how to relate to it and reduce vulnerability to worries and anxieties. Irimi meditation invites a stance of how to be with difficulty instead of what to do about difficulty. As you learn to relate with acceptance and spaciousness to worry and anxiety and their manifestations in the body, new ways to respond to the challenge will open up.

The assignment is to do the Irimi practice on 6 days out of 7 days, that is, every day until the next session with 1 day of rest.

3. *3-minutes breathing space: Regular 3MBS and 3MBS on worry*

Please, keep doing the regular 3MBS a few times a day as you did for the last assignment. It is like taking a brief mental break.

In addition, start to do the 3MBS on worry whenever you see a challenge. As a rule of thumb practicing three times a day work works well for most people.

4. *Practicing one strength a day*

Doing what we are good at is pleasurable and does not require effort. Yet even strengths need to be cultivated, otherwise they atrophize like muscles you never use.

Look at your VIA results of character strengths and choose one strength a day (preferably each day a different one) and implement it intentionally. For example, if humor is your strength make someone who feels a little depressed or miserable laugh. If fairness is a strength you could stand up for a colleague who does not get what he or she deserves. There are thousands of possibilities to exercise your strengths and it feels good to be imaginative when you implement them.

5. *Practicing transforming dislikes*

Consider this an Aikido exercise of getting close to adversity:

Once a day decide to do something you actually dislike, for example, eating something you do not find tasty, listening to a kind of music you would normally turn off, reading a newspaper you find boring, or talking to a person you prefer to avoid.

It is a way of opening your horizons and consciously changing your relationship with your dislikes. Experiment with this and make notes in your journal. We will share your experiences in the next session.

6. *Watching movies*

In preparation for what we will discuss in Session 6, watch one of these classic films: *The Great Gatsby* with Robert Redford and Mia Farrow or *The Treasure of Sierra Madre* with Humphrey Bogart. It is an exercise you can do together with friends or family members. Besides being fun it might help explain to your close relations that you are participating in a MBSAT training program. It might help you to elicit their support to help you maintain your discipline and keep practicing. Integrating your significant others may be very important for your progress.

Handout 4 of Session 5: "Guest House" by Rumi

This being human is a guest house
Every morning a new arrival.
A joy, a depression, a meanness,
some momentary awareness comes as an unexpected visitor.
Welcome and entertain them all!
Even if they are a crowd of sorrows,
who violently sweep your house
empty of its furniture,
still treat each guest honorably.
He may be clearing you out
for some new delight.
The dark thought, the shame, the malice,
meet them at the door laughing,
and invite them in.
Be grateful for whoever comes,
because each has been sent
as a guide from beyond.

Session 6

Note 17: POMO Meditation

1. The script

POMO (Powerful Money) meditation starts like the sitting meditation on breath and body by bringing the awareness to your breathing with the rhythm of your abdomen and then briefly scanning your body. Practitioners sometimes call this a body sweep.

After approximately 10 minutes, when your mind is calm and your attention has expanded to the whole body, invite into your consciousness a situation that is concerned with money. It is useful to recall an experience as early in your life as possible as money concerns can begin in early childhood. Alternatively it is acceptable to recall an actual experience concerning an issue with money. Give yourself some time, open your mind, and see what emerges.

When you have an experience in your mind, remember the circumstances as vividly as you can and keep the situation in your mind. Stay with it, whatever it is. The feelings, thoughts, and sensations that come up are the raw material to begin experiencing the relation between you and money and the significance of money in your life.

Can you identify the feelings? How does this experience manifest itself in this moment in your body? Are there perhaps any sensations of tightness in different parts of the body? Are your shoulders raised or hunched? Is your jaw clenched? What else is there? What impulses have you discovered?

Remember that there is no intention to change what you are feeling, sensing, or thinking. The idea is to become aware of your experience and to recognize that it is part of you. These thoughts, feelings, and sensations have been with you for most of your life, unconsciously or semi-consciously. Recognizing them and moving towards them in an Irimi attitude, embracing and accepting them can produce a shift in the way you relate to money.

Give this process enough time so that you can immerse yourself in the experience, explore it and stay with it, and then slowly and gently come back to the surface. When you feel ready, slowly disengage your attention from your discoveries and move it toward your breath. Once again feel your breath flowing in and out in the area around your belly. Stay with this soothing movement for the last few moments before you open your eyes.

2. Guidelines

POMO Meditation is a discovery practice that comprises three short meditation practices: (a) POMO I: The past, (b) POMO II: The present, and (c) From POMO to MIMO. The intention is to guide participants into an inquiry about their relationship with issues of money.

As usual the meditation starts with awareness of breath and body. The same guidelines apply as for the meditation on breath and body in Session 3.

It is the second part that is dedicated to the discovery process. Invite participants to bring their attention to a situation related to money. It can be a situation from their past, preferably in the participants' early years when they were growing up, or it can be a challenge currently related to money. Invite the participants to recall whatever incident they want to work on and remember as vividly as possible the different aspects of the situation. The more vividly they recall the experience, the higher the possibility to parse the experience into different components (feelings, thoughts, body sensations, and behavioral impulses).

Sometimes it is useful to provide some universal examples to stimulate the discovery process. Here are a number of possible memories. If one of these situations happens to be relevant for the participants they could focus on it as a starting point to recall a real incident in their life.

Suggestions to access memories

a. Recalling an incident in childhood or adolescence where you desired something (a bicycle or motorcycle, skiing, travelling, a toy) that your parents could not afford or were not willing to purchase.

   Invite participants to recall their wishes at the time with all the fervor as well as the arguments with their parents. Those arguments about how everyone at school had it and you were the only outsider. If the participants grew up in a family with limited resources most probably their parents told them that they didn't have the means to afford the wish. Or they could have been growing up in an affluent family but the parents didn't agree with their wishes. Can the participants recall their feelings or emotions? What are they? Can they sense these feelings or emotions in the body? Do they have any particular thoughts vis-à-vis their friends at the time?

b. Possible current situations:
   - A neighbor buys an expensive new car that you cannot afford.
   - A colleague gets a promotion with a substantial salary increase and you are passed over.
   - A friend goes on vacation to an exotic place that you cannot afford.

c. Examples for participants working in environments of affluence (bankers, tax consultants or lawyers for high-net worth individuals, salespersons in high-end segments, etc.):
   A relevant suggestion for these participants could be to recall their experience when they are in direct contact with their very wealthy clients. What feelings and thoughts come up in such interactions?

After guiding the participants and helping them identify a situation, the teacher should invite participants to focus their attention on the effects of these memories on their present experiences. Can they recognize the manifestations of this experience in their body sensations? Maybe pulsing in their temples or their heart? Any pressure in the head? What feelings and thoughts emerge?

Further suggestions for guiding this practice are identical to those described for Irimi meditation on difficulty in Session 5. In spite of the overlap some are repeated here, because they are crucial for the experiential learning process:

a. Suggest participants imagine their issues around money as bundles of energy that can be transformed with an attitude of acceptance.
b. Remind them to breathe into the difficulties in their body and breathe out from them with an attitude of curiosity and acceptance.
c. Explain that the aim is not to change the body sensations or their intensity, but to soften the way they are held in awareness and the way we relate to them.
d. Always remind participants that they have the choice to get back to mindful breathing if the experience gets too intense.

3. *Inquiry*

a. In exploring their experiences with money during the meditation, have they discovered patterns of thinking or feeling that are driving their current behavior in relation to money and with regard to work and earning their living?
b. What are the dominant emotions when they are confronted with money issues?
c. Are there connections with how they relate to other difficulties in life?
d. What intense feelings or sensations about money have resulted from breathing in and breathing out?
e. How do they feel now at the end of the practice?

To close the inquiry and wrap up the lesson distribute the figure on the dynamics of money accumulation in Handout 1 and discuss it with the participants. Ask them whether they recognize some of the same dynamics in their own behavior or whether it is different and if so, in what way?

4. *Psycho-educational points*

Essential lessons from the meditation on money are:

a. Money issues are potent drivers of behavior.
b. Money issues are linked with worrying and anxiety. More skillful responses to money issues reduce worrying and anxiety and vice versa: more equanimity helps normalize the relation to money.
c. Money issues are constants in our lives. Meditation will not eliminate them but we can learn to relate to them with awareness and acceptance in other words with an attitude of MIMO (Mindful Money).
d. Money issues tend to seep into relationships. Becoming aware of cognitive and behavioral patterns in relation to money can help improve human relations.
e. Meditating on money creates spaciousness as it facilitates decentering and helps recognize thoughts as mental events, not facts.
f. Focusing on breathing and on the body allows people to disengage from sticky money thoughts.
g. Decreasing the importance of money as an extrinsic motivator allows to increase the potential of creativity at work.

Note 18: Exercise on Money and Opportunity Costs (MOC)

1. *The script*

MOC is designed to explore the relative value of money and how contextual situations can shake long-held beliefs, values, and ideas about the significance of money.

The exercise starts by presenting a brief scenario, letting participants reflect on it with closed eyes for a few moments, and then asking them to share their reactions: What thoughts came up? What feelings, body sensations, and impulses to act?

The scenario suggested is an adaptation of David's life experience presented in the introduction to the exercise (Section 12.3.2).

Scenario

Imagine you just achieved a big breakthrough. After working strenuously for years you landed a unique deal that earned you millions. You "made it" and feel in heaven. At the same time you think you have to take advantage of the momentum and continue to work hard.

Shortly afterwards, out of the blue, the person closest to you is diagnosed with a life-threatening disease. You might imagine that it is your child, your life-long partner, or someone else who is key to your happiness in life. The physicians tell you there is not much they can do. Even the most sophisticated treatment is most likely ineffective.

Invite participants to close their eyes and imagine this scenario as if it was just happening to them. In case some of them have actually experienced something similar, ask them to recall their own experience, however painful it may have been.

After a few moments let the participants slowly open their eyes and share their impressions:

2. Guidelines and inquiry

Start with an open dialogue to gather impressions freely. Then draw a table on a board in the room (whiteboard or blackboard) and start entering the contributions of the participants to the conversation. You could make four columns for example: thoughts, feelings, changes in relation to work or business, and changes in relation to money. It can be similar to the table established in Session 3.

3. Psycho-educational points

a. The relative value of money.
b. Tradeoffs in life.
c. Money and well-being.
d. Things that money cannot buy (example: the life of Steve Jobs).

Note 19: 3-Minutes Breathing Space on Money Worry (3MBS-Money Worry)

1. *The script*

While the theme of the sitting meditation is on money, this 3MBS is on money *worry*. The two practices look at money from different angles and have different functions. The sitting meditation cultivates awareness and helps discover conditioning (mental, emotional, and behavioral patterns). The 3MBS-Money Worry is like the other mini-meditations. It is designed for immediate application when a pressing need for recollection arises—in this case when something worries you about money. In our society money is likely to be the one thing that provokes more worries than anything else. It represents our livelihood and our position in the social fabric.

The 3MBS-Money Worry is a very effective practice to curb unproductive worrying about finances and reinforces a calmer attitude that is more conducive to good solutions. It is best to practice it as soon as money worries set in and as often as necessary.

The three steps to follow are very similar to the 3MBS-Worry, which actually covers a wider array of worries.

Step 1: Start directing your attention towards your inner experience at the present moment: becoming aware of your BETA. Notice and acknowledge them. Then give your money worry an explicit label in the same way that you labeled other worries in the plain 3MBS-Worry of Session 5. Just specify silently in your mind what you are concerned about, e.g.,

I worry about paying my bills.
I worry about the expensive car I would like to buy.
I worry about maintaining my standard of living.
I worry about the private school I want to send my kids to.

Giving your worry a name helps to put it in perspective and makes it less overwhelming.

Step 2: As with the 3MBS-Worry shift the awareness now to your breath and start counting silently: in 1, out 1—in 2, out 2—and so forth. When you reach 5 start again with: in 1, out 1, etc. Alternatively you might repeat in your mind: inhaling, exhaling, inhaling, if this is more helpful and takes your mind off the money worries.

Step 3: After a few moments of breathing and counting expand your awareness to your whole body. Notice your sensations, your posture, and your facial expression with gentle acceptance. Try to stay with this attitude as you bring the practice to a close and resume your activities. You can always return to the practice whenever the worries surface again.

2. *Guidelines*

a. As with the more general 3MBS-Worry invite participants to specifically name their money worries. This helps the decentering process.
b. Make it clear that there ought to be no judging or self-criticizing when labeling worries. There is no moralizing involved, only exploring, being aware, and accepting.
c. Remind participants to take the attitude of awareness and acceptance with them when they return to their normal activities.
d. Remember to announce each step clearly. It gives the signal to shift the awareness to the next point of attention.

3. *Inquiry*

a. Find out how the participants feel after the practice. Money worries are sometimes linked to shame or embarrassment, consciously or unconsciously. If this is the case point out that they are not alone in this. We all have encountered similar worries.
b. Ask the participants whether they found specific descriptions and language for their worries about money. If necessary help them be more explicit.
c. Remind them that the intention of the practice is to become aware and look at what is there with acceptance. There is no reason to be judgmental or self-critical.
d. Suggest that counting or repeating "inhaling, exhaling" is simply a technique to interrupt the infinite loops created by worrying thoughts.

4. *Psycho-educational points*

a. Awareness with gentle acceptance reduces the pressure to produce instant solutions. It generates the wisdom to wait for the right answers to the problem.

b. We are all prone to money worries. There is no need to feel singled out or to seek fault with oneself.
c. It is good to repeat the practice as many times as necessary. Just keep doing it, until you feel relief.
d. The rules and techniques for money worries are almost the same as with general worries. The main difference is that money worries tend to be pervasive and especially intense.

Note 20: Easterlin Paradox and Kahneman–Deaton Happiness Benchmark: Two Mini-Lectures (Optional)

The aim is to offer participants a wider framework that allows them to put their personal concerns in perspective. Their personal worries are part of universal socio-economic phenomena, reflected in macro-economics and the subject of serious research in economic science, including behavioral economics. Being aware of these wider connections may take some pressure off individual anxieties about money.

For these reasons it is advisable to provide brief presentations of the Easterlin paradox and the Kahneman–Deaton happiness benchmark. The findings are authoritative and carry weight in part because of their distinguished authors (Kahneman and Deaton are both Nobel prize laureates and Easterlin is an economics professor, member of the US National Academy of Sciences and other prestigious institutions). The mini-lectures are marked as optional for teachers who feel uncomfortable with the topics because they have had little or no contact with economics. However, the concepts are actually quite easy to grasp. For anyone determined to better understand the human condition in today's world the two articles recommended should be interesting and quite easy to read.

Articles:

a. The happiness–income paradox revisited.
Easterlin, R. A., Angelescu McVey, L., Switek, M., Sawangfa, O., & Smith Zweig, J. (2010). *PNAS*, *107*(52), 22463–22468.
b. High income improves evaluation of life but not emotional well-being.
Daniel Kahneman (Nobel Prize, 2000) and Angus Deaton (Nobel Prize 2015). (2010). *PNAS*, *107*(38), 16489–16493.

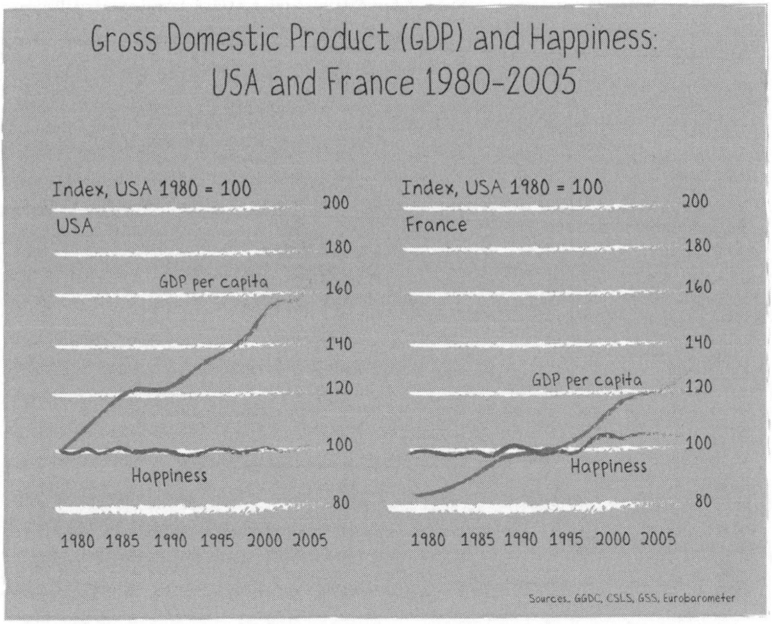

Figure 12.4 Gross Domestic Product (GDP) and Happiness: United States and France 1980–2005. *Source*: Adapted from GGDC, CSLS, GSS, and Eurobarometer.

1. *The script*

In essence the teacher will present a brief explanation of the two concepts based on the articles and supported by the figures and the summaries below. Then he or she will invite the participants to discuss how they can relate the concepts to their own experiences.

To facilitate the process there is a figure for each mini-lecture that the teacher can distribute (Handouts 2 and 3). The teacher could also project the figures or collect the exhibits after the discussion.

2. *The Easterlin Paradox*

a. *Summary*

While economies have kept growing over recent decades and by many measures the standard of living has improved (accessibility of education, health services for example, infrastructure and mobility, etc.), surveys have found that the level of subjective well-being or happiness has stagnated. If material wealth makes people happy, then the well-being/happiness curve should also have risen, yet this is not the case. This contradicts the predominant assumption that the better off you are, the happier you are.

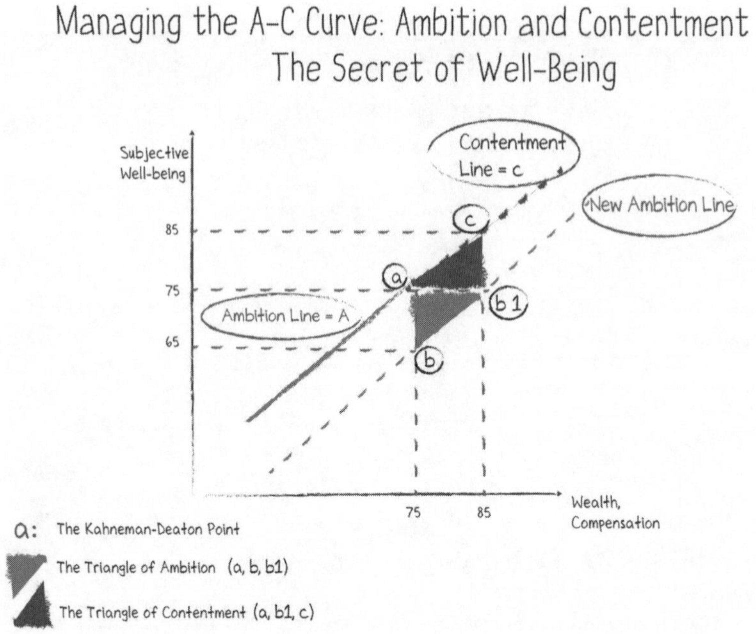

Figure 12.5 Managing the A-C Curve: Ambition and Contentment. The Secret of Well-Being. *Source*: Juan Humberto Young.

The main reason for this counterintuitive finding is the human tendency to become accustomed to money and comfort, the so-called treadmill effect. As one gets accustomed to improvements the level of happiness relapses to the former level and aspirations and wishes take on larger dimensions. Social comparison compounds this cycle of striving for more. As higher income provides access to other social circles, new desires and ambitions develop based on comparison with others.)

Figure 12.5 explains a dynamic psychological process. (This figure is not a representation of economic theory but a simplified illustration of psychological phenomena after getting an economic reward visualizing either contentment or a shift in aspiration by wanting even more, assuming a 1:1 relation between money and happiness.

Let us assume that someone, for example, a woman named Bobby, has worked hard and reached an income level of 75 units. With this income she achieves 75 units of well-being (point a). She takes a MBSAT training course and learns about mindful ways with money. In thinking about her situation (point a) she feels pleased and decides to consider her work a calling instead of merely a means to earn more money. Obviously, like everybody else she would welcome a salary raise but she is content. This implies that her ambition line A now becomes her contentment line C, in the graph visible as an extension of line A.

As Bobby is engaged with her job before long she gets a salary raise of 10 units so that her income is now 85. Since she is on contentment line C her well-being also increases and reaches 85 units (point c). Her overall increase in well-being is represented by the triangle of contentment between the points a, b1, and c.

Changing the scenario let us assume that Bobby did not have a chance to take a MBSAT course and that she stays in the same mindset of ambition once she has achieved 75 units of income. Fairly soon she will be subject to the treadmill effect and to social referencing, thus wanting more of everything: a higher salary, a more attractive car, a more prestigious home, and so on.

At this particular moment, when the discontent sets in, a new ambition line gets created. This implies that she is no longer at point (a) but shifts to point (b) in accordance with her new aspirations. Unfortunately for Bobby, this implies that her well-being drops to 65 units, as this is all her income of 75 will get her on her new ambition line. The reduction in well-being is represented by the triangle of ambition between the points a, b, and b1.

Bobby now starts to struggle hard to get a promotion and after a while she gets a salary raise of 10 units. As the graph shows this brings her to point b1. It is not much of an advancement, however, because this increase in income actually brings her back to the well-being level of 75 units, where she was before.

What might happen is that Bobby starts repeating this cycle of striving, and achieving, then becoming discontented and unhappy over and over again, never feeling completely happy and satisfied, slipping into the treadmill trap—the type of dynamics we have also seen in the graph the dynamics of money accumulation (Figure 12.2, also included in Handout 1).

The conclusion is this: If your goal is happiness in life, maintain your line of aspirations and turn your ambition line into a contentment line.

In case the concept of the contentment line seems abstract and difficult to connect to your reality, you might think of the following experience that inspired me to design this exercise. It happened in Denmark where my company's board held the yearly review meeting. After an intense debate I went out for a stroll in the city of Copenhagen with a guide. Knowing that the Danish rank almost at the top of the worldwide happiness scale I asked the guide what the secret of the Danish people was to reach such high levels of happiness. He answered: "I'm not sure whether we are so exuberantly happy, but one thing I know: we are content. We pay a lot of taxes, close to 60% of our income, yet we see what we pay for and reap the benefits. My son for example is going to the university and I don't have to worry about financing his studies. It is not just that I don't have to pay tuition—my son gets a small salary during his education to help with living expenses. Everybody here in Denmark has this opportunity. This gives you satisfaction. And that is actually our secret: to be satisfied and content with life. That is what we are here in Denmark: content, and probably it is the reason for our ranking." A question likely to emerge during inquiry is how to move from an ambition line to a contentment line. An explanation I have found useful is to present three different orientations towards work (Wrzesniewdki et al., 1997): (a) the job as a means to provide for necessities with focus on financial rewards, (b) a career view of work with a focus on advancement and social status, and (c) work as a calling with a focus on meaning and enjoyment. A strategy for the transition towards contentment may be found in a calling orientation to work that provides intrinsic motivation.

If a critical mass of people could realize the secret of being content, the Easterlin paradox would disappear into thin air and the happiness trend would start to point upwards.

b. *Inquiry for Easterlin paradox*

- Ask the participants if the concept reflects their observations of life.
- Discuss with the participants whether they recognize their own behavior in the graphs.
- For skeptical participants doubting the findings it can be helpful to point out that the focus here is subjective, *emotional* well-being, that is, the frequency of positive emotions in daily life.
- You can also venture some open questions as to what connections the participants make between the concept of the paradox and what they have learned so far in the MBSAT program.

3. *Kahneman–Deaton happiness benchmark*

a. *Summary*

In a large empirical study the two Nobel laureates found that there is a certain level of income beyond which subjective well-being does not increase further, even if income continues to rise.

This finding contradicts the widespread belief that the more money you have, the happier you must be.

The authors introduce some careful distinctions:

- The finding applies to well-being defined as the emotional quality of an individual's everyday life—the frequency and intensity of experiencing joy and affection or stress, sadness, anger, and so on, that makes life pleasant or unpleasant.

- Life satisfaction is a cognitive evaluation and refers to the thoughts that people have about their life. Life satisfaction keeps growing without a specific ceiling when income continues to rise.
- Very low income means both low subjective well-being and low life satisfaction.

The overall conclusion remains that "high income buys life satisfaction but not happiness" (Kahneman & Deaton, 2010, p. 16489).

Looking specifically at the United States Kahneman and Deaton found that the threshold is an annual income of $75,000. Above this benchmark they found no significant increase in subjective well-being. The sum of $75,000 is an average of the values they found in different US states.

Obviously, this figure will be different in different countries and it will also vary over time. The key insight is that there is a limit to how much well-being money can produce. Beyond this point well-being must be nourished from other sources, prominent among them mindfulness and the mindset cultivated by mindfulness practices such as equanimity and acceptance.

A sample of Kahneman's and Deaton's findings are reported in Figure 12.6 (reduced number of states).

b. *Guidelines for the Kahneman–Deaton Happiness benchmark*
After presenting the concept to the participants a main point of discussion may be to offer possible explanations for the happiness benchmark. Naturally the teacher will invite the participants to share their views based on their personal experience. The participants' contributions can lead to generalized conclusions.

Plausible explanations that could apply generally include:

a. Wealth can generate worries:
   - It can increase responsibility, for example, if you are in business and care for employees.
   - It may lead to risky investments that create headaches.
   - It might trigger addictive behavior to accumulate more and more money.
b. Money is no insurance against difficulties such as health issues, conflicts in relations, defeats in other areas (e.g., politics, sports)
c. There are many things money cannot buy such as authentic friendship, love, trust, and so on.

Ultimately money may help a person to live comfortably but it is not a necessary condition for happiness.

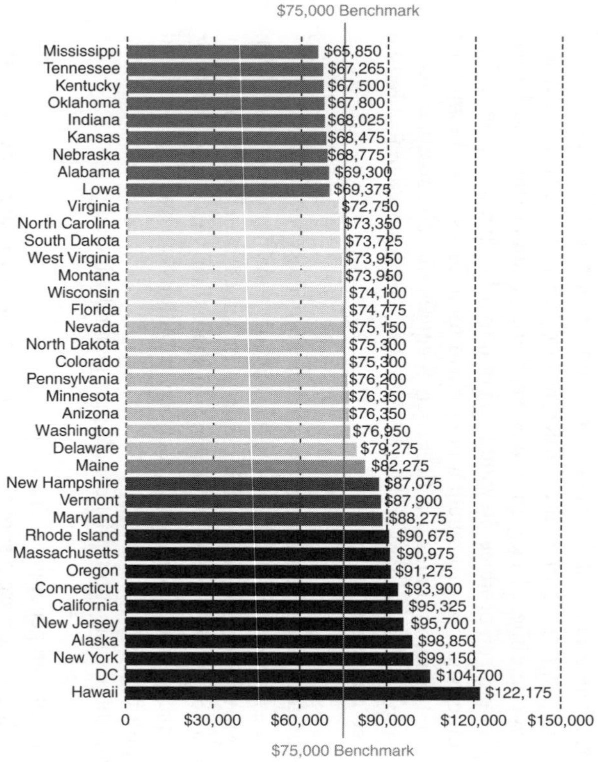

Figure 12.6 High Income Improves Evaluation of Life but not Emotional Well-Being. *Source*: Kahneman et al. (2014).

c. *Inquiry for the Kahneman–Deaton happiness benchmark*

a. Ask participants whether the concept of a happiness threshold makes sense to them.
b. Probably they have already been asking themselves whether they can nominate a value that would apply to them or their environment. Is this the case and have they actually quantified it? Even if participants are not willing to disclose figures, it would be interesting to know their thinking.
c. What are the conclusions they have reached about the happiness benchmark: For them personally? For society in general?

4. Psycho-educational points

a. The two mini-lectures emphasize the idea that the value of money is relative.
b. They reduce the priority often attributed to the pursuit of wealth.
c. They drive home the message that we must cultivate other, complementary sources of happiness.
d. They can motivate the practices of the MBSAT program and search for sustainable well-being.

Note 21: Mindful Positive Self (MPS): Second Take

1. The script

The task now is to explain to participants the second part of establishing their MPS self-portraits.

As explained in Section 12.3.5. the main steps in the second part are as follows:

a. Remembering personal stories of fulfilling moments and adding them to the feedback from contacts.
b. Analyzing all the narratives collected—your own and feedback from others.
c. Complementing the results with information from other sources (prizes, pictures, quotes from letters or emails, etc.).
d. Establishing a vivid, evocative self-portrait of oneself in moments of fulfillment: the main part will be an essay that can be accompanied or complemented by pictures, mementos, or whatever the participants consider important.

Handout 4 provides the practical details the participants need to realize their self-portraits.

2. *Guidelines*

a. In our society it is unusual to highlight one's strengths. Explain to participants that this is not the time to be shy. It is about creating a vision for their personal development and therefore it is alright to be confident and bold, all the more as their self-portraits are supported by external sources and survey results.
b. Working on the self-portrait awakes emotions. Tell participants to welcome them as they create positive energy.
c. Encourage participants by explaining the philosophy behind training methods in sport. Sports coaches concentrate on further developing their trainees' strengths. This is known to generate greatness whereas working on weaknesses only brings about average achievements and mediocrity.
d. Explain to the participants how to handle weaknesses so they do not feel uncomfortable when concentrating on strengths.

Weaknesses should be taken care of only to the point where they do not drag down the overall performance. They should be managed with a minimum investment of energy, just enough to avoid a negative impact on strengths and fulfillment. Sometimes they can be handled by delegating the tasks to other people or by moving into another field of activity altogether. In any case the maxim is to manage weaknesses, not fight a losing battle to eliminate them. And then focus on strengths.

3. *Psycho-educational points*

a. The self-portrait is a vision that can guide us towards a life with more moments of flourishing.
b. Participants should let go of conditioning that results in self-doubts and self-criticism.
c. Establishing the self-portrait has a healing and inspiring effect.
d. Defining one's mindful positive self builds positive resources and resilience.
e. Positive self trains the participants to perceive strengths and potentials in others.
f. Positive self generates know-how and ideas on how to develop human resources through a positive approach.

Session 6—Handouts and Homework

Handout 1 of Session 6: POMO Meditation

This meditation is a discovery practice. Its intention is to become more aware of our conditioning in relation to money—our emotional, cognitive, and behavioral patterns—without judging or moralizing. Finding out what drives us is liberating simply because it provides us with more choices.

More than any other topic money has the capacity to hijack our minds, cause worries, and propel us into a doing mode. The reason is the central role money plays in our society as a means to sustain our livelihood and to position ourselves in society. It is nothing to be embarrassed about.

Often personal money-related characteristics are shaped early in life by feelings of deprivation or social comparison and peer pressure. This can create endless loops of perceived needs and attempts to satisfy them. Figure 12.2 provides a visual representation of this dynamic. It starts with loops 1 and 2. If we are lucky we can escape the spin at some point and experience satiation, contentment, and well-being (loop 3). If, on the contrary, our feelings

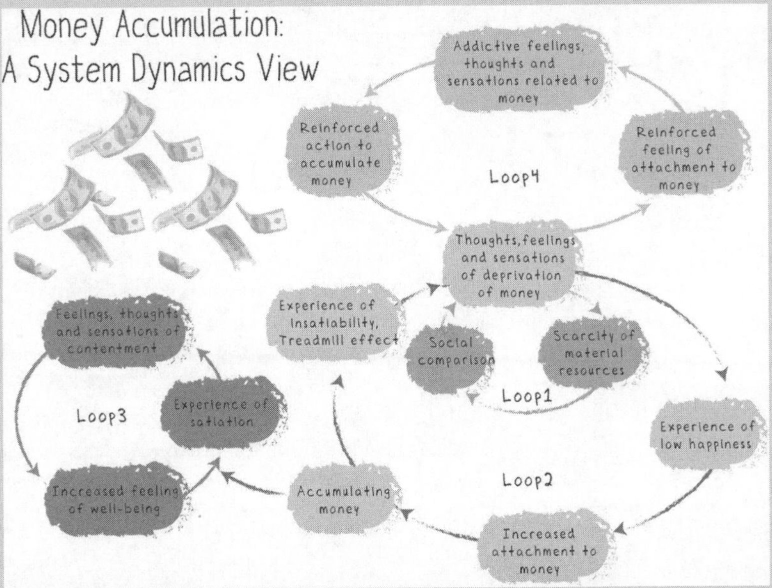

Figure 12.2 Money Accumulation: A Systems Dynamics View. *Source*: Juan Humberto Young.

of attachment to money become stronger a pattern of behavior can develop that borders on addiction (loop 4).

The POMO meditation starts with awareness of breath and body. When we are settled in a being mode we bring our attention to a situation related to money and explore the thoughts feelings and body sensations that come up, without judging them or wanting to change them. The audio files provided will guide you through the meditation.

It can be revealing to be aware of a situation of the past, preferably a memory from childhood or early adolescence. If it is difficult to retrieve these memories then a participant can focus on a current situation related to money. Maybe other memories will occur later. The main focus of the practice is to parse the experience into different components and become aware of feelings, thoughts, body sensations, and behavioral impulses.

End the practice by returning to awareness of breath and body, gently surfacing from the meditation.

Practice this meditation on 6 days till the next session with 1 day of rest.

Handout 2 of Session 6: Gross Domestic Product (GDP) and Happiness

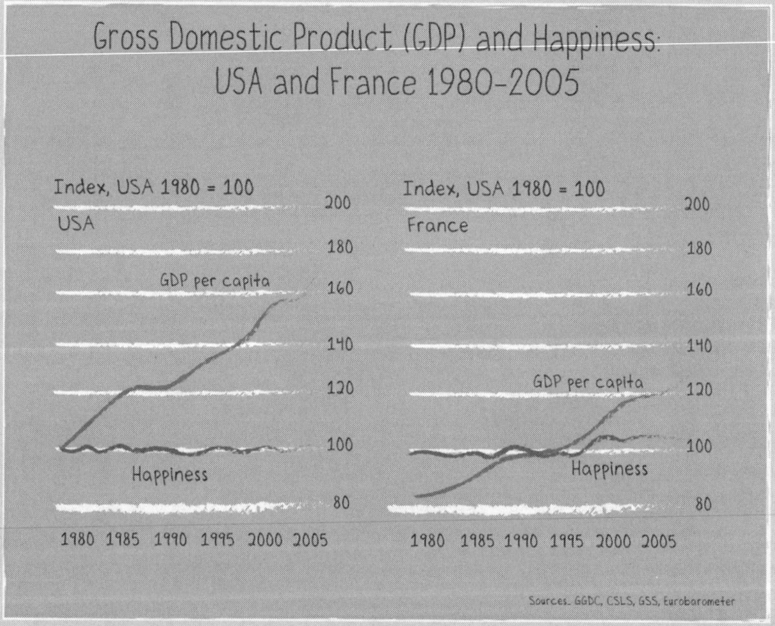

Figure 12.4 Gross Domestic Product (GDP) and Happiness: United States and France 1980–2005. *Source*: Adapted from GGDC, CSLS, GSS, and Eurobarometer.

Handout 3 of Session 6: High Incomes Improves Evaluation of Life but not Emotional Well-Being

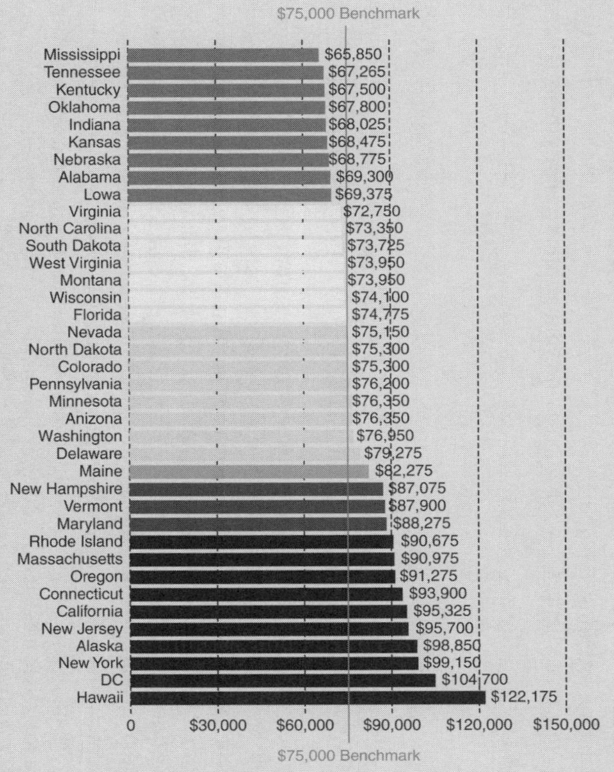

Figure 12.6 High Income Improves Evaluation of Life but not Emotional Well-Being. *Source*: Adapted from D. Kahneman and A. Deaton, cited by Short in *Huffington Post* 07/17/2014.

Handout 4 of Session 6: 3-Minutes Breathing Space on Money Worry (3MBS-Money Worry)

Whenever you feel that you are worrying about money issues do this three step mini-meditation, preferably several times a day.

The three steps are the same as in the 3MBS on worry in general with the only difference that you focus on worries specifically related to money. See if you can be as precise as possible in labeling your money worry: for example, "I am worrying right now about rising interest on my mortgage," or "I am worrying about not reaching the financial objectives of my department," and so on.

Remember to count your in-breaths and out-breaths in Step 2 or repeat "inhaling, exhaling, inhaling."

Notice the changes in your worries and your attitude towards them as you do this practice.

Handout 5 of Session 6: Mindful Positive Self (MPS): Second Take

By now the responses to your feedback requests from people who know you will have been received. For the next session you have to complete the second part and "paint" or realize your mindful, positive self-portrait.

Your self-portrait is the basis for an action plan that we will elaborate in Sessions 7 and 8 as a tool for your personal development that you can take with you and use when the MBSAT program comes to an end. Therefore, it is crucial that you complete your portrait before Session 7.

Set about realizing your portrait with optimism and without being shy. We are so used to feedback involving criticism that it can feel awkward to focus on your strengths and achievements and highlight only the best in you. Don't worry about such feelings. Just remember that this is a vision that will serve as your vision for the future and inspire you. And it is not fantasy but grounded in real events and supported by observations from others and from survey results.

These are the next steps:

Your own best-self stories

In addition to the feedback from your contacts all of us remember stories of moments when we personally felt soaring and carried away by the good qualities we possess. Write these stories down and add them to your collection of best moments.

Analyze all the stories collected (your own and the feedback)
The more abundant the material the better it is. Now it must be systematized in order to shape the features for the self-portrait. A practical way is to start analyzing the stories with the help of a table—record the salient points of each story in columns or rows:

- What was the positive behavior displayed?
- What strengths seemed to be in the action?
- What were the circumstances?
- What was the positive outcome?
- Other important elements depending on the data available.

Perhaps the table already provides a clear picture or else it can be the basis for a second, interpretative table, indicating for example:

- Circumstances that bring out the best in me.
- My patterns of behavior in moments of fulfillment.
- My signature strengths and qualities.
- My feelings in these very best moments.

Combine with other sources of information
Important inputs for the self-portrait are your character strengths resulting from the values in action (VIA) survey that you did as a home assignment after Session 4. In addition it is a good idea to add any other complementary information you find relevant, perhaps quotes from letters or emails you received, congratulations for achievements, pictures, prizes and trophies, and so on. Tap into your imagination.

"Painting" your MPS self-portrait
Now it's time you "paint" yourself in the most vivid colors and from the best perspective, knowing that this impressive picture is really you, since it is all based on factual information. You could, for example, add a relevant quote from a feedback or mention an example of an event to support each of your statements. A central part of the self-portrait is an essay describing yourself based on all the data and material you have gathered. Below is a self-portrait of one participant as an illustration (in German). The idea is not that you imitate it. It is a good example because it conveys the impression that the person drawing the portrait really felt what he wanted to say. If you follow your heart in the same way, and are authentically engaged in describing yourself in your best moments, your portrait will be great in your own way.

The author of the portrait complements his drawing in the essay saying that he has two legs, that is, two signature strengths that ground him: kindness and love of learning. Strengths that form his spine and give him stability are persistence and forgiveness. He backs up his statements with examples demonstrating his respective strengths.

This person likes to draw. Drawing is not a necessity. Your portrait can also be plain in form. As long as it is authentic and really represents all of your good sides then that is fine. To show you a different example you will find another self-portrait in the form of an essay in Handout 6. It is the self-portrait of a student in a Master level course I taught at a university in Switzerland.

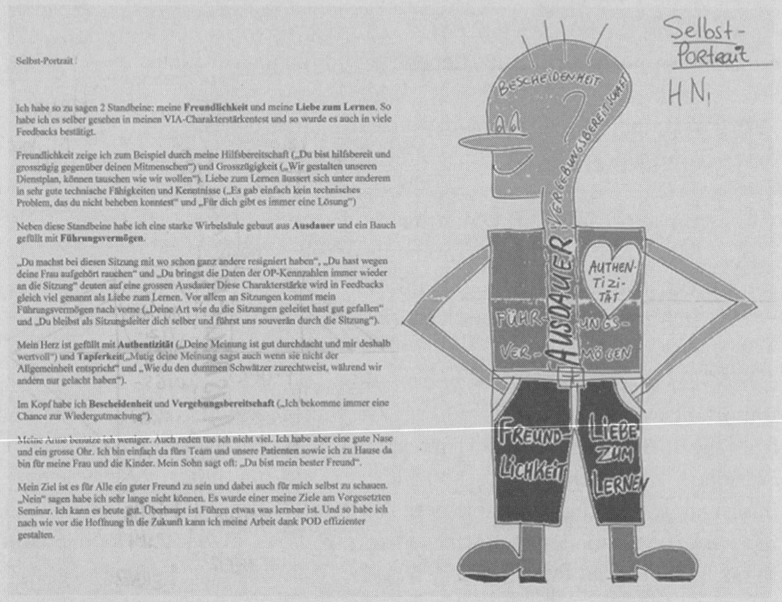
Selbst-Portrait !

Ich habe so zu sagen 2 Standbeine: meine **Freundlichkeit** und meine **Liebe zum Lernen**. So habe ich es selber gesehen in meinen VIA-Charakterstärkentest und so wurde es auch in viele Feedbacks bestätigt.

Freundlichkeit zeige ich zum Beispiel durch meine Hilfsbereitschaft („Du bist hilfsbereit und grosszügig gegenüber deinen Mitmenschen") und Grosszügigkeit („Wir gestalten unseren Dienstplan, können tauschen wie wir wollen"). Liebe zum Lernen äussert sich unter anderem in sehr gute technische Fähigkeiten und Kenntnisse („Es gab einfach kein technisches Problem, das du nicht beheben konntest" und „Für dich gibt es immer eine Lösung")

Neben diese Standbeine habe ich eine starke Wirbelsäule gebaut aus **Ausdauer** und ein Bauch gefüllt mit **Führungsvermögen**.

„Du machst bei diesen Sitzung mit wo schon ganz andere resigniert haben", „Du hast wegen deine Frau aufgehört rauchen" und „Du bringst die Daten der OP-Kennzahlen immer wieder an die Sitzung" deuten auf eine grossen Ausdauer Diese Charakterstärke wird in Feedbacks gleich viel genannt als Liebe zum Lernen. Vor allem an Sitzungen kommt mein Führungsvermögen nach vorne („Deine Art wie du die Sitzungen geleitet hast gut gefallen" und „Du bleibst als Sitzungsleiter dich selber und führst uns souverän durch die Sitzung").

Mein Herz ist gefüllt mit **Authentizität** („Deine Meinung ist gut durchdacht und mir deshalb wertvoll") und **Tapferkeit**(„Mutig deine Meinung sagst auch wenn sie nicht der Allgemeinheit entspricht" und „Wie du den dummen Schwätzer zurechtweist, während wir andern nur gelacht haben").

Im Kopf habe ich **Bescheidenheit** und **Vergebungsbereitschaft** („Ich bekomme immer eine Chance zur Wiedergutmachung").

Meine Arme benutze ich weniger. Auch reden tue ich nicht viel. Ich habe aber eine gute Nase und ein grosse Ohr. Ich bin einfach da fürs Team und unsere Patienten sowie ich zu Hause da bin für meine Frau und die Kinder. Mein Sohn sagt oft: „Du bist mein bester Freund".

Mein Ziel ist es für Alle ein guter Freund zu sein und dabei auch für mich selbst zu schauen. „Nein" sagen habe ich sehr lange nicht können. Es wurde einer meine Ziele am Vorgesetzten Seminar. Ich kann es heute gut. Überhaupt ist Führen etwas was lernbar ist. Und so habe ich nach wie vor die Hoffnung in die Zukunft kann ich meine Arbeit dank POD effizienter gestalten.

Figure 12.7 Selbst-Portrait. *Source*: Juan Humberto Young.

Handout 6 of Session 6: Example of a Master Student's Mindful, Positive Self-Portrait (MPS)

By: *Student (anonymous)**
For: *Juan Humberto Young, DM*

Doing the MPS was very interesting, not only because it helps to know myself better, but also because it was a unique occasion to question people about me. It is something I am not used to doing and often people prefer

* The Positive Self-Portrait is rendered verbatim as the student wrote it including some linguistic peculiarities as the student's mother tongue was German, not English.

Figure 12.8 Example of a Master Student's Mindful, Positive Self-Portrait. *Source*: Juan Humberto Young.

criticizing than talking about our strengths. The questioned people were surprised by my request and I think that it leads to a reflection on themselves too. Most people were interested by this original exercise and even wanted to do their own MPS. Therefore, I really like the "questioning" step as it led to rich and profound dialogues.

Moreover, I found it interesting to compare the results of the MPS to those of the VIA test which indicated that my top five strengths are love of learning, curiosity, perseverance, humor, modesty, whereas the last strengths are thankfulness, leadership, and teamwork. The perception of myself given by the VIA test generally fit to the views of questioned people, however, I had some surprises.

I have interviewed individuals from different backgrounds to have a more complete vision from my daily life. Therefore, I talked to people involved in my professional experience (who worked with me), in my academic experience (students and teachers), and those I consider as most important in my private life (best friends, family, boyfriend). I saw that among these different groups, some commonalities exist, but also differences. It was interesting to see how I adapt myself accordingly to the role I have to play in a given situation (work, family, etc.). It seems that some strengths are only used in one of the dimensions of my life whereas others are constantly involved. Thus, I will present you my MPS in three parts which correspond to the dimensions in which the positive behaviors appeared: the common basis, the competitive, and then the intimate environment.

1. *The basis*

Some strengths were quoted by all the questioned people: perseverance, humor, curiosity (and the related love of learning). Indeed, it seems that they represent my most developed strengths as they were immediately given by the people, and they are mobilized on a regular basis. As a consequence people see me like a person who constantly acquires and uses information (curiosity) in order to achieve goals (perseverance). However, my goals are not accomplished at the expense of others as I have strong interpersonal strengths which are showed by humor and kindness. First, I want to highlight that these results correspond to my top 5 in the VIA test.

The curiosity was often illustrated by my passion of museums, documentaries, trips in new regions of the world… One said: "you always ask questions and you always need more information than others. The funniest thing is that when we are not sure about something, for example last time we debated about the death circumstances of Bob Marley, you immediately go on Wikipedia to check the information whereas others do not have the curiosity to look for the information."

Then, the humor was often illustrated by stories about some jokes I made at work, home, or school in order to cheer up people (it seems that people remember my humor better when it helps them to overcome their bad mood). However, not only the jokes were quoted but also my ability to laugh about others' jokes. It seems much appreciated that I laugh easily with people and not about them, and it contributed to reinforce interpersonal relationships. For example, a colleague of my internship said: "it was nice to laugh with you in order to evacuate the high pressure the boss put on us. I remember that after the awful meetings of Monday morning during which our results were criticized, we made like a 'laughing' break in order to feel better. I think that it brought us closer and improved our whole week."

Lastly, the perseverance was illustrated with completely different stories according to the person interviewed. Indeed, whereas the humor and curiosity were explained with relatively resembling examples, the perseverance appeared in differentiated examples. For example, my professional background spoke about my perseverance to reach the fixed objectives which help them to maintain the motivation too. At school, people talked about my constant fight to improve my knowledge for courses like mathematics. Indeed, even if I fail once, I always will try to do better next time, even if it requires many efforts. In my private circle, people said more about the events of my life and relate them to the courage I showed in front of the obstacles. For example, my best friend said: "You don't have an easy life and I think that many people would be depressed at your place. You are extremely positive, optimistic, and courageous otherwise you would not have achieved your goals. I think about your cancer during the preparatory class (2 years class after the high school necessary in France to enter the elite business schools known as grandes écoles). You were several times at the hospital and missed many courses, however you never thought about failing, did not give up and you do not show to others the difficulties you lived."

After these basis strengths, which are present in all the dimensions of my daily life, I will now speak about other positive behaviors used in a more limited way and which I even discover for the first time with this exercise.

2. *In a competitive environment (school, work)*
The academic and professional environments are especially competitive as it is important to have the best results to succeed. People who were with me at school or work evoked systematically my capacity to avoid excesses and civic strengths like teamwork and leadership. I want to notice here that I was already aware of my modesty and self-control (even if I thought that I use them more widely which is apparently not the case) whereas my ability to manage people was completely new for me. Indeed, like the VIA test showed, I really do not think to be able to lead people; however, it seems that I do it without being aware of it. Maybe it is due to the fact that I have the image of the "traditional" leader in mind which is autocratic and creates a hierarchy. As I do not like this authoritarian style, I never thought that other types exist and that we can manage people in a different manner.

The anecdotes about my leadership and ability to work in team were especially numerous in the academic background (as my professional experience is limited). For example, in my business school I was at the head of an Arts Society and I decided about the events to organize, how to finance them… One of the members said: "You managed to create a community which was ready to work as interim not for personal aims, but for giving the money to the association. We organized nice events even if we were only 10 and it would have been not possible without you: you gave us our aims, motivated us, reminded us about the important things to do, etc." Another friend talked about a big project we had to do for our high school degree, she underlined that it was me who organized the team work, for example by creating a voting system, by distributing the work, etc. Even my superior of my internship said that I succeed to supervise some people for little projects.

Moreover, people said that I am a self-regulated person as they cannot imagine me having excessive reactions even in critical moments.

Indeed, I think that especially in my public life I am very prudent as I do not really know the people I meet; therefore I manage to control myself. As a consequence, the interviewed person said that I was very respectful of the rules and people. For example, during my internship I had an impulsive chief and he could be very aggressive. A colleague said to me that it was impressive that I never reacted violently to his unjustified criticism as others have done. "Some cried, others shouted or left the room, but you stay serene and prefer be prudent in your answers. I think it explains why the boss listened more attentively to your comments as you react in a moderate way."

Contrary to the competitive environments, people in my private life never spoke about my modesty and self-control as sometimes I have some strong reactions. Indeed, events in the private sphere touch me too much that I have not succeeded yet to look at them with distance, which would enable more temperance. Therefore, as I am now aware of it, I will try to be more balanced in my private life, even if I think that it will not be easy as jealousy, betrayal of trust, etc. of close people harm more than of others people (from school, work, etc.)

3. *Intimate environment*
Lastly, I saw that several strengths are only used in front of close people like friends or family members: critical thinking, open-mindedness, and fairness. The first ones complete my curiosity. I may use them only in my private life, and not at school or work, as I have not dared yet to criticize the knowledge of the teachers and highly experienced people. Indeed, I sometimes estimate that I am too young to contest the knowledge of other people. For me, they represent an authority which I am not able yet to question and I have first to learn enough before activating my critical thinking. The fairness is very present in my private life as I do not like inequities. I express easily my disagreements when people are not well treated whereas in public life I feel less powerful so I am more prudent and so do not always react in front of injustices. Here again, the observations will help me to extend my positive behaviors in all the dimensions of my life and not only in my private life.

About fairness, a family member said for example, that I do not like the discrimination of minorities: "I remember when I said negative words about homosexuals you immediately react and defend this minority." My mother gave another example: "You always fight against stereotypes. For example, when I said that the Arabian immigrants of France steal a lot, you find counter-arguments in order to show me that I was wrong."

The arguments I mobilize to defend my ideals are related to the critical thinking. Indeed, I try to analyze the ideas of people and do not accept them as the "truth." I do not appreciate stereotypes and people underlined that my open-mindedness helps me to take into account different dimensions of an issue, often ignored by others. For example, my mother gave me the example of my orientation choice. In France, for the high school degree, you have three possibilities for the orientation, scientific, economic, and literary. The general idea is that the scientific orientation is the best and my mother wanted me to choose that as I had the required grades. However, she changed her mind: "You convinced me that the economic orientation was better for you as it seems more diversified, with courses you would appreciate. You explained me well that the scientific orientation is not always the best. The choice was unusual and few teachers support your decision. However, you were right as today you study what you like in a good university."

As a conclusion, I want to underline that the questioned people talked about strengths I underestimated like leadership and therefore I think that the MPS completes well the VIA test in order to know one's strengths. Moreover, it helps to see that several strengths are less used and it gave me concrete means to work on them. Indeed, it will help me to develop positive attitudes like the fairness in all the dimensions of my life.

More globally, I see that I have many strengths and it is a very positive image. They are related between them and nourish each other. For example, my curiosity is linked to my open-mindedness which contributes to the fairness, which may improve my social intelligence, etc.

Lastly, I also saw that especially the strengths related to knowledge and courage characterize me whereas those linked to transcendence (spirituality, appreciation of beauty, etc.) are less developed and perceived by the people. It is the first time I see myself in this way and it will help me in my professional life, especially for my job research. I know what I am good at and what I like therefore I will find more easily the "ideal" job and organization which valorize my strengths and so where I can be engaged and happy.

Session 7

Note 22: Meditation on Friendliness

Some preliminary remarks on the focus of friendliness meditation may be useful because there are several possible focal points to choose from.

Usually only one or two people are addressed in a single practice. The easiest choice is a person that is actually likeable and generates spontaneous feelings of friendliness. Eventually the practice can expand by focusing on a person for whom we have neutral feelings and then moving on to someone we find difficult or to someone for whom we even feel animosity because the person has angered us or because we simply dislike them. Besides these four choices (likeable, neutral, difficult, and disliked person) an obvious focus for friendliness meditation is the self. Is there a need for cultivating friendliness towards ourselves, when there is widespread self-interest and narcissism in our consumer society? The answer is a resounding yes. First of all many people are hard pressed to hold onto their jobs or to make ends meet. Second, as strange as it may seem, it can be quite difficult to befriend yourself. As mentioned earlier in this chapter we are taught from early age to excel, to be perfectionists and to not be quitters. Hence we have a tendency to drive ourselves mercilessly in the pursuit of our goals. The other side of all this striving is self-doubt and self-contempt whenever we fall short of our personal benchmarks and objectives. We have a tendency to compare ourselves with others and define ambitious goals that sometimes stretch our abilities beyond their limits. This is why friendliness meditation focused on the self makes sense.

There are other orientations for friendliness meditation. Besides single individuals it can be valuable to include a whole team in the meditation (not necessarily our own team at work), even a company or another kind of institution. As the focus gets wider, we may not know the people involved personally. We may wish to include them in the meditation, because it is an organization whose goals we value or an organization that we wish to move in a positive direction. It could be the company we work for. It could also be our society as a whole or mankind, making it all-inclusive.

Focusing on people or these more abstract entities in friendliness meditation is not equivalent to praying for them. It is just an open and friendly awareness, a benevolence that warms our own hearts, yet in doing so something will always change for the better. The spirit of friendliness is contagious and the warmth we create is a kind of energy. By doing this we are intentionally opening our hearts and cultivating attitudes of friendly cooperation.

There are four fundamental orientations with respect to this practice:

- Wishing safety from harm for oneself and others.
- Wishing physical health and absence from physical suffering for oneself and others.
- Wishing mental health and absence from worry, anxiety, and sadness for oneself and others.
- Wishing flourishing states and acceptance for oneself and others.

Usually these wishes are expressed by the prefix "may I be..." or "may the person XYZ be...," for example, "may I be healthy" or "may my neighbor be healthy." Although the wish could or could not be fulfilled, the very fact of generating friendly thoughts has beneficial effects. In contrast, affirmative phrases such as "I want to be healthy" or "I want to be happy" convey a resolute claim that can produce a negative effect because it might highlight the shortfall between a desire and a current reality.

Let us look once again at the people we might include in our friendliness meditation:

- A person we like.
- A person that provokes no particular feeling in us (a neutral or indifferent relationship).
- A person we dislike.
- A person we consider difficult.
- Ourself.
- A group of persons that we might know—or maybe not.
- An organization, company, or institution we are part of—or maybe not.
- All of society or humanity.

In the script below for the first meditation on friendliness we focus on three choices: a person we like, a neutral person, and ourselves. This will allow a thorough exploration of this meditation.

1. The script

This is a sitting meditation. By now the first phases of any sitting meditation are a familiar process: settling into an upright position, shifting from a doing to a being mode by focusing on the breath, then expanding the awareness to the entire body and acknowledging without judging any feelings, thoughts, or body sensations that are present.

When you feel you have arrived at a state of calm and open awareness let the image of a person who you love or very much appreciate, a person that evokes warm feelings in you, come into your mind. It could be someone you have been in contact with recently or someone whose memory you cherish. If no particular person comes to your mind, give it some more time. It does not need to be a person you know intimately. It could be someone you met accidentally but who has been very kind to you.

Now begin by wishing the person all the good things that you think might be important to them. It is like showering a person in kind and loving thoughts. Put your wishes in words, silently repeating for example "may you be healthy," "may you find happiness," or "may you find peace of mind."

The invocation "may you ..." is a standard phrase in this type of meditation. It works well for practitioners as it expresses an encompassing wish that the person may do well. To that prefix can be added whatever is relevant for the particular person and whatever you feel you really wish him or her. If it sounds artificial to you, you could alter the sentence and silently repeat what sounds right for you and comes from your heart.

You can repeat several different wishes for the same person. While reiterating the wishes you can follow the same order or vary the sequence in the way that best suits you. If it becomes too strenuous mentally you could resort to a simple rhythmic repetition, for example repeating the following four wishes over and over again:

- Wishing you authentic happiness.
- Wishing you a healthy body.
- Wishing you a healthy mind free from defilements.
- Wishing you authentic friendliness.

These four wishes encompass practically everything in life and might be enough to generate the warmth this meditation aims to achieve. To go with the rhythm of the same wishes can also help you to stay in a being mode, aware of one's feelings and body sensations instead of getting completely drawn into thinking processes.

After a while disengage from the image of that person and let someone else you feel more or less neutral to arise in your mind. It could be an employee that turned out to be a difficult team member and although you do not personally dislike him or her you have not really been able to connect with them (a difficult person). It could also be a colleague with whom you have little interaction and the few contacts you have are mostly mechanical (a neutral person). Or you might think of a person you see once in a while on your way to work or when you buy groceries (a person you hardly know). Extend to this person the same wishes of happiness, health, and well-being. As you probably know little about this person, the four prototype wishes mentioned above may be the easiest.

This exercise may be more challenging. It may be harder to develop authentic warmth when compared to the person you first focused on. When you find it difficult, you could remind yourself that this person is just another human being with the same needs and wishes we all have: just like you this person would like to be happy and healthy. Humans have much more in common than we usually think. Reminding us of what we share makes it easier to extend friendliness to others.

Then, when you feel ready, you may shift your attention to yourself. You know your own worries and the things you long for. So why not wish that you may find what you are looking for? Start formulating the wishes that come from your heart and would mean so much to you. Or use the four standard wishes above to include everything: may I be happy, may I be healthy, may I be at peace, may I live with ease.

If this feels unfamiliar or odd, you might remind yourself that you are just another human being and deserve happiness like everybody else, just like the person you did not know very well and had no particular feelings for. If it still feels strange to wish yourself the best, just stay aware of your feelings, thoughts, and body sensations as they arise, remaining open and accepting your experience without judgment. Maybe you can explore what inhibits you from wishing yourself well. Maybe you can generate a warm understanding about where that obstacle comes from. Perhaps you can formulate the wish that this barrier may dissolve.

As always you can return to your breathing, this trusted friend that accompanies us everywhere and provides an anchor when we feel carried away. This is your breath, your body, your experience. May I be happy, may I live with ease….

When your breathing is calm, slowly return from your inner world and start expanding your attention to the room again, gently beginning to move and bringing the practice to an end.

It is worth reminding yourself that in order to be able to send love to others you must have a stock of love that is healthy and not egotistical. As Lao Tzu said over 2,000 years ago:

> This how the best people are:
> In their heart, they love what is deep;
> In personal relationships, they love kindness;
> In their words, they love truth.
> In the world, they love peace.
> In personal affairs, they love what is right.
> In action, they love choosing the right time.
> It is because they do not compete with others
> That they are beyond the reproach of the world.

2. *Guidelines*

a. For most people the four focal points—a loving person, a neutral and a difficult person, and self—represent a progression from easy to increasingly difficult. The teacher can encourage the participants to think of the previous step and replicate the process of wishing and creating the warm feelings they experienced before.
b. With the neutral person it may be useful to point out that encounters with persons we do not know well, and feel mostly indifferent towards, are our most common interaction. Especially in big organizations and in cities, we make contact with dozens if not hundreds of people we have little or no relation with. If we can learn to extend friendliness to all those strangers the world we live in will become a more pleasant place.
c. If some participants have difficulty in extending wishes to themselves, let them know that they are not alone and that this is a common phenomenon in Western societies. These participants will benefit most from friendliness meditation in the long run.
d. Make it quite clear to the participants that the most important element in this practice is not the content of the wishes but the warm feeling that should accompany them.

3. *Inquiry*

a. Start with open questions and find out from the participants what worked well and what was difficult.
b. Ask participants what neutral or difficult persons came to their mind and in what way they experienced that friendliness meditation might have an impact.

c. Find out how it went with friendliness to self and how it made them feel during and after this part of the meditation.
d. Have they found formulations to express wishes to themselves, for example? If so they should share their formulations, it might help their colleagues.
e. If they found friendliness directed to themselves too difficult, have they been able to find out where the difficulty comes from or is it a diffuse feeling? If so the teacher might briefly point out the cultural factors such as perfectionism and self-criticism that can be barriers as discussed above in Section 13.1.6.

4. Psycho-educational points

a. All human beings share the same wishes to be happy and to live with ease. We have more in common than we think.
b. By extending friendliness to fellow human beings we can make life easier for everyone, including ourselves.
c. If our friendliness is not returned right away it may happen later. In any case the friendly person benefits from a warm heart. A cold heart means emotional distress and is therefore detrimental to psychic and physical health, independent of whether the friendliness is returned or not.
d. Friendliness to self brings inner peace and a feeling of being whole.
e. Friendliness to self helps review priorities and goals in life.

Note 23: Active Constructive Responding: A Positive Communication Approach

Distribute Handout 1 that depicts the corresponding graphic or use a beamer/overhead projector to view the graph together. Prompted by the examples in the graph the participants will certainly contribute their own experiences regarding verbal and non-verbal communication. The more examples from the participants the richer the learning will be.

The main psycho-educational point is to learn how to communicate and become more sensitive to the people close to us. The more actively constructive we are ourselves, the less defensive behavior we will provoke, the smoother our communication and the more productive and pleasant our relations will be.

This is a practical implementation of friendliness and will greatly benefit from regularly practicing friendliness meditation.

Note 24: Albert Einstein: Is the Universe Friendly?

Einstein's reflection is presented in Handout 2. The handout can be distributed or alternatively the text can be beamed on a screen or wall in the room.

To manage the time within the session schedule it is probably convenient to have someone in the group read the reflection aloud and then have a very brief inquiry. An interesting point to make might be that even the great scientists cannot give a conclusive answer on the nature of the universe. We still keep searching long after Einstein's passing and maybe will search forever, because the more we know the more we realize that there are still so many questions unanswered.

In the end it is a question of choice as to what we decide to believe from the alternatives Einstein presents to us. But the consequences of the choices will determine the future of mankind, as he beautifully illustrates.

In defining our view we have to remember what we learned from positive psychology, namely that we have a disposition to pay more attention to negative information and take positive information for granted. It is in our interest to correct the balance consciously in favor of a friendly view of the universe. It will make our lives more fulfilling.

Note 25: Strengths, Opportunities, and Positive Action—SOPA Part I

1. *The script*

The starting point is to briefly explain to participants the nature and the purpose of the SOPA working model based on the introduction above (see Section 13.3.4):

- SOPA is a strategic tool using a positive approach that has been developed and tested over several years by the author of this book.
- SOPA is introduced in the MBSAT program as a complement to the mindful positive self-portrait (MPS). The intention is to establish an action plan that helps to advance participants on the path to realizing the MPS and gives support after the completion of the MBSAT program. To underscore this connection the SOPA graphic is included in Handout 4.
- In this session we start with the foundation of the action plan by preparing to take stock of what is present: (a) assets available including

character strengths, (b) current activities, and (c) opportunities. For this purpose the participants will receive templates in the form of tables and the home assignment is to fill in these tables carefully and thoughtfully in order to create a well-founded action plan.

After this short explanation the tables provided in the handouts may be distributed. Instead of handing out all three together it is better to distribute them one at a time and to discuss each table in turn: what the columns and the rows are and what elements are needed to complete the table.

The inventory of current activities is the easiest table to fill in and should be distributed first. A possible example of a weekly activity is the one mentioned previously: "working late x times a week." The criteria determining whether a current activity is mentioned can be the time it occupies (the more time the more important is the activity) or the impact it has on the participant's life. Participating in a professional association for example, may not take much time and not require frequent activity, but might be important for a person's future career.

The second table to distribute can be the inventory of assets. This may require more explanation. Participants are encouraged to think of all kinds of factors that might be helpful for their future professional or personal development. The teacher's dilemma is that the best explanation may be examples, but examples tend to limit thinking and channel the imagination instead of stimulating new ideas. Therefore ask the participants for examples and only provide additional illustrations if there are no useful inputs from the group.

In principle there are two categories of assets: material and immaterial ones. Among the first category would be resources such as a vehicle or an available physical space that could help in the founding phase of a new company. Examples for immaterial resources might include diplomas, specific know how, useful contacts, and character strengths. Participants should be encouraged to think hard when they fill in the table at home. If the space on the table is too limited, the participants might create their own, larger tables in the A3 format or photocopy the table provided.

The third table, the inventory of opportunities, requires even more careful reflection. It involves two skills: the capacity to analyze the environment to identify needs and demands and the creative ability to uncover new possibilities. The table is subdivided into columns corresponding to different areas of life (work, family, leisure, social activities) and this is useful to structure the reflections. To find the appropriate elements participants can formulate personal questions like:

- What possibilities exist in the area “work” to increase my engagement in what I am doing?
- What measures could increase quality time with my family?
- Where and how could I get to know more people personally (as opposed to internet friendships) and have a more active social life?
- How could I contribute to well-being beyond my workplace and family and get the satisfaction of doing something meaningful?

At the root of such questions are wishes and motives. These desires help to mobilize energy.

2. *Guidelines*

The SOPA working model is a tool to realize the mindful positive self (MPS) and participants should continuously make the connection and keep their MPS in mind as they fill in the tables.

In addition to the explanations provided in the discussion about the tables, the teacher could suggest that the participants help each other with ideas and advice if they get stuck with this home assignment.

It is best for the participants to start thinking and jotting down notes in the tables from day 1. In the interval between now and the eighth and last session they should continue to refine their entries by adding, correcting, and enriching.

3. *Inquiry*

As this is preparatory work the inquiry consists only of asking the participants whether they have further questions.

4. *Psycho-educational points*

a. The SOPA exercise is an experiential learning process that shows participants that personal growth can be systematically planned as opposed to simply drifting.
b. Most probably the participants will discover more assets and opportunities than they anticipated when they first looked at the empty tables. Knowing about assets and opportunities provides confidence, hope, and optimism.

Note 26: 3-Minutes Breathing Space on Friendliness (3MBS-Friendliness)

1. *The script*

This version of 3MBS creates a warm feeling and energy and you will implement it with pleasure.

Step 1: Start gathering your awareness by acknowledging your BETA. Be friendly and accepting with yourself and let be what there is. There is no need for judging or improving. Just being here.

Step 2: Focus on your breath and let in- and out-breaths gently rock you in the rhythm of your abdomen as it expands and contracts, expands and contracts.

Step 3: When you feel calm awareness, bring to your mind a person that you feel is in need of friendliness. It could be yourself. Maybe you feel exhausted and under pressure. Then this 3MBS-Friendliness is like a comforting massage. Or perhaps you will choose to focus on someone at work that you have noticed having a hard time or someone in your private life, maybe a person who is lonely or sad and needs support.

Keep the picture of that person in your mind or remain aware of yourself and silently start to form wishes. For example: May this person find her way. May this person get support. May this person feel at ease again.

You can formulate any wishes that come from your heart. Your focus should not be on thinking or on searching for smart wordings. Just let warmth arise from your heart for whoever you are thinking of, even if this means that your words feel unclear and mumbled.

Alternatively you can return to the standard wishes and let yourself be carried by the rhythm of repetition:

- Wishing you authentic happiness.
- Wishing you a healthy body.
- Wishing you a healthy mind free from defilements.
- Wishing you authentic friendliness.

When you feel it is good then slowly and gently disengage from the wishes and come back to your surroundings, taking the feelings of kindness and empathy with you to your current tasks.

2. Guidelines

a. You may explain to the participants that it is much more than a figure of speech to mention the heart in connection with friendliness. There is in fact biological evidence that feelings of love are enabled by a nerve called the vagus nerve that runs from deep inside the brain to the heart. (Porges, 2011).
b. You may also mention that the vagus nerve is linked with the breathing rate as mentioned in Chapter 7 in connection with the body scan (Section 7.3.2). Therefore, 3MBS-Friendliness integrates several aspects that jointly foster positivity and loving kindness.

3. Inquiry

a. It is probable that it requires some practice to summon the warm feelings quickly enough to do this mini-practice in the short time assigned, especially if the focus is on difficult persons or if a participant finds it difficult to focus on him or herself. In case the inquiry raises these kind of questions encourage the participants to persist with the mini-practice. The sitting meditation on friendliness that is practiced in parallel will naturally help facilitate 3MBS-Friendliness.
b. You may ask the participants about their reasons for choosing the persons they decided to focus on. Is it because they feel the person is in need of friendliness or because they like the person? Are there other reasons, maybe feelings of guilt or of helplessness (wanting to help and realizing the impossibility)?
c. What feelings emerged during and after the mini-practice?

4. Psycho-educational points

a. Friendliness does not depend on spontaneous liking. Cultivating friendliness toward those people that we find difficult is a tool designed to improve our personal relations and help avoid unnecessary tensions and confrontation.
b. Friendliness toward ourselves often gets neglected during the day, especially during busy and hectic times. Stepping back and doing 3MBS-Friendliness on our self helps foster emotional and physical health.
c. Friendliness towards strangers has the potential to change the world.
d. Friendliness is an ingredient of strategic awareness. Positive emotions have been demonstrated to increase creativity and openness, hence the capacity to perceive new perspectives. (See Chapter 2, Section 2.2.)

Note 27: How to Acquire Talented People

The sixteenth-century tale of Samurai wisdom is a text to be read aloud as a group. It is reproduced in Handout 3.

The main learning outcome is that friendliness and love create a positive energy that attracts good things in life. Hence if we cultivate friendliness in as many areas of life as possible, the more issues will resolve themselves effortlessly.

Session 7—Handouts and Homework

Handout 1 of Session 7: Active Constructive Responding: Connecting a Friendly Heart with a Friendly Tongue

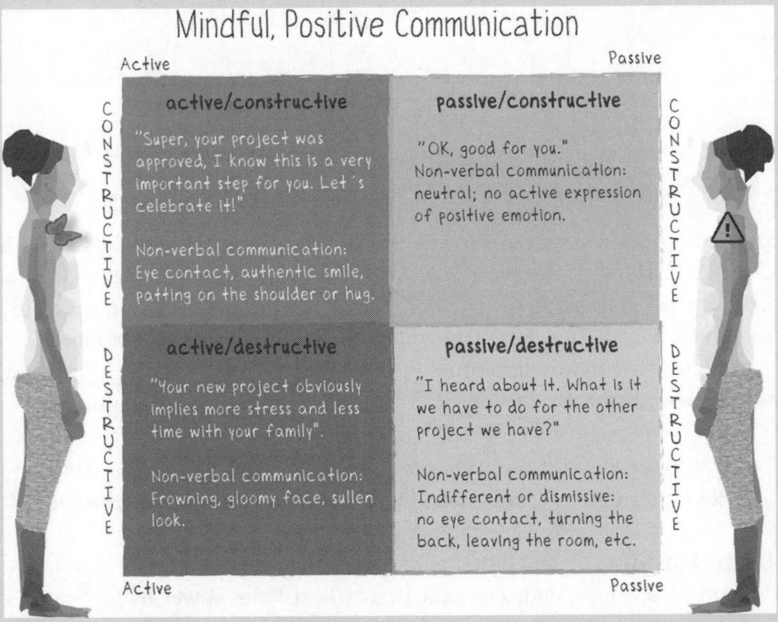

Figure 13.3 Mindful, Positive Communication. *Source*: Juan Humberto Young.

Handout 2 of Session 7: Albert Einstein: Is the Universe Friendly?

I think the most important question facing humanity is: "Is the universe a friendly place?" This is the first and most basic question all people must answer for themselves.

For if we decide that the universe is an unfriendly place, then we will use our technology, our scientific discoveries and our natural resources to achieve safety and power by creating bigger walls to keep out the unfriendliness and bigger weapons to destroy all that which is unfriendly and I believe that we are getting to a place where technology is powerful enough that we may either completely isolate or destroy ourselves as well in this process.

If we decide that the universe is neither friendly nor unfriendly and that God is essentially "playing dice with the universe," then we are simply victims to the random toss of the dice and our lives have no real purpose or meaning.

But if we decide that the universe is a friendly place, then we will use our technology, our scientific discoveries and our natural resources to create tools and models for understanding that universe. Because power and safety will come through understanding its workings and its motives.

God does not play dice with the universe.

Source: from www.awakin.org

Handout 3 of Session 7: How to Acquire Talented People: A Sixteenth-Century Samurai Tale

Before Lord Katsushige passed on his position as lord to his son, he gave him a note consisting of twenty items. All of the items were recommendations from Lord Katsushige's own father, Naoshige, the revered founder of the clan. Now his advice was being handed down to the third generation.

Among the items was the recounting of a father-to-son talk between Naoshige, the then Lord and clan leader, and Katsushige when he was a young man.

Lord Naoshige:	In order to rule the nation, you should have able men.
Son Katsushige:	Do you mean I have to pray to Buddha and the gods for the appearance of these men?
Lord Naoshige:	You pray to God for things beyond human power and endeavor. Yet it is within your power to get talented people to appear.
Son Katsushige:	How is this possible?

LORD NAOSHIGE: Irrespective of any matter, things gather around him who loves them. If he loves flowers, every variety of flower will begin to gather around him, even though he has not had a single seed until that time. And, in due course, there will grow a flower of the rarest kind. Likewise, if you love people, the result will be the same. Make a point of loving and respecting.

Source: Yamamoto, edited by Stone (2002, pp. 40–41).

Handout 4 of Session 7: Strengths, Opportunities, and Positive Action: SOPA Part I

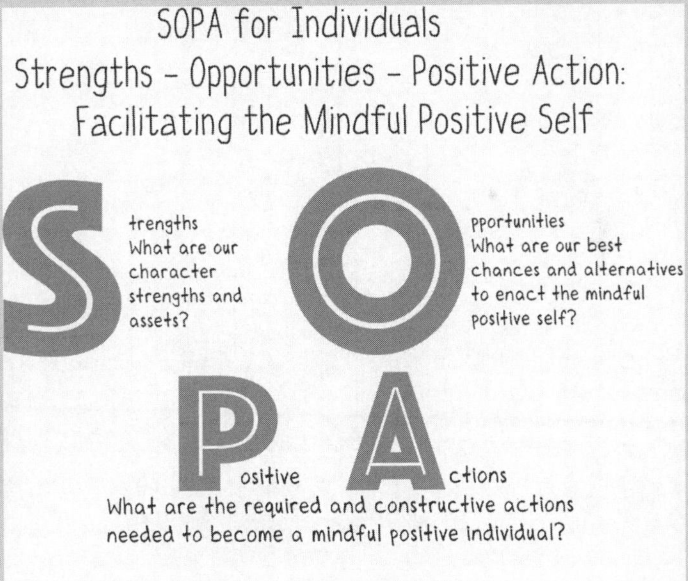
SOPA for Individuals
Strengths - Opportunities - Positive Action:
Facilitating the Mindful Positive Self
S trengths
What are our character strengths and assets?
O pportunities
What are our best chances and alternatives to enact the mindful positive self?
P ositive
A ctions
What are the required and constructive actions needed to become a mindful positive individual?
SOPA
Focus on the Mindful Positive Vision of Self

Figure 13.4 SOPA for Individuals. Strengths—Opportunities—Positive Action: Facilitating the Mindful Positive Self. *Source*: Juan Humberto Young.

Handout 5 of Session 7: Strengths, Opportunities, and Positive Actions: SOPA Part I

Inventory of Activities (See Handout 8 for tips.)

Table 13.1 SOPA (Strengths, Opportunities, and Positive Actions) Phase I: Inventory of Activities. *Source*: Juan Humberto Young.

SOPA (Strengths, Opportunities, and Positive Actions) Phase I: Inventory of Activities				
	Activities			
	Work	Family	Leisure	Social
Daily Activities	Driving to work	Dinner with family	Watching the news	Texting or calling friends
Weekly Activities	Planning the following week	Grocery shopping for a week	Playing tennis	Going out with friends
Monthly Activities	Review of monthly performance	Checking and paying bills	Concert	Volunteering in foundation
Yearly Activities	Yearly personnel evaluation	Family vacation	Spa treatment	Annual meeting of alumni association

Handout 6: Strengths, Opportunities, and Positive Actions: SOPA Part I

Inventory of Assets (See Handout 8 for tips.)

Table 13.2 SOPA (Strengths, Opportunities, and Positive Actions) Phase I: Inventory of Assets.
Source: Juan Humberto Young.

SOPA (Strengths, Opportunities, and Positive Actions) Phase I: Inventory of Assets											
Assets											
Work	Mobilization of Asset		Family	Mobilization of Asset		Leisure (Personal Hobbies)	Mobilization of Asset		Social (Group and Civic Activities, Social Projects)	Mobilization of Asset	
	Easy	Difficult		Easy	Difficult		Easy	Difficult		Easy	Difficult
Professional training	✔		Cooking abilities	✔		Kindle reader / ibook	✔		Facebook account	✔	

Handout 7: Strengths, Opportunities, and Positive Actions: SOPA Part I Inventories of Opportunities (See Handout 8 for tips.)

Table 13.3 SOPA (Strengths, Opportunities, and Positive Actions) Phase I: Inventory of Opportunities. *Source*: Juan Humberto Young.

SOPA (Strengths, Opportunities, and Positive Actions) Phase I: Inventory of Opportunities											
Opportunities											
Work	Cost of Realization		Family	Cost of Realization		Leisure (Personal Hobbies)	Cost of Realization		Social (Group and Civic Activities, Social Projects)	Cost of Realization	
	High	Low		High	Low		High	Low		High	Low
Promotion to vacant higher position	✔		Gourmet cooking once a week		✔	Learning Aikido	✔		Foundation for helping immigrants	✔	

Handout 8 of Session 7: Home Practice for the Week Following Session 7

May you be gently reminded to use the home record form to keep track of your practice.

1. Meditation on friendliness

The sitting meditation on friendliness, although considered very important for developing a truly mindful, positive mindset, is assigned for 4 out of 7 days in order to provide enough time to do Part I of the SOPA exercise carefully, because it is the foundation for your personal strategic plan to be completed in Session 8.

When you do the meditation on friendliness the most important component is that you actually feel genuine kindness towards the person you are focusing on, no matter who it is, including yourself. It is preferable not to become too drawn into thinking processes when formulating well-sounding wishes. It is more important to feel authentic warmth for the person. This will foster your relationship with him or her more effectively and positively. The audio files provided will guide you through the different phases of the meditation.

When you choose a third person as your focus (after calling to your mind a loving individual and before starting to focus on yourself) it may be useful to focus on a difficult person or someone for whom you might feel animosity as opposed to a person that is simply indifferent to you. You might be able to comprehend the practice sooner and it would probably enrich the group inquiry in Session 8.

During the week it may be interesting for you to observe how the meditation makes you feel and whether you note some impact on your relations and if so in what ways.

2. 3-Minutes Breathing Space on Friendliness (3MBS-Friendliness)

Whenever you notice unfriendly or cold feelings towards someone (it could be impatience, tension, or frustration, anger) please do 3MBS-Friendliness.

Remember to separate the three steps. The cultivation of friendliness is part of Step 3.

It will be interesting to observe your environment closely as you do the 3MBS-Friendliness frequently.

3. Practicing the positive communication approach: Active/constructive

Practice active/constructive communication wherever you are in contact with other people. Start by observing which quadrant of the graph in Handout

1 you are located in: How often are you passive/constructive instead of active/constructive? Are you sometimes destructive, passively or actively?

As you practice meditation on friendliness, see if you can make the connection between "friendly heart" and "friendly tongue" more often. When you notice that you are not in the active/constructive quadrant, experiment with reframing your communication. Keep observing and experimenting as you go about your daily activities just by staying alert and being aware of the dynamics of communication.

4. *Practicing one strength daily*

In the interval between Session 5 and Session 6 you practiced one of your VIA character strengths daily.

This is a practice that does not require more time in your schedule. All you need to do is consciously make a point of infusing one of the activities you are doing with one of your VIA character strengths. For example, if social intelligence is your strength, see if you can help improve cooperation in your team. Or if humility is your strength, why not include an outsider in your workplace, club, or association, someone others ignore or avoid. This action would also relate to other strengths such as social responsibility and kindness.

5. *Strengths, opportunities and positive actions—SOPA Part I*

The SOPA model is a tool to realize your mindful positive self (MPS). Therefore, put your self-portrait beside you when you complete Part I of SOPA and see what connections emerge and how you can animate your ideas.

The inventory of activities is the easiest table to fill in. The criteria for mentioning a current activity can be the time it requires or the impact it has on your life. Your membership of a professional association may not take much time but it could be important for your career. Another example of an entry in the table could be "working late x times a week" because of the importance this has on your life. If the space is too limited on the table provided, you might create your own, perhaps an A3 format or simply photocopy the table.

When completing the table inventory of assets it helps to think of factors that are potentially helpful for your professional or personal development. There are two categories of assets: material and immaterial ones. Among the first category would be resources such as a vehicle or an available physical space that could help in the founding phase of a new company. Examples for immaterial resources might include diplomas, specific know how, useful contacts, and character strengths.

The third table, the inventory of opportunities, involves two skills: (a) the capacity to analyze the environment to identify needs and demands and (b) the creative ability to uncover new possibilities. The table is subdivided into columns corresponding to different areas of life (work, family, leisure, social activities) and this is useful to structure the reflections. To find the appropriate elements you may formulate personal questions like:

- What possibilities exist in the area "work" to increase my engagement in what I am doing?
- What measures could increase quality time with my family?
- Where and how could I get to know more people personally (as opposed to internet friendships) and have a more active social life?
- How could I contribute to well-being beyond my workplace and family and get the satisfaction of doing something meaningful?

At the root of such questions are motives. If you think about your wishes in the context of your mindful positive self more ideas will come to your mind. You will be astonished how much you discover.

It is also useful to get in touch with colleagues and exchange ideas with them. It is advisable to start jotting down notes in the tables from day 1 and to keep refining the entries day after day by adding, correcting, enriching, and so on. It is a discovery process that takes shape gradually. And it is exciting—it is about your future!

Session 8

Handout 1 of Session 8: Strengths, Opportunities, and Positive Actions: SOPA Part II

In Part I you have prepared all the material needed for Part II:

- An inventory of your current activities (daily, weekly, monthly, yearly).
- An inventory of your assets (intrinsic and extrinsic).
- A list of opportunities you have identified to achieve more mindfulness and positivity in your life.

SOPA Part II is the completion of your mindful positive self plan, based on the material above and the mindful, positive self-portrait that is your vision.

SOPA Part II consists of two phases.

Phase 1: The task in this phase is to sift through your activities and decide whether they need to be boosted in order to increase mindfulness and positivity or whether they should be trimmed or maybe even dropped altogether. You may also recognize new activities that do not exist yet but would help you to achieve your goal of being more mindful and positive. These are activities that need to be generated.

Figure 14.1, presents visually, the four options you have as you go through your activities inventory: **boost, trim, drop, or generate.**

To facilitate this task you may use the MBSAT SOPA worksheet provided in this handout. You can start by listing your activities in the left column and then checking one of the four options in the columns to the right.

To orient you there are three examples in the worksheet. If you do not have enough space you could make photocopies or replicate the table on your computer.

Phase 2: In Phase 2 you continue to complete the MBSAT SOPA worksheet.

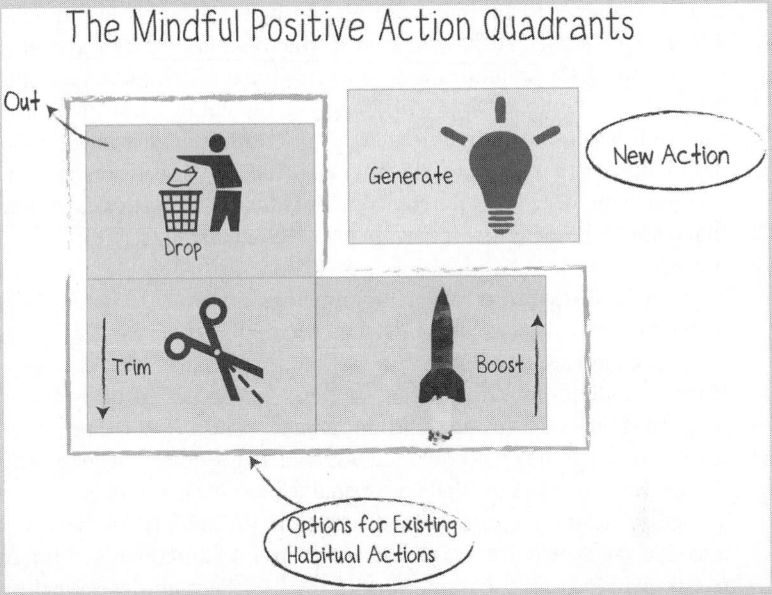

Figure 14.1 The Mindful Positive Action Quadrants. *Source*: Juan Humberto Young.

- You start by connecting the activities with the **opportunities** identified in the inventory of opportunities, asking about each activity: What opportunity does it support? The respective opportunity is entered in the adjacent column.
- Then you identify and fill in your **assets** and personal **character strengths** that support each activity and give them a positive quality.
- Next you determine under the heading of flourishing function what **barriers** the respective activity helps **to reduce**. If it is an activity that you decide to drop, the respective activity is probably not helpful at all and you may leave the columns empty.

The worksheet mentions three barriers in particular. They are based on a framework used in MBSAT that is called evolutionary leadership theory (ELT). ELT has been widely researched and defines three fundamental barriers to mindful and positive personal growth:

a. **Bio-social mismatch**: This means that our mental and behavioral patterns are still shaped by ancient times when leaders and their group of followers had to survive under harsh circumstances. They had to move from one shelter to another, hunting and fighting dangerous animals. The related archaic behavior and instinctive survival reflexes have turned into obstacles in the modern world. Today individuals, and especially leaders, must have a wide range of capabilities and be able to foresee future trends, generate new ideas, and skillfully manage social interactions and relationships. The questions on the worksheet are therefore whether a specific activity helps reduce ancient survival modes that tend to be defensive or aggressive, ego-centered, territorial, and possessive.

b. **Cognitive biases and errors:** Human beings are prone to many faulty cognitive patterns. A list of the most common of these biases and errors is included in the handout.

c. **Human tendency for dominance:** This tendency is also archaic in origin. In ancient times the strongest group members and the clan chiefs were better fed, had more choices to mate, and had many other privileges. This disposition to dominate others has remained a common human trait.

d. Under the heading of flourishing function in the SOPA worksheet, you also analyze whether each activity helps fulfill **fundamental human needs**. MBSAT uses the framework of the so-called self-determination theory (SDT), another robust scientific foundation. It has identified three fundamental human needs that motivate and drive our behavior: the need for autonomy, the need for competence, and the need for relatedness. In other words we want to be able to make decisions, we have a need to feel competent in what we are doing, and we are social beings who need to be in contact with others. In the SOPA worksheet you analyze which one of these essential needs each of your activities helps to fulfill. If an activity does not contribute to any of the three basic needs it probably should be dropped.

Once you have completed the MBSAT SOPA worksheet you will have a portfolio of ideas and insights as to how you can realize your vision of a mindful positive self. You can keep updating the worksheet and modifying the entries as you continue on your path of personal growth in the coming weeks, months, and years.

Frequent Biases Affecting Decisions

Action-oriented biases

Excessive optimism. Tendency for people to be overly optimistic, overestimating the likelihood of positive events and underestimating negative ones.
Overconfidence. Overestimating our skills relative to others' and

consequently our ability to affect future outcomes. Taking credit for past outcomes without acknowledging the role of chance.

Perceiving and Judging Biases

Confirmation bias. Placing extra value on evidence consistent with a favored belief and not enough on evidence that contradicts it. Failing to search impartially for evidence.

Groupthink. Striving for consensus at the cost of a realistic appraisal of alternative courses of action.

Misaligning of incentives. Seeking outcomes favorable to one's organizational unit or oneself at the expense of collective interests.

Framing Biases

Loss aversion. Feeling losses more acutely than gains, making us more risk-averse than a rational calculation would recommend.

Sunk-cost fallacy. Paying attention to historical costs that are not recoverable when considering future courses of action.

Escalation of commitment. Investing additional resources in an apparently losing proposition because of the effort, money, and time already invested.

Controllability bias. Believing one can control outcomes more than is actually the case and causing a misjudgment of the riskiness of a course of action.

Stability Biases

Status quo bias. Preferring the status quo in the absence of pressure to change.

Present bias. Valuing immediate rewards very highly and undervaluing long-term gains.

Anchoring and insufficient adjustment. Rooting decisions in an initial value and failing to sufficiently adjust away from that value.

Table 14.1 MBSAT SOPA Worksheet (SOPA Phase II). *Source*: Juan Humberto Young.

MBSAT SOPA Worksheet (SOPA Phase II)												
Activities	Opportunities	Character Strengths and other Assets	Flourishing Function						Positive Actions			
			Reducing Evolutionary Barriers			Fulfilling SDT Needs						
			Bio-social Mismatch	Cognitive Biases	Human Tendency for Dominance	Need for Autonomy	Need for Competence	Need for Relatedness	Generate	Boost	Trim	Drop
Spending more time with family	Longer dinner at home	Love, Kindness, Cooking abilities			✓			✓		✓		
Diet: eating less meat	Meat substitutes readily available in supermarkets	Persistence		✓			✓				✓	
Communication: Interrupting others while they speak	Meeting at the office, conversation with family	Self-regulation, Social Intelligence, MBSAT Training		✓	✓			✓				✓
Working mindfully and positively to compete for a new opening in the organization	Opening of a higher position in the organization	Social Intelligence, Leadership, etc. Additional professional training			✓	✓	✓	✓	✓	✓		

Note: Please go to the book's website and kindly download a larger size copy of this table.

Handout 2 of Session 8: Review of the 8-week MBSAT Program

It is time to take stock of what we have learned in the past 8 weeks and reflect on the essence of the MBSAT program. The MBSAT program overview (Table 14.2) presents a summary of all the practices and exercises and their benefits.

The table reviews benefits from different perspectives and connects them with the other dimensions of the program, including the scientific foundations and frameworks:

We check what **goals** of mindfulness and positive psychology are served by the practices and exercises.

We analyze what evolutionary **barriers** are reduced by the program by comparing them to the corresponding section in the MBSAT SOPA worksheet (see Handout 1 of this Session).

We determine what fundamental human **needs** are fulfilled by the practices and exercises (also in Handout 1).

- The overview contains four major subdivisions:
  a. Session themes, practices, and exercises.
  b. MBSAT's scientific foundations: mindfulness and positive psychology.
  c. Mindful positive function:
     Reducing evolutionary barriers and fulfilling fundamental human needs (SDT).
  d. Benefits: skills and insights

These major subdivisions are further subdivided to reflect essential learning outcomes:

Mindfulness is classified in the four BETA components: Body sensations, Emotions/feelings, Thoughts and Action impulses—the areas that meditation makes us aware of.

Positive psychology is schematized according to PERMA: positive emotions, engagement and flow, relationships, meaning in life, and positive accomplishment. For example the three good things exercise of Session 2 connects with the P of PERMA, namely positive emotion.

Reducing evolutionary barriers—part of the heading mindful positive function—is subdivided in the same way as in the SOPA worksheet: biosocial interaction mismatch, cognitive biases and errors, and human tendency for dominance. Each practice and exercise is analyzed from the point of view of which barrier it helps to reduce.

The second part of mindful positive function is the fundamental human needs of autonomy, competence, and relatedness according to self-determination theory (SDT). We check what practices and exercises fulfill these needs.

Table 14.2 MBSAT Program Overview. *Source*: Juan Humberto Young.

MBSAT´s Program Overview																				
8-Week Program				MBSAT´s Scientific Foundation									Mindful Positive Function							
				Mindfulness – BETA				Positive Psychology					Reducing Evolutionary Barriers			Fulfilling SDT Needs				
Session Nº	Theme	Practices	Exercises	Body	Emotions	Thoughts	Action Impulses	P	E	R	M	A	Bio-Social Interaction Mismatch	Cognitive Biases and Errors	Power Tendency for Dominance	Need for Autonomy	Need for Competence	Need for Relatedness	Skills	Insights
1	Robotic Living - Automatic Pilot	Body Scan		✓	✓									✓		✓			Directing attention volitionally	Awareness of Body sensations
			Raisin Exercise	✓	✓	✓	✓							✓		✓			Shifting from doing to being mode	Experiencing the richness of life in the present moment
			Building MBSAT´s Formal Mindfulness Practice Habit	✓	✓	✓	✓	✓	✓	✓	✓	✓	✓	✓	✓	✓	✓	✓	Building a mindful positive habit	Adaptive craving for a positive purpose
2	Living Above the Neck		Three Good Things (TGT)					✓						✓		✓	✓		Cultivating gratitude	So many good things in life we normally don´t see
		Mindfulness of the Breath		✓	✓									✓		✓	✓		Dealing with mind wandering	Awareness of the patterns of the mind
			BETA Exercise		✓	✓								✓		✓	✓		Connecting thoughts, emotions, body sensations and behavioral impulses	Our interpretations of events influence our experience
3	Recollecting Our Mind	Breath-and-Body Sitting Meditation		✓	✓									✓		✓	✓		Using breath and body sensations to focus awareness	Becoming aware of patterns of the mind and how they connect with body sensations
		Three-Minutes Breathing Space (3MBS)		✓	✓	✓	✓							✓			✓		Using Mindfulness in daily life	Moving into the present moment and away form doing into being mode
		Mindful Stretching and Mindful Salsa		✓	✓			✓		✓				✓				✓	Awareness of body in movement	The richness of body sensations and the accompanying healing effects
			Positive BETA Reframing					✓	✓					✓		✓	✓		Switching mood from negative to positive	Ability to increase the positivity ratio (ratio of positive to negative events or emotions)
			Character Strengths						✓				✓	✓	✓	✓	✓	✓	Identifying and learning to better use character strengths	Living an engaged life and living in "flow"
4	Constriction of Experience- Like and Dislike (Our worried and Anxious Mind)	Sitting Meditation on Breath, Body, Sounds, Thoughts and Open Awareness		✓	✓	✓	✓							✓		✓	✓		Using the breath, sounds, thoughts, and open awareness to be present to our moment-to moment experience	Recognition of our full experiences in awareness including worries and difficulties; decentering from thoughts by bringing attention to our body
		Mindful Walking		✓									✓			✓			Awareness of body in movement	Managing mind wandering and staying present with daily activities
			Defining the territory of anxiety and worry									✓		✓		✓	✓		Identifying the cyles of worry and anxiety	Ability to exit the worry cycle
		Three Minutes Breathing Space Focusing on Strengths		✓	✓	✓	✓		✓				✓			✓	✓	✓	Moving from doing to being mode and responding skillfully with strengths	Ability to respond to difficulty skillfully and from character strengths
5	Strategic Awareness I: Mindful Real Options (MROs)	Irimi Meditation		✓	✓	✓	✓					✓		✓		✓	✓		Ability to renecognize aversion patterns and moving directly into difficulty	Allowing difficulties and opening up Mindful Real Options (MROs)
		Three-Minutes-Breathing Space on Worry		✓	✓	✓	✓					✓	✓	✓		✓	✓		Switching form a driven worrying-doing mode to an accepting being mode	Responding skillfully with acceptance
			Mindful Positive Self (First Take)									✓	✓	✓	✓	✓	✓	✓	A mindful positive vision of oneself	The mindful positive self is achievable
6	Strategic Awareness II: From POMO (Powerful Money) to MIMO (Mindful Money)	POMO Meditation I, II and III		✓	✓	✓	✓	✓	✓	✓	✓	✓	✓	✓	✓	✓	✓	✓	Recognizing cognitive, emotional and behavioral patterns related to money	Using awareness of the relation to money to change patterns of behavior (MIMO)
		Three-Minutes-Breathing-Space on Money		✓	✓	✓	✓	✓	✓	✓	✓	✓	✓	✓	✓	✓	✓	✓	Switching mindset away from money worries	Enetering a zone of being with expanded awareness about more skillful ways with money
			Money and Opportunity Costs			✓	✓				✓			✓	✓	✓	✓	✓	Trade-offs of money	Recognizing the relative value of money
			Mindful Positive Self (Second Take)									✓	✓	✓	✓	✓	✓	✓	Designing the mindful positive vision blueprint	The magnet effect of mindful positive vision (motivating towards achieving the vision)
7	Strategic Awareness III: Opening the Heart	Meditation on Friendliness			✓	✓	✓			✓					✓			✓	Opening the heart: developing friendliness to others and to self	Befriending ourselves and the world is possible
		Three Minutes Breathing Space on Friendliness			✓	✓	✓			✓					✓			✓	Befriending ourselves and others in a moment	Befriending ourselves and others in a brief moment in daily life is possible
			Active/Constructive Responding							✓					✓			✓	Connecting a friendly heart with a friendly tongue	Changing pattern of communication is possible and desirable
			Strengths, Opportunities and Positive Actions-SOPA Part I	✓	✓	✓	✓	✓	✓	✓	✓	✓	✓	✓	✓	✓	✓	✓	Designing the Mindful Positive Plan for personal growth	Discovering the growth mindset of perceiving multiple possibilities
8	Minding Your BETA	Three Minutes Breathing Space on Strategic Awareness		✓	✓	✓	✓							✓		✓	✓	✓	Switching from doing mode to being mode with strategic awareness	Strategic awareness as prospection in being mode and in the present moment
			Strengths, Opportunities and Positive Actions-SOPA Part II	✓	✓	✓	✓	✓	✓	✓	✓	✓	✓	✓	✓	✓	✓	✓	Accomplishing the Mindful Positive Plan for personal growth	Discovery of one´s potential to become a mindful positive self

Note: Please go to the book's website and kindly download a larger size copy of this table.

Clearly the practices and exercises have multiple effects: they can reduce one of the barriers and at the same time help fulfill one of the basic needs. For example, the contribution of Irimi meditation consists of reducing cognitive biases and errors (in many ways the source of our difficulties) and at the same time it fulfills our needs for autonomy and competence as it helps people gain the ability to handle difficulties skillfully.

Finally, the benefits of the MBSAT program are subdivided into skills and insights gained. For example, with the meditation on a person's relationship with money one of the skills gained is the ability to recognize what one's cognitive, emotional, and behavioral patterns regarding money are and the insight is that we can use this awareness to change the patterns, if so desired.

Handout 3: The Living Zone of the Mindful, Positive Individual

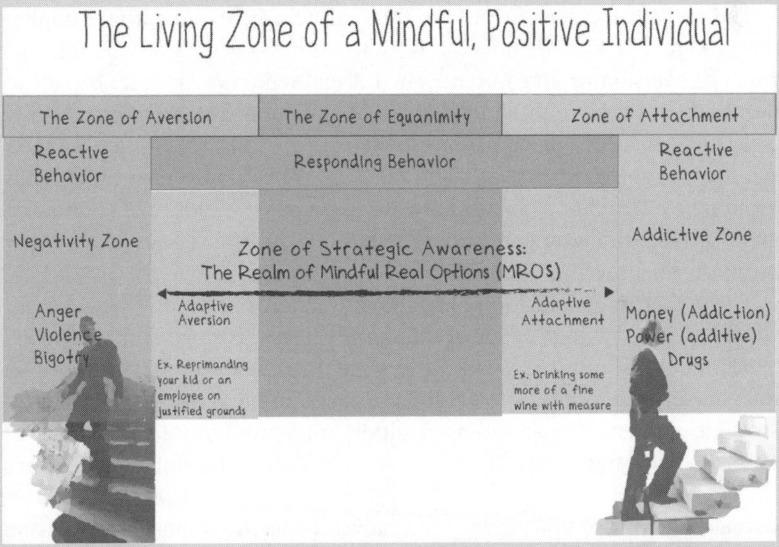

Figure 14.2 The Living Zone of a Mindful, Positve Individual. *Source*: Juan Humberto Young.

The purpose of the MBSAT program is to provide training for practices and skills that allow individuals to make decisions that can lead to a life characterized by mindful and positive states.

With MBSAT there are three essential zones in which a person's life can unfold. They are depicted in Figure 14.2.

- *The Zone of Aversion*: Whenever dislike arises in us we are in the zone of aversion. We try to stay away from what we dislike or ban it from our lives.
- *The Zone of Attachment*: We enter the zone of attachment when we like something and wish to keep it and preserve the pleasurable feeling that comes with it.
- *The Zone of Equanimity*: This is the zone of balance and serenity where ideally the lives of mindful, positive individuals can develop.

Life in the first two zones, aversion and attachment, is characterized by reactive behavior: the doing mode in automatic pilot, impulsiveness with little awareness, and compulsive patterns. It is a life of reactivity.

In the zone of equanimity individuals live their lives more consciously and calmly. Equanimity is the ability to regulate our cognitive and emotional state and to adapt the intensity and quality of our responses, based on strategic awareness that allows for lucidity, a wider perspective, and objectivity.

The art of living for most of the time in the zone of equanimity implies that we are able to respond adaptively when life's events carry us into the zones of aversion or attachment. The normal tendency is to get caught in negativity or mired in different degrees of addiction. The art of equanimity is to realize that aversion and attachment can vary considerably in both their significance and their intensity and to adapt our response accordingly thus avoiding overreactions. Such moderate responses are indicated in the diagram as adaptive aversion and adaptive attachment. These areas imply responsive behavior as opposed to knee-jerk reactions.

The two areas of transition of adaptive aversion and adaptive attachment when combined with the zone of equanimity form the broad domain of strategic awareness. In other words, if it is not possible to stay permanently in the zone of equanimity, we can at least maintain ourselves in the realm of strategic awareness, responding skillfully and mindfully to situations of aversion and attachment. This is the area where Mindful Real Options (MROs) emerge.

Imagine, for example, that an employee or team member provokes an adverse situation by handing in a much-needed report late or losing an important client. As that employee's supervisor or colleague you could let yourself drift into the negativity zone, go red with anger, shout, or even insult the failing person and that could make the situation worse (it could result in the employee walking out, a drop in morale, or other possible consequences). Alternatively you could reprimand him or her with fairness, albeit firmly, pointing out the damage and taking measures to prevent similar situations in the future (for example, establish checks before the deadline is reached or offer additional personnel training). These responses will help you to remain in the zone of strategic awareness and resolve the situation with wisdom and friendliness.

The same applies to situations in the zone of attachment, for example, going out for dinner with friends and having more than usual of a very fine wine in the animated ambience of the group without losing your composure or doing something foolish.

Obviously, the aim is to stay in the zone of strategic awareness that coincides with the zone of responding behavior and MROs.

By continuing the practices of MBSAT the ability to avoid reactive behavior and avert negativity or addiction will rise. Over time we can build a special space within the world around us, a personal world that acts as an antidote to daily turmoil.

If today's world is characterized by VUCA (Volatility, Uncertainty, Complexity, and Ambiguity) the personal world of mindful, positive practitioners has the qualities of WECO (Wisdom, Equanimity, Compassion, and Open Awareness). An illustration of these two contrasting worlds is presented in Handout 6 of this session.

Handout 4 of Session 8: A Tale of Equanimity and Open Mindset

Good thing, Bad thing, Who knows? (A Sufi Tale)

There was once a farmer who owned a horse and had a son.

One day his horse ran away. The neighbors came to express their concern: "Oh, that's too bad. How are you going to work the fields now?" The farmer replied: "Good thing, Bad thing – Who knows?"

In a few days, his horse came back and brought another horse with her. Now, the neighbors were glad: "Oh, how lucky! Now you can do twice as much work as before!" The farmer replied: "Good thing, Bad thing – Who knows?"

The next day, the farmer's son fell off the new horse and broke his leg. The neighbors were concerned again: "Now that he is incapacitated, he can't help you around the farm, that's too bad." The farmer replied: "Good thing, Bad thing – Who knows?"

Soon, the news came that a war broke out, and all the young men were required to join the army. The villagers were sad because they knew that many of the young men would not come back. The farmer's son could not be drafted because of his broken leg. His neighbors were envious: "How lucky! You get to keep your only son." The farmer replied: "Good thing, Bad thing – Who knows?"

Source: YogiMir (2013)

Handout 5 of Session 8: Course Evaluation

As the program comes to a close your feedback on the program by answering the questions below would be much appreciated.

Value of the Program

How beneficial have the following themes been for you?

Please give a score from 1 through 10 where 1 means "not at all beneficial" and 10 means "extremely beneficial."

Theme **Score (1–10)**

Living with awareness and conscious choice
(*versus* being on automatic pilot)..

Knowing experience directly through your senses
(*versus* through thinking) ....

Being here, now, in this moment
(*versus* dwelling in the past or future) ....

Approaching all experience with interest
(*versus* avoiding the unpleasant) ....

Allowing things to be as they are
(*versus* needing them to be different) ....

Seeing thoughts as mental events
(*versus* as necessarily true and real)..

Taking care of yourself with kindness and compassion
(*versus* focusing on achieving goals regardless of the cost to you and others) ....

Relating skillfully to money
(*versus* being driven by compulsion or reaction in relation to money) ....
....

Overall, has MBSAT improved your decision-making skills for well-being?
(*versus* no improvement at all) ....

Has your strategic awareness increased in your opinion?
(*versus* no increase at all) ....

Handout 6 of Session 8: The Overall Goal of MBSAT: From VUCA to WECO

From VUCA to WECO:

From the VUCA world around us
(a world of Volatility, Uncertainty, Complexity, Ambiguity)
to a personal world of WECO
(Wisdom, Equanimity, Compassion and Open Awareness)

Figure 14.3 The Institutionalized World of VUCA/The Goal. *Source*: Juan Humberto Young.

Final Words and Acknowledgments

When participants have completed this program they will have learned to calm their minds, open their hearts and experience their lives more integrally by accessing the embedded wisdom of their body and recognizing the visceral information that reveals more about what really is going on in their lives than what they think they know.

The skills gained in the first half of the program will have created the necessary scaffolding for the second part of the program: the last 4 weeks of the course in which participants gain a discerning and evaluative ability defined as strategic awareness, the skill that can help them build Mindful Real Options and take lucid decisions for building and sustaining well-being, their own as well as that of others.

The program is not easy. It takes committed work to develop practical wisdom, equanimity, friendliness, and open awareness, the qualities that serve as the nutrients for strategic awareness—qualities that cannot be purchased but need to be cultivated, nurtured, and refined over time. Any serious attempt to improve one's life experience, which is what MBSAT is about, will invariably encounter discomfort. The key is to allow increasing levels of difficulty while gaining new possibilities to grow. Those who have mindfully, positively, and diligently maintained their practice during the 8 weeks will know and understand the true value of the course. They might already be less distracted. They might find it easier to concentrate and have more patience, even in situations they would otherwise find annoying. They will have gained resilience to weather skillfully the challenges of a VUCA life and the ability to move into a WECO life. People who have known them for many years or who are close to them might be commenting: "You are different, so much nicer to be with and work with. How come?" In just the 8 weeks of practice their brain has begun to transform and grow by increasing gray-matter density in the hippocampus area that is associated with learning and memory as well as in processes associated with self-awareness, compassion, and introspection (McGreevey, 2011; Singleton et al., 2014).

Mindfulness-Based Strategic Awareness Training: A Complete Program for Leaders and Individuals, First Edition. Juan Humberto Young.

Companion website: www.wiley.com/go/humbertoyoung/mbsat

Having identified their mindful positive self, participants will have discovered their potential and their goodness and will be ready to put it in action with their personal SOPA blueprint. It is hoped that with the practices of MBSAT participants will have acquired useful skills to reduce the reactivity of their conditioned mind and learned to respond in more skillful ways to the inherent challenges of life. MBSAT, by allowing you to reinvent yourself, is a challenging, positively disruptive program, appropriate for our disruptive times. As such it is an ongoing project and an invitation to continue with the different practices in order to find out what works best for you. In essence MBSAT is about remembering to mind your BETA as visualized in Figure 0.1.

This book is really the voice of so many individuals who have accompanied me on my journey and helped shape the person I am today: Monika, my wife, with her sharp mind and Swiss precision; both of my parents, Juan Humberto and Eva Maria with their love, care, and attention as I was growing up; my teachers, some now my friends, without whose ideas this book could not have been written, in particular M. Seligman, C. Peterson, B. Fredrikson, S. Srivastva, D. Copperrider, D. Boland, J. Aram, and R. Reich; researchers and authors whose work has helped me to develop my ideas, amongst others M. Van Vugt, E. Deci, and R. Ryan. I owe a huge debt to the ground-breaking work on secular mindfulness practices to J. Kabat-Zinn and the "MBCT Three" (Z. Siegel, J. Teasdale, and M. Williams); to J. Peacock for his "not so cozy" introduction to Buddhist psychology (as he says: if this stuff is not disturbing you, it isn't working); to E. Riggs for her skillful and gentle supervision of my mindfulness teaching practices and the other members of the Oxford Mindfulness Center; to K. Janjöri and T. Krayenbühl of my time at UBS who helped me understand Swiss leadership and culture. I am also deeply grateful to my colleagues at IE University: M. Chaskalson, M. Fernandez de Villata, P. Huang, D.M. Hosking, J. Liedtka, L. Newman, T. Rashid, B. Schmitt, and A. Stutzer; my clients and business partners; and my students at both University of Saint Gallen, Switzerland, and IE University, Madrid.

Special thanks goes to the editorial team of Wiley & Sons: Sakthivel Kandaswamy, Roshna Mohan and Fionnguala Sherry-Brennan, and to Maria Linares who did such a wonderful job helping me with the illustrations.

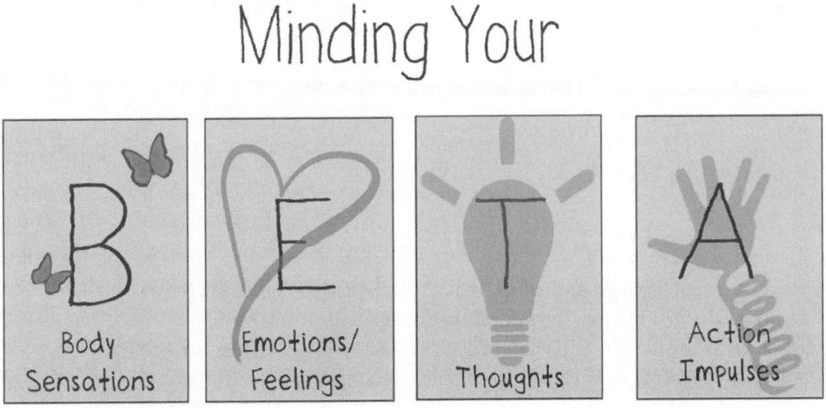

Figure 0.1 Minding Your BETA. *Source*: Juan Humberto Young.

References

Admati, A., & Hellwig, M. (2013). *The bankers' new clothes: What's wrong with banking and what to do about it*. Princeton, NJ and Oxford, England: Princeton University Press.

Amabile, T. M. (1983). *The social psychology of creativity*. New York, NY: Springer.

Amabile, T. M. (1998). How to Kill Creativity. *Harvard Business Review*, September–October 1998.

Añalayo (2004). *Satipatthana: The direct path to realization*. Cambridge, MA: Windhorse Publications.

Anderson J. (2015) 'The point is you're greedy: Trader called 'ringmaster' at rate-rigging trial. *Sydney Morning Herald*. May 27, 2015.

Ariely, D., & Norton, M. I. (2008). How actions create – not just reveal – preferences. *Trends in Cognitive Sciences*, *12*(1) (January), 13–16.

Babiak, P., & Hare, R. D. (2006). Nice suit. Would a snake wear such a nice suit? In *Snakes in suits – When psychopaths go to work* (pp. 5–17). New York, NY: Harper.

Baer, R. A. (2003). Mindfulness training as a clinical intervention: A conceptual and empirical review. *Clinical Psychology: Science and Practice*, *10*, 125–143.

Barrett, L. F., & Bar, M. (2009). See it with feeling: Affective predictions during object perception. *Philosophical Transactions of the Royal Society*, *364*, 1325–1334.

Baumeister, R. F., Bratslavsky, E., Finkenauer, C., & Vohs, K. D. (2001). Bad is stronger than good. *Review of General Psychology*, *5*, 323–370.

Bennett, N., & Lemoine, G. J. (2014). What VUCA really means for you. *Harvard Business Review*. January–February.

Bishop, S. R., Lau, M., Shapiro, S., Carlson, L., Anderson, N. D., Carmody, J. … Devins, G. (2004). Mindfulness: A proposed operational definition. *Clinical Psychology: Science and Practice*, *11*(3), 230–241.

Board, B. J., & Fritzon, K. (2005). Disordered personalities at work. *Psychology, Crime & Law*, *11*(1), 17–32.

Bodhi, B. (2011). What does mindfulness really mean? A canonical perspective. *Contemporary Buddhism*, *12*(1), 19–39.

Mindfulness-Based Strategic Awareness Training: A Complete Program for Leaders and Individuals, First Edition. Juan Humberto Young.

Companion website: www.wiley.com/go/humbertoyoung/mbsat

Boehm, J. K., & Kubzansky, L. D. (2012). The heart's content: The association between positive psychological well-being and cardiovascular health. *Psychological Bulletin, 138*(4), 655–691.

Bögels, S., & Restifo, K. (2014). *Mindful parenting, a guide for mental health practitioners.* New York, NY: Springer.

Bolier, L., Haverman, M., Westerhof, G. J., Riper, H., Smit, F., & Bohlmeijer, E. (2013). Positive psychology interventions: A meta-analysis of randomized controlled studies. *BMC Public Health, 13*, 119. doi: 10.1186/1471-2458-13-119

Borkovec, T. D., Alcaine, O. M., & Behar, E. (2004). Avoidance theory of worry and generalized anxiety disorder. In R. G. Heimberg, C. L. Turk, & D. S. Mennin (Eds.), *Generalized anxiety disorder – Advances in research and practice* (77–109). New York: Guilford.

Boyatzis, R., & McKee, A. (2005). Mindfulness – an essential element of resonant leadership. In R. Boyatzis & A. McKee (Eds.), *Resonant leadership* (Chapter 6). Cambridge, MA: Harvard Business School Press.

Boyer, E. L. (1997). *Scholarship reconsidered: Priorities of the professoriate.* San Francisco, CA: Jossey-Bass.

Brewer, J., Worhunsky, P. D., Gray, J. R., Tang Y. Y., Weber, J., & Kober, H. (2011). Meditation experience is associated with differences in default mode network activity and connectivity. *Proceedings of the National Academy of Science*, USA, *108*(50), 20254–20549.

Brickman, P., & Campbell, D. (1971). Hedonic relativism and planning the good society. In M. H. Apley (Ed.), *Adaptation-level theory: A symposium* (pp. 287–302). New York, NY: Academic Press.

Brickman, P., Coates, D., & Janoff-Bulman, R. (1978). Lottery winners and accident victims: Is happiness relative? *Journal of Personality and Social Psychology, 36*(8), 917–927.

Brown, K. W., & Ryan, R. M. (2004). Perils and promise in defining and measuring mindfulness: Observations from experience. *Clinical Psychology: Science and Practice, 11*(3), 242–248.

Brown, K. W., Ryan, R. M., & Creswell, J. D. (2007). Mindfulness: Theoretical foundations and evidence for its salutary effects. *Psychological Inquiry, 18*, 211–237.

Brown, K.W. et al. (2009) When what one has is enough: Mindfulness, financial desire discrepancy and subjective well-being. *Journal of Research in Personality*, 43, 727–736.

Buczynski, R., & Porges, S. (2013) *Body, brain, behavior: How polyvagal theory expands our healing paradigm.* Transcripts of a webinar session at the National Institute for the Clinical Application of Behavioral Medicine.

Butler, G., & Hope, T. (2005). *Manage your mind – the mental fitness guide* (Reprint of 1986 Rev. Ed.), Oxford, England: Oxford University Press.

Candido, C. J. F., & Santos, S. P. (2015). Strategy implementation: What is the failure rate? *Journal of Management and Organization, 21*(20), 237–262.

Chadwick, P. (2014). Mindfulness for psychosis. *The British Journal of Psychiatry, 204*, 333–334.

Cohn, M., & B. Fredrickson. (2009) Positive Emotions. In *Oxford Handbook of Positive Psychology* (Chapter 3). Oxford University Press.

Csikszentmihalyi, M. (1990, new edition in 2008). *Flow: The psychology of optimal experience.* New York, NY: Harper & Row.

Dalai Lama (n.d.). *A letter from our founder*. The Center for Compassion and Altruism Research and Education, Stanford School of Medicine. Retrieved from http://ccare.stanford.edu/education/about-compassion-cultivation-training-cct/a-letter-from-our-founder/

Dalai Lama (2010) *Mind and Life XX – Altruism and Compassion in Economic Systems: A Dialogue at the Interface of Economics, Neuroscience, and Contemplative Sciences*. Conference, Zurich, Switzerland.

Damasio, A. (2006). *Descartes' error: Emotion, reason, and the human brain* (Rev. ed.). New York, NY: Penguin.

Dane, E., & Brummel, B. (2013). Examining workplace mindfulness and its relations to job performance and turnover intention. *Human Relations, 67*(1), 105–128.

Danner, D. D., Snowdon, D. A., & Friesen, W. V. (2001). Positive emotions in early life and longevity: Findings from the nun study. *Journal of Personality and Social Psychology, 80*(5), 804–813.

Deci, E. L., & Ryan, R. M. (2000). The "what" and "why" of goal pursuits: Human needs and the self-determination of behaviour. *Psychological Inquiry, 11*, 227–268.

Deckersbach, T., Hölzel, B., Eisner, L., Lazar, S. W., & Nierenberg, A. A. (2014). *Mindfulness-based cognitive therapy for bipolar disorder*. New York, NY: Guilford Press.

Desbordes, G. et al. (in press). Moving beyond Mindfulness: Defining Equanimity as an Outcome Measure in Meditation and Contemplative Research. *Mindfulness*.

Ditto, B., Eclache, M., & Goldman, N. (2006). Short-term autonomic and cardiovascular effects of mindfulness body scan meditation. *Annals of Behavioral Medicine, 32*, 227–234.

Dreyfus, G. (2011). Is mindfulness present-centred and non-judgmental? A discussion of the cognitive dimensions of mindfulness. *Contemporary Buddhism, 12*(1), 41–54.

Duhigg, C. (2012). *The power of habit: Why we do what we do and how to change*. London, England: Random House.

Dutton, K. (2013). *The wisdom of psychopaths: What saints, spies, and serial killers can teach us about success*. London, England: Arrow Books.

Dweck, C. S. (2006). *Mindset, The new psychology of success*. New York, NY: Random House.

Easterlin, R., & Angeluscu, L. (2009). *Happiness and growth the world over: Time-series evidence on the happiness–income paradox*. Discussion Paper No. 4060, March. Germany: The Institute for the Study of Labor in Bonn.

Easterlin, R. A., Angelescu McVey, L., Switek, M., Sawangfa, O., & Smith Zweig, J. (2010). The happiness-income paradox revisited. *Proceedings of the National Academy of Sciences, USA, 107*(52), 22463–22468.

Ekman, P. (2003). *Emotions revealed: Recognizing faces and feelings to improve communication and emotional life*. New York, NY: Henry Holt and Company.

Emmons, R. A., & Mishra, A. (2012). Why gratitude enhances well-being: What we know, what we need to know. In K. Sheldon, T. Kashdan, & M. F. Steger (Eds.), *Designing the future of positive psychology: Taking stock and moving forward*. New York, NY: Oxford University Press.

Epel, E. S., Puterman, E., Lin, J., Blackburn, E., Lazaro, A., & Berry Mendes, W. (2012). Wandering minds and aging cells. *Clinical Psychological Science, 15*, 1.

Estés, C. (1996). *Women who run with the wolves*. New York, NY: Ballantine Books.

Farb, N., Daubenmier, J., Price, C. J., Gard, T., Kerr, C., Dunn, B. D., … Mehling, W. E. (2015). Interoception, contemplative practice, and health. *Frontiers in Psychology, 6*, Article 763.

Fredrickson, B. (2003). The value of positive emotions. *American Scientist, 91*(4), 330–335.
Fredrickson, B. L., Cohn, M. A., Coffey K. A., Pek, J., & Finkel, S. M. (2008). Open hearts build lives: Positive emotions, induced through loving-kindness meditation, build consequential personal resources. *Journal of Personality and Social Psychology, 95*(5), 1045–1062.
Freedman, L. (2013). *Strategy, a history*. Oxford, England: Oxford University Press.
Galinsky, A. D., Magee, J. C., Inesi, M. E., & Gruenfeld, D. H. (2006). Power and perspectives not taken. *Psychological Science, 17*(12), 1068–1074.
Gallup, Inc. (2015) State of the American Manager: Analytics and Advice for Leaders. *Special Report*. Retrieved from http://www.gallup.com/services/182138/state-american-manager.aspx
Gethin, R. (2015). Buddhist conceptualizations of mindfulness. In K. W. Brown, J. D. Creswell, & R. M. Ryan (Eds.), *Handbook of mindfulness: Theory, research, and practice* (pp. 9–41). New York, NY: Guilford Publications.
Gilbert, D. T., & Wilson, T. D. (2007). Prospection: Experiencing the future. *Science, 317*, 1351–1354.
Gino, F., & Pierce, L. (2009). The abundance effect: Unethical behaviour in the presence of wealth. *Organizational Behavior and Human Decision Processes, 109*, 142–155.
Glomb, T. M., Duffy, M. K., Bono, J. E., & Yang, T. (2011). Mindfulness at work. *Research in Personnel and Human Resources Management, 30*, 115–157.
Goswami, A. (1995). *The self-aware universe*. New York, NY: Penguin Putman.
Grabovac, A. D., Lau, M. A., & Willett, B. R. (2011). Mechanisms of mindfulness: A Buddhist psychological model. *Springer Science + Business Media*, 6 April. doi: 10.1007/s12671-011-0054-5
Gross, J. J. (2002). Emotion regulation: Affective, cognitive, and social consequences. *Psychophysiology, 39*, 281–291.
Hafenbrack, A. C., Kinias, Z., & Barsade, S. G. (2014). Debiasing the mind through meditation: Mindfulness and the sunk-cost bias. *Psychological Science, 25*(2), 369–376.
Hamel, G., & Prahalad, C. K. (1989). Strategic intent. *Harvard Business Review*, May-June.
Haselton, M. G., & Nettle, D. (2006). The paranoid optimist: An integrative evolutionary model of cognitive biases. *Personality and Social Psychology Review, 10*(1), 47–66.
Hayes, S. C., Strosahl, K. D., & Wilson, K. G. (2012). *Acceptance and commitment therapy*. New York, NY: The Guilford Press.
Hoffman, S. G., Asmundson, G. J., & Beck, A. T. (2013). The science of cognitive therapy. *Behavioral Therapy, 44*(2), 199–212.
Hogan, R. (2006). *Personality and the fate of organizations*. Hillsdale, NJ: Erlbaum.
Hogan, R., & Kaiser, R. (2005). What we know about leadership. *Review of General Psychology, 9*, 169–180.
Hölzel, B. K., Lazar, S. W., Gard, T., Schuman-Oliver, Z., Vago, D. R., & Ott, U. (2011). How does mindfulness meditation work? Proposing mechanisms of action from a conceptual and neural perspective. *Perspectives on Psychological Science, 6*(6), 537–559.
Hsee, C.K. et al. (2013). Overearning. *Psychological Science, 24*(6), 852–859.
James, W. (1961). *Psychology: The Briefer Course. New York:* Harper & Row Publishers.
Jayson, S. (2012). Bad bosses can be bad for your health. *USA Today*, 5 August 2012. Retrieved from http://usatoday30.usatoday.com/news/health/story/2012-08-05/apa-mean-bosses/56813062/1

Jazaieri, H. et al. (2016). A wandering mind is a less caring mind: Daily experience sampling during compassion meditation training. *The Journal of Positive Psychology, 11*(1), 37–50.

Jung, C. G. (1933). *Modern man in search of a soul.* New York, NY: Harcourt, Inc.

Kabat-Zinn, J. (1994). *Wherever you go, there you are: Mindfulness meditation for everyday life.* London, England: Piatkus.

Kabat-Zinn, J. (2012). Mindfulness and democracy. *Mindfulness, 3*(3), 249–250.

Kabat-Zinn, J. (2013). *Full catastrophe living – How to cope with stress, pain and illness using mindfulness meditation.* (Rev. ed.). London, England: Piatkus.

Kahneman, D. (2003). Maps of bounded rationality: psychology for behavioral economics. *The American Economic Review, 93*(5), 1449–1475.

Kahneman, D., & Deaton, A. (2010). High incomes improves evaluation of life but not emotional well-being. *Proceedings of the National Academy of Science (PNAS),* USA, *107*(38), 16489–16493.

Kahneman, D., & Klein, G. (2009). Conditions for intuitive expertise. *American Psychologist, 64*(6), 515–526.

Kang, Y., Gruber, J., & Gray, J. R. (2013). Mindfulness and de-automatization. *Emotion Review, 5*(2), 192–201.

Kaplan, R. E., & Kaiser, R. B. (2006). *The versatile leader.* San Francisco, CA: John Wiley & Sons, Inc.

Karelaia, N., & Reb, J. (2014). Improving decision making through mindfulness. *INSEAD Faculty and Research Working Paper* 2014/43/DSC, In J. Reb & P. Atkins (Eds.), *Mindfulness in organizations* (pp. 163–189). Cambridge, England: Cambridge University Press.

Kaufman, A. C. (2015). Stephen Hawking says we should be really scared of capitalism, not robots. *The Huffington Post,* August 10. Retrieved from http://www.huffingtonpost.com/entry/stephen-hawking-capitalism-robots_us_5616c20ce4b0dbb8000d9f15

Kets de Vries, M. (2006). Making sense of "fuck-you money" and beyond. *INSEAD Working Paper* 2006/45/EFE.

Kets de Vries, M. (2007). Money, money, money. *Organizational Dynamics, 36*(3), 231–243.

Kiken, L. G., & Shook, N. J. (2011). Looking up: Mindfulness increases positive judgments and reduces negativity bias. *Social Psychological and Personality Science, 2*(4), 425–431.

Killingsworth, M., & Gilbert, D. (2010). A wandering mind is an unhappy mind. *Science, 330*(6006), 932.

Kirk, U. Brown, K.W., Downar, J. (2015). Adaptive neural rewards processing during anticipation and receipt of monetary rewards in mindfulness meditators. *SCAN, 10,* 792–759.

Kirk, U., Downar, J., & Montague, P. R. (2011). Interoception drives increased rational decision-making in meditators playing the ultimatum game. *Frontiers in Neuroscience, 5*(49). doi: 10.3389/fnins.2011.00049

Kok, B. E., Coffey, K. A., Cohn, M. A., Catalino, L. I., Vacharkulksemsuk, T., Algoe, S. B., … Fredrickson, B. L. (2013). How positive emotions build physical health: Perceived positive social connections account for the upward spiral between positive emotions and vagal tone. *Psychological Science, 24*(7), 1123–1132.

Kringelbach, M., & Phillips, H. (2014). *Emotion, pleasure and pain in the brain.* Oxford, England: Oxford University Press.

Kuan, T-f. (2008). *Mindfulness in early Buddhism.* New York, NY: Routledge.

Kuoppala, J., Lamminpää, A., Liira, J., & Vainio, H. (2008). Leadership, job well-being, and health effects – a systematic review and a meta-analysis. *Journal of Occupational and Environmental Medicine, 50*(8), 904–915. doi:10.1097/JOM.0b013e31817e918d

Kuyken, W., Watkins, E., Holden, E., White, K., Taylor, R. S., Byford, S., ... Dalgleish, T. (2010). How does mindfulness-based cognitive therapy work? *Behavioral Research and Therapy, 48*(11), 1105–1112.

Langer, E. J. (1989). *Mindfulness.* Cambridge, MA: Da Capo Press.

Layous, K., & Lyubomirsky, S. (2014). The how, why, what, when, and who of happiness: Mechanisms underlying the success of positive interventions. In J. Gruber & J. Moscowitz (Eds.), *Positive emotion: Integrating the light sides and dark sides* (pp. 473–495). New York, NY: Oxford University Press.

Lazar, S. W., Kerr, C. E., Wasserman, R. H., Gray, J. R., Greve, D. N., Treadway, M. T., ... Fischl, B. (2005). Meditation experience is associated with increased cortical thickness. *Neuroreport, 16*(17), 1893–1897.

Leahy, R. L. (2003). Insatiability. In *Psychology and the economic mind- cognitive processes and conceptualization* (pp. 141–160). New York, NY: Springer Publishing Company.

Lieberman, M. D. (2013). *Social: Why Our Brains Are Wired to Connect.* New York: Crown Publishers.

Loewenstein, G. F., Weber, E. U., Hsee, C. K., & Welch, N. (2001). Risk as feelings. *Psychological Bulletin, 127*(2), 267–286.

Lyubomirsky, S., Sheldon, K. M., & Schkade, D. (2005). Pursuing happiness: The architecture of sustainable change. *Review of General Psychology, 9*(2), 111–131.

Maslow, A. H. (1943). A theory of human motivation. *Psychological Review, 50*, 370–396.

Mason, M. F., Norton, M. I., Van Horn, J. D., Wegner, D. M., Grafton, S. G., & Macrae, C. N. (2007). Wandering minds: The default network and stimulus-independent thought. *Science, 315*(5810), 393–395.

Maturana, H. R., & Verden-Zöller, G. (1997). *Liebe und spiel* (3rd ed.). Heidelberg, Germany: Auer.

McCown, D. (2013). Building a multidimensional model. In *The ethical space of mindfulness in clinical practice – An exploration essay* (pp. 138–171). London, England and Philadelphia, PA: Jessica Kingsley Publishers.

McCraty, R., & Childre, D. (2004). The grateful heart: The psychophysiology of appreciation. In R. A. Emmons & M. E. McCullough (Eds.), *The psychology of gratitude* (pp. 230–255). New York, NY: Oxford University Press.

McGreevey, S. (2011). Eight weeks to a better brain. *Harvard Gazette*, January 21. Retrieved from http://news.harvard.edu/gazette/story/2011/01/eight-weeks-to-a-better-brain/

McIntosh, W. D., Harlow, T. F., & Martin, L. L. (1995). Linkers and nonlinkers: Goal beliefs as a moderator of the effects of everyday hassles on rumination, depression and physical complaints. *Journal of Applied Social Psychology, 25*(4), 1231–1244.

Mooneyham, B., & Schooler, J. (2013). The costs and benefits of mind-wandering: A review. *Canadian Journal of Experimental Psychology, 67*(1), 11–18.

Nettle, D. (2005). *Happiness: The science behind your smile.* Oxford, England: Oxford University Press.

Newman, J. D., & Harris, J. C. (2009). The Scientific Contributions of Paul D. MacLean (1913-2007). *The Journal of Nervous and Mental Disease, 197*(1), 3–5.

Nilsson, U. (2008). The anxiety- and pain-reducing effects of music interventions: A systematic review. *AORN Journal, 87*(4), 780–807. doi:10.1016/j.aorn.2007.09.013

Nolen-Hoeksema, S., Wisco, B. E., & Lyubomirsky, S. (2008). Rethinking rumination. *Association for Psychological Science, 3*(5), 400–424.

Olendzki, A. (2010). *Unlimiting mind – The radically experiential psychology of Buddhism.* Boston, MA: Wisdom Publications.

Ostafin, B. D., & Kassman K. T. (2012). Stepping out of history: Mindfulness improves insight problem solving. *Consciousness and Cognition, 21*, 1031–1036.

Pinniger, R., Brown, R. F., Thorsteinsson, E. B., & McKinley, P. (2012) Argentine tango dance compared to mindfulness meditation and a waiting-list control: A randomised trial for treating depression. *Complementary Therapies in Medicine, 20*(6), 377–384.

Porges, S. W. (2011). *The polyvagal theory, neurophysiological foundations of emotions, attachment, communication, self-regulation.* New York, NY and London, England: W.W. Norton & Company.

Ryan, R. M., Huta, V., & Deci, E. L. (2008). Living well: A self-determination theory perspective on eudaimonia. *Journal of Happiness Studies, 9*, 139–170.

Ryan R. M., & Deci, E. L. (2000). Self-determination theory and the facilitation of intrinsic motivation, social development, and well-being. *American Psychologist, 55*(1), 68–78.

Sapolsky, R. (2004). Why zebra's don't get ulcers (Reprint). New York, NY: Henry Holt and company.

Schouten, R., & Silver, J. (2012). The almost psychopath. In *Almost a psychopath: Do I (or does someone I know) have a problem with manipulation and lack of empathy?* (pp. 14–60). Center City, MN: Hazelden/Harvard Health Publications.

Segal, Z. V., Williams, J. M. G., & Teasdale, J. D. (2013). *Mindfulness-based cognitive therapy for depression.* London, England and New York, NY: The Guilford Press.

Seligman, M. (2011). *Flourish.* Sydney, Australia: Heinemann.

Seligman, M. E. P., Railton, P., Baumeister, R. F., & Sripada, C. (2013). Navigating into the future or driven by the past. *Perspectives on Psychological Science, 8*(2), 119–141.

Shapiro, S. L., Carlson, L. E., Astin, J. A., & Freedman, B. (2006). Mechanisms of mindfulness, *Journal of Clinical Psychology, 62*, 373–386.

Short, K. (2014). Here Is The Income Level At Which Money Won't Make You Any Happier In Each State. *Huffington Post* 07/17/2014.

Siegel, D. J. (2009). Mindful awareness, mindsight, and neural integration. *The Humanistic Psychologist, 37*, 137–158.

Singleton, O., Hölzel, B. K., Vangel, M., Brach, N., Carmody, J., & Lazar, S. W. (2014). Change in brainstem gray matter concentration following a mindfulness-based intervention is correlated with improvement in psychological well-being. *Frontiers in Human Neuroscience, 8*(33), 1–7.

Smith, A. (1776/1904). *An inquiry into the nature and causes of the wealth of nations.* London, England: Methuen R. & Co.

Stanley, E. A., Schaldach, J. M., Kiyonage, A., & Jha, A. P. (2011). Mindfulness-based mind fitness training: A case study of a high-stress predeployment military cohort. *Cognitive and Behavioral Practice, 18*, 566–576.

Stone, J. F. (Ed.). (2002). *Bushido – The way of the Samurai. Based on the Hagakure by Tsunetomo Yamamoto.* Garden City Park, NY: SquareOne Classics.

Tang, Y.-Y., Britta, K., Hölzel, B. K., & Posner, M. I. (2015). The neuroscience of mindfulness meditation. *Nature Reviews Neuroscience, 16*, 213–225.

Teasdale, J. D., Segal, Z. V., & Williams, J. M. G. (2003). Mindfulness training and problem formulation. *Clinical Psychology: Science and Practice, 10*(2), 157–160.

Vago, D. R., & Silbersweig, D. A. (2012). Self-awareness, self-regulation, and self-transcendence (S-ART): A framework for understanding the neurobiological mechanisms of mindfulness. *Frontiers in Human Neuroscience, 6*, 296.

van Vugt, M., & Ronay, R. (2014). The evolutionary psychology of leadership: Theory, review, and roadmap. *Organizational Psychology Review, 4*(1), 74–95.

Veenhoven, R. (2008). *Happiness in the USA*. Erasmus University Rotterdam: World Database of Happiness.

Wegner, D. M., Schneider, D. J., Carter III, S. R., & White, T. L. (1987). Paradoxical effects of thought suppression. *Journal of Personality and Social Psychology, 53*(1), 5–13.

Weick, K. E., & Sutcliffe K. M. (2006). Mindfulness and the quality of organizational attention. *Organization Science, 17*(4), 514–524.

Weng, H. Y., Fox, A. S., Shackman, A. J., Stodola, D. E., Caldwell, J. Z., Olson, M. C., … Davidson, R. J. (2013). Compassion training alters altruism and neural responses to suffering. *Psychological Science, 24*, 1171–1180.

Williams, J. C., & Lynn, S. J. (2010). Acceptance: An Historical and Conceptual Review. *Imagination, Cognition and Personality, 30*(1), 5–56.

Wilson, T. D., Wheatley, T., Meyers, J. M., Gilbert, D. T., & Axsom, D. (2000). Focalism: A source of durability bias in affective forecasting. *Journal of Personality and Social Psychology, 78*(5), 821–836.

Wrzesniewski, A. et al. (1997). Jobs, Careers, and Callings: People's Relations to Their Work. *Journal of Research in Personality, 31*, 21–33.

YogiMir (2013). *Good thing, bad thing, who knows*. Retrieved from http://www.yogalifestylecoach.com/presentmoment.html

Further Reading

Alznauer, M. (2013). *Natürlich führen*. Heidelberg, Germany: Springer Gabler.

Amishi, A. P., Stanley, E. A., Kiyonaga, A., Wong, L., & Gelfand, L. (2010). Examining the protective effects of mindfulness training on working memory capacity and affective experience. *Emotion*, *10*(1), 54–64.

Armenta, C., Bao, K. J., Lyubomirsky, S., & Sheldon, K. M. (2014). Is lasting change possible? Lessons from the hedonic adaptation prevention model. In L. M. Sheldon & R. E. Lucas (Eds.), *Stability of happiness: Theories and evidence on whether happiness can change* (1st ed., pp. 57–74). Amsterdam, The Netherlands: Elsevier.

Ash, C. (2008). Happiness and economics: A Buddhist perspective. *University of Reading, CIP Working Paper No. 2008-059*, 1–20.

Austin, J. H. (2012). Meditating selflessly at the dawn of a new millennium. *Contemporary Buddhism*, *13*(1), 61–81.

Avent-Holt, D., & Tomaskovic-Devey, D. (2014). A relational theory of earnings inequality. *American Behavioral Scientist*, *58*(3), 379–399.

Baer, R. A. (2010). Self-compassion as a mechanism of change in mindfulness- and acceptance-based treatments. In R.A. Baer (Ed.), *Assessing mindfulness and acceptance processes in clients* (pp. 135–154). Oakland, CA: Context Press.

Baltes, P. B., & Smith, J. (2008). The fascination of wisdom – its nature, ontogeny, and function. *Perspectives on Psychological Science*, *3*(1), 56–64.

Barrett, L. F., & Bar, M. (2009). See it with feeling: Affective predictions in the human brain. *Royal Society Philosophical Transactions B*, *364*, 1325–1334.

Batchelor, M. (2011). Meditation and mindfulness. *Contemporary Buddhism*, *12*(1), 157–164.

Batchelor, S. (1997). *Buddhism without beliefs – A contemporary guide to awakening*. New York, NY: Riverhead Books.

Baumann, S. L. (2008). Wisdom, compassion, and courage in the wizard of Oz: A humanbecoming hermeneutic study. *Nursing Science Quarterly*, *21*(4), 322–329.

Mindfulness-Based Strategic Awareness Training: A Complete Program for Leaders and Individuals, First Edition. Juan Humberto Young.

Companion website: www.wiley.com/go/humbertoyoung/mbsat

Baumeister, R. F., Vohs, K. D., & Tice, D. M. (2007). The strength model of self-control. *Association for Psychological Science, 16*(6), 351–355.

Bazerman, M., & Tenbrunsel, A. (2011). Blind spots: The roots of unethical behaviour at work. *Rotman Magazine,* Spring, 53–57.

Bédard, M., Felteau, M., Marshall, S., Cullen, N., Gibbons, C., Dubois, S., ... Moustgaard, A. (2014). Mindfulness-based cognitive therapy reduces symptoms of depression in people with a traumatic brain injury: Results from a randomized controlled trial. *Journal of Head Trauma Rehabilitation, 29*(4), E13–E22.

Bien, T. (2009). Paradise lost: Mindfulness and addictive behavior. In F. Didonna (Ed.), *Clinical handbook of mindfulness* (pp. 289–298). New York, NY: Springer Science + Business Media.

Bihari, J. L. N., & Mullan, E. G. (2012). Relating mindfully: A qualitative exploration of changes in relationships through mindfulness-based cognitive therapy. *Mindfulness, Springer Science + Business Media.* Published online September 2012. doi:10.1007/s12671-012-0146-x

Block-Lerner, J., Adair, C., Plumb, J. C., Rhatigan, D. L., & Orsillo, S. M. (2007). The case for mindfulness-based approaches in the cultivation of empathy: Does nonjudgmental, present-moment awareness increase capacity for perspective-taking and empathic concern? *Journal of Marital and Family Therapy, 33*(4), 501–516.

Blumenthal, J. (2009). Toward a Buddhist theory of justice. *Journal of Global Buddhism, 10,* 321–349.

Boddy, C. R. (2006). The dark side of management decisions: Organisational psychopaths. *Management Decision, 44*(10), 1461–1475.

Boddy, C. R. P., Ladyshewsky, R., & Galvin, P. (2010). Leaders without ethics in global business: Corporate psychopaths. *Journal of Public Affairs, 10,* 121–138.

Borkovec, T. D. (2002). Life in the future versus life in the present. *American Psychological Association, D12,* 76–80.

Boyatzis, R. E., Jack, A., Cesaro, R., Khawaja, M., & Passarelli, A. (2010). Coaching with compassion: An fMRI study of coaching to the positive or negative emotional attractor. *Case Western Reserve University* January 2010: 1–38 (unpublished, available with authors' permission).

Boyatzis, R. E., Smith, M. L., & Beveridge, A. J. (2012). Coaching with compassion: Inspiring health, well-being, and development in organizations. *The Journal of Applied Behavioral Science, 49*(2), 153–178.

Boyatzis, R. E., Smith, M. L., & Blaize N. (2006). Developing sustainable leaders through coaching and compassion. *Academy of Management Learning & Education, 5*(1), 8–24.

Boyce, B. (2014). What happens after now? *Mindful,* February, 71–76.

Boyd, J. W., & Metcalf, E. (2012). Almost addiction, but very much a concern. In *Almost addicted – Is my (or my loved one's) drug use a problem?* (pp. 19–38). Center City, MN: Hazelden/Harvard Health Publications.

Brantley, J. (2007). Applying mindfulness to fear, anxiety & panic. In *Calming your anxious mind: How mindfulness and compassion can free you from anxiety, fear, and panic* (pp. 199–212). Oakland, CA: New Harbinger Publications.

Brazier, C. (2014). Beyond mindfulness: An other-centred paradigm. In M. Bazzano (Ed.). *After mindfulness – New perspectives on psychology and meditation* (Reprinted rev. ed., pp. 23–36). New York, NY: Palgrave Macmillan.

Broderick, P. C. (2005). Mindfulness and coping with dysphoric mood: Contrasts with rumination and distraction. *Cognitive Therapy and Research*, *29*(5), 501–510.

Brown, K. W., & Ryan, R. M. (2003). The benefits of being present: Mindfulness and its role in psychological well-being. *Journal of Personality and Social Psychology*, *84*(4), 822–848.

Brown, K. W., Kasser, T., Ryan, R. M., Alex Linley, P. P., & Orzech, K. (2009). When what one has is enough: Mindfulness, financial desire discrepancy, and subjective well-being. *Journal of Research in Personality 43*, 727–736.

Burden, A. (2011). MBCT and addiction: Developing compassionate mind. *Presentation at Bangor University 2011 Conference.*

Burns, D. (2013). Living with the devil we know. *Psychotherapy Networker*, January/February, 28–35 & 56.

Canetti, E. (1992). Elements of power. In *Crowds and power* (pp. 327–328). London, England: Penguin Books.

Care, N. S. (2000). Others' needs. In *Decent people* (pp. 67–102). Lanham, MD: Rowman & Littlefield Publishers.

Carlson, E. N. (2013). Overcoming the barriers to self-knowledge: Mindfulness as a path to seeing yourself as you really are. *Perspectives on Psychological Science*, *8*(2), 173–186.

Chadwick, P. (2005). Mindfulness groups for people with psychosis. *Behavioural and Cognitive Psychotherapy*, *33*, 351–359.

Chancellor, J., & Lyubomirsky, S. (2014). Money for happiness: The hedonic benefits of thrift. In M. Tatzel (Ed.), *Consumption and well-being in the material world* (pp. 13–47). Dordrecht, The Netherlands: Springer.

Chaskalson, M. (2011). *The mindful workplace – Developing resilient individuals and resonant organizations with MBSR*. Chichester, England: John Wiley & Sons.

Chen, G., & Zhu, D. H. (2014). The fallout of CEO narcissism. *INSEAD Knowledge*, June 2. 2014: 1–3. Retrieved from www.knowledgeinsead.edu

Cheng-Kar, P., & Tian Po, S. O. (2012). From mindfulness to meta-mindfulness: Further integration of meta-mindfulness concept and strategies into cognitive-behavioral therapy. *Mindfulness*, *3*, 104–116.

Chiesa, A., Calati, R., & Serretti, A. (2011). Does mindfulness training improve cognitive abilities? A systematic review of neuropsychological findings. *Clinical Psychology Review*, *31*, 449–464.

Chugh, D., & Bazerman, M. (2007). Bounded awareness: What you fail to see can hurt you. *Rotman Magazine*, Spring, 21–25.

Coffey, K. A., Hartman, M., & Fredrickson, B. L. (2010). Deconstructing mindfulness and constructing mental health: Understanding mindfulness and its mechanisms of action. *Mindfulness*, *1*, 235–253.

Condon, P., Desbordes, G., Miller, W. B., & DeSteno, D. (2013). Meditation increases compassionate responses to suffering. *Psychological Science*, *24*(10), 2125–2127. doi: 10.1177/0956797613485603

Crabtree, S. (2013). Worldwide, 13% of employees are engaged at work. *Gallup*, October 8. Retrieved from www.gallup.com/poll/165269/worldwide-employees-engaged-work.aspx

Crane, R. (2009). *Mindfulness-based cognitive therapy*. (Rev. ed.). New York: Routledge.

Crane, R., Eames, C., Kuyken, W., Hastings, R. P., Williams, M. G., … Surawy, C. (2013). Development and validation of the mindfulness-based interventions-teaching assessment criteria (MBI:TAC). *Assessment, 20*(10), 1–8.

Csikszentmihalyi, M. (1990). *Flow: The psychology of optimal experience.* New York, NY: Harper and Row.

Csikszentmihalyi, M. (1999). If we are so rich, why aren't we happy? *American Psychologist, 54*(10), 821–827.

Cullen, M. (2011). Mindfulness-based interventions: An emerging phenomenon. *Mindfulness, 2*, 186–193.

Damasio A., & Damasio H. (2006). Minding the body. *Daedalus, 135*(3), 15–22.

De Silva, P. (2014). *An introduction to Buddhist psychology and counselling – pathways of mindfulness-based therapies.* New York, NY: Palgrave Macmillan.

Decety, J. (2010). The neurodevelopment of empathy in humans. *Developmental Neuroscience, 32*, 257–267.

DeLong, T. J. (2011). *Flying without a net: Turn fear of change into fuel for success.* Boston, MA: Harvard Business Review Press.

Depraz, N. (2003). *On becoming aware. A pragmatics of experiencing.* Amsterdam, The Netherlands: John Benjamins Publishing.

Desbordes, G., Negi, L. T., Pace, T. W. W., Wallace, B. A., Raison, C. L., & Schwartz, E. L. (2012). Effects of mindful-attention and compassion meditation training on amygdala response to emotional stimuli in an ordinary, non-meditative state. *Frontiers in Human Neuroscience, 6*, 1–15.

Desmukh, V. D. (2006). Neuroscience of meditation. *The Scientific World Journal, 6*, 2239–2253.

Deyo, M., Wilson, K. A., Ong, J., & Koopman, C. (2009). Mindfulness and rumination: Does mindfulness training lead to reductions in the ruminative thinking associated with depression? *Explore, 5*(5), 265–271.

Dobkin, P. L., Hickman, S., & Monshat, K. (2014). Holding the heart of mindfulness-based stress reduction: Balancing fidelity and imagination when adapting MBSR. *Mindfulness, 5*(6), 710–718. doi:10.1007/s12671-013-0225-7

Dorjee, D. (2010). Kinds and dimensions of mindfulness: Why it is important to distinguish them. *Mindfulness, 1*, 152–160.

Dreeben, S. J., Mamberg, M. H., & Salmon, P. (2013). The MBSR body scan in clinical practice. *Mindfulness, 4*(4), 394–401. doi:10.1007/s12671-013-0212-z

Dunkley, C., & Stanton, M. (2014). Mindfulness as a skill – Case examples. In *Teaching clients to use mindfulness skills – a practical guide* (pp. 83–96). London, England and New York, NY: Routledge.

Dunning, D., & Fetchenhauer, D. (2013). Behavioral influences in the present tense: On expressive versus instrumental action. *Perspectives on Psychological Science, 8*(2), 142–145.

Dutton, K. (2013). Wisdom from psychopaths? A scientist enters a high-security psychiatric hospital to extract tips and advice from a crowd without a conscience. *Scientific American Mind, January 1*, 36–53.

Dutton, K., & McNab, A. (2014). Uncouple behaviour from emotion. In *The good psychopaths guide to success – How to use your inner psychopath to get the most out of life* (pp. 297–327). London, England: Bantam Press.

Elliott, J. C., Wallace, B. A., & Giesbrecht, B. (2014). A week-long meditation retreat decouples behavioural measures of the alerting and executive attention networks. *Frontiers in Human Neuroscience, 8*, 1–8.

Emanuel, A. S., Updegraff, J. A., Kalmbach, D. A., & Ciesla, J. A. (2010). The role of mindfulness facets in affective forecasting. *Personality and Individual Differences, 49*(7), 815–818. doi:10.1016/j.paid.2010.06.012

Ennenbach, M. (2012). *Praxisbuch Buddhistische psychotherapie – Konkrete behandlungsmethoden und anleitung zur selbsthilfe*. Oberstdorf, Germany: Windpferd.

Epstein, M. (1986). Meditative transformations of narcissism. *The Journal of Transpersonal Psychology, 18*(2), 143–158.

Epstein, M. D., & Lieff, J. D. (1981). Psychiatric complications of meditation practice. *The Journal of Transpersonal Psychology, 13*(2): 137–147.

Epstein, R. M. (1999). Mindful practice. *JAMA – Journal of the American Medical Association, 282*(9), 833–839.

Epstein, R. M. (2003). Mindful practice in action (I): Technical competence, evidence-based medicine, and relationship-centered care. *Family, Systems & Health, 21*(1), 1–9.

Epstein, R. M. (2003). Mindful practice in action (II): Cultivating habits of mind. *Family, Systems & Health, 21*(1), 11–17.

Erhard, E., & Jensen, M. (2014). Putting integrity into finance. *Rotman Magazine*, Spring, 19–23.

Evans, S., Ferrando, S., Findler, M., Stowell, C., Smart, C., & Haglin, D. (2008). Mindfulness-based cognitive therapy for generalized anxiety disorder. *Journal of Anxiety Disorders, 22*, 716–721.

Farb, N. A. S., Anderson, A. K., & Segal, Z. V. (2012). The mindful brain and emotion regulation in mood disorders. *Psychiatry, 57*(2), 70–77.

Feldman, C., & Kuyken, W. (2011). Compassion in the landscape of suffering. *Contemporary Buddhism, 12*(1), 143–155.

Finkelstein, S., Whitehead, J., & Campbell, A. (2008). Inappropriate self-interest: A beguiling and unconscious influence on decision making. In *Think again: Why good leaders make bad decisions and how to keep it from happening to you* (pp. 107–129). Boston, MA: Harvard Business Press.

Freeman, D., & Freeman, J. (2012). *Anxiety – A very short introduction*. Oxford, England: Oxford University Press.

Fukukura, J., Helzer E. G., & Ferguson, M. J. (2013). Prospection by any other name? A response to Seligman et al. (2013). *Perspectives on Psychological Science, 8*(2), 146–150.

Gardner, H. (2007). The ethical mind. Interview. *Harvard Business Review*, March, Reprint R0703B: 1–6.

Gelles, D. (2012). The mind business – yoga, meditation mindfulness: Why some of the West's biggest companies are embracing Eastern spirituality. *Financial Times, August 24*, 1–10.

Gendlin, E. T. (2003). If you can't find a felt space. In *Focusing – How to gain direct access to your body's knowledge* (pp. 83–101). (Reprinted Rev. Ed. 1981). London, England: Rider.

Germer, C. (2006). You gotta have heart. *Psychotherapy Networker*, January/February, 1–6.

Germer, K., & Neff, K. D. (2013). Self-compassion in clinical practice. *Journal of Clinical Psychology: In Session, 69*(8), 1–12.

Gethin, R. (2011). On some definitions of mindfulness. *Contemporary Buddhism, 12*(1), 263–279.
Gilpin, R. (2008). The use of Theravāda Buddhist practices and perspectives in mindfulness-based cognitive therapy. *Contemporary Buddhism, 9*(2), 227–251.
Giluk, T. L. (2010). *Mindfulness-based stress reduction: facilitating work outcomes through experienced affect and high-quality relationships.* University of Iowa, IA.
Gino, F., Moore, D., & Bazerman, M. (2013). *See no evil: Why we overlook other people's unethical behaviour.* Rotman Magazine, Fall, 29–32.
Goldstein, J. (2013). Clearly knowing: Cultivating clear comprehension. In *Mindfulness: A practical guide to awakening* (pp. 13–20). Boulder, CO: Sounds True Inc.
Goldstein, J. (2013). Contemplating the five aggregates. In *Mindfulness: A practical guide to awakening* (pp. 195–202). Boulder, CO: Sounds True Inc.
Goldstein, J. (2013). Mindfulness: A practical guide to awakening. interview. *Insight Journal,* October, *18*, 1–9. Retrieved from www.bcbsdharma.org/2013-10-18-insight-journal/
Goldstein, J. (2013). The wholesome and unwholesome roots of mind. In *Mindfulness: A practical guide to awakening* (pp. 101–110). Boulder, CO: Sounds True Inc.
Goleman, D. (2013). The focused leader: How effective executives direct their own – and their organizations' – attention. *Harvard Business Review,* December, 3–11.
Goleman, D. (2014). Interview. *Rotman Management*, Winter, 10–14.
Gombrich, R. (2012). What the Buddha thought. Interview. *Tricycle,* Fall, 62–65 & 101–102.
Graham, J., Nosek, B. A., Haidt, J., Iyer, R., Koleva, S., & Ditto, P. H. (2011). Mapping the moral domain. *Journal of Personality and Social Psychology, 101*(2), 366–385.
Hadot, P. (1995). Reflections on the idea of the "cultivation of the self." In *Philosophy as a way of life – Spiritual exercises from Socrates to Foucault* (pp. 206–214). Oxford, England: Blackwell Publishing.
Hansen, D. (2012). A guide to mindfulness at work – toxic emotions disrupt the workplace. *Forbes,* October 31. Retrieved from http://www.forbes.com/sites/drewhansen/2012/10/31/a-guide-to-mindfulness-at-work/#29be909a6870
Hanstede, M., Gidron, Y., & Nykliček, I. (2008). The effects of a mindfulness intervention on obsessive-compulsive symptoms in a non-clinical student population. *The Journal of Nervous and Mental Disease, 196*(10), 776–779.
Hart, R., Ictzan, I., & Hart, D. (2013). Mind the gap in mindfulness research: A comparative account of the leading schools of thought. *Review of General Psychology, 17*(4), 453–466.
Haselton, M. G., & Nettle, D. (2006). The paranoid optimist: An integrative evolutionary model of cognitive biases. *Personality and Social Psychology Review, 10*(1), 47–66.
Hawley, L. L., Schwartz, D., Bieling, P. J., Irving, J., Corocan, K., Farb, N. A. S. … Segal, Z. V. (2014). Mindfulness practice, rumination and clinical outcome in mindfulness-based treatment. *Cognitive Therapy Research, 38*, 1–9.
Hede, A. (2010). The dynamics of mindfulness in managing emotions and stress. *Journal of Management Development, 29*(1), 94–110.
Herdt, J., Bührlen, B., Bader K., & Hänny, C. (2012). Participation in an adapted version of MBCT in psychiatric care. *Mindfulness, 3*, 218–226.
Hertenstein, E., Rose, N., Voderholzer, U., Heidenreich, T., Nissen, C., Thiel, N., … Külz, A. K. (2012). Mindfulness-based cognitive therapy in obsessive-compulsive disorder – a qualitative study on patients' experiences. *BMC Psychiatry, 12*, 185. doi:10.1186/1471-244X-12-185

Higgins, T., & Summers, N. (2014). If only they had listened … how a GM lifer spent years trying to warn the company, and how it silenced him. *Bloomberg Businessweek, June 20*, 48–53.

Hofmann, S. G., Grossman, P., & Hinton, D. E. (2011). Loving-kindness and compassion meditation: Potential for psychological interventions. *Clinical Psychology Review, 31*(7), 1126–1132.

Hofmann, S. G., Moscovitch, D. A., Pizzagalli, D. A., Litz, B. T., Kim, H-J., & Davis, L. L. (2005). The worried mind: Autonomic and prefrontal activation during worrying. *American Psychological Association, 5*(4), 464–475.

Hogan, J., Hogan, R., & Kaiser, R. B. (2010). Management derailment. In S. Zedeck (Ed.), *American Psychological Association Handbook of Industrial and Organizational Psychology*, (Vol. 3, pp. 555–575). Washington, DC: American Psychological Association.

Hoppes, K. (2006). The application of mindfulness-based cognitive interventions in the treatment of co-occurring addictive and mood disorders. *CNS Spectrums, 11*(11), 829–841, 846–851.

Hsee, C. K., Zhang, J., Cai, C. F., & Zhang, S. (2013). Overearning. *Psychological Science, 24*(6), 852–859.

Huffington, A. (2013). Less stress, more living. *Huffington Post, March 27*, 1–3.

Huppert, F. A., & So, T. (2009). What percentage of people in Europe are flourishing and what characterizes them? *Prepared for the OECD/SQOLS meeting "Measuring subjective well-being: an opportunity for NSOs?* FAH TS OECD briefing document. Florence, July 23/24, 1–7.

Hutcherson, C. A., Seppala, E. M., & Gross, J. J. (2008). Loving-kindness meditation increases social connectedness. *American Psychological Association, 8*(5), 720–724.

Jacobson, N. P. (1983). The self-surpassing oneness. In *Buddhism & the contemporary world* (pp. 151–163). Carbondale, IL: Southern Illinois University Press.

Jha, A. P. (2013). Being in the now. *Scientific American Mind*, March/April, 26–33.

Jinpa, T. (2015). *A fearless heart, how the courage to be compassionate can transform our lives.* New York, NY: Hudson Street Press.

Kabat-Zinn, J. (2005). Mindfulness and democracy. In *Coming to our senses – Healing ourselves and the world through mindfulness* (pp. 551–554). New York, NY: Hyperion.

Kabat-Zinn, J. (2011). Heartfulness. *4Slick Video.* Retrieved from https://www.youtube.com/watch?v=6aaJtBKwK9U

Kabat-Zinn, J. (2011). Some reflections on the origins of MBSR, skillful means, and the trouble with maps. *Contemporary Buddhism, 12*(1), 281–306.

Kabat-Zinn, J., Bauer-Wu, S., & Siegel, D. (2011). The healing power of mindfulness. Interview by B. Boyce. *Shambala Sun*, January, 42–48.

Kahneman, D. (2011). Interview by A. Jarden. *International Journal of Wellbeing, 1*(1), 186–188.

Kahneman, D., & Riis, J. (2005). Living and thinking about it: Two perspectives on life. In F. Huppert, N. Baylis, & B. Keverne (Eds.), *The science of well-being: Integrating neurobiology, psychology, and social science* (pp. 285–304), Oxford, England: Oxford University Press.

Kaiser, R. B. (Ed.). (2010). Developing flexible and adaptive leaders for an age of uncertainty [Special Issue]. *Consulting Psychology Journal: Practice and Research, 62*(2).

Kaiser, R. B., & Hogan, R. (2010). How to (and how not to) assess the integrity of managers. *Consulting Psychology Journal: Practice and Research, 62*, 216–234.

Kang, Y., Gruber, J., & Gray, J. R. (2012). Mindfulness and de-automatization. *Emotion Review, 5*(2), 192–201.

Kang, Y., Gruber, J., & Gray, J. R. (2014). Mindfulness, deautomatization of cognitive and emotional life. In *The Wiley Blackwell handbook of mindfulness* (pp. 168–175). Oxford, England: Wiley.

Kanov, J. M., Maitlis, S., Worline, M. C., Dutton, J. E., Frost, P. J., & Lilius, J. M. (2004). Compassion in organizational life. *American Behavioral Scientist, 47*(6), 808–827.

Kasser, T. (2002). The chains of materialism. In *The high price of materialism* (pp. 73–86). Cambridge, MA: MIT Press.

Kerkhof, A. (2010). Worrying for advanced students. In *Stop worrying: Get your life back on track with CBT* (2nd ed., pp. 147–172) New York, NY: McGraw-Hill Education.

Kerr, C. E., Sacchet, M. D., Lazar, S. W., Moore, C. I., & Jones, S. R. (2013). Mindfulness starts with the body: Somatosensory attention and top-down modulation of cortical alpha rhythms in mindfulness meditation. *Frontiers in Human Neuroscience, 7*, Article 12: 1–15.

Kets de Vries, M. F. R. (2009). Meditations on money. In *Sex, money, happiness, and death – The quest for authenticity* (pp. 73–102). New York, NY: Palgrave Macmillan.

Kets de Vries, M. F. R. (2012). The psychopath in the C Suite: Redefining the SOB. *INSEAD Working Paper* 2012/119/EFE, 1–38.

Kets de Vries, M. F. R. (2014). The art of forgiveness: Differentiating transformational leaders. In *Mindful leadership coaching – Journey into the interior* (pp. 42–67). New York, NY: Palgrave Macmillan.

Kets de Vries, M. F. R. (2014). The psycho-path to disaster with SOB executives. *Organizational Dynamics, 43*, 17–26.

Kets de Vries, M. F. R. (2014). The psycho-path to disaster: Coping with SOB executives. In *Mindful leadership coaching – Journey into the interior* (pp. 104–133). New York, NY: Palgrave Macmillan

Kinder, G. (1999). Vision: Seeing far, inside and outside. In *Seven stages of money maturity – Understanding the spirit and value of money in your life* (pp. 265–288). New York, NY: Random House.

Knapton, S. (2014). Mindfulness therapy adopted by stressed Britons. *The Telegraph*. Retrieved from www.telegraph.co.uk/science/science-news

Konnikova, M. (2014). No money, no time. *International New York Times*, June *13*, 1–8.

Kumar, S. M. (2002). An introduction to Buddhism for the cognitive-behavioral therapist. *Cognitive and Behavioral Practice, 9*, 40–43.

Kunzmann, U., & Baltes, P. B. (2003). Wisdom-related knowledge: Affective, motivational, and interpersonal correlates. *Personality and Social Psychology Bulletin, 29*(9), 1104–1119.

Kuyken, W., & Evans, A. (2013). Mindfulness-based cognitive therapy (MBCT). *Presentation at University of Exeter*, March 26. Retrieved from www.exeter-mindfulness-network.org

Kuyken, W., Crane, R., & Dalgleish, T. (2012). Does mindfulness based cognitive therapy prevent relapse of depression? *British Medical Journal, 345*, e7194. doi:10.1136/bmj.e7194

Kuyken, W., Pasesky, C. A., & Dudley, R. (2009). The case conceptualization crucible: A new model. In *Collaborative case conceptualization – Working effectively with clients in cognitive-behavioral therapy* (pp. 25–58). New York, NY: Guilford Press.

La Forge, R. (2005). Aligning mind and body: Exploring the disciplines of mindful exercise. *ACSM's Health & Fitness Journal, 5*, 7–14.

Langer, E., & Beard, A. (2014). Mindfulness in the age of complexity. Interview. *Harvard Business Review*, March 2014. Reprint R1403D: 2–7.

Layous, K., & Lyubomirsky, S. (2013). How do simple positive activities increase well-being? *Current Directions in Psychological Science, 22*(1), 57–62.

Layous, K., Chancellor, J., & Lyubomirsky, S. (2014). Positive activities as protective factors against mental health conditions. *Journal of Abnormal Psychology, 123*(1), 3–12.

Leahy, R. L. (2005). Understanding worry. In *The worry cure: Seven steps to stop worry from stopping you* (pp. 11–26). New York, NY: Harmony Books.

Leroy, H., Anseel, F., Dimitrova, N. G., & Sels, L. (2013). Mindfulness, authentic functioning, and work engagement: A growth modeling approach. *Journal of Vocational Behavior, 82*, 238–247.

Levinthal, D., & Rerup, C. (2006). Crossing an apparent chasm: Bridging mindful and less-mindful perspectives on organizational learning. *Organization, 17*(4), 502–513.

Levitt, H. M. (1999). The development of wisdom: An analysis of Tibetan Buddhist experience. *Journal of Humanistic Psychology, 39*(2), 86–105.

Lief, J., Thich Nhat Hanh, Salzber, S., & Tarrant, J. (2014). The real problem with distraction: It keeps you from enlightenment. *Shambala Sun*, May, 43–48.

Lilius, J. M., Worline, M. C., Dutton, J. E., Kanov, J. M., & Maitlis, S. (2011). Understanding compassion capability. *Human Relations, 64*(7): 873–899.

Linden, M., & Muschalla, B. (2007). Anxiety disorders and workplace-related anxieties. *Journal of Anxiety Disorders, 21*, 467–474.

Lloyd, B. (2010). Power, responsibility and wisdom: Exploring the issues at the core of ethical decision making. *Journal of Human Values, 16*(1), 1–8.

Loy, D. (2013). Why Buddhism and the West need each other: On the interdependence of personal and social transformation. *Journal of Buddhist Ethics, 20*: 401–421.

Loy, D. R. (2003). Buddhist social theory? In *The great awakening – A Buddhist social theory* (pp. 1–52). Boston, MA: Wisdom Publications.

Mace, C. (2007). Mindfulness in psychotherapy: An introduction. *Advances in Psychiatric Treatment, 13*, 147–154.

Mace, C. (2008). *Mindfulness and mental health: Therapy, theory and science.* London: Routledge.

Maex, E. (2011). The Buddhist roots of mindfulness training: A practitioner's view. *Contemporary Buddhism, 12*(1), 165–175.

Marques, L., & Metcalf, E. (2013). What is "almost anxious"? In *Almost anxious – Is my (or my loved one's) worry or distress a problem?* (pp. 9–24). Center City, MN: Hazelden/Harvard Health Publications.

McCown, D., Reibel, D., & Micozzi, M. S. (2011). Authenticity, authority and friendship. In *Teaching mindfulness* (pp. 91–136). New York, NY: Springer.

McCown, D., Reibel, D., & Micozzi, M. S. (2011). Towards an "empty" curriculum. In *Teaching mindfulness* (pp. 137–220). New York, NY: Springer.

McManus, F., Muse, K., & Surawy, C. (2011). Mindfulness-based cognitive therapy (MBCT) for severe health anxiety. *Healthcare Counselling and Psychotherapy Journal,* January, 19–23.

Meeks, T. W., & Jeste, D. V. (2009). Neurobiology of wisdom – a literature overview. *Archives of General Psychiatry*, *66*(4), 355–365.

Miller, G. (2009). A quest for compassion. *Science, 324*: 458–459.

Mitroff, I. I., & Linstone, H. A. (1996). *The unbounded mind: Breaking the chains of traditional business thinking*. Oxford, England: Oxford University Press.

Mogilner, C. (2010). The pursuit of happiness: Time, money, and social connection. *Psychological Science, 21*(9), 1348–1354.

Molinsky, A. L., Grant, A. M., & Margolis, J. D. (2012). The bedside manner of homo oeconomicus: How and why priming and economic schema reduces compassion. *Organizational Behavior and Human Decision Processes, 119*, 27–37.

Moneta, G. B. (2014). *Positive psychology, a critical introduction*. New York, NY: Palgrave Macmillan.

Nanda, J. (2010). Embodied integration, reflections on mindfulness-based cognitive therapy (MBCT) and a case for mindfulness-based existential therapy (MBET). *Existential Analysis, 21*(2), 331–350.

Ng, E. (2014). Towards a dialogue between Buddhist social theory and "affect studies" on the ethico-political significance of mindfulness. *Journal of Buddhist Ethics, 21*, 346–377.

Niemiec, R. M. (2012). Mindful living: Character strengths interventions as pathways for the five mindfulness trainings. *International Journal of Wellbeing, 2*(1), 22–33.

Niemiec, R. M. (2014). Mindfulness-based strengths practice. In *Mindfulness & character strengths – A practical guide to flourishing* (pp. 141–152). Boston, MA: Hogrefe.

Niemiec, R. M., Rashid, T., & Spinella, M. (2012). Strong mindfulness: Integrating mindfulness and character strengths. *Journal of Mental Health Counseling, 34*(3), 240–253.

Norton, M. I. (2014). The domino effect of greed. *The Scientific American, March/April*, 24–25.

Norton, P. J. (2012). Anxiety disorders and the transdiagnostic perspective. In *Group cognitive-behavioral therapy of anxiety* (Chapter 1). New York, NY/London, England: The Guilford Press.

O'Connor, R. C., & Williams, J. M. G. (2014). The relationship between positive future thinking, brooding, defeat and entrapment. *Personality and Individual Differences, 70*, 29–34.

Olendzki, A. (2008). The real practice of mindfulness. *Buddhadharma Practitioner's Quarterly*, Fall, 1–6.

Olendzki, A. (2009). Mindfulness and meditation. In F. Didonna (Ed.). *Clinical handbook of mindfulness* (pp. 37–44). New York, NY: Springer Science + Business Media.

Orsillo, S. M., Roemer, L., & Barlow, D. H. (2003). Integrating acceptance and mindfulness into existing cognitive-behavioral treatment for GAD: A case study. *Cognitive and Behavioral Practice, 10*, 222–230.

Pappas, N. (2011). *On awareness: A collection of philosophical dialogues*. New York, NY: Algora Publishing.

Parker, J. D. A., Taylor, G. J., & Bagby, R. B. (2001). The relationship between emotional intelligence and alexithymia. *Personality and Individual Differences, 30*(1), 107–115.

Parks, A. C., & Schueller, S. M. (Eds.). (2014). *Positive psychological interventions*. Oxford, England: Wiley Blackwell.

Paulson, S., Davidson, R., Jha, A., & Kabat-Zinn, J. (2013). Becoming conscious: The science of mindfulness. *New York Academy of Sciences, 1303*, 87–104.

Payutto, P. (1990). Sammāsati: An exposition of right mindfulness (Dhammavijaya Bhikkhu, Trans.). Bangkok, Thailand: Bhuddhadhamma Foundation.

Peacock, J. (2008). Suffering in mind: The aetiology of suffering in early Buddhism. *Contemporary Buddhism, 9*(2), 209–226.
Peacock, J. (2012). Mindfulness & the cognitive process. *Insight Journal,* Barre Center for Buddhist Studies. June 6, 1–11. Retrieved from http://www.bcbsdharma.org/2012-06-05-insight-journal/
Peacock, J. (2014). *Sati* or mindfulness? Bridging the divide. In M. Bazzano (Ed.). *After mindfulness – New perspectives on psychology and meditation* (pp. 3–22). New York, NY: Palgrave Macmillan.
Pech, R. J., & Slade, B. W. (2007). Organisational sociopaths: Rarely challenged, often promoted. *Why? Society and Business Review, 2*(3), 254–269.
Perich, T., Manicavasagar, V., Mitchell, P. B., & Ball, J. R. (2014). Mindfulness-based approaches in the treatment of bipolar disorder: Potential mechanisms and effects. *Mindfulness, 5,* 186–191.
Peterson, C., & Seligman, M. (2004). *Character strengths and virtues.* Oxford, England: Oxford University Press.
Phelan, J. P. (2012). Friendliness to the self. *Mindfulness, 3,* 165–167.
Pickert, K. (2014). The mindful revolution. *Time,* February 3, 36–42.
Piet, J., & Hougaard, E. (2011). The effect of mindfulness-based cognitive therapy for prevention of relapse in recurrent major depressive disorder: A systematic review and meta-analysis. *Clinical Psychology Review, 31,* 1032–1040.
Pollak, S., Pedulla T., & Siegel, R. D. (2014). Bringing mindfulness into psychotherapy. In *Sitting together: Essential skills for mindfulness-based psychotherapy* (pp. 1–26). New York, NY/London, England: The Guilford Press.
Polman, P. (2014). Business, society, and the future of capitalism. *McKinsey & Company,* May, 1–5.
Quoidbach, J., Gilbert, D. T., & Wilson, T. D. (2013). The end of history illusion. *Science, 339,* 96–98.
Rapgay, S., & Bystrisky, A. (2009). Classical mindfulness – an introduction to its theory and practice for clinical application. *New York Academy of Sciences, 1172,* 148–162.
Rasmussen, M. K., & Pidgeon, A. M. (2011). The direct and indirect benefits of dispositional mindfulness on self-esteem and social anxiety. *Anxiety, Stress & Coping, 24*(2), 227–233.
Reb, J., Narayanan, J., & Chaturvedi, S. (2012). Leading mindfully: Two studies on the influence of supervisor trait mindfulness on employee well-being and performance. *Mindfulness, 5*(1), 36–45. doi:10.1007./s12671-012-0144-z.
Reeves, A., McKee, M., & Stuckler, D. (2014). Economic suicides in the Great Recession in Europe and North America. *The British Journal of Psychiatry, 205*(3), 246–247. doi:10.1192/bjp.bp.114.144766
Reyes, D. (2012). Self-compassion: A concept analysis. *Journal of Holistic Nursing 30*(2), 81–89.
Rimes, K. A. (2011). Pilot study of mindfulness-based cognitive therapy for trainee clinical psychologists. *Behavioural and Cognitive Psychotherapy, 39,* 235–241.
Riskin, L. L. (2009). Awareness and ethics in dispute resolution and law: Why mindfulness tends to foster ethical behavior. *South Texas Law Review, 50,* 493.
Robinson, H., & Graham Fuller, V. (2003). *Understanding narcissism in clinical practice.* London, England: Karnac Books.
Rodriguez, T. (2014). That missing feeling – alexithymia, a little-known personality trait, reveals the profound power of emotional awareness over health. *Scientific American Mind, 25,* 66–71.

Roemer, L., & Orsillo, S. M. (2002). Expanding our conceptualization of and treatment for generalized anxiety disorder: Integrating mindfulness/acceptance-based approaches with existing cognitive-behavioral models. *American Psychological Association, D12*, 54–68.

Ronningstam, E. (2005). Asset or disruption? Narcissism in the workplace. In *Identifying and understanding the narcissistic personality* (pp. 135–158). Oxford: Oxford University Press.

Ruedy, N. E., & Schweitzer, M. E. (2010). In the moment: The effect of mindfulness on ethical decision making. *Journal of Business Ethics, 95*, 73–87.

Ryan, T. (2012). *A mindful nation: How a simple practice can help us reduce stress, improve performance, and recapture the American spirit.* Carlsbad, CA: Hay House Inc.

Salmon, P., Lush, E., Jablonski, M., & Sephton, S. E. (2009). Yoga and mindfulness: Clinical aspects of an ancient mind/body practice. *Cognitive and Behavioral Practice, 16*, 59–72.

Salzberg, S. (1995). *Loving-kindness – The revolutionary art of happiness.* Boston, MA/London, England: Shambala.

Salzberg, S. (2011). Mindfulness and loving-kindness. *Contemporary Buddhism, 12*(1), 177–182.

Sauer, S., & Baer, R. A. (2010). Mindfulness and decentering as mechanisms of change in mindfulness- and acceptance-based interventions. In R. A. Baer (Ed.), *Assessing mindfulness and acceptance processes in clients* (pp. 25–50). Oakland, CA: Context Press.

Schumpeter, J. (2013). The mindfulness business – Western capitalism is looking for inspiration in Eastern mysticism. *The Economist*, 16 November. Retrieved from www.economist.com

Schwartz, B., & Sharpe, K. (2006). Practical wisdom: Aristotle meets positive psychology. *Journal of Happiness Studies, 7*, 377–395.

Scott, B. A., Colquitt, J. A., Paddock, E. L., & Judge, T. A. (2010). A daily investigation of the role of manager empathy on employee well-being. *Organizational Behavior and Human Decision Processes, 113*, 127–140.

Semple, R. J., & Lee, J. (2011). Understanding the problem of anxiety. In *Mindfulness-based cognitive therapy for anxious children – A manual for treating childhood anxiety* (pp. 25–39). Oakland, CA: New Harbinger Publications.

Shapiro, S. L., Schwartz, G. E. R., & Santerre, C. (2002). Meditation and positive psychology. In C. R. Snyder & S. J. Lopez (Eds.). *Handbook of positive psychology* (pp. 632–645). Oxford, England: Oxford University Press.

Siegel, R. D., Germer, C. K., & Olendzki, A. (2009). Mindfulness: What is it? Where did it come from? In F. Didonna (Ed.), *Clinical handbook of mindfulness* (pp. 17–35). New York, NY: Springer Science + Business Media.

Siew, B., & Khong, L. (2009). Expanding the understanding of mindfulness: Seeing the tree and the forest. *The Humanistic Psychologist, 37*, 117–136.

Siew, B., & Khong, L. (2013). Being a therapist, contributions of Heidegger's philosophy and the Buddha's teachings to psychotherapy. *The Humanistic Psychologist, 41*, 231–246.

Singh, N. N. (2008). Mindfulness approaches in cognitive behavior therapy. *Behavioural and Cognitive Psychotherapy, 36*, 659–666.

Sipe, W. E. B., & Eisendrath, S. J. (2012). Mindfulness-based cognitive therapy: Theory and practice. *The Canadian Journal of Psychiatry, 57*(2), 63–69.

Sjøgren, K. (2013). The boss, not the workload, causes workload depression. *ScienceNordic,* October 27 Retrieved from http://sciencenordic.com/boss-not-workload-causes-workplace-depression

Snyder, R., Shapiro, S., & Treleaven, D. (2012). Attachment theory and mindfulness. *Journal of Child and Family Studies, 21*, 709–717.

Southwick, S. M., & Charney, D. S. (2012). The science of resilience: Implications for the prevention and treatment of depression. *Science, 338*, 79–82.

Speer, A. (1995). Organized improvisation. In *Inside the Third Reich* (pp. 287–300). London, England: Phoenix.

Sripada, C., Railton, P., Baumeister, R. F., & Seligman, M. E. P. (2013). Reply to comments. *Perspectives on Psychological Science, 8*(2), 151–154.

Stanley, E. A., & Jha, A. P. (2009). Mind fitness – improving operational effectiveness and building warrior resilience. *JFQ – Joint Force Quarterly, 55*, 144–151.

Stanley, E. A., & Schaldach, J. M. (2011). Mindfulness-based mind fitness training (MMFT). *Mind Fitness Training Institute,* January. Retrieved from http://docplayer.net/4549378-Mindfulness-based-mind-fitness-training-mmft.html

Stanley, S. (2012). Mindfulness: Towards a critical relational perspective. *Social and Personality Psychology Compass, 6*(9), 631–641.

Stein, D. J. (2013). What Is a mental disorder? A perspective from cognitive-affective science. *La Revue canadienne de psychiatrie, 58*(12), 656–662.

Sterman, J. D. (2000). *Business dynamics, systems thinking and modeling for a complex world.* New York, NY: McGraw-Hill.

Stern, V. (2009). Why we worry. Chronic worrying stems from a craving for control. *Scientific American Mind,* November/December, 41–47.

Sternberg, R. J. (2004). What is wisdom and how can we develop it? *American Academy of Political and Social Science,* January (Annals), 164–277.

Surawy, C., McManus, F., Muse, K., & Williams, J. M. G. (2015). Mindfulness-based cognitive therapy (MBCT) for health anxiety (hypochondriasis): Rationale, implementation and case illustration. *Mindfulness, 6*, 382–392. doi:10.1007/s12671-013-0271-1

Teasdale, J. D., & Chaskalson, M. (Kulananda). (2011). How does mindfulness transform suffering? I: The nature and origins of *dukkha. Contemporary Buddhism, 12*(1), 89–102.

Teasdale, J. D., & Chaskalson, M. (Kulananda). (2011). How does mindfulness transform suffering? II: The transformation of *dukkha. Contemporary Buddhism, 12*(1), 102–124.

Teper, R., Segal, Z. V., & Inzlicht, M. (2013). Inside the mindful mind: How mindfulness enhances emotion regulation through improvements in executive control. *Current Directions in Psychological Science, 22*(6), 449–454.

Thurman, R. A. F. (1988). Nagarjuna's guidelines for Buddhist social activism. In F. Eppsteiner (Ed.), *The path of compassion: Writings on socially engaged Buddhism.* (Rev. 2nd ed., pp. xx–xx). Berkeley, CA: Parallax Press.

Treviño, L. K., Weaver, G. R., & Reynolds, S. J. (2006). Behavioral ethics in organizations: A review. *Journal of Management, 32*(6), 951–990.

Troy, A. S., Shallcross, A. J., Davis, T. S., & Mauss, I. B. (2013). History of mindfulness-based cognitive therapy is associated with increased cognitive reappraisal ability. *Mindfulness, 4*, 213–222.

Tsai, C., & Hsee, C. (2008). Hedonomics in consumer behavior. *Rotman Magazine,* Spring, 45–49.

Tse-fu, K. (2012). Cognitive operations in Buddhist meditation: Interface with Western psychology. *Contemporary Buddhism*, *13*(1), 35–60.

Vallerand, R. J. (2000). Deci and Ryan's self-determination theory: A view from the hierarchical model of intrinsic and extrinsic motivation. *Psychological Inquiry*, *11*(4), 312–318.

Van Doesum, N. J., Van Lange, D. A. W., & Van Lange, P. A. M. (2013). Social mindfulness: Skill and will to navigate the social world. *Journal of Personality and Social Psychology*, *105*(1), 86–103.

Van Vugt, M. (2006) Evolutionary origins of leadership and followership. *Personality and Social Psychology Review*, *10*, 354–372.

Van Vugt, M., & Ahuja, A. (2010). *Selected: Why some people lead, why others follow, and why it matters. The evolutionary science of leadership*. London, England: Profile Books.

Van Vugt, M., Hogan, R., & Kaiser, R. (2008). Leadership, followership, and evolution: Some lessons from the past. *American Psychologist*, *63*, 182–196.

Vohs, K. D., Mead, N. L., & Goode, M. R. (2006). The psychological consequences of money. *Science*, *314*, 1154–1156.

Wahbeh, H., Lane, J. B., Goodrich, E., Miller, M., & Oken, B. S. (2014). One-on-one mindfulness meditation trainings in a research setting. *Mindfulness*, *5*, 88–99.

Walsh, R., & Shapiro, S. L. (2006). The meeting of meditative disciplines and Western psychology – a mutually enriching dialogue. *American Psychologist*, *61*(3), 227–239.

Walton, G. M. (2014). The new science of wise psychological interventions. *Current Directions in Psychological Science*, *23*(1), 73–82.

Weaver, G. R., Reynolds, S. J., & Brown, M. E. (2014). Moral intuition: Connecting current knowledge to future organizational research and practice. *Journal of Management*, *40*(1), 100–129.

Weick, K. E., & Sutcliffe, K. M. (2007). *Managing the unexpected: Resilient performance in an age of uncertainty*. Oxford, England: Jossey-Bass.

Weng, H. Y., Fox, A. S., Shackman, A. J., Stodola, D. E., Caldwell, J. Z. K., Olson, M. C., ... Davidson, R. J. (2013). Compassion training alters altruism and neural responses to suffering. *Psychological Science*, *24*(7), 1171–1180.

Westbrook, D., Kennerley, H., & Kirk, J. (2011). *An introduction to cognitive behaviour therapy – Skills and applications* (2nd Ed.). Los Angeles: Sage.

Wilkinson, R., & Pickett, K. (2009). Equality and sustainability. In *The spirit level – Why more equal societies almost always do better* (pp. 215–228). London, England: Allen Lane.

Williams, J. M. G. (2008). Mindfulness, depression and modes of mind. *Cognitive Therapy Research*, *32*(6), 721–733. doi:10.1007//s10608-008-9204-z

Williams, J. M. G., & Kabat-Zinn, J. (Eds.). (2013). *Mindfulness – Diverse perspectives on its meaning, origins and applications*. London, England/New York, NY: Routledge.

Williams, M. J. (2014). Serving the self from the seat of power: Goals and threats predict leaders' self-interested behavior. *Journal of Management*, *40*(5), 1365–1395.

Williams, P. B. (2013). Practicing wisdom by mindfulness. *Wisdom Research, University of Chicago*, September, 1–4. Retrieved from http://wisdomresearch.org/forums/t/1242.aspx

Worsfold, K. E. (2013). Embodied reflection in mindfulness-based cognitive therapy for depression. *The Humanistic Psychologist*, *41*, 54–69.

Yook, K., Lee, S. H., Ryu, M., Kim, K. H., Choi, T. K., Suh, S. Y., … Kim, M. J. (2008). Usefulness of mindfulness-based cognitive therapy for treating insomnia in patients with anxiety disorders. *The Journal of Nervous and Mental disease*, *196*(6), 501–503

Young-Eisendrath, P. (2009). The transformation of human suffering: A perspective from psychotherapy and Buddhism. *Psychoanalytic Inquiry – Topical Journal for Mental Health Professionals, 28*(5), 541–549.

Zellner Keller, B., Singh, N. N., & Winton, A. S. W. (2014). Mindfulness-based cognitive approach for seniors (MBCAS): Program development and implementation. *Mindfulness, 5*: 453–459.

Zollo, M. et al. (2008). *Understanding and responding to societal demands on corporate responsibility (RESPONSE): Final report* (pp. 6–108). INSEAD, Copenhagen Business School, Bocconi, Impact and the Leon Kozminski Academy of Entrepreneurship and Management. Retrieved from www.academia.edu/2837333/Understanding_and_responding_to_societal_demands_on_corporate_responsibility_RESPONSE_Sixth_framework_programme

Index

Mindfulness-Based Strategic Awareness Training: A Complete Program for Leaders and Individuals, First Edition. Juan Humberto Young.

Companion website: www.wiley.com/go/humbertoyoung/mbsat